DECENT WORKING TIME

New trends, new issues

ABOUT THE EDITORS

Jean-Yves Boulin, *Sociologue au Centre National de la Recherche Scientifique (CNRS); chercheur à l'Institut de Recherche Interdisciplinaire en Socio-économie (IRIS) à l'Université de Paris–Dauphine.*

Michel Lallement, *Professeur de sociologie, Laboratoire Interdisciplinaire pour la Sociologie Économique (LISE), Centre National de la Recherche Scientifique (CNRS) and Conservatoire National des Arts et Métiers (CNAM), Paris.*

Jon C. Messenger, *Senior Research Officer, International Labour Office (ILO), Conditions of Work and Employment Programme, Geneva, with the lead responsibility for its sub-programme on working time and work organization.*

François Michon, *Économiste, Directeur de recherches au Centre National de la Recherche Scientifique (CNRS)–MATISSE and Université de Paris I Panthéon–Sorbonne; chercheur associé à l'Institut de Recherches Économiques et Sociales (IRES).*

Decent working time

New trends, new issues

Edited by Jean-Yves Boulin, Michel Lallement,
Jon C. Messenger and François Michon

INTERNATIONAL LABOUR OFFICE • GENEVA

Jean-Yves Boulin, Michel Lallement, Jon C. Messenger and François Michon (eds.)
Decent working time: New trends, new issues
Geneva, International Labour Office, 2006

Hours of work, flexible hours of work, arrangement of working time, trend, developed countries. 13.05.1

ISBN 978-92-2-117950-4

ILO Cataloguing in Publication Data

Typeset by Magheross Graphics, France & Ireland *www.magheross.com*
Printed in Switzerland   PCL

FOREWORD

Working time has been a central workforce issue since the beginning of the Industrial Revolution, and a central issue of labour policy since at least the adoption of the Factories Act of 1844 in the United Kingdom limiting the working hours of women and children. Working time was also the subject of the very first international labour standard, the Hours of Work (Industry) Convention, 1919 (No. 1). Over the years, working time has continued to be central to the work of the International Labour Organization (ILO), which has adopted international standards on a variety of working time related subjects, including not only standards establishing limits on working hours, but also those providing for minimum weekly rest periods, paid annual leave, protections for night workers and equal treatment for part-time workers.

The ILO has defined a concept of "decent work" that involves "promot[ing] opportunities for women and men to obtain decent and productive work, in conditions of freedom, equity, security and human dignity" (ILO, 1999, p. 6). This vision of decent work animates all the ILO's efforts across four broad strategic objectives: advancing fundamental principles and rights at work; promoting employment; strengthening social protection; and expanding social dialogue. During the past few years, different programmes within the ILO have worked to apply the broad concept of decent work to their specific fields of inquiry. Based upon both the existing international labour standards on working time and recent research on working time trends and developments focusing on industrialized countries, five significant dimensions of "decent working time" have recently been proposed: working time arrangements should be healthy; "family-friendly"; promote gender equality; advance enterprise productivity; and facilitate worker choice and influence over their hours of work (Messenger (ed.), 2004).[1] These five dimensions of "decent working time" provide a broad policy framework – grounded in long-standing ILO principles such as equality of opportunity and treatment between women and men in the world of work[2] – that establishes a basis from which to consider how the goal of decent work can be advanced in the area of working time.

In its programme of work on working time and work organization, the ILO is seeking to advance "decent working time" by two related means of action:

- building its knowledge base via information collection and research on a range of issues, including national laws on working time, actual hours of work, various types of "flexible" working time arrangements (e.g., part-time work, flexi-time), rest periods and paid annual leave, etc.; and

- applying this expanded knowledge base to provide practical tools and technical advisory services to assist ILO constituents (governments and employers' and workers' organizations) to develop and implement appropriate policies and practices regarding working time and work organization – both at the national level and in the workplace.

In addition, the ILO is in the process of considering the implications of the recent *General Survey* report on two of the most important inter-national labour standards on working time, the Hours of Work (Industry) Convention, 1919 (No. 1) and the Hours of Work (Commerce and Offices) Convention, 1930 (No. 30) (ILO, 2005).[3] This report, based on survey questionnaires submitted by ILO member States regarding their working time laws and practices, concluded that, while "it remains important and relevant to provide for minimum standards of working hours . . . the changes that have taken place since these two instruments were adopted warrant their revision" (ibid., p. 105). While at the present time there is no consensus for such a revision, having access to the best available information regarding working time trends and developments will help to inform the decision of the ILO's Governing Body regarding the appropriate course of action to take with respect to these two standards. It will also inform any potential future discussion of working time, such as at a Tripartite Meeting of

---

[1] Each of these five dimensions of "decent working time" is discussed at length in the concluding chapter of this volume.

[2] This principle is enshrined in a number of international labour Conventions, most notably the Discrimination (Employment and Occupation) Convention, 1958 (No. 111).

[3] This report was prepared by the ILO's Committee of Experts on the Application of Conventions and Recommendations.

Experts[4] or at the International Labour Conference – the body that ultimately makes the decisions on the adoption and revision of international labour standards.

As the premier network of international researchers in the field of working time, the International Symposium on Working Time – ISWT (Le Séminaire International sur le Temps de Travail – SITT) represents an important source of knowledge regarding working time trends and developments, as well as an essential forum for the exchange of ideas. As such, the ISWT/SITT network offers an important resource for assisting the ILO with building its knowledge base regarding working time and informing any future discussions and debates on this subject. The Symposium itself, which is held every few years, brings together scholars in the field of working time to address new trends and new issues in working hours and the organization of working time from across the industrialized world.

The Ninth International Symposium on Working Time, convened in Paris on 26–28 February 2004 and co-sponsored by the ILO, focused on the profound changes that have been occurring in the nature of working time, and indeed in the nature of the employment relationship itself. The new trends that have emerged over the past decade or two – such as the increasing use of results-based employment relationships for managers and professionals; an increasing fragmentation of time to more closely tailor staffing needs to customer requirements (e.g., short-hours part-time work); and the dramatic expansion of operating/opening hours with the move towards a 24-hour and 7-day economy – have resulted in a growing diversification, decentralization and individualization of working hours, as well as an increasing tension between enterprises' business requirements and workers' needs and preferences regarding their hours. This new reality has raised some new issues as well, such as those regarding increasing employment insecurity and instability; time-related social inequalities, particularly in relation to gender; workers' ability to balance their paid work with their personal lives; and even the synchronization of working hours with social times, such as community activities.

The results of the Ninth International Symposium on Working Time provide a better understanding of current developments in working time across the industrialized world; how those developments vary across different countries and under different sets of socio-economic circumstances; and the public and enterprise policies that are the best suited to addressing these

---

[4] A proposal to conduct a Tripartite meeting of Experts on Working Time will be considered by the ILO's Governing Body in March 2006.

developments. The carefully selected set of papers from the Paris Symposium that is presented in this volume represents an important contribution to building our knowledge base from some of the leading scholars in the field of working time. As such, these papers provide a wealth of information for policy-makers, the social partners and academics, and will also assist the ILO in further developing and refining the proposed policy framework for advancing "decent working time".

Jon C. Messenger
Senior Research Officer
International Labour Office
Geneva

References

International Labour Office (ILO). 1999. *Decent work*. Report of the Director-General to the International Labour Conference, 87th Session (Geneva).

—. 2005. *Hours of work: From fixed to flexible? General Survey of the reports concerning the Hours of Work (Industry) Convention, 1919 (No. 1) and the Hours of Work (Commerce and Offices) Convention, 1930 (No. 30)*, Report III (Part 1B), International Labour Conference, 93rd Session (Geneva).

Messenger, J.C. (ed.). 2004. *Working time and workers' preferences in industrialized countries: Finding the balance* (London and New York, Routledge).

CONTENTS

7   **The French 35-hour week: A decent working time pattern? Lessons from case studies**

Pascal Charpentier, Michel Lallement, Florence Lefresne and Jocelyne Loos-Baroin

Tables

Figures

Boxes

ACKNOWLEDGEMENTS

We would like to offer our thanks to each of the authors who contributed to this volume. Their efforts are greatly appreciated, and the excellence of their contributions has made an enormous difference to the overall quality of this publication.

The various chapters in this book are taken from the highlights of the work presented at the Ninth International Symposium on Working Time (ISWT) conference. This conference was held in Paris in February 2004 by a network of four research teams: MATISSE–Centre National de la Recherche Scientifique (CNRS) and Université de Paris I–Panthéon Sorbonne; Laboratoire Interdisciplinaire pour la Sociologie Économique (LISE) (CNRS and the Conservatoire National des Arts et Métiers (CNAM)); Institut de Recherche Interdisciplinaire en Socio-économie (IRIS) (CNRS and Université de Paris IX–Dauphine); and lastly, l'Institut de Recherches Économiques et Sociales (IRES)–France (Noisy-le-Grand). In addition to receiving the backing of the ILO, the initiative was supported by the European Foundation for the Improvement of Living and Working Conditions (Dublin) and the European Trade Union Institute (Brussels). We would like to take this opportunity to thank all the bodies that enabled this conference to take place, and especially the ILO for its constant support of the ISWT network – of which this book is the most recent evidence.

We would also like to express our appreciation to several individuals from the International Labour Office who also made important contributions to this report. First, we would like to thank François Eyraud, Director of the Conditions of Work and Employment Programme, and Jean-Pierre Laviec, who headed the International Institute for Labour Studies, for their support for both the Symposium and this publication. We would also like to thank

Rosemary Beattie and May Hofman of ILO Publications for their invaluable advice regarding publication matters, as well as their considerable efforts to move this manuscript through the various stages of the publication process. Finally, we are particularly grateful to Jared Turner, Mariela Dyrberg, Elizabeth Teague, Judith Oppenheimer and Beverley Coult, who deserve special thanks for all their assistance with editing, formatting and proofreading the manuscript.

INTRODUCTION

Jean-Yves Boulin, Michel Lallement and François Michon

The International Symposium on Working Time (ISWT) is an interdisciplinary research network set up in the late 1980s. In the ensuing period there has been no lack of policies and debates on this issue. These include the processes of reducing working time and increasing the flexibility of working time; the growth of part-time working; the consequences of these policies on employment and working conditions; and the transformation of social working time norms, brought about as much by the reductions of working time as by the sizeable new types of flexibility introduced into schedules and working patterns established in most industrialized countries. All these matters have constituted the crux of the work carried out by the ISWT. In particular, its research has aimed to examine, analyse and evaluate government working time policies and the strategies of employers and trade unions in the main countries of the industrialized world (Europe, North America, Japan and Australia) from the perspective of international comparison. The effects of these policies and strategies on employment, working and living conditions have also been a focus for research.

The work has highlighted the distinctive national industrial relations characteristics, particularly in terms of the methods for organizing industrial relations and family relations. It has shown how these distinctive features are taken into account and reinforced by the choice of employment policies, and how their effects intersect with those of the economic constraints impacting on the policies and methods of the organization and reduction of working time. The research has also stressed the effect of industry-specific differences on the methods of organizing working time, by highlighting, for example, that service-sector activities differ considerably from the industrial model on which the economic literature has long been based. Lastly, this work has heavily emphasized the social inequalities developing in the field of working time, in particular gender-based ones.

This book is the second collection of ISWT research to be published by the International Labour Organization (ILO).[1] The first (Bosch et al., 1994) marked the completion of the network's initial phase of activity. The goal was thus to review and assess the policies, concerns and methods of regulating working time in the industrialized countries. This phase was encapsulated in the building up of a research network in a period during which international comparison as a methodology ultimately became dominant within academic concerns.

A good decade or so later, economic and social concerns and stakes are greatly changed, especially in terms of working time. This second book uses the "decent working time" perspective advocated by the ILO to evaluate the recent transformations of working time and of the policies implemented in the last few years: the use of instruments for increasing the flexibility of working time, methods for reducing as well as extending working time; the intensification and degradation of working conditions as well as changes in the social organization of time (working time, time devoted to other activities, time set aside for leisure and family) to ensure "lifelong learning" and greater "work–life balance"; and the growth of new time-related social inequalities (in particular issues specific to small and medium-sized enterprises (SMEs) – women, managerial staff, older workers, etc.). This evaluation framework is obviously a fruitful one.

The various chapters in this book are taken from the highlights of the work presented at the Ninth International Symposium on Working Time (ISWT) conference. During this conference, a sizeable body of contributions stressed the powerful relationships bringing together the various facets of the change that working time is going through: the changes in working hours and, as a result, in the organization of working time, and the time set aside for family and leisure. The difficulties of harmonizing "supply side" and "demand side" have been identified and studied using concepts such as "working time gaps" and "decent-work deficits". Many contributions have emphasized the effects of such changes on the control that employees (and the organizations representing them) might have over their working time, and the losses of autonomy to which they are subject in terms of their working patterns. The processes involved in the social construction of time, productive and social-time periods, have been described using a range of methodologies (surveys, data analysis, etc.). It was underlined at the conference that the social

---

[1] These two books do not make up the ISWT's entire published output. To consult the findings of other research undertaken in the network, see Michon and Taddei (1991); Bosch et al. (1994); Anxo et al. (1995); Bosch et al. (1997).

construction constituted by "working time" is indeed part and parcel of the general process of transforming productive organizations and the employment relationship, and also how much employees' relationships with their own personal time are heterogeneous or even individualized, and in any case vary widely among different groups of workers. Naturally the gender issue is crucial to this variation, and can be found virtually everywhere in the thread of this book's arguments. Indeed, it is around such concerns that this book is structured.

In this collection, international comparative studies stand alongside national case studies. In Part I, this book attempts to describe the "New Stakes and Policies" in the industrialized countries and, using a range of approaches, examines the transformations and adjustments between productive and social organizations, preferred choices, and individual and collective constraints.

This section of the book thus begins with a long-term review of 20 years of the transformations of working time, economic and social stakes and working time policy objectives implemented in the industrialized countries. In Chapter 1, Jean-Yves Boulin, Michel Lallement and François Michon explore the point of the concept of "decent working time" in the design, drafting and assessment of policy. The authors identify some limits and paradoxes, and even a few apparent contradictions, which they suggest may be raised by the decent working time approach, in particular with respect to the European Employment Strategy. How can increasing working time be reconciled with the implementation of work–life balance policies? How can the productive flexibility demanded by business be reconciled with individual flexibility to take the wishes and needs of employees into account? These two issues generate another one: "Should working time policies therefore be reconfigured to more effectively anchor them in the decent working time approach?"

In Chapter 2, Gerhard Bosch links the analysis of working time with an overview of the changes in the standard employment relationship. In doing so, he argues against a number of theories which form the conventional wisdom about the breakdown and erosion of this employment norm and which some attribute to the coming of the information society. Without denying the existence of major changes, which he describes using empirical data, he suggests paving the way for a new model of a flexible labour relationship that resonates with the concerns inherent in decent working time – that is, the promotion of internal flexibilities of labour organization within firms, the extension of lifelong learning to all individuals, the growth of care structures, etc.

Sangheon Lee and Deirdre McCann clearly share Bosch's concern, that is, to contribute to thinking through the growing trend towards the individualization of the labour and employment relationship in the most beneficial possible industrial relations context (Chapter 3). Building on Sen's theory of "capabilities", Lee and McCann stress the significance of industrial relations infrastructure and more generally of institutions, in order to make working time schemes viable enough for individuals to accept. The authors then discuss practical legal steps that can bolster genuine decent working time: equal treatment with regard to wages, benefits, promotions and so on for full- and part-time workers; entitlement, if the employee so wishes, to withdraw from the labour market to bring up children, and so on. What is at stake, the authors add, is to place an entire legal infrastructure at an employee's disposal: an infrastructure whose actual utilization does not generate more inequalities than already exist in the labour market.

Dominique Anxo, Jean-Yves Boulin and Colette Fagan (Chapter 4) demonstrate how viewing working time from a life-course perspective leads to imagining new forms of the organization of time, in order that individuals may more effectively adjust their own time between paid work and other family-oriented, social and leisure activities. Of course, life-course arrangements are becoming more diverse, as the authors point out, but much remains to be done. The writers emphasize how much, from this viewpoint, the embedding of working time policies in a life-course perspective and the concept of decent working time are intimately connected. The life-course perspective offers a solid basis for advancing decent working time, while the latter suggests that numerous criteria can be used for assessing the effectiveness of these life-course policies.

Lastly, to end the first section of the book, Jill Rubery, Kevin Ward and Damian Grimshaw's Chapter 5 presents the findings of a survey on the various reconfigurations of the employment relationship now under way in the United Kingdom. They emphasize the degree to which working time lies at the crux of these transformations. Their interpretative framework locates companies' management of working time at the intersection of: (i) employment relationships that develop between employees, employers and their representatives; (ii) the organization of productive activities; and (iii) the domestic sphere. Their findings describe two new working time arrangements that have developed in British firms: on the one hand, a results-based employment system, characterized by long hours, and, on the other hand, a more fragmented time-based system. Their work confirms that a clear deterioration in the job satisfaction of British employees in terms of their working hours can now be witnessed.

Part II focuses on "Individual Choices and Collective Options", and examines the real nature of the individual preferences that are used to justify systems of flexible working time organization. It introduces some assessments (from the decent working time perspective) of the comparative merits of the regulations that either promote individual choices or introduce collective amendments to working time.

The book's second part begins with an essay by Didier Fouarge and Christine Baaijens (Chapter 6) that puts forward an assessment of the effects of the Adjustment of Working Hours Act introduced by the Dutch Government in July 2000. This policy's goal was to oblige employers to allow employees to seek longer or shorter individual working hours, in order to obtain their preferred hours. The authors' findings show the minimal impact (over a very short period, however) of the measures comprising the Adjustment of Working Hours Act. Only a small proportion of employees dissatisfied with their working hours managed to adjust them to their needs; moreover, the majority of the changes made were obtained through changing jobs, whereas the Adjustment of Working Hours Act aimed to reach this goal without employees having to change jobs. These findings show that upward adjustments in working hours can be made more easily than downward adjustments, and that men's working time preferences are more stable than women's. All these findings imply that decent working time has a long way to go even in the Netherlands – a country that, however, is exemplary in terms of the large-scale presence of part-time workers who have supposedly actually opted to work those hours.

Pascal Charpentier, Michel Lallement, Florence Lefresne and Jocelyne Loos-Baroin question to what extent the French 35-hour-week experiment has contributed to the improvement of decent working time (Chapter 7) in that country. Basing their work on four firm monographs, enabling an in-depth longitudinal analysis of the implementation process and the effects of the second Aubry Act to be carried out, they link various constituent criteria for decent working time – most importantly the opportunities for employees' choice and control over their working time, working and employment conditions on the one hand, and companies' economic performance requirements on the other. Refusing to gloss over the potential for conflict within this range of criteria, they aim to identify the types of combinations that can exist within companies. First, the authors make no attempt to hide their surprise when they find that a reduction in working time of this scope was desirable neither for employers nor for employees. Yet both groups responded negatively to later attempts to back-pedal over the 35-hour week. Second, they point out that if the compromises made by the parties concerned have established working time arrangements that are not entirely satisfactory, almost nobody thinks of scrapping them. The authors here stress the degree to which the stability of the organization of working time that results from a compromise within a firm is a significant dimension that should be incorporated in the concept of decent working time.

Lonnie Golden devotes Chapter 8 to the issue of overemployment in the United States: the fact that employees work longer hours than those they would actually like, the exact opposite of what decent working time suggests. Although the incidence of overemployment is actually relatively limited in the United States (despite substantial variation among the available empirical studies), the phenomenon is highly concentrated in particular industries, occupations, and categories of workers, especially women and the parents of young children. The author identifies that in the United States (as well as in the United Kingdom), substantial overemployment coexists with an even higher level of underemployment (i.e., people who have shorter working hours than those to which they aspire). He makes the same observation as Fouarge and Baaijens: to enable actual working hours and working time preferences to coincide, employees usually have to change jobs. Yet, unlike Fouarge and Baaijens, he makes a plea for the introduction of collective rules allowing American workers to exercise a minimum of control over their working schedules, so that they can alter their working time depending on the various phases and events in their working and personal lives.

In Chapter 9, Mara Yerkes and Jelle Visser look at whether part-time work, and specifically *the one-and-one-half earner model* developed in the Netherlands, fits with the decent working time criteria. The authors compare part-time working conditions in three countries in which part-time working is particularly widespread – Germany, the Netherlands and the United Kingdom. In these countries, as elsewhere, part-time working is a form of employment in which women predominate massively, and they nicely illustrate the continuing prevalence of the *male breadwinner model*. Yet part-time working does not really match the preferences of women except in the Netherlands – where, indeed, it has been completely normalized, with an equivalent set of rights established in law. However, part-time work is still very much marred by discriminatory treatment in the other two countries. Yet, although part-time working seems to match the criteria for decent working time in the Netherlands, one question posed by Yerkes and Visser is why this form of employment is still occupied overwhelmingly by women.

Part III – "Flexibilities and Conditions of Work" – addresses new forms of flexibility in working time and their twin effects on working conditions and non-working time. Nicole Gadrey, Florence Jany-Catrice and Martine Pernod-Lemattre (Chapter 10) focus on the working conditions of unskilled white-collar workers in the service industries in France. These researchers show how the temporal availability required from unskilled clerical workers brings into play the dimensions of timing, variability and predictability of work schedules, and thus constitutes a crucial aspect of the hardships faced by today's service-sector workforce. This temporal availability criterion seems to raise questions about the concept of decent working time that are all the more relevant, as it is indeed a central element of the changes currently impacting on working conditions.

Oddly (but is it really that odd?), a similar examination based on temporal availability is repeated in relation to the highly skilled work accomplished by managers. Jouko Nätti, Timo Anttila and Mia Väisänen (Chapter 11) attempt to delineate the features of the new working time regime that is now emerging in Finland in the field of knowledge work, more specifically among managers. They note the extension of what they refer to as "the ambiguity of working time" – the impossibility of really setting temporal limits, and the lengthening of working times well beyond the norms contained in collective agreements. Although managers' work is still characterized in principle by a large degree of autonomy, this does not prevent negative outcomes impinging on managers' social and family lives, especially those who show a marked preference for shorter hours – that is, this is a kind of lack of decent working time.

In Chapter 12, Thomas Haipeter describes the new methods for injecting flexibility into working time established in German companies – in particular the working time accounts systems, which are decentralized, negotiated systems exempt from the norms contained in sector-level collective agreements, and which aim more effectively to meet employees' individual needs. He looks at the risk of the erosion of collective standards that the growth of these company systems brings about, and the difficulties encountered by the unions and works councils on this issue. Above all, he observes that works councils are struggling to get flexible working time systems implemented at company level. Obtaining negotiated rules at that level which assumes a genuinely "normative power" is not possible without serious difficulties because, in the face of market constraints, these rules carry little weight. The criteria for achieving decent working time seem, therefore, to be difficult to satisfy using this method, without a more centralized form of regulation – although strong, proactive works councils can make a difference.

The fourth section of this book – "Quality, Efficiency and Inequalities" – suggests linking the theme of decent working time to the issues of quality of work, economic efficiency and social inequalities. In his study of Japan (Chapter 13), Thierry Ribault offers an initial explanation by theorizing that the structural transformations related to Japan's shift to service-sector activities have had determining impacts on time management. Using a framework borrowed from the French "conventions school", he shows in more detail that three types of systems interact: income, family and temporal availability. Analysing the interaction between these various components sheds light on the determining role of the age and gender variables in the process of decommodification now under way in the Japanese economy. In the picture he draws, Ribault demonstrates that atypical work schedules are becoming more widespread; this is the case among young workers, as well as in the category of men occupying normal forms of employment. Women are found more in part-time employment statuses (*pâto*), especially when they reach an intermediate age, at which point, the issue of the compatibility between occupational and domestic commitments arises. Finally, as in other countries, the distribution of domestic tasks is changing slowly – proof that although, with the help of flexible working, the distribution of time is changing in the occupational sphere, such changes are much less obvious when the focus is on the personal sphere.

The study by Paul Bouffartigue and Jacques Bouteiller (Chapter 14) reveals concerns that converge with those structuring the argument of the preceding chapter. Unlike that chapter, however, this one is comparative in two ways – it analyses three different countries (Belgium, Spain and France), and two different professions (nurses and bank managerial staff). One of the major findings of this investigation is that dynamics specific to each occupational group seem to take precedence over the social characteristics structuring the organization of work and industrial relations in each country. From this perspective, also, gender emerges as a determinant at all three levels studied here, that is, "formalized time", "represented time" and "experienced time". There are, however, still some irreducible societal effects (e.g., part-time working is much less widespread in Spain) against a general backdrop of changes in working time which, in all three countries, link the intensity of work, flexibility, and the growing diversity of employment statuses and situations.

This trend towards the reconfiguration of time worked is also at the crux of the analysis undertaken by Isik Zeytinoglu and Gordon Cooke (Chapter 15). More precisely, they investigate the determining factors of regular weekend work in Canada, starting from the understanding that behind such a form of working time organization a series of problems deserving attention can be identified – such as its effects on health and social life; its real impacts on productive efficiency; and the creation of new forms of inequality in which weekday workers and weekend workers are on either side of a dividing line. Without claiming to have answers to all the questions directly related to decent working time, Zeytinoglu and Cooke contribute empirical evidence, thanks to a statistical analysis of the factors that are associated with weekend working. In any society that some people happily imagine is open 24 hours a day, 7 days a week, in this case Canada, weekend workers are often people who have a number of disadvantages: lower education and skill levels, temporary contracts and part-time work (although here they are often covered by collective agreements). Although a testimony to the power of the trend towards extending working time beyond the boundaries of the standard work-week, weekend work is not the province of only a small minority of employees.

To end the book, or rather *not* to end it, Jon Messenger offers an interpretative synthesis of the various contributions to this volume summarized above. Based on the findings that he highlights, as well as the unanswered questions that he identifies (of which there are still many), he outlines some prospective approaches that could build on and enrich the decent working time policy framework. Finally, he sketches an agenda for future research on working time that will, we hope, provide a structure for much future work.

References

Anxo, D.; Bosch, G.; Bosworth, D.; Cette, G.; Sterner, T.; Taddei, D. (eds.). 1995. "Utilisation des équipements et horaires de travail. Comparaison internationale", in *INSEE Méthodes* (Paris), Nos. 49–51, September.

Bosch, G.; Dawkins, P.; Michon, F. (eds.). 1994. *Times are changing: Working time in fifteen industrialised countries* (Geneva, ILO International Institute for Labour Studies).

—; Meulders, D.; Michon, F. (eds.). 1997. *Le temps de travail, nouveaux enjeux, nouvelles normes, nouvelles mesures* (Working time: new issues, new norms, new measures) (Brussels, Editions du Dulbea).

Michon, F.; Taddei, D. (eds.). 1991. "Le travail en équipes et le temps de travail dans les pays développés", in *Économies et Sociétés*, Vol. XXV, Nos. 9–10, Sept./Oct. (série Économie du Travail, AB/17).

PART I

NEW STAKES AND POLICIES

DECENT WORKING TIME IN INDUSTRIALIZED COUNTRIES: ISSUES, SCOPES AND PARADOXES

1

Jean-Yves Boulin, Michel Lallement and François Michon

1.1 INTRODUCTION

Changes in working time and in the life course (its length, patterns and timetables) as economic and social issues – and even the stated objectives of working time policies – are, all things considered, very similar in the large developed economies. Trends in working time, related concerns and policies have knock-on effects upon one another, and explain these changes. Moreover, in the contemporary context of international competition due to global-ization, each country is seeking explanations for others' success and trying to reproduce the "winning formula" at home. Although the issues in each country seem more convergent than ever, on closer inspection there are still considerable national differences, both in working time and in the ways of understanding the main issues of the moment and translating them into objectives and policy instruments. There is an interminable list of distinctive regional and national characteristics, particularly distinguishing the North American continent from Europe, the British Isles from continental Europe, northern from southern Europe and so on. So it is this mixture of shared and specific dynamics and concerns which at the same time marks the field of working time.

This chapter attempts to analyse the ways in which the trends and stakes of working time have changed during recent decades (section 1.2). The utility of the concept of "decent working time" will then be examined in the light of these changes, by emphasizing its heuristic contribution, and the perspectives and implications that the term suggests in respect of working time policy (section 1.3). The limits and even the paradoxes of such a concept when applied to a heterogeneous world of national spaces can thus be stipulated. The paradoxes and contradictions of policies, in this case EU ones, will then be stressed (section 1.4). Finally, we will show how the notion of "decent working time" suggests some reconfigurations of these policies (section 1.5).

1.2 WORKING TIME: ISSUES AND POLICIES OVER THE LAST DECADES

Let us first note that the reduction of working time is a long-standing phenomenon. Estimates of annual working time put forward by Maddison (2001) trace the path covered since the early twentieth century: from roughly 2,600 hours per person in the years before the Second World War to between 1,400 and 1,800 hours now, depending on the country. Naturally, these estimates are approximate, especially those for the earliest period. The comparability of national data is highly problematic, but in regard to current levels, the long-term trend is incontestable (figure 1.1).

Economic prosperity plus sustained growth, whose stability seems assured, and full employment, characterize the 30 "glorious" years in industrialized countries between the immediate post-war period of reconstruction and the first oil crisis. In the 1960s and 1970s, the threat hanging over the economic future seemed to be that of labour shortages, entailing a growth bottleneck and destabilizing inflation. To make up for these shortages, new workforce seams were mined: immigration and the large-scale entry of women into the labour market. Working patterns simultaneously intensified, and shift work became more widespread in order to make better use of heavy equipment. On the other hand, a policy of improving working conditions appeared to be indispensable.

The observation of the hardships involved in "timed and repetitive" tasks imposed by assembly lines in the car-manufacturing industry in Europe and the United States nicely encapsulates the concerns of that era in the industrialized world, and the interest shown in the experiments in reorganizing labour engaged in by some American and Scandinavian car manufacturers to enrich work, increase the organizational autonomy of assembly-line workers, and break the mandatory alignment of everybody's working patterns and timetables with the imperatives of a standardized form of organization. Such experiments were also aimed at reducing and reorganizing working time, but with a view to diminishing the hardship of the labour force's working conditions. The range of concerns then was far smaller than that later attributed to working time policies. In particular, the objectives of "flexibility" lay within much more restrictive parameters than those of today. One such initiative was to implement individual flexi-time schemes – a

Figure 1.1   Annual hours worked per person employed (total employment),
1913–1998

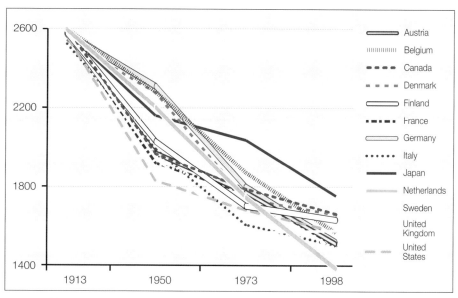

Source: Maddison (2001).

system of time organization enabling each worker to obtain greater levels of
personal satisfaction with his/her constraints and wishes, etc. by satisfying the
time needs of individuals first – even though the restrictive parameters of
labour force requirements (i.e. attracting new groups into the workforce) were
always there (Rehn, 1972).

This "golden age" appears to have gone for good. The oil crises of the
mid-1970s ushered in a new era. Due to uncertain growth and rising
unemployment, the stakes had changed. The emblematic employment
relationship of the period, that is, a permanent full-time contract and a job
"for life", at least in the large industrial firms, is now giving way to a large
number of forms of atypical and more "flexible" employment contracts. The
fight against unemployment and for job creation has dominated the political
and industrial relations agendas of many European countries. The reduction
of working time, followed by the organization and reduction of working
time (the goal of reducing working time thus combining with that of flexible
reorganization of work in order to improve productive efficiency) have
been addressed in Europe as employment and work-sharing policies
(Gauvin and Michon, 1989). It is hardly surprising that the economic and
social stakes related to the issues of working time have been largely
transformed as a result.

The requisite conditions for the success of policies for reducing collective working time standards have been talked about for a long time in continental Europe, in France and Germany particularly. A vigorous revival in job creation was initially expected, but this was slowed down by insufficient economic growth. Next, solid productivity gains were expected to ensue, despite the short-term contradictions between these objectives. It was hoped that the competitiveness jeopardized by increased production costs following the reduction of working time – which was nonetheless indispensable if the job creation effects were to be fully realized in the long term – would thus be restored. The debate in particular underlined the extent to which the pay-related measures accompanying the reduction in working time and its impacts on the organization and patterns of work are key elements in the effectiveness of such policies. On the other hand, for increasing part-time working, the objectives put forward were very different. These meant reducing the contradictions between career and family duties, and fostering women's engagement with the labour market.

Yet at the end of the twentieth century, the long-term trend toward the reduction of working time slowed noticeably, especially in a few countries, the most notable of which were Canada, Sweden, the United Kingdom and the United States.[1] Europe, on the one hand, and the North American continent and the United Kingdom, on the other, are not really treading the same path. Moreover, the spectrum of working times is broad – apparently broader now than at the beginning of the century, if recent data are compared with Maddison's estimates (figure 1.2).

The very broad aggregate figures naturally hide a number of differences between countries, operating in one way or another. The annual working times *per person employed* quoted above, apart from the fact that they refer to all employees and non-salaried workers, including those on leave schemes, differ widely from one country to the next. These also include part-time workers. We know there was a rapid growth in part-time work in the final quarter of the last century. It grew at varying rates however, from one country to another. Consequently, the levels reached are not particularly comparable. In Europe, there is a world of difference between the levels observed in the Netherlands, the country that is a byword for part-time working, and southern European countries such as Greece, Italy, Spain and even France. This difference accounts for a considerable proportion of the reduction of working time witnessed over this period, using indicators for average annual working time that incorporate part-time work in several countries that have expressly

---

[1] These long-term elements conceal several particular national distinctions. In Sweden, for example, the increase in annual working time heading towards previous levels is basically explained by a lengthening of working time for part-timers.

Figure 1.2   Annual hours worked per person employed (total employment),
             1973–2003

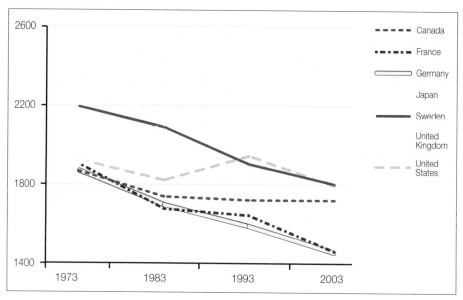

Source: OECD (1996; 2004).

chosen to foster its growth. For some, the entire reduction in working time
recorded using such indicators can, in these countries, be explained by the
growth of part-time working. In the 1970s and 1980s, then, the reduction of
working time recorded is not always due to cutting collective working time.
Two genuine national strategies of reduction of working time have been
witnessed in Europe: fostering part-time employment (the Netherlands or the
United Kingdom); and reducing full-time working hours (Denmark, France
and Germany) (Bosch et al., 1994; 1997). Some countries accorded such high
priority to one of these two strategies that they appear to be almost exclusive
of one another (figure 1.3).

    Now the strategic choices are definitely less clearcut. As early as 1998, the
European Commission stressed the limits of a policy of reducing working time,
and obviously preferred the expansion of part-time work and new forms of
employment. The growth of part-time working, however, is only one aspect of
the directions adopted, out of many. The crucial objective has indeed become
that of increasing employment rates and improving the quality of employment,
rather than reducing unemployment (Math, 2002). The priority previously
accorded to the reduction of collective working time in the countries that had
chosen this option are thus substituted by the priorities of more flexible and
more individualized regulations. The individualized regulations whose

Figure 1.3   Proportion of part-time work in total employment, 1990 and 2003

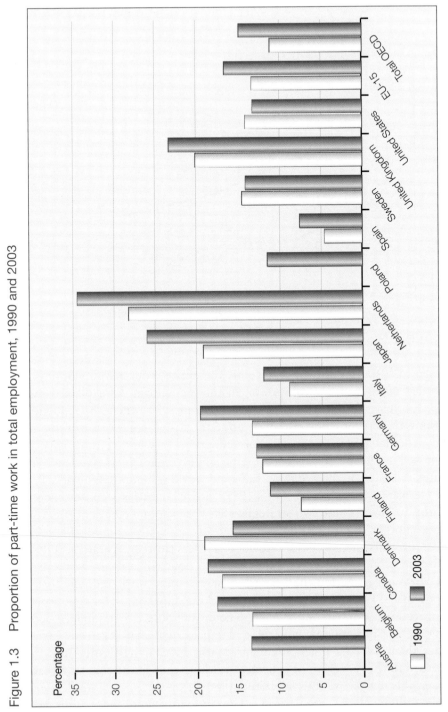

Source: OECD (2004).

extension is sought have enabled more flexible and varied working times to be devised, such that everyone can manage them at their own convenience. Yet above all, these regulations are not focused solely on weekly working time, but address the whole of working life. Lastly, although the basic idea has been to relax collective regulations, and enable each individual to organize his/her own working time and career, the issue is opening the option to extend working time as much as it is to reduce it, even to the point of "working longer hours to earn more money", as the slogan goes in France. The extension of weekly flexi-time schemes and annualized working time to enable greater levels of flexibility has already been propounded, but so have the broadening of overtime options, possible longer working hours, the availability of training time throughout one's career, the postponement of retirement and so on.

Is the point always to provide more choices for workers? While there is growth in part-time employment, long working hours are actually making a comeback. This therefore produces a growing dispersion of weekly working times. Anxo and O'Reilly (2000) observe such a change over an 11-year period in Germany and the United Kingdom. Lee (2004, pp. 41–43) notes the sometimes astonishing frequency of working weeks lasting 50 hours and more, amounting to, for example, 20 per cent of American and Australian employees and 26 per cent of Japanese employees in 2000. Campbell (2004, p. 10) argues that, in Australia, "the trend towards longer hours is the dominant one for full-time employees. It is widespread and strong, spreading well beyond the ranks of managers and based on patterns of not just extended but often very extended and extremely extended hours." If the growth of shift work and atypical hours (evening, night, weekend work, etc.) is added to the picture, the situation is obviously far from one in which a typical single model predominates with few exceptions – i.e. the same hours every day, weekends off, annual leave during the summer holidays, if, of course, we were to use a caricature to summarize this model.

The OECD (2004) shows that the United States now enjoys a basic competitive advantage over Europe: a far higher total number of hours worked per capita. The resulting discrepancy is allegedly a major determining factor affecting relative performance regarding economic growth. A total number of hours worked per capita includes not only employment data but also reflects demographic changes, and in some way measures the population's productive performance. The growth in employment rates due particularly to the large-scale mobilization of women has had a positive impact on productive performance in Europe. Yet the longer period of education prior to accessing the labour market, the lowering of the retirement age, the increase in the amount of training received during one's working life, mass unemployment and, lastly, unfavourable demographic changes have weighed in the opposite direction.

According to the OECD (2004), although time in paid work is associated with major economic and social challenges to the governments of OECD countries and working time policies still need to be activated, the current challenges are completely different. The reduction of working time is clearly no longer an instrument to be considered. On the contrary, increasing the population's productive performance is at the top of the agenda. Among the available instruments, working time flexibility is still highly favoured, but is this actually the type of flexibility that was envisaged by the OECD back in the 1970s?

All these overhauls of the organization of working time and time set aside for people's private lives have contributed to the high degree of organizational flexibility sought by companies, and are probably a more effective response to the inevitable fluctuations and contingencies of a workload now calculated down to the last detail. All of this simultaneously enables the economically active (at least we hope it does), and especially economically active wage earners, to achieve better trade-offs between their working lives, their income requirements and their out-of-work activities on one side, and their family and personal choices and constraints on the other. However, the path between the two is narrow, and is strewn with pitfalls. This is the path that the reforming zeal derived from the concept of "decent working time" attempts to clear.

1.3 FROM DECENT WORK TO DECENT WORKING TIME

Because in all of the "developed" countries, the turning point represented by the introduction of flexibility has had many pathological consequences for working and employment conditions, it is easy to see that, by remaining true to its mission, an institution such as the ILO might foster new research and actions in order to have its own input into the world of work across the globe, including the industrialized countries. The concept of "decent working time" was designed with this purpose. It reworks the ILO's concept of "decent work", applicable to all types of working environments, in order to address the issue of working time first in industrialized countries. However, it is hardly controversial to say that the same issues are raised in completely different ways in the developing world. Understandably and fortunately, pragmatism is holding its ground against reforming zeal on this point. Isn't this approach problematic, however, from the perspective of researchers anxious to retain their axiomatic neutrality? If the concepts of "decent work" and "decent working time" are used for heuristic purposes, therefore enabling the two ideas to be examined, the answer is a resounding "no".

1.3.1 "Decent work"

The concept of "decent work" was formulated by the International Labour Organization to refer to satisfactory working and employment conditions.[2] The term first appeared in the Director-General's Report during the 87th Session of the International Labour Conference in 1999. The ILO's stated goal was the possibility for both men and women to obtain "productive work under conditions of freedom, equity, security and dignity, in which rights are protected and adequate remuneration and social coverage are provided" (ILO, 1999a, p. 15). A further requirement was added: a "tripartite approach and social dialogue". This means, as indicated in a later report (ILO, 1999b), that there should be a genuine freedom for trade union action, and a collective bargaining process without which a minimum level of regulation would be impossible. An initial stake of this semantic formula is, according to the ILO, to reveal a discrepancy between the reality of work and employment and individuals' "aspirations". The ILO calls this a "decent work deficit", which may be attributable to "the absence of sufficient employment opportunities, inadequate social protection, the denial of rights at work and shortcomings in social dialogue" (ILO, 2001, p. 8). In other words, again, behind this "decent work deficit" stand realities as variable as unemployment and under-employment, precarious working conditions, various forms of mutually compounding discrimination, and the absence of basic social rights.

In distinguishing four pillars of "decent work", the ILO was seeking above all to try to "normalize" working and employment conditions in the most varied workplaces, on a global scale: formal and informal economies, wage earners and the self-employed, the most modernized and the most traditional industries, men's work as well as women's, etc. The stated objectives are thus ambitious, and address subjects with different statuses. The first two sets of variables that inform "decent work", that is, access to employment (including pay levels) and social protection (including working conditions), are the products of rules and practices that can be broken down and compared, but whose norms vary dramatically from one country to the next. This is precisely why the ILO acknowledges the premise that, in terms of job security and income, the minimum that could be expected for workers necessarily varies depending on the country's level of and capacity for development. Workers' rights (freedom of association, no discrimination in

---

[2] The term "decent work" is difficult to translate. In English, "the word decent has quite a specific meaning. If you say, I have a decent job, a decent income, it is a positive expression – the job or income is good, it meets your expectations and those of your community, but it is not exaggerated – it falls within the reasonable aspirations of reasonable people" (Rodgers, 2002, p. 15). By emphasizing four constitutive dimensions of work and employment relations (employment, social protection, workers' rights and bargaining), the ILO thus avoids the moral connotation that a clumsy translation might evoke.

employment, the rejection of all forms of forced labour, minimum age for employment, etc.) constitute a different type of norm since they make claims to virtually universal status, and the production of a range of differing rules is made conditional on the set of variables previously referred to. From this perspective, "social dialogue" is, in the opinion of the ILO, a prerequisite for "decent work". Social dialogue is not only the benchmark for freedom of expression and the observance of rights, but it also facilitates the ways in which disputes are dealt with; has an impact in procuring greater social equity; and makes it easier to actually implement labour and job-related policies, etc.[3]

As Ghai (2002) argues, this "decent work" approach is above all a way of packing a concept with a set of longstanding ILO topics and concerns. Moreover:

> The notion of decent work not only forces us to view work along all its different dimensions but also invites us to explore the relationships between these dimensions. Hopefully this should help bring out the complementarities and conflicts among the components of decent work more clearly than in the past (Ghai, 2002, p. 2).

In classifying these components of "decent work", the ILO is not simply placing all the desirable objectives in the global workplace on the same level, but also setting out the necessary conditions for improvement to take place (material resources, law, social dialogue). Lastly, it is encouraging the establishment of hierarchies among the objectives to be attained for the actual implementation of "decent work", based on the assumption that "the question of priorities must depend upon societal values, socio-economic institutions and levels of prosperity and wealth" (ibid., p. 3).

This is a crucial point. It implies, quite rightly, that for the promotion of "decent work", priorities are not necessarily similar in every country, and there may even be an incompatibility of goals due to the specific characteristics of institutional configurations:

> For instance, an agrarian regime characterized by a relatively equal distribution of land generally provides greater livelihood security and more even income distribution than one featuring a few large landowners and widespread

---

[3] By late 2004, there were 76 contributions of various formats (reports, discussion papers, conference papers, web pages, book chapters, etc.) listed in the ILO's in-house publications. Altogether, one-third were programmatic statements, dealing with general approaches to "decent work", etc.; one-fifth included this issue in a national or comparative study, with a clear focus on Africa and Latin America (in terms of "decent work" deficits), on the one hand, and a slight inclination toward Scandinavian models on the other (which, in the case of Sweden, and the role of women in its labour market, emerge as potentially useful normative configurations). The rest of the work was thematic, with priority accorded to vocational training, poverty, the informal economy and gender. There were also more sporadic treatments of "social welfare", "equality", "pay", "migration", "illness" and "labour rights".

landlessness and tenancy. Similarly, the presence of communal and cooperative institutions in some societies can provide an important cushion against insecurity and risks before the development of insurance schemes and social security financed by the state and employer (ibid.).

More generally, it is well understood that certain variables determine others. This is true for legislation and rules that derive from collective bargaining, as well as for available state funding and each country's dominant forms of socialization, which in turn are determining elements for the construction of local, regional and national forms of social solidarity.

Based on the argument outlined above, Ghai (2002) puts forward the theory that among the determining institutional variables, the most significant are: per capita income, sector-level structures, workforce employment status, public expenditure on employment as a proportion of national income and lastly, the public sector's role in the national economy. Based on this theory, he then constructs three models to which the concept of decent work can be applied. The first, the "classical" model, relates to the wealthiest nations (the United States, Western Europe and Scandinavia). Its characteristics are well known: high GDP; wage earning as the predominant form of employment; a poverty rate (i.e. the percentage of people with income worth below 50 per cent of the median income) oscillating between a little over 5 per cent (Finland) and more than 25 per cent (the United States); acknowledgement of the role of trade unions and the existence of collective agreements (with coverage rates of 25–90 per cent of employees), etc. The second model is that of the former "socialist" countries. Despite the diverse situations of the countries in this category, they share a level of national income that puts them in the middle of the world hierarchy, with their social security systems undergoing radical transformations and the rebirth of industrial relations. Lastly, there is the "development" model, the most heterogeneous in that it includes "the rest of the world", or more precisely the least wealthy nations. Here, the agricultural sector dominates the economy (employing 60–80 per cent of the active population); the informal economy is vigorous; the number of wage earners still very low and trade unionism still in its infancy; public expenditure on social welfare is much lower than in other countries; and poverty is a reality for a large segment of the population. Although rather contrived, this schema enables the conceptual "nail" to be hit on the head: like other general concepts such as wealth, education, culture, etc., "decent work" is relevant only if it can be adapted to a very broad spectrum of social contexts.

Only if this basic methodological imperative is kept in mind can the genuine significance of the few available indicators for characterizing

Table 1.1   Breaking down "decent work"

Components of "decent work"	Some possible indicators of "decent work"
Employment	• Access to employment: activity rate, employment rate, unemployment rate.
	• Pay: proportion of the population below a relative income or absolute poverty line.
Social protection	• Proportion of national income spent on social welfare.
	• Percentage of employees covered by unemployment, sickness, old age, accident, and maternity insurance.
	• Working conditions: working-time indicators, prevalence of night work, prevalence of weekend work, prevalence of work-related accidents and occupational mortality rate.
	• Human development: mortality rate, malnutrition indicator, literacy rate, access to water, presence of secondary schools.
Rights at work	• Presence and prevalence of child and forced labour.
	• Prevalence of gender and ethnic discrimination (identifiable in terms of pay, career, etc.).
	• Freedom of association or lack of it (measurable by an index of civil liberties), unionization rate, coverage rate for employees by collective agreements.
Employees' representation and social dialogue	• Right to negotiate or lack of it, percentage of workers covered by basic rights enshrined in legislation and collective agreements.
	• Rules facilitating economic democracy or lack of them.
	• Participation of social partners in national economic and social policy, or lack of it.

national spaces (and even classifying them, as Ghai suggests) be assessed (table 1.1).[4]

One can easily get the feeling when reading this table that not all the indicators enjoy the same status: the ones that particularly relate to the last two components of "decent work" are thus difficult to compare with the other indicators. It is therefore a genuine intellectual challenge to find a formula to express decent work through these possible indicators of "decent work". However, in the comparison of the 22 developed countries he constructs,

---

[4] For an even more exhaustive presentation and discussion of the issue of "decent work" indicators, see the special edition of *International Labour Review* (ILO, 2003) devoted to that topic.

Ghai (2002) picks up the gauntlet. In order to accomplish this goal, he begins by ranking the countries by each indicator used. He then adds up these rankings to obtain an overall "decent work" league table in which the leading positions are taken by the Scandinavian countries (Sweden 1st, Denmark 2nd, Norway 3rd and Finland 4th), followed by Australia (5th), Germany (6th) and Canada (7th). At the bottom of the league come France (20th), Ireland (21st) and Spain (22nd). The United States and Japan take joint 15th place. After having built up an overall economic performance indicator (growth of per capita income, growth and average inflation rate) for the 1990–98 period, the author juxtaposes the results with those for "decent work". No significant correlation then emerges between the economic performance and "decent work" results.

From a researcher's viewpoint, this typology is both useful and unsatisfactory. It is useful in so far as it provides a documented table of "decent work" performance by country, and in that it substantially validates the idea that certain national spaces (those in Scandinavia first and foremost) are able to put their particular ethical and social solidarity requirements into practice. However, it is unsatisfactory (and Ghai is fully aware of this) in that indicators and rankings can only squeeze the social breadth of the relevant countries and conceal, among others, the fact that "decent work" performance is perhaps above all the product of an interaction among institutions rather than the expression of a sum of actions and indicators.

1.3.2 Time and "decent work"

From the perspective of the ILO, Messenger (ed.) (2004) has suggested applying the concept of "decent work" to working time. The goal here is to critically examine, using "decent working time", five dimensions of working time: its effects on health, the juggling of family life and work, gender equality, productive efficiency, and workers' capacity to influence their working hours. By using this method, Messenger fully accepts the normative concern which calls, through greater knowledge of the practices relating to working time, for an improvement in the effects of working time on health and safety; the prioritization of "family-friendly" policies (priority given to family life rather than exclusively to childcare strategies); the use of working time as a lever for promoting gender equality; a campaign for more effective work–life balance that might allow the two birds of "decent working time" and "productive working time" to be killed with one stone; and lastly, for workers' margins of autonomy regarding the control of their working time to be broadened.

As citizens, we can only approve and support this pragmatic concern. From a researcher's perspective, however, several comments immediately come to mind. The first is that the concept of "decent working time" grants an insight whose major advantage is to help understand a multifaceted subject in a synthetic form (the length, quality and distribution of working time, its consequences for employment levels, etc., are merely some of the relevant aspects). The question that arises, however, is that of the interaction between these components: are they actually completely independent of each other? Isn't analysing and acting on one simply (directly or indirectly) the same as analysing and acting on another? So, for example, it is difficult to observe and study autonomy in the choice of working time without simultaneously raising the issue of the relationships between working time and family life, as well as gender equality. From this angle, the various components of "decent working time" do comprise, at least pragmatically speaking, a useful set that provides *a broad policy framework from which to consider how the goal of decent work can be advanced in the arena of working time* (Messenger (ed.), 2004). On another level, however, it is worth debating the way in which an apparently similar subject can, in different countries, contain different meanings, and consequently can be the foundation for policies with ultimately very different (potentially positive or negative) impacts, even when the original intention seems generous – e.g. increasing the numbers of men as well as women working part time in order to heighten male involvement in the domestic arena.[5]

Let us return to the first of the two points. The issue here is to extend the "decent working time" approach advocated by the ILO into a system, so that we can more effectively capture the multiple dimensions of time-related practices. To this end, we suggest submitting highly diverse national and subnational realities to an empirical comparison. Two areas of reflection seem to merit consideration. The first is the comparison of purely quantitative approaches to working time (e.g., daily and weekly working time, the proportion of part-time workers, etc.) with more qualitative measurements (e.g., working conditions, effects on health, etc.). The second calls for the opposition between work and employment to be taken into account, based on the understanding that, following Maruani (1994), we can define: (i) "work" as any human activity directed at the production of goods and services considered useful, as well as the set of conditions for performing this activity; and (ii) "employment" as the methods for accessing the labour market and the translation of labour activity in terms of social status and role. The intersection of these two areas suggests an avenue to explore, in the field of study opened up particularly by Supiot (1999), whose book contains elements supporting this

---

[5] This raises the question of the relevance of "best practice", which might be used to promote good employment conditions, equality and rights, but would need to be applied differentially, as so many areas would be involved, and also has some risks in that such practices may be viewed as a substitute for setting norms.

point (see also the contributions in this volume by Anxo, Boulin and Fagan (Chapter 4) and Rubery, Ward and Grimshaw (Chapter 5)).

Our second point concerns the cross-cutting nature of the various subjects that make up "decent working time". We know that making international comparisons can by its very nature be a hazardous exercise. In terms of working time, Michon (2003) uncovered many difficulties and traps that are not easy to avoid whenever one is dealing with a large group of countries. It is, however, important to adopt a critical stance towards what appears to be obvious. Take the example of part-time work. The functions and implications of this specific form of short-hours employment differ from one social context to another. Using the same terminology now defined in Europe as a job involving 30 hours per week or less, regardless of the full-time working week, it covers "marginal" part-time jobs with very short hours (around 20 hours or less, virtually corresponding to a half-time job), which are by far the most numerous in some countries, and long-hours part-time jobs (almost 30 hours, corresponding to four-fifths of a full-time job), which are the norm elsewhere. What is there in common between France, where part-time working is seen, in the case of women, as a form of labour market peripheralization, and Germany and the Netherlands (and to a lesser extent the United Kingdom), where the connotation of part-time work is much more positive? In Germany and the Netherlands, part-time work is not viewed as an economic crisis-management instrument at the expense of one section of the active population, but as an instrument that, used as early as the 1950s and 1960s, enabled women to earn some independence by accessing the labour market in this way. A comparative analysis of "decent working time" forces us, it can be observed, to transcend the simple consideration of general indicators to get straight to the crux of social variations (e.g., the relative weight of the various institutions and the relationships between them; the weight of history; dominant forms of solidarity, etc.) in which working and employment time refer to highly idiosyncratic stakes, practices and policies.

A key component of decent work, the notion of "decent working time", whose ideal-type contours have just been set out, cannot cover the same concrete realities and implementation conditions without reference to the economic and social development of the world's various geographical areas. Moreover, its implementation cannot be extricated from the nature of the industrial relations systems, methods and conditions for industrial relations dialogue and even the values and representations attached to the various amounts of working time and time set aside for people's private lives. As defined by the ILO, the concept of decent working time stands as a universal in terms of its structuring principles, but it is clear that today its implementation can only be achieved by taking into consideration the specific situations of the various large groups of countries. The prevalent situation with regard to working time in what are now called the "emerging nations" (e.g., 7-day working weeks; 10–12-hour working days; child labour; very few paid holidays; pension provisions that are non-existent or not applied due to very low life expectancy in those countries, etc.) involves stakes which are of a different nature from those pertaining to developed economies.

1.4 PARADOX AND CONTRADICTIONS OF POLICIES TODAY

In the following argument, we shall confine ourselves to the analysis of the policies of developed countries[6] by examining the current trends in working time, i.e. first, which political stakes structure contemporary change, and then what questions these pose with respect to the concept of decent working time.

1.4.1 Working time policies in Europe: Paradoxical precepts

The paradoxical nature of current working time policy enacted in the EU can be seen in the objectives set by the European Commission for the revision of the European directive on working time (Directive 93/104, box 1.1). For the Commission (European Commission, 2004), a working time policy must:

• ensure a high level of protection of workers' health and safety in terms of working time;

• afford companies and Member States greater flexibility in the management of working time;

• enable a better balance between working and family life to be achieved; and

• avoid imposing unreasonable constraints on companies, particularly on small and medium-sized enterprises (SMEs).

Although the goal of bringing all these criteria together can only be welcomed, one element of the revision plan immediately raises doubts regarding its feasibility. The Commission's plan includes, among other things, the option of making employees work up to 65 hours per week, since the possibility of exemption from the maximum 48-hour week established in the 1993 directive can be activated by collective agreement or even by introducing it directly into an individual contract (the so-called "opt-out"

---

[6] More precisely to the old EU-15, which is the subject of many of the contributions to this book.

Box 1.1   The revision of the 1993 European Working Time Directive [1]

The European Union (EU) Working Time Directive sets the maximum weekly working time at 48 hours, including overtime, with this 48 hours being calculated as an average over a maximum 4-month period; a maximum of 8 hours' night work on average over a 24-hour period; a minimum daily rest period of 11 consecutive hours; a minimum weekly one-day rest period; and 4 weeks of paid leave per year. All EU Member States were to have incorporated these rules into their national statute books by 23 November 1996. In April 2003, Italy completed this process, becoming the last of the EU-15 members to have done so.

The directive allows two justifications for exemptions. The 4-month reference period used for the calculation of weekly averages can be extended to 6 or even 12 months by collective agreement. An "opt-out" clause grants employers exemption from the weekly maximum if employees agree this threshold. This exemption is now so widespread in the United Kingdom that almost one in five employees works more than 48 hours per week.

In January 2004, the European Commission planned to revise the directive with two objectives. The first was to redefine working time in order to respond to the problems generated by recent European Court of Justice (ECJ) rulings concerning the nature of "on-call" time. The second was to more effectively monitor the use of the two types of exemptions applicable to the calculation of average and maximum working hours. The proposals for revisions tabled by the Commission have been facing strong opposition from the Member States, particularly the United Kingdom. In these countries, it is now probably considered that the basic point is not to set boundaries, but rather to offer the broadest possible choices that would allow the entire range of economic and social needs to be met – i.e. short working hours (part-time work for example), but also very long hours. In many countries with relatively low wages, and more generally in areas of work that require low levels of skill and pay low wages, very long hours of work enable workers to improve their total earnings.

[1] Directive 93/104/EC, 23 November 1993. Cf. EIRO (2004), "Commission consults on review of working time Directive", EIRO on-line, http://www.eiro.eurofound.ie/2004/02/ feature/eu0402202f.html

provision). Yet virtually all the available studies on the subject show that working long hours has negative implications for workers' health; that it compromises work-life balance; and lastly, since it is men who most often work such long hours, that it does not facilitate gender equality. This type of contradiction can be found in the three currently dominant trends regarding working time in developed countries.

The extension of working hours

EU membership for ten new Member States, in which norms governing employment and pay are clearly worse than those in force in the 15 older Member States, has led to a trend towards an extension of working time in several countries, such as Germany, France (which is currently experiencing a challenge to the 35-hour week), the Netherlands, Sweden, etc. Although this trend is still confined to a few companies and industries that are facing the new stakes of economic competition in a more immediate way than others, it currently appears to be viewed by many developed countries as the most appropriate response to economic globalization. It does not encounter, for example, any legislative or collectively agreed obstacles any more than it runs counter to the dominant representations of a country such as the United States (Golden, Chapter 8, in this volume; Golden and Figart, 2000). This development then is part of a logic of cost competitiveness that aims to cut hourly labour costs, since very frequently the extension of working time is implemented without any increase in pay. Such an approach (the economic relevance of which this is not the place to discuss) heralds a break with the trend towards shorter working hours that had held sway in several European countries over the previous 20 years (see above). It also attests to a change in the nature of the instruments used for fostering economic growth, which, as far as the smooth running of the labour market was concerned, was assumed to be derived from the extension of the flexibility of working time and the development of a variety of forms of employment.

Work–life balance

For more than a decade, the issue of work–life balance has been one of the significant elements in European policy impacting on the length and organization of working time through the adoption of directives and recommendations, some of which have become the subjects of prior agreements between the social partners (part-time work, parental leave). It has already been emphasized that this dimension of work–life balance has been grasped as basic to the EU policy guidelines adopted in Lisbon in 2000, then reiterated in subsequent summits (in Barcelona, Stockholm and Laeken): the development of a knowledge-based society and an increase in employment rates, particularly for women, but also for younger and older people. The inclusion of the latter two categories additionally allows the concept of social time to be extended to all the time spent outside work – not only time spent with one's family. In practice, this institutional context has been a driver for the implementation of legislative provisions on parental leave or granting entitlements for changing to part-time hours (e.g., a Dutch law in July 2000 establishing a reversible option for moving from full- to part-time working; a 2001 law in Germany granting an entitlement for changing to part-time work). Collectively agreed provisions have also been negotiated in some sectors and companies offering employees the option of taking longer parental leave than the European basic norm (3 months); a temporary reduction in working time; and various working time modifications for family reasons (Den Dulk, 2001). In the United Kingdom, following several government initiatives aimed at encouraging the social partners to come up with "family-friendly" working time arrangements, the British Trade Union Confederation (TUC) launched a campaign in the late 1990s called "Changing Times", which aimed at spurring unions to negotiate the establishment of working time options that would enable a greater degree of work–life balance to be achieved. This prospect of a better relationship between working and family life thus gave rise to a wide variety of methods for reorganizing working time which has increased the process of diversifying working time schemes: long paid leaves and possibilities for career breaks; part-time work; variable working hours; a compressed working week; job-sharing; teleworking; the annualization of working time; and work schedules based on school hours (European Foundation, 2002).

Life-course working time policy

The European Employment Strategy begun in Luxembourg and endorsed at the Lisbon and Barcelona summits has also contributed to the growing number of working time provisions fostering the idea of older people remaining in the workforce, and a proactive labour market policy (designed to increase employment rates) through concepts such as lifelong learning. De facto, a process is now under way in Europe of the "destandardization" of the life courses of employees who are experiencing sometimes involuntary "career breaks" (i.e. unemployment), but who can also take advantage of new working time provisions enabling them to train throughout their lives and temporarily get involved in other activities (care, voluntary work, leisure, etc.) via the emergence of new working time provisions such as the *Droit individuel à la formation* ("Individual Training Entitlement") established in France in 2004 and the working time accounts in force in many companies in Germany, France, the Netherlands and Scandinavia (Boulin and Hoffmann, 1999; Naegele et al., 2003; Anxo and Boulin, 2005, 2006).

1.4.2 Current trends in working time and decent working time

These current trends in working time policy supplement rather than replace the policies in force over the last two decades that have contributed to the development of forms of reorganizing working time designed with the aim of granting greater productive flexibility to businesses (see section 1.2). Even firms themselves have spurred the emergence of initiatives in terms of work–life balance, in so far as productive flexibility has resulted in the growth of atypical working schedules and new forms of working time (especially the annualization of working hours), which are generally imposed on employees. This leads to a growing interference that blurs the boundaries between working life and life outside work, and raises questions regarding the relationship between working time and other forms of social time.

From the point of view of decent working time, the current trends in working time policies in developed countries contain contradictory elements. Although the policies enacted to procure a balance between the various types of social time, such as life-course policies, are, depending on the conditions in which they are implemented, integral parts of a philosophy based on the concept of decent working time, the potential extension of individual working hours is on a collision course with this approach for at least four main and mutually compounding reasons.

First, the possibility of detrimental outcomes from recent changes in working time duration (i.e. longer hours), and even the reorganization of working time – in terms of worker satisfaction certainly, but first and foremost in terms of difficult working conditions and occupational health – is obviously a decisive issue (Golden and Figart, 2000; Askenazy, 2004). A recent Austrian survey has shown that levels of stress rise proportionately with increases in working time (European Foundation, 2004).[7] Van Echtelt (2004) demonstrates that, for employees, overtime is a source of time-related pressure, and difficulties arise from trying to reconcile occupational and domestic constraints; that this may, however, be fully compensated for when occupational tasks are such that they can procure personal satisfaction; and finally that, on the other hand, the negative effects of overtime are not compensated for by the financial benefits that overtime work provides. The OECD (2004) has pointed out that around 20 per cent of men work long hours in all of its member States, with some countries being particularly affected by this phenomenon (Iceland, Japan, Republic of Korea, Mexico, New Zealand, Turkey, the United Kingdom, etc.). Moreover, working time flexibility – which often used to go hand in hand with a reduction in working time – has also had negative impacts on workers' health, due in particular to the twin trends of the intensification and the "densification" of working time (i.e. the elimination of unproductive time during the working day). The

---

[7] These findings come from the Austrian "work climate" survey (*Arbeitsklima-index*), which is based on a standardized survey of 1,800 respondents questioned in two interviews carried out over a 6-month period. It was commissioned by the Upper Austrian Chamber of Labour and carried out by the Institute for Empirical Social Research (IFES) and the Institute for Social Research and Analysis.

compounding effect of these two trends that seems to emerge with the development of extended working schedules may, from the perspective of working conditions, have disastrous effects. Studies carried out by the European Foundation for the Improvement of Living and Working Conditions (Merllié and Paoli, 2001; Boisard et al., 2003) stress the clear worsening of working conditions that occurred in Europe between 1990 and 2000, at the same time as the collective working week was being reduced and part-time working was on the rise. These same studies also demonstrate the diversification of working patterns; the growing importance of market constraints; and the demands placed on working time patterns by rigorous deadlines. It was argued for a time that contemporary forms of the reorganization of work had increased the autonomy of the people performing it and reduced the time pressures on them. However, no evidence of this can be found in the above-mentioned aggregate statistics. The pressure of deadlines and customer demands now seems to have replaced the pace of the assembly line – the very symbol of Taylorism and its excesses that were criticized during the 1960s and 1970s.

Second, long hours are an obstacle to attaining a work–life balance (see, e.g., Schor, 1991; Jacobs and Gerson, 2004). As the OECD (2004, p. 48) underlines: "The greatest difficulty in finding a balance between work and family life is very significantly linked to the presence of children in the household, to being younger and working longer hours or in more demanding jobs, or being self-employed." The Austrian survey on long hours referred to above demonstrates the negative impact of long hours on work–life balance: 62 per cent of respondents working 20 or fewer hours per week rate their own ability to reconcile work with family life as "very good", while only 39 per cent of those working between 35 and 40 hours and 29 per cent of those working more than 45 hours per week do so (European Foundation, 2004, p. 1). A DARES[8] study also shows that it is particularly the self-employed and managerial staff – i.e. those who usually work long hours – who experience the greatest difficulty in finding an adequate work–life balance (Garner et al., 2004). The findings in the two pieces of work referred to above converge in their indication that working atypical hours, most particularly at night, or having irregular or unpredictable working schedules makes achieving a good work–life balance more difficult. Clearly, here as well the compounding effect of the two trends is not going to help resolve the issue of the relationship between work and family life. The current trend in the context of a culture of long hours is to use services that assist in finding a good work–life balance to help alleviate these problems and to transfer the negative externalities of the organization of

---

[8] DARES is a section of the French Ministry of Labour that undertakes statistical surveys on employment conditions.

working time onto society as a whole, in the hope that time-related aspects of public policies at a municipal council level, whose objectives greatly exceed solely an adjustment function (see Boulin and Mückenberger, 2002), will enable these problems to be tackled.

Third, long working hours run counter to gender equality, and one might say counter to equality in general. As witnessed above, it is mostly men who work longer than 45-hour weeks, which also means that their contribution to educational and domestic tasks is still marginal in most developed countries (Gershuny, 2000). Because of this, women in many countries where schemes facilitating work–life balance are not very developed face a choice between engaging in paid work or bringing up children – a dilemma dramatically expressed in the decline in fertility rates in countries such as Spain and Italy. Unintended discriminatory negative effects on social equality stem from the fact that services assisting the search for a good work–life balance – for example, those that enable both parents to stay in the labour market, even when they have small children – are only accessible to those with higher incomes, which in turn consolidates the traditional division of labour at the foot of the social ladder.

Finally, long hours militate against both encouraging older workers to stay in the workforce and the prospects of developing life-course policies. Indeed, we know that it is those who have experienced the hardest working conditions, particularly in terms of hours or those who began to work at a young age, who leave or wish to leave the labour market prematurely.

1.5 RECONFIGURING WORKING TIME POLICIES BASED ON THE CONCEPT OF DECENT WORKING TIME

In respect of the current trends in working time, it should be stressed that neither work–life balance policies nor life-course working time policies are automatically rooted in the philosophy of decent working time. Many options offered to employees lead to gender discrimination and social inequalities due to the ways in which they are implemented and the systems of representation still dominant with regard to "downshifting". Those countries in which parental leave and other career-break mechanisms are paid, and in which social welfare regimes include them, are few and far between (Anxo and Boulin, 2005). Similarly, male entry rates into these schemes are still low, even where there are accompanying incentive systems, such as in Sweden. The same observation can be made regarding men's movement into part-time employment. As in the case with long-term leave, it is more the employers' responses that are questionable, in that such a decision, when made by male employees, is perceived by the former as a sign of the latter's lack of interest in their jobs. The Act of July 2000 enabling Dutch employees to reduce or increase their working time thus seems to have been little used so far (see Fouarge and Baaijens, Chapter 6 in this volume). Similarly, studies show that the take-up rate for working time accounts at the employee's initiative is still rather poor, especially for long-term working time accounts (Eberling et al., 2004).

Should working time policies therefore be reconfigured to more effectively anchor them in the decent working time approach? This is one of the questions that this book attempts to answer. From reading what has already been argued, it appears that a prerequisite is to break out of the trap of paradoxical precepts – especially that of wanting to simultaneously increase working time and institute work–life balance policies. Additionally, it should be emphasized that the increase in per capita working time does not inevitably entail the growth of a long-hours culture. Research shows that, although a considerable proportion of full-time employees want to reduce their working time, in particular those working overtime, another group – most clearly those in "marginal" part-time work with very short hours – actually want to increase their hours (see, e.g., Bielenski et al., 2002). Moreover, a rise in employment rates (and thus in per capita hours) can also occur if individuals who are currently outside of the labour market are able to enter employment with working hours that are not minimal.[9] Any solutions must take into consideration the various situations prevalent in each country: where there is a high employment rate for all age groups, among both men and women, and for the various ethnic groups, the increase of working time for those working part time seems a heuristic avenue (this is true of the Scandinavian countries and, to a lesser extent, of the Netherlands). Alternatively, where employment rates are generally low, or low for particular age, gender or ethnic groups, their integration into the labour market must be sought (this is true of France, Germany, and generally among the European "Mediterranean-model" countries).

Obviously, however, things also depend on social contexts. In a study cited by the OECD (2004, p. 55), for example, Golden shows that American workers who want more freedom of choice regarding their working hours often have to agree to long, atypical or unpredictable hours (Golden, 2001). This finding seems paradoxical in terms of our observation that this type of timetable is incompatible with family life.

A second avenue to explore is the compatibility between productive and individual flexibility, which raises the twin issues effectively highlighted in the

---

[9] As the OECD rightly notes, policies aiming to increase employment rates do not take into account the generally low number of hours worked by the members of under-represented groups when they are integrated into the active population. On the contrary, choosing the one-dimensional perspective of increasing the number of hours worked per member of the active population tends to neglect the determining significance of the extensive margin of labour supply (OECD, 2004).

1993 European Directive on working time, which "sets out the principle of adjusting work to mankind, which entails, on an individual level, that every person is in control of his/her time, and collectively, that collective time away from work be preserved" (Supiot, 1999, p. 127). These two issues are, first, the matter of workers' independence in the area of time and the influence they can have on their working schedules and, second, the issue of finding out whether non-working time is included in the regulation of working time and at what level (e.g., national legislation, regional, sector, company, etc.).

If our starting point is the observation that workers who can exercise a degree of control over the organization of their working time mention fewer problems in finding a decent work–life balance (OECD, 2004),[10] the findings of the survey on working conditions carried out by the Dublin-based European Foundation for the Improvement of Living and Working Conditions (European Foundation, 2001) demonstrate how much remains to be done: around one-third of all employees state that the number of hours they work varies from day to day, and approximately one-quarter state that they work different days from week to week; a little over one in four men and women say that their hours change at least once a month, and only about half of this group is given more than one day's notice of such changes; and, while 50 per cent to 60 per cent of all workers enjoy a degree of latitude in the choice of when to take breaks and paid holiday, only one-third say they actually have "control" over their working schedules. To respond to these power imbalances in terms of determining work schedules – which means, in the final analysis, reducing the employer's authority and the employee's subordination – we must look at which lines of inquiry enable us to make "chosen schedules" more widespread, and consider at which levels collective regulation of individual working time choices can be carried out. From this perspective, the law that came into force in the Netherlands as of July 2000 seems a fruitful path to follow, on the condition that the way in which it is to be implemented be specified at the sectoral level. Yet examples of companies in which genuine regulation of individual choice has been implemented show that collective bargaining can play its part in this area as well (Anxo and Boulin, 2006; Den Dulk, 2001). One further condition for greater autonomy being granted to employees in setting their work schedules and working patterns lies in the reconfiguration of social welfare systems in order that they include paid periods outside work as a part of the normal career path (as is true for parental leave in Sweden and other Scandinavian countries), and in order to confer

---

[10] Yet this point is not corroborated by all the studies. Work carried out by Garner et al. (2004) suggests that "People who set their own hours flag up more problems than those whose working time is set by a company, whether shift-work or a timetable that may change on a daily basis" (p. 3).

practical content on the neologism "flexicurity". From this point of view, the thinking currently being done in the Netherlands about the reconfiguration of the social welfare system from a life-course perspective deserves ongoing and more detailed attention (Leijnse et al., 2002).

If, as Alain Supiot emphasizes, "the personal needs and wishes of the workers must be addressed in the organization of work schedules" (Supiot, 1999, p. 136), this assumes, for example, the implementation of "policies aiming to reduce the opportunity cost devoted to work, via finer adjustment of work schedules to other daily activities" (OECD, 2004, p. 52). Such an approach means that working time and its regulation can be viewed from a societal perspective, with working time thus becoming one form of social time among others that has to be examined in terms of its relationship with other periods of social time. Legally speaking, this results in "considering time no longer solely as working time, like a measurement of the work/pay exchange, but also as a subjective experience, i.e. as part of the worker's life course" (Supiot, 2001, p. 127). In terms of action, this shows the whole point of local time policies (or time-related policies decided on a municipal council level), is to demonstrate that regulation should no longer apply to every form of social time taken individually, but rather to the relationship between the various types of social time (Boulin and Mückenberger, 2002).

Lastly, the final question and an extreme ambition, but one for which we must indeed provide some tentative theoretical and practical answers: in a knowledge-based society, is time still a relevant indicator for measuring work?

References

Anxo, D.; Boulin, J.-Y. (coordinators). 2005. *Working time options over the life course: Changing social security structures* (European Foundation for the Improvement of Living and Working Conditions, Luxembourg, Office for Official Publications of the European Communities).

—; —; (coordinators). 2006. *Working time options over the life course: New work patterns and company strategies* (European Foundation for the Improvement of Living and Working Conditions, Luxembourg, Office for Official Publications of the European Communities).

—; O'Reilly, J. 2000. "Working time regimes and transitions in comparative perspective", in J. O'Reilly, I. Cebrian and M. Lallement (eds.): *Working time changes: Social integration through transitional labour markets* (Cheltenham, United Kingdom, Edward Elgar).

Askenazy, P. 2004. *Les désordres du travail : Enquête sur le nouveau productivisme* (Paris, Editions du Seuil).

Bielenski, H.; Bosch, G.; Wagner A. 2002. *Working time preferences in sixteen industrial countries* (Dublin, European Foundation for the Improvement of Living and Working Conditions).

Boisard, P.; Cartron, D.; Gollac, M.; Valeyre, A. 2003. *Time and work: Duration of work* (Dublin, European Foundation for the Improvement of Living and Working Conditions).

Bosch, G.; Dawkins, P.; Michon, F. (eds.). 1994. *Times are changing: Working time in fifteen industrialised countries* (Geneva, ILO).

—; Meulders, D.; Michon, F. (eds.). 1997. *Le temps de travail, nouveaux enjeux, nouvelles normes, nouvelles mesures (Working time: New issues, new norms, new measures)* (Brussels, Editions du Dulbea).

Boulin, J.-Y; Hoffmann, R. 1999. *New paths in working time policy* (Brussels, European Trade Union Institute (ETUI)).

—; Mückenberger, U. 2002. *La ville à mille temps* (La Tour d'Aigues, France, Editions de l'Aube/Datar).

Campbell, I. 2004. "Employer pressures and overtime: Exploring the causes of extended working hours in Australia", paper presented at the Ninth Conference of the International Symposium on Working Time, Paris, 26–28 February.

Den Dulk, L., 2001. *Work–family arrangements in organizations: A cross-national study in the Netherlands, Italy, the United Kingdom and Sweden* (Amsterdam, Thela-Thesis).

Eberling, M.; Hielscher, V.; Hildebrandt, E.; Jürgens, K. 2004. *Prekäre Balancen, Flexible Arbeitszeiten zwischen betrieblicher Regulierung und Individuellen* (Berlin, Ansprüchen, Sigma).

European Commission. 2004. *Proposition de directive du Parlement Européen et du Conseil.* SEC, (2004) 1154, 22 September.

European Foundation for the Improvement of Living and Working Conditions. 2001. *Third European Survey on Working Conditions 2000* (Dublin).

—. 2002. *The reconciliation of work and family and collective bargaining.* (Dublin).

—. 2004. "Long working hours in Austria", in *News Updates*, 1 December 2004 (Dublin).

Garner, H; Méda, D; Senik, C. 2004. *La difficile conciliation entre vie professionnelle et vie familiale*. DARES, Premières Synthèses, Ministère de l'emploi, du travail et de la cohésion sociale, No. 50.3, Dec.

Gauvin, A.; Michon, F. 1989. "Work sharing public policy in France 1981–1986", in S. Rosenberg (ed.), *The State and the labor market*, collection: Studies in work and industry (New York, Plenum Publishing).

Gershuny, J. 2000. *Changing times: Work and leisure in post-industrial society* (Oxford, Oxford University Press).

Ghai, D. 2002. "Decent work: Concepts, models and indicators, Discussion paper no. 139" (Geneva, ILO).

Golden, L. 2001. "Flexible work schedules: What are we trading off to get them?", in *Monthly Labor Review*, Mar., pp. 50–67.

—; Figart, D.M. (eds.). 2000. *Working time: International trends, theory and policy perspectives* (London and New York, Routledge).

International Labour Office (ILO). 1999a. *Decent work*, Report of the Director-General to the International Labour Conference, 87th Session (Geneva).

—. 1999b. *Decent work and protection for all: A priority for the Americas*, Report of the Regional Director to the 14th Regional Meeting of ILO Member States of the Americas (Lima, Peru)

—. 2001. *Reducing the decent work deficit*, Report of the Director-General to the International Labour Conference, 89th Session (Geneva).

—. 2003. *International Labour Review Special Issue: Measuring Decent Work*, Vol. 142, No. 2.

Jacobs, J.A.; Gerson, K. 2004. *The time divide: Work, family, and gender inequality* (Cambridge, MA, Harvard University Press).

Klander, J. 2002. "The future of the Nordic Welfare Model", working paper for ILO staff, January.

Lee, S. 2004. "Working-hour gaps: trends and issues", in J.C. Messenger (ed.): *Working time and workers' preferences in industrialized countries: Finding the balance* (London and New York, Routledge).

Leijnse, F.; Goudsward, K.; Plantenga, J.; Van den Toren, J.P. 2002. *A different attitude to security: Life course, risk and responsibility* (The Hague, Ministry of Social Affairs and Employment).

Maddison, A. 2001. *The world economy: A millennial perspective* (Paris, OECD).

Maruani, M. 1994. "Marché du travail et marchandage social", in M. Lallement (ed.): *Travail et emploi: Le temps des métamorphoses* (Paris, L'Harmattan).

Math, A. 2002. "Retournement conjoncturel et emploi", in *Chronique internationale de l'IRES*, No. 78 (Retournement conjoncturel et emploi – numéro spécial), September, pp. 34–45.

Messenger, J. 2004. "Finding the balance: Working time and workers' needs and preferences in industrialized countries. A summary of the report and its implications for working time policies", paper presented at the Ninth International Symposium on Working Time, Paris, 26–28 February.

—. (ed.). 2004. *Working time and workers' preferences in industrialized countries: Finding the balance* (London and New York, Routledge).

Michon, F. 2003. "Sur la comparaison internationale des temps de travail", in M. Lallement and J. Spurl (dir.): *Stratégies de la comparaison internationale* (Paris, CNRS Éditions), June, pp. 189–97.

Naegele, G.; Barkholdt, C.; de Vroom, B.; Goul Andersen, J.; Krämer, K. (coordinators). 2003. *A new organization of time over working life* (Dublin, European Foundation for the Improvement of Living and Working Conditions).

Organisation for Economic Co-operation and Development (OECD). 2004. *OECD employment outlook 2004* (Paris, OECD).

Paoli, P., Merllié, D. 2001. *Third European survey on working conditions 2000* (Luxembourg, Office for Official Publications of the European Communities).

Rehn, G. 1972. "Prospective views on patterns of working time", Manpower and Social Affairs Directorate (Paris, OECD).

Rodgers, G. 2002. "Decent work as a goal for the global economy", unpublished mimeograph.

Schor, J. 1991. *The overworked American: The unexpected decline of leisure* (New York, Basic Books).

Supiot, A. 1999. *Au-delà de l'emploi: Transformations du travail et devenir du droit du travail en Europe* (Paris, Flammarion).

—. 2001. *Beyond employment: Changes in work and the future of labour law in Europe* (Oxford, Oxford University Press).

Van Echtelt, P. 2004. "Working overtime: When does it harm well-being?", paper presented at the Ninth Conference of the International Symposium on Working Time, Paris, 26–28 February.

WORKING TIME AND THE STANDARD EMPLOYMENT RELATIONSHIP

2

*Gerhard Bosch**

2.1   INTRODUCTION

When social scientists today debate the employment relationship of the traditional full-time core worker, the so-called standard employment relationship (SER), they speak almost exclusively of erosion and crisis rather than of change. The predominant notion is that the SER of the past is breaking up in favour of a diversity of non-standard atypical employment relationships that are no longer held together by any common bond, so that it no longer makes any sense to assume that there is any dominant form of employment relationship. For example, in his monumental work on the information society, Manuel Castells wrote that "the traditional form of work, based on full-time employment, clear-cut occupational assignment, and a career pattern over the lifecycle is being slowly but surely eroded away" (Castells, 1996, p. 268). He notes, moreover, that this applies not only to unskilled workers, but also, and particularly, to highly qualified knowledge workers (ibid., p. 267). The reasons he and other authors advance this can be summarized as follows:

- The new information and communications technologies (ICTs) are leading to the spatial restructuring of established productive systems. Corporate structures and forms of work organization geared to the long term are being replaced by virtual networks and frequently shifting forms of cooperation geared to the short term.

---

* Vice President, Institut Arbeit und Technik (Institute for Work and Technology) Gelsenkirchen, Germany and Professor of Sociology at the University Duisburg–Essen, Germany.

- The "half-life" of workers' skills and qualifications is declining because of the increasing pace of technological change. As a result, specialist knowledge that has tended hitherto to have a stabilizing effect over the course of the working life is being more rapidly devalued, so that in the future workers can expect to have to change jobs and occupations several times in their lives.

Self-evidently, these arguments share a common basis. Because of the disintegration of its spatial and social ties, labour is regarded as divisible and combinable at will. For most theoreticians of the information society, the current paradigm can be expressed as follows: "external structural change is replacing internal structural change". As is usually the case when such paradigms are formulated, this is meant not only as an empirical observation but also as a normative proposition. The new forms of employment are, it is argued, superior to the allegedly sluggish and conservative employment model of the past. The message is clear: "External structural change is more flexible and thus more efficient than internal structural change, because it is not hampered by so many rules. Only what is known can be regulated, not innovations." By virtue of its technological determinism, this paradigm is also universal. Its paean of praise to external labour market mobility turns it, perhaps unwittingly, into a propaganda vehicle for the so-called "Anglo-Saxon" model of deregulated labour markets that encourages external mobility.

Only a few contributors to the debate (Beynon et al., 2002; Bosch, 2002, 2004; Wagner, 2000b) have examined the chances of the SER's survival or reconstruction; outlined some starting points for the political action that needs to be taken; and developed some approaches to a new SER that would be viable in future. These opportunities for shaping the future of the SER and developing new norms for employment relationships are the subject of this chapter. These opportunities are also important for achieving the goal of decent work,[1] which up to now has been defined by the ILO (1999) largely in terms of good standards achieved in the traditional employment relationship. In order to uncover these buried starting points for action, the various lines of argument alluded to above need to be unpicked step by step. The fact that they are so intertwined makes it very difficult to obtain a clear view of the overall situation. It is not sufficient to check the numerous statements of fact against the findings of empirical research. The world of work is in such a state of upheaval that statistical surveys on the diffusion of particular forms of employment relationships merely provide snapshots of a moving object. In

---

[1] The ILO (1999) defines decent work in the following way: "Decent work is the converging focus of all its (the ILO's) four strategic objectives: the promotion of rights at work; employment; social protection; and social dialogue. It must guide its policies and define its international role in the near future."

order to make a film out of these snapshots, not necessarily one with a happy ending but at least with a comprehensible story, we have to get to grips with the forces driving the change. Only then will we be in a position not only to consider the future, but also to understand the causes of change, and hence identify shifts in trends and points of intervention for political action. What interventions are proposed is a normative decision – and not one that can be inferred simply from the analysis. However, whether or not any opportunities for action are revealed at all depends very much on the quality of the analysis.

The paradigm of work organization in the information society formulated by Castells and others is empirically indefensible, normatively questionable and, because of differences in societal configurations, not universal in scope. This will be demonstrated in what follows. I begin by outlining what the standard employment relationship actually is and why it was regarded as "standard" during a long period of high economic growth. Here, particular attention will be devoted to analysing the connection between the standard employment relationship and standard working hours (section 2.2). In section 2.3, selected empirical findings on the development of employment relationships in various countries are presented. I then turn to an examination of the various causes of the change in employment relationships and their effects on the SER. What emerges from this examination is that much of what is attributed to the computerization of society has quite different causes. It will be shown that new technologies are only one of several equally important causes of the changes that have occurred in the standard employment relationship (section 2.4). Since paradigms can be combated only with other paradigms and not with facts (Kuhn, 1967), I would like to propose an alternative paradigm which, in contrast to that formulated by Castells, takes as its starting point a balance between external and internal change on the one hand and, on the other, more working time options for employees to choose from (section 2.5). An alternative paradigm is necessary, because otherwise all other options will be closed off. Castells will of course be proved absolutely right if his view becomes so dominant that it pushes all other approaches and possibilities into the background.

2.2   THE DEFINITION AND FUNCTION OF THE SER

The traditional SER has been defined as a "stable, socially protected, dependent, full-time job . . . the basic conditions of which (maximum working hours per day and week, rest times, pay, social transfers etc.) are regulated to a minimum level by collective agreement or by labour and/or social security law" (Bosch, 1986, p. 165). The full-time nature of the job, its stability and the social standards linked with permanent full-time work are the key elements in this definition. Only full-time employment guarantees a family wage and an adequate level of social protection, while a stable job places the relations between employer and employee on a long-term footing. Nolan's starting point is the social function of the SER for employers. He argues that what distinguishes this employment relationship from other forms of exchanges is the "attempt by employers to reconcile ... two problems – of securing workers' cooperation and a surplus product" (Nolan, 1983, p. 303). Harvey (1999) and Clarke (1991) identify the wage form as the key criterion in assessing the approach to future time inherent in employment forms. In the SER, in contrast to day labour, workers are paid not only for the days they work, but also for times when they are not working or are investing in their capacity for work (through learning on the job, initial and further training, health and safety at work and so on). The object of the contract is not only today but also to-morrow, with many mutual obligations enshrined therein. These obligations may include, on the employee's side, exclusivity of employment with one organization and, on both sides, a commitment to a minimum period of employment and rules for terminating the contract. Esping-Andersen (1990) argues that workers are not commodities like other inputs to production because they must survive and reproduce both themselves and the society they live in. As commodities they could easily be destroyed by even minor contingencies such as illness, and by macro-events like the business cycle. Decommodification is a precondition for a tolerable level of individual welfare and security. The welfare state, including job protection and the entitlements linked to the SER, reflects responses to pressure for decommodification (Esping-Andersen, 1990, p. 37). He differentiates between three types of welfare systems: the social-democratic (example Sweden), the corporatist (example Germany), and the neo-liberal (example United States). The purpose of welfare state regulations in the social-democratic and corporatist models is to protect that special commodity *labour* from the vagaries of the market. The various social protection measures create buffers between the market and employment relationships that guarantee workers an income, at least for a transitional period when they are not working, or are working less, because of illness, accident, unemployment, short-time working, etc.

The various analytical perspectives on the SER can be summarized by reviving the concept of decommodification – not, as Esping-Andersen sees it, as relating only to the provision of social security by the welfare state – but with its original wider meaning. The term, which was, to the best of my knowledge, first coined by Briefs (1927), who spoke of decommercialization, and Polyani (1957), covered all the social protection measures of a welfare state that create buffers between the market and employment relationships. These buffers are rooted, first, in the supra-enterprise welfare state and, second, in the employment contract itself, which is not concluded, as it is with day labourers, for the here and now, but contains elements of future security. For example, owing to protection against dismissal, enterprises are obliged to conclude longer-term employment contracts, and under certain conditions, such as holiday, illness, unemployment, accident or continuing training, employees still receive money when they are not working, and, thanks to compulsory insurance, part of the wage goes towards provision for retirement. Third, there is also the issue of making use of the commodity *labour* once the contract has been concluded. Time limits are set for this utilization. Employees' capacity for work is maintained over the long term by protecting workers from excessive demands, for example by establishing maximum working times and holiday entitlements (Bosch, 1999). Private life is made easier to plan by establishing a standard working time and rules that have to be adhered to when deviations from that norm are necessary (payment of premiums, giving notice of changes to working time). The first two dimensions can be described as external decommodification and the third as internal decommodification of employment relationships. Working time regulations play a part in all three dimensions.

Thus the SER enables employees to plan for the long term. This applies not only to the planning of everyday life, such as the use of leisure time, but also to workers' investment, and that of family members, in their own capacity for work, for example through education and training. Social protection and the constraining of corporate decision-making by rules (protection against dismissal, for example) increase employees' bargaining power in the labour market, which they are able to deploy effectively in representing their interests. Above all, they have been able to obtain for themselves a share of the increase in economic productivity and compensation for their own willingness to be flexible (e.g., through the payment of overtime premiums). In this way, the SER has been a significant instrument for the reduction of social inequality.

If only welfare state regimes are compared, there is a danger that the function of the SER for firms and the economy as a whole will be overlooked, a point underlined by Nolan (1983). Firms also benefited from the standards laid down by the SER during the period of stable economic growth and mass production. In the past, work organization in both the manufacturing industry and the service sector was based on full-time employment and the 8-hour day associated with it, and on the 48-hour and, later, the 40-hour week. This traditional form of working time was the main pillar of work organization systems and was generally taken for granted. Thus employees' standard working time was not simply an externally imposed regulation but found its equivalence in firms' work organization systems. This is the main reason why traditional forms of work organization became second nature to both employees and firms. The standard working time laid down in the SER and the dismissal protection it provided meant that ad hoc personnel decisions became costly, leading firms to plan their personnel deployment very carefully. The high-productivity increases achieved in the 1960s and 1970s showed that they made intensive use of their freedom of action within the framework laid down by the SER in order to reorganize and rationalize labour deployment.

This focus on decommodification has been criticized from a gender perspective because "in order to enjoy rights to 'de-commodification' it is essential to be a potential participant in the labour market. Some welfare states act to restrict women's role to the domestic or family sphere, while others encourage and promote the participation of all citizens" (Rubery and Grimshaw, 2003, p. 87). In the corporatist model, as in the German model, the traditional male breadwinner model is still further stabilized by a number of reinforcing measures, such as morning-only school, the inadequate supply of childcare facilities, the so-called *splitting* system for assessing married couples' tax liability and the system of deriving married women's social security entitlements from their husbands' SER. On the basis of criticism of the traditional paternalistic model, Orloff (1993) actually demanded the right for women "to be commodified" (ibid., p. 318). However, this formulation is misleading. What Orloff really means is a right to paid employment, and not the dismantling of all the protective provisions of the SER. To recommodify the SER would only mean replacing a woman's dependence on her husband with dependence on the market. This is an important distinction, since only some, but by no means all, of the regulations involved in the traditional SER impede employment of women. Today many working women, even in the corporatist welfare model, enjoy the protection of many SER regulations, and the new, more flexible, SER in the social-democratic model has developed not by deregulating the old model but through reregulation. In the 1950s and 1960s the Scandinavian welfare states also supported traditional household structures with a male breadwinner and were gradually transformed into the social-democratic welfare states of today, which is based on the assumption that all fit adults are in employment. We will see that the switch from derived entitlements to individual rights in European welfare states is one of the major drivers of change in the SER.

It is clear from the various definitions and attributions of function that the SER is of value not only to employees but also to firms and society as a whole. Employees are protected from the vagaries of the markets and can make long-term plans for themselves and their families. Firms benefit from a reliable framework within which to plan their work organization and are able to rely on their employees' willingness to cooperate in return for the security they enjoy. In society as a whole, inequalities are reduced and families are enabled to invest in their members' human capital. With the traditional household division of labour, the SER could fulfil these functions only if the single male breadwinner worked full time and earned a family wage. However, examination of the various models of the welfare state has revealed that alternatives very definitely exist. In order to develop our analysis, therefore, it is important to make a distinction between the substance of the SER and its form. The substance is determined by the functions set out above. However, the forms (full-time employment, family wage, rigid forms of work organization based on the 8-hour day or full-time employment) can change.

2.3   THE EVOLUTION OF THE SER IN THE EU

Contrary to all the forecasts made by Castells and others, there has been no sign of an end to the SER. In the EU-15, between 1992 and 2003 the proportion of people in self-employment fell from 16.1 per cent to 14.8 per cent. The proportion of employees with fixed-term contracts rose from 11.1 per cent to 12.8 per cent and the proportion of part-time employees from 14.2 per cent to 18.2 per cent (European Commission, 2004). Permanent full-time employment is still the predominant employment relationship. In this context, there are interesting differences between individual countries. In southern Europe in particular, the proportion of people in self-employment has fallen, particularly in the primary sector. In some countries there are very high proportions of employees with fixed-term contracts (Spain and the United Kingdom), or their proportion has increased rapidly in recent years (Belgium, Ireland, Portugal). In Austria, Belgium, France, Germany, Ireland, the Netherlands and the United Kingdom, as the numbers of women in employment have risen, there has also been a rapid increase in the proportion of part-time employees, but in Denmark, part-time employment has decreased and in Sweden it has remained unchanged. Both the proportions of part-time employees and the rate of women in employment are low in southern Europe. Since part-time work is primarily structured as women's work, any attempt to explain these trends must look first at the conditions under which family responsibilities and paid work can be reconciled.

Obviously, the expansion of fixed-term or temporary employment can, under certain conditions, undermine the SER (e.g., Spain). One possible reason for this may lie in excessive regulation of the SER, which induces firms to confine themselves largely to revocable personnel decisions when adjusting employment levels. Another reason may be inadequate levels of flexibility within the workforce (because of skill deficiencies, for example), which encourages firms to opt for external flexibility.

Part-time and full-time work are often looked at as different forms of employment relationships. Blyton and Turnbull (1994) subdivided the labour force into three broad categories: a core of full-time workers, a periphery of part-time, temporary, and homeworkers together with the self-employed, and, finally, the unemployed (p. 53). This polarized view of full-time and part-time work might make sense in the British context but should not be generalized. In some European countries, the hours worked by full-timers and part-timers are beginning to converge as a result of an increase in part-timers' hours and a reduction in those of full-timers. In Denmark, for example, it became possible for many women to work the reduced full-time norm when the generalized reduction of working time from 40 to 37 hours was introduced. At the same time, female part-timers now tend to work 30 hours per week rather than the 20 hours they used to work 10 years ago. The reduction of men's working time has certainly also helped to change the family division of labour and women's labour market behaviour (figure 2.1a). In Germany, these developments are only in their early stages and are masked in particular by the strong growth in marginal part-time employment among women (figure 2.1b). In the United Kingdom, on the other hand, full-time and part-time employment are tending rather to diverge. The de facto full-time norm among men is far in excess of 40 hours. Obviously unions have lost or never gained control over actual working hours. Long working hours are a strong indicator for an inner recommodification of the SER. The large volume of overtime worked by men means that married women with children, despite an advantageous school system with relatively long hours, have to be content with marginal part-time jobs, so that the gap between full-time and part-time employment has widened even further in recent years. In contrast to Denmark (figure 2.1c), part-time work is also largely unregulated; it is less well paid than full-time work, so there is little incentive for households to substitute the low wages earned by female part-timers for men's overtime, which attracts premium payments. A longitudinal survey would probably show even more clearly that the differences between full-time and part-time employment are becoming more fluid in Denmark. Temporary rather than permanent part-time working, with a return to full-time employment, has become part of a normal work history, particularly as a result of flexible parental leave arrangements.

The empirical evidence presented up to this point has provided only snapshots of the diffusion of certain employment forms. Such snapshots cannot reveal whether or not the SER is being eroded from within by increasing job turnover, which has increased instability over the course of the working life. Auer and Cazes (2002) investigated the evolution of average job tenure in various industrialized countries. They found, surprisingly, that employment stability in most countries had increased (table 2.1). In some countries (Ireland, the United States) job tenure has increased because of the high growth rates and the high level of recruitment of new workers. Auer and

Figure 2.1　Distribution of usual weekly working hours for dependent employees, 1992 and 2002

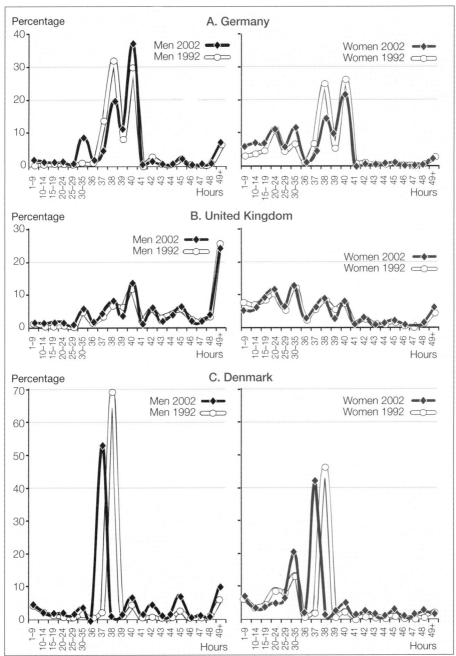

Source: European Labour Force Survey 1992, 2002 (calculations: S. Schief, Institut Arbeit und Technik).

49

Table 2.1   Average employment tenure, 1992–2000

Country	1992	2000	Percentage change 1992–2000
Belgium	11.0	11.5	4.5
Denmark	8.8	8.3	−5.7
Germany	10.7	10.5	−1.9
Finland[1]	n.a.	10.1	−5.6
France	10.4	11.1	6.7
Greece	13.5	13.5	0.0
Ireland	11.1	9.4	−15.3
Italy	11.9	12.2	2.5
Japan	10.9	11.6	6.4
Luxembourg	10.1	11.4	12.9
Netherlands	8.9	9.1	2.2
Portugal	11.1	11.8	6.3
Spain	9.9	10.1	2.0
Sweden[1]	n.a.	11.5	8.5
United Kingdom	8.1	8.2	1.2
United States[2]	6.7	6.6	−1.5
EU (14)[3]	10.5	10.6	1.6
Average	10.2	10.4	2.1

Notes: [1] Change from 1995 to 2000. [2] Average tenure data refer to 1991 instead of 1992. For US and Japan, data refer to 1998 instead of 2000. [3] Without Austria.
n.a. not available

Source: Auer and Cazes (2002), p. 25.

Cazes controlled for economic growth rates and the age structure of workers and came to the conclusion that "we do not find any general and systematic trend towards declining tenure" (p. 29). A number of other writers (e.g. Erlinghagen and Knuth, 2004; Doogan, 2001) have reached similar conclusions. Erlinghagen (2004) actually shows that the increasing integration of women into the German labour market has been accompanied by an increase in the stability of employment of part-time employees in particular.

With international comparisons of this kind, one must be aware that apparently comparable statistical categories are often being used to measure very different things. Because of the low level of statutory dismissal protection and the decline in trade union power and influence in the United Kingdom and the United States, a permanent, full-time job in the large areas not covered by a collective agreement in these countries frequently offers no more protection than a temporary contract, so that ultimately it matters little to employers or employees which kind of contract is concluded. It is hardly surprising, therefore, that, after the far-reaching deregulation of recent decades, there is less debate on the SER in the United States and the United Kingdom to match that being conducted, for example, in Germany. In the neo-liberal model, permanent full-time work is decommodified only to a limited extent, if at all.

2.4   THE CAUSES OF THE CHANGE IN THE SER

In empirical terms, this means that the forecast erosion of the SER cannot be identified as a universal trend. In this chapter it will be shown that the new ICTs are not the only reason for a change in employment relationships, and that other causes play an equally important part. In particular, new technologies are embedded in enterprises' work organization, and do not affect employment relationships directly, but only indirectly. In this section, an attempt will be made to bring out the various causes of change. A distinction will be made here between the following six significant factors: (1) the flexibilization of product markets; (2) rising employment rates among women; (3) the combining of education/training and work; (4) rising educational levels among the working population; (5) the employment situation; and (6) the regulation or deregulation of the labour market.

1.   *Flexibilization of product markets.* The continuity and predictability of working time in the traditional SER did not become possible until product markets were similarly organized. The manufacturing industry was dominated by mass production, which enabled firms to deal with fluctuating demand by holding stocks, and less by varying working time. In many service industries, standard working time was safeguarded by fixed opening hours. These arrangements have changed. Mass production shifted to low-wage countries a long time ago and goods are now produced virtually exclusively to order. It is no longer possible to keep parts in stock for the growing number of possible variants; thus stocks can no longer serve as a buffer between market and production and their role has been taken by working time. At the same time, opening hours in many service industries have been extended and hence also the time frame within which customer flows of varying volumes have to be served. In addition, and particularly in knowledge-intensive forms of work, such as software production, there is the pressure of deadlines in project work, which is a consequence of, among other things, the diminishing half-life of innovations. In a generally more flexible economy, firms cannot survive with the old, rigid employment forms. A return to the early industrial

forms of hiring and firing offers a solution only in the case of low-level jobs. In other jobs, employers are increasingly dependent on skilled workers, whom they wish to retain even in times of crisis in order not to lose the considerable investment they have made in their know-how. Consequently, they seek to increase internal flexibility. The rise in job tenure, despite more turbulent markets, has been possible as a result of greater internal flexibility. Employees today are better and, more importantly, more broadly educated and are therefore more versatile (Bosch, 2000). Moreover, flexible working times mean there are considerable internal reserves of labour that can be drawn on in the event of fluctuations in demand. More and more firms today prefer to eliminate hours of work rather than dismiss employees. Research has shown that the new ICTs enable companies to manage and control higher levels of internal and external flexibility than in the past, but they are a neutral tool, not an independent driving force behind any particular form of flexibility.

2. *Rising employment rates among women.* Female employment rates have risen considerably in recent years in most of the developed industrialized countries and according to all forecasts will continue to increase further in the years to come. This additional labour supply is not, like that of men in the single breadwinner model, free of the burden of reproductive work but rather has to combine paid work with domestic responsibilities. The working hours and employment forms that women are in a position to accept depend primarily on the social organization of childcare. In countries with an inadequate childcare infrastructure, many women will be able only to look for part-time employment or have to remain childless. The inadequate provision of care facilities for children under 3 and morning-only schooling are the reasons why women with children in the Netherlands or Germany either seek part-time employment or, because of these restrictions, decide, perhaps reluctantly, not to have children, which is reflected in the sharply falling birth rate. Substantial differences between the wages of men and women will mean that, for financial reasons, households are likely to opt for longer working hours for men and shorter working hours for women. Another important factor affecting the distribution of working hours between men and women is pay differences between men and women (incentives offered by the tax and social security systems for non-employment or marginal part-time employment (Dingeldey, 2000)). Thus an increase in women's employment that is not accompanied by changes in the wider social environment is a phenomenon with the capacity to blow apart the traditional SER (albeit one that is concealed by the decline in the birth rate), and can be defused only by a reorganization of childcare.

3. *The combining of education/training and work.* As higher education has expanded, so the number of high-school and university students seeking employment has risen. Many industries (call centres, for example) have based their work organization systems and locational decisions on this specific labour supply. In the EU, the percentage of young people aged between 15 and 29 who are combining part-time work and education rose between 1987 and 1995 from 22 per cent to 33 per cent (European Commission, 2000). In Germany, a growing percentage of students are seeking employment, usually part-time employment. In 1991 the employment rate among students was 51 per cent, but in 2003, 68 per cent of the some 2 million students were in employment (Deutsches Studentenwerk, 2003). The Eurobarometer showed an increase in occasional employment among young people aged between 15 and 24 from 13 per cent in 1997 to 15 per cent in 2001 (Eurobarometer, 2001, p. 103). Thus as a result of the expansion of the education system and the consequent extension of the *youth phase* of the life course, employment forms are becoming increasingly differentiated, particularly among younger people; temporary and part-time jobs have become *standard*, albeit temporary employment forms that are not the last points on individual career trajectories.

4. *Rising educational levels among the working population.* In today's knowledge society, a good education will increasingly serve as an entry ticket to the labour market. In most countries, the employment rate for highly qualified men and women is significantly higher than that for the less well qualified (figure 2.2). For the more highly qualified, the influence of educational level on labour market position is now greater than that of gender. Incidentally, this also applies to working time and employment forms. The higher the qualification level, the longer the average working times and the lower the part-time employment rate tends to be. Thus as qualification levels among the working population rise, the demand for permanent, full-time employment also rises. In this respect, the risk to the SER comes from quite another direction. Working times are especially increasing among highly qualified workers, and a permanent, full-time contract no longer fulfils its classic function of protecting workers against excessive demands (Wagner, 2000a). Overlong working hours may lead to internal recommodification, while external decommodification is maintained. Such an internal recommodification can be observed in the United Kingdom (figure 2.3).

5. *The employment situation.* The SER is a regulated employment relationship. Only by laying down minimum standards can employment

Figure 2.2   Employment rates for men and women (aged 15–64) by educational qualifications in the EU-15, 2002

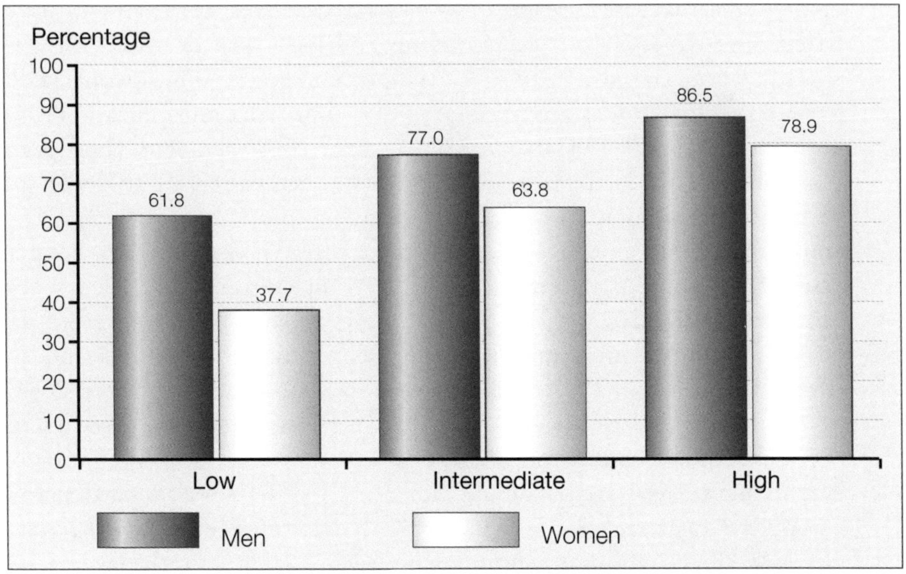

Source: European Labour Force Survey 1992, 2002 (calculations: S. Schief, Institut Arbeit und Technik).

relationships in very different firms and industries and among very different groups of employees acquire the common characteristics required for the development of a societal standard. If central regulations (on working time or dismissal protection, for example) were abolished, then employees would have to negotiate their employment conditions individually. Under such circumstances, only a small proportion would enjoy the same level of protection as under the SER. In some countries, such as the United Kingdom or the United States, labour market deregulation has been a contributory factor in the wholesale undermining of the SER. However, deregulation of the SER is not the only problem, since excessive regulation, as well as the regulations governing other employment forms, can have similar effects. If the SER is too rigid, firms will increasingly resort to other employment forms, as the example of temporary work in Spain shows. Since complete decommodification in a market economy is not possible, a balance has to be struck between security and flexibility. However, the reason for the use of other employment forms may also be that they are under-regulated. If these employment forms give firms unrestricted freedom to take the decisions they wish to take, as is the case, for example, with marginal part-time jobs in Germany, then the regulatory *gap* between the various employment

Figure 2.3   Share of employees usually working more than 48 hours per week, 1992 and 2002

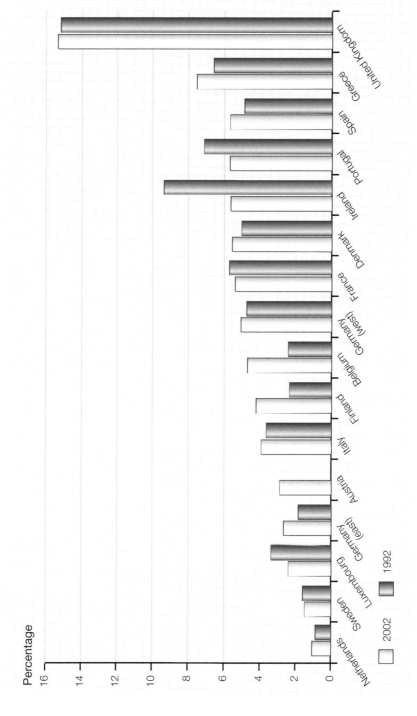

Percentage

Source: European Labour Force Survey 1992, 2002 (calculations: S. Schief, Institut und Technik).

forms can give rise to a powerful *suction effect* pulling standards irresistibly downwards. On the other hand, the more strongly all forms of part-time work are regulated, the more similar they become in all aspects to the SER, with working time remaining then as the only significant difference.

6. *Regulation/deregulation of the labour market.* Full employment and economic growth formed the background against which the SER came into existence mainly in the 1950s and 1960s. High unemployment, on the other hand, together with labour market regulation, has been the most important factor in the dissolution of the SER. As unemployment rises, competition in the labour market increases and employees' bargaining power declines. Firms are able to shift a greater share of market risks on to workers' shoulders and will offer only less well-protected employment forms. Many workers are unable to realize their employment preferences, so that they have to accept involuntary part-time work or temporary employment. However, as unemployment decreases, employers have to compete for labour, which is in shorter supply, and improve employment conditions. Under such circumstances, they will even be happy to resort to standardized employment forms, since these standards limit employees' demands as well, thereby removing disputes over distribution from the everyday life of the workplace. Thus a reduction in unemployment, which is to be expected in the years to come, not least for demographic reasons, may strengthen the SER on a lasting basis.

All six of these factors may alter the significance of the traditional SER in various ways. If the temporal and functional flexibility within the SER is not developed further in comparison with the rigid Taylorist forms, in increasingly flexible product markets enterprises will increasingly switch to external forms of flexibility, such as fixed-term contracts or temporary workers. If women's opportunities for integration into the labour market are not improved by means of improvements in childcare, equal wages and career prospects with men, and flexible working hours during phases of child-rearing and other domestic care, there will be a polarization between part-time and full-time work, resulting in a lessening of the SER's importance as has happened in the United Kingdom. When unemployment is chronically high, competition between insiders and outsiders will undermine the SER. Policy can play a widely varying part here. In the social-democratic model, it can develop a new, more flexible, SER via reregulation, something that has already been achieved in the Scandinavian countries. However, by recommodifying employment relationships, as has happened in the United States, it can also create a new form of equality between the sexes via the market, with high employment rates, great insecurity as regards employment, and long working hours for men and women – in other words, also creating internal recommodification. Since it makes no sense to select the expansion of the education and training system as an indicator of the crisis in the SER, particularly since career trajectories are likely to be stabilized by the expansion of the education system, it would be sensible to base future investigations of the diffusion of the SER on employees aged 25 and over.

2.5   APPROACHES TO A NEW, FLEXIBLE SER

It could be shown that the dissolution of the SER is not an inevitable development, determined by the use of the new ICTs. Castells also expresses some doubts about his own all too deterministic comments. At some points, Castells refers to the importance of the experience and knowledge of an established workforce[2] and at others calls into question the universalism of the "Anglo-Saxon" model and emphasizes the possibility of alternative routes to social development.[3] He seems not entirely unimpressed by the findings of innovation research, industrial sociology and labour market research which, from various perspectives, point to the increasing importance of spatial proximity, stable relationships and close social communication in knowledge-based work and to differences in societal development trajectories. This has far-reaching consequences for the structuring of employment relationships, which can be described as follows: it is true that the technical possibilities for dividing up work processes and rapidly assembling the parts at any location have increased. However, only standardized activities whose contents are known and have been codified can be divided up and put back together again. In innovative work environments, additional, as yet uncodified knowledge is created. This includes, on the one hand, knowledge derived from experience, without which the productive potential of new technologies cannot be developed. On the other hand, it includes new knowledge that has not yet become standard. True, companies make efforts to decode such knowledge in order to incorporate it into technologies or to be able to pass it on through vocational training. However, these efforts come up against certain constraints, since demand for standard products is constantly decreasing and

---

[2] Thus he writes, for example: " the nature of the informational work process calls for co-operation, team work, worker's autonomy and responsibility, without which new technologies cannot be used up to their potential" (Castells, 1996, p. 246).

[3] Thus he argues that working and employment conditions are by no means necessarily determined by information technologies: "these trends do not stem from the structural logic of the informational paradigm, but are the result of the current restructuring of capital–labour relationships, helped by the powerful tools provided by new information technologies" (Castells, 1996, p. 273).

firms are constantly chasing after new knowledge because of the ever-quickening pace of innovation. Since the uncodified knowledge is embodied in individuals or teams and is not transferable, or if it is, only at considerable cost, it is economically efficient for firms to build up skilled workforces and to invest in their skills. They offer these core workforces security and in return expect a high degree of flexibility, together with the motivation and commitment required to mobilize the uncodified knowledge.

However, the traditional SER, based on Taylorist production structures and the male sole wage earner, cannot survive unchanged. The question of what policy changes will be sought is a normative issue, but at the same time it is also a question of efficiency. A welfare state and its labour and social laws cannot be funded unless they are embedded in efficient economic structures, and they themselves make a contribution to efficiency. As in the old SER, efficiency and social security must be combined under new production conditions and new household structures.

One of the starting points of this analysis was the fact that a changed SER should be created not by deregulating the old model, but via reregulation. In order to be able to describe the levels of reregulation more precisely, it is helpful to begin by describing the additional functions of a new SER. The old SER was intended to achieve the following goals: (1) protection of employees against economic and social risks; (2) reduction of social inequality; and (3) an increase in economic efficiency. The simultaneous realization of these goals made it possible to achieve decent work standards (ILO, 1999) through compromises between the interests of employees, firms and society as a whole. These objectives have been achieved to a large extent. Social inequalities in the developed European welfare states have been reduced, employees were well protected against the major economic and social risks, and companies have been able to develop highly productive forms of work organization within the framework laid down through the SER. The old objectives are still current, but three further goals have to be added to them. The first of these is equal access for men and women to the employment system, the second support for lifelong learning in order to improve employability in a rapidly changing economy, and the third increased flexibility in the workplace. This would add the functions underlined in figure 2.4 to the traditional functions of the SER. The new SER thus created would be similar in its substance to the old one, but its form would be adapted to the changed social conditions.

There will be a change in working hours in particular, as a result of the new needs of enterprises and of employees themselves. Enterprises will distribute their working hours more flexibly over the year or over more than one year, and employees too, in altered household structures, will not always work regularly.

Figure 2.4   Functions of the old and the new SER

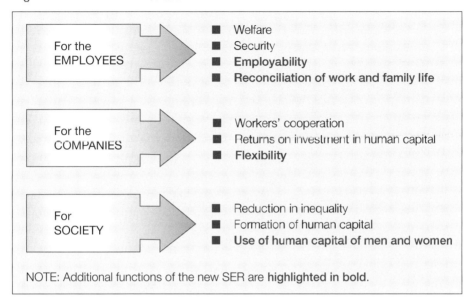

If both partners in a couple are economically active, the man will no longer have to earn the family wage by himself. If both partners combine paid work and family responsibilities, career paths will become more flexible. Workers will alternate between periods of full-time employment, part-time employment and career breaks (parental or educational leave). Flexible career paths of this kind differ from market-driven "human capital portfolios" (Carnoy et al., 1997) in that they are decommodified. Changes in employment forms over the life course are not only enforced but also self-selected and socially protected.

Just like the traditional SER, its replacement must be socially embedded and supported. The following structures in particular are crucial elements in the institutional framework required for its successful realization:

1. *Promotion of internal flexibility in flexible work organization systems.* Flexible working times over the life course lead to increased employee turnover. At the same time, firms are operating in more turbulent markets. These increased demands for flexibility can be met only by developing decentralized forms of work organization. Any attempt to combine business efficiency with increased time sovereignty for employees inevitably raises the question of work organization. There are now numerous examples of innovative forms of work organization that show that such a synthesis can be made to work successfully (Lehndorff, 2001). Employees must adopt a more flexible attitude than in the classic

SER towards both working time and their sphere of deployment. Limits must, however, be set to the temporal flexibility of employees via protective norms (maximum working hours, breaks and rest periods, notice periods for changing working hours).

2. *Promotion of lifelong learning.* In the knowledge society, there is a risk, even with short career breaks, that skills and qualifications will become obsolete. Thus social protection can no longer be confined to passive transfers for those experiencing difficulties in achieving labour market integration, as it was in the past; rather, as the quid pro quo for the establishment of more flexible forms of work organization, it must improve opportunities for lifelong learning.

3. *Development of the public childcare infrastructure for children under 3 and for those of school age (all-day schooling).* Extension of the childcare system must take priority over financial transfers that support economic inactivity among women (e.g. child-rearing allowance) and also over any increase in child benefits. Only if the social infrastructures are reliable do mothers and fathers have genuine freedom to choose how to organize their labour supply.

4. *Increased opportunities for choosing working hours.* The rigid full-time standard seriously restricted individual choice of working hours. Surveys of employees' working time preferences across Europe (Bielenksi et al., 2002) show that most employees would prefer a weekly working time within the 25- to 38-hour range. In most countries, however, individual preferences still founder on the rigid division between full-time and part-time work, which must be relaxed. More men, reluctant to shift to part-time work with its attendant discriminations but more than willing to contemplate a few hours' reduction in their working time or blocks of free time distributed over several years, would then be likely to reduce their working hours. In this way, it would be possible to share out the volume of paid work, not only among women but also between the sexes.

5. *Derived entitlements to social security should be replaced by individual rights.* Independent social protection for women will have to be built up primarily through continuous economic activity. When women are economically active in their own right, then some derived rights, such as widows' pensions, would be claimed less and less and could probably be abolished. Equal treatment for different lifestyles and the ending of tax subsidies for married couples without children (e.g. the tax-splitting system for married couples) will help to encourage women to enter the labour market and hence build up their own social security entitlements.

Figure 2.5   Internal change in occupational and internal labour market

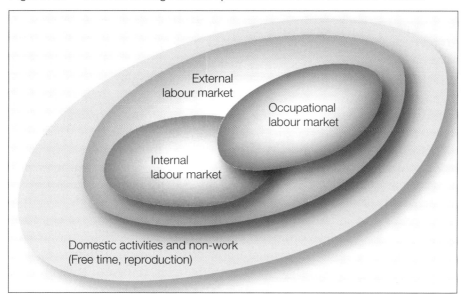

The first two points can be integrated by developing occupational labour markets, i.e. the risks involved for the individual in changing jobs can be reduced and at the same time enterprises' internal flexibility can be increased. Castells would object that the half-life of qualifications is declining and hence recognized occupations no longer afford workers any protection in the labour market. However, he does not make sufficient distinction between the various levels of qualifications. When it is used, general knowledge lasts a lifetime; basic knowledge of a trade or occupation also has a long half-life but must be continuously supplemented; specialist knowledge is being renewed ever more rapidly. High-quality vocational training, updated through further training and experience, allows workers to change employer without loss of status. Since occupational labour markets have developed in Germany right down to the lower qualification categories, there are particularly good opportunities here for encouraging the extended internal mobility we have outlined. Figure 2.5 shows the considerable possible overlap between internal and occupational mobility. Because job tenure has remained largely stable, the regulations on dismissal protection and social security arrangements associated with the long-established SER have not become outdated. However, they must be expanded to include support for occupational training and further training, in order to safeguard workers' employability. Investment in qualifications will in future become even more important than monetary compensation in the event of dismissal.

This is also an advantage for companies. Interfirm cooperation can function only on the basis of communicable stocks of knowledge and shared know-how. Communicable stocks of knowledge are acquired through standardized vocational training, while familiarity with comparable work processes and interfirm exchanges of experiences make it possible to acquire a minimum level of know-how that is at least reciprocal. In order to keep frictional losses in interfirm networking as low as possible, it is rational for firms to employ workers with a vocational training whose contents can be communicated to other firms and to locate themselves in regions with a large number of potential partners who, by virtue of their physical proximity, can exchange their know-how with each other and, in the case of complex processes, plan to cooperate on a long-term basis, thereby making their investment in the development of shared know-how more worthwhile.

What might an SER capable of fulfilling such a complex list of objectives look like? The Scandinavian model demonstrates one possible way forward. Its starting assumption is a certain degree of flexibility in patterns of labour market behaviour, in which working time is freely chosen in the individual stages of the working life. Full-time work for both partners can be combined with paid and unpaid career breaks and periods of part-time work, depending on individual situations and needs. During career breaks, only socially *recognized* activities, such as child-raising or further training, are paid for, while the realization of other individual preferences remains unpaid. The choices open to employees with children are extended by a highly developed childcare system. Workers who have opted for such flexible patterns of labour market behaviour are protected from poverty in old age by minimum pensions. Moreover, a narrowing of the gender pay gap reduces the negative incentives for a redistribution of paid work between men and women. At the same time as changes were being made to the traditional family model, the Scandinavian countries also invested more than other countries in education and training and the development and diffusion of new forms of decentralized work organization and the introduction of semi-autonomous work groups.[4] The recent extension of the occupational labour market by creating new IT occupations can also be regarded as a reference point in the sphere of the new ICTs (Bosch, 1999).

---

[4] In Norway, for example, the first programmes on work organization and the introduction of autonomous work groups were jointly implemented by the unions and the employers' organizations as early as in the 1960s. The purpose of the first generations of these programmes tended to be the improvement of the working conditions; nowadays, however, the state-supported "Enterprise Development 2000 Programme" is more focused on improvements in competitiveness (Bosch, 1997, p. 222).

References

Auer, P.; Cazes, S. 2002. "The resilience of the long-term employment relationship", in P. Auer and S. Cazes (eds.): *Employment stability in an age of flexibility* (Geneva, ILO).

Beynon, H.; Grimshaw, D.; Rubery, J.; Ward, K. 2002. *Managing employment change. The new realities of work* (Oxford, Oxford University Press).

Bielenski, H.; Bosch, G.; Wagner, A. 2002. *Working time preferences in sixteen European countries* (Dublin, European Foundation for the Improvement of Living and Working Conditions).

Blyton, P.; Turnbull, P. 1994. *The dynamics of employee relationship* (Basingstoke and London, Macmillan).

Bosch, G. 1986. "Hat das Normalarbeitsverhältnis eine Zukunft?" in *WSI-Mitteilungen*, Vol. 39, No. 3, pp. 163–76.

—. 1997. "Flexibility in the Norwegian labour market in a comparative perspective", in J.E. Dølvik and A.H. Stehen (eds.): *Making solidarity work? The Norwegian labour market model in transition* (Oslo, Scandinavian University Press), pp. 211–47.

—. 1999. "Working time: Tendencies and emerging issues", in *International Labour Review*, Vol. 138, pp. 131–49.

—. 2000. "The dual system of vocational training in Germany: Is it still a model?", in D.G. Tremblay and P. Doray (eds.): *Vers de nouveaux modes de formation professionnelle? Rôle des acteurs et des collaborations* (Quebec, Quebec University), pp. 91–114.

—. 2002. "Auf dem Weg zu einem neuen Normalarbeitsverhältnis? Veränderung von Erwerbsläufen und ihre sozialstaatliche Absicherung", in K. Gottschall and B. Pfau-Effinger (eds.): *Zukunft der Arbeit und Geschlecht: Diskurse, Entwicklungspfade und Reformoptionen im internationalen Vergleich* (Opladen, Leske & Budrich), pp. 107–34.

—. 2004. "Towards a new standard employment relationship in Western Europe?", in *British Journal of Industrial Relations*, Vol. 42, Issue 4, Dec. 2004, pp. 617–36.

Briefs, G. 1927. "Gewerkschaftswesen und Gewerkschaftspolitik", in *Handwörter-buch der Staatswissenschaften*, Vol. 4, 4th edition (Göttingen), pp. 1108–50.

Carnoy, M.; Castells, M.; Benner, C. 1997. "Labour markets and employment practices in the age of flexibility: A case study of Silicon Valley", in *International Labour Review*, Vol. 136, No. 1, pp. 27–48.

Castells, M. 1996. *The rise of the network society* (Oxford and Malden, Blackwell).

Clarke, L. 1991. *The significance of wage forms: The example of the British construction industry*, Thirteenth annual conference of the International Working Party on Segmentation Theory (Bremen, Germany).

Deutsches Studentenwerk. 2003. *Die wirtschaftliche und soziale Lage der Studierenden in der Bundesrepublik Deutschland 2003. 17. Sozialerhebung des Deutschen Studentenwerks* durchgeführt durch HIS.

Dingeldey, I. (ed.). 2000. *Erwerbstätigkeit und Familie in Steuer- und Sozialversicherungs-systemen: Begünstigungen und Belastungen verschiedener familialer Erwerbsmuster im Ländervergleich* (Opladen, Leske & Budrich).

Doogan, K. 2001. "Insecurity and long-term employment", in *Work, Employment & Society*, Vol. 15, pp. 419–41.

Erlinghagen, M. 2004. *Die Restrukturierung des Arbeitsmarktes: Arbeitsmarktmobilität und Beschäftigungsstabilität im Zeitverlauf* (Wiesbaden: VS-Verl. für Sozialwiss. Zugl.: Duisburg, Univ., Diss.).

—; Knuth, M. 2004. "The evolution of labour market dynamics in West Germany from the doom of industrialism to the dawn of the service economy", in *Economia & Lavoro*, Vol. 38, pp. 91–113.

Esping-Andersen, G. 1990. *The three worlds of welfare capitalism* (Cambridge, Cambridge Polity Press).

Eurobarometer. 2001. *Les jeunes Européens en 2001*, Eurobaromètre 55.1, INRA August 2001 at: http://europa.eu.int/comm/public_opinion/archives/eb/ebs_151_fr.pdf.

European Commission. 2000. *Employment in Europe* (Luxembourg, Office for Official Publications of the European Community).

—. 2004. *Employment in Europe 2004* (Luxembourg, Office for Official Publications of the European Community).

Harvey, M. 1999. "Economies of time: A framework for analysing the restructuring of employment relations", in A. Felstead and N. Jewson (eds.): *Global trends in flexible labour* (Basingstoke and London, Macmillan Business), pp. 21–32.

ILO. 1999. *Decent work*, Report of the Director-General, 87th International Labour Conference (Geneva).

Kuhn, T. 1967. *Die Struktur wissenschaftlicher Revolutionen (The structure of scientific revolutions)* (Frankfurt, Suhrkamp-Verlag).

Lehndorff, S. 2001. *Weniger ist mehr. Arbeitszeitverkürzung als Gesellschaftspolitik* (Hamburg, VSA Verlag).

Nolan, P. 1983. "The firm and labour market behaviour", in G.S. Bain (ed.): *Industrial relations in Britain* (Oxford, Blackwell), pp. 281–310.

Orloff, A.S. 1993. "Gender and the social rights of citizenship: The comparative analysis of gender relations and welfare state", in *American Sociological Review*, Vol. 58, pp. 303–28.

Polyani, K. 1957. *The great transformation* (Boston, Beacon Press).

Rubery, J.; Grimshaw, D. 2003. *The organization of employment: An international perspective* (New York, Palgrave Macmillan).

Wagner, A. 2000a. "Arbeiten ohne Ende? Über die Arbeitszeiten hochqualifizierter Angestellter", in *Institut Arbeit und Technik: Jahrbuch 2000*, pp. 258–75 (Gelsenkirchen, Institut Arbeit und Technik).

—. 2000b. "Krise des Normalarbeitsverhältnisses? Über eine konfuse Debatte und ihre politische Interessenorientierung", in Claus Schäfer (ed.): *Geringer Löhne – mehr Beschäftigung?* pp. 200–46 (Hamburg, Niedriglohn-Politik).

WORKING TIME CAPABILITY: TOWARDS REALIZING INDIVIDUAL CHOICE   3

*Sangheon Lee and Deirdre McCann**

Don't mourn for me, friends, don't weep for me never,
For I'm going to do nothing for ever and ever.

Epitaph written for herself by an old charwoman,
as quoted in Keynes, 1930

It is high time to rid ourselves of the notion that leisure for
workmen is either "lost time" or a class privilege.

Henry Ford, 1926

[T]ime must be conceived of not only in terms of working
time, as a measure of the trading of labour for pay, but also as a
subjective experience, i.e. as time in the life of the worker.

Alain Supiot, 1999

3.1   INTRODUCTION

The assumption of economic theory that workers exercise free choice over their working time has always stood in stark contrast with their day-to-day experiences at the workplace. The charwoman's epitaph is a reminder of how working time was perceived during the period of early industrialization, when it was gradually established as a way of disciplining workers in the factory system and protecting the workplace from the pre-industrial lifestyle, generating "a clear demarcation between 'work' and 'life'" (Thompson, 1967).

* The authors are Research Officers in the Conditions of Work and Employment Programme (TRAVAIL) at the International Labour Office in Geneva, Switzerland. They are grateful for comments on an earlier draft of this chapter provided by Iain Campbell, François Eyraud, Enrique Fernández Macías, Michelle Gallant, Lonnie Golden, Jon Messenger, Jouko Nätti and Barbara Pocock. The views expressed in this chapter are those of the authors and do not necessarily reflect those of the International Labour Office.

Hours spent outside work were seen simply as "lost" time. From the workers' perspective, this process meant in practice the subordination of their lives to production demands, and a disregard for their lives outside of work. Gradually, however, the importance of guaranteeing "free time" or "leisure" for workers was recognized, and perceptions of working time changed. Time outside of work came to be recognized, by Henry Ford among others, not as lost time, but as essential for both the quality of working life (predominantly health and safety) and economic progress (Ford, 1926). Indeed, the economic value of leisure ("a workman would have little use for an automobile if he had to be in the shops from dawn until dusk" (ibid., p. 614)) has often been seen as the driving force in the post-war prosperity that was generated by the Fordist system (Aglietta, 1979). During this period, the issue of working time regulation was centred on the reduction of working hours to achieve the standard of the 8-hour day and 40-hour week.

While Ford predicted a further universal reduction of daily working hours as the probable next step, instead, "the historical trends towards a progressive standardization of working time have given way to a *diversification, decentralization and individualization* of working hours" (Anxo et al., 2004a, p. 2; see also Bosch, Chapter 2 in this volume). At the same time, there have been increasing demands for the reconceptualization of working time to "embrace workers' lives as a whole and guarantee the harmony of the various kinds of time making up these lives" (Supiot, 2001, p. 85). As part of this call for the reconceptualization of working time, the issue of workers' choice and influence over their working hours has taken central stage, as evidenced by the growing body of theoretical, empirical and policy studies on this issue (Anxo et al., 2004a and 2004b). As a result, evidence has accumulated regarding the extent to which actual working time reflects workers' needs and preferences, and the reasons for mismatches between these two.

However, despite this increasing recognition of variations in workers' needs and preferences, and the importance of realizing them through increasing workers' choice and influence, conflicting views have been put forward regarding how to capture and interpret workers' preferences and what needs to be done to increase worker choice. In particular, it is interesting to note that the shift in focus to individualized working time has paved the way, in some countries, for the resurgence of market fundamentalism: the belief that the individualization of working time means a reduced role for "universal" policy interventions, such as limitations on working hours. This has been accompanied by a Hayekian belief that workers' preferences are best communicated through market transactions, and that social interventions would simply distort this process. In contrast, several countries have taken a different route, towards increasing social interventions, including through the introduction of social policies that aim to help workers better realize their preferences over their working time arrangements.

This chapter aims to provide a research and policy framework for these issues by arguing that *real* individualization based on workers' needs and preferences requires strong, not weak, social support. We believe that the "capabilities approach" developed by Sen provides a promising avenue for better understanding and elaborating the issues related to choice and preferences in the area of working time; evaluating the policy interventions intended to advance them; and suggesting some considerations for future policy directions. This is because the capabilities approach gives *individual* workers and their preferences a central role without falling into the trap of ontological or methodological individualism – due to its explicit recognition of the role of institutions in facilitating individual capabilities and its recognition of "preference formation through social interaction" (Sen, 1999, p. 253). As a result, the capabilities approach offers an alternative framework within which workers' preferences can be interpreted and realized.

Section 3.2 develops the concept of *working time capability* based on Sen's capabilities approach. Relying on this concept, section 3.3 reviews existing studies on working time preferences, focusing in particular on different ways of understanding preferences among those workers in part-time work and those with long working hours. Section 3.4 draws on recent literature on capabilities and social rights to discuss the types of social support that are needed, with the goal of improving working time capabilities for individual workers, by focusing on the role of individual rights to influence working hours and outlining their primary forms. This chapter concludes in section 3.5 by drawing on the working time capability approach to suggest some of the considerations that need to be addressed in the future development of policies to advance individual influence over working hours.

3.2　THE CAPABILITIES APPROACH AND WORKING TIME

In an attempt to evaluate individuals' well-being in terms of their *real* opportunity to pursue their desired objectives, Sen has proposed the concept of capabilities. Capability refers to "the alternative combinations of functionings that are feasible for [individuals] to achieve" or "the substantive freedom to achieve alternative functioning combinations" (Sen, 1999, p. 75). These functionings reflect "the various things a person may value doing or being" (ibid.), which naturally have individual variations. This conceptual framework differs fundamentally from the outcomes-based approaches typical of mainstream economics, which concentrate on the "choices" made without considering the options from among which they were selected. Under the capabilities approach, having x when there is no alternative should be distinguished from choosing x when substantial alternatives exist: "fasting is not the same thing as being forced to starve" (ibid., p. 76).

A central aspect of the capabilities approach is that a person's capability is determined by "conversion factors", which include not only personal characteristics, such as mental and physical conditions, but also social characteristics, including social norms and institutions.[1] The role of social conversion factors is particularly significant in the analysis of the labour market. Deakin, who has applied the capability approach to the labour market, has emphasized the relevance of this aspect of the capabilities approach in reformulating the concept of social rights in the age of neo-liberal reforms (2004). He suggests that "a key role for social rights is to act as conversion factors which extend the range of alternative functionings available to individuals" (p. 48). This aspect of capabilities is discussed in more detail in section 3.4.

The capabilities approach holds the potential of specific applicability to the field of working time, particularly with regard to workers' ability to exercise choice over the duration and arrangement of their working hours. The capabilities approach to working time is basically concerned with the opportunities given to workers to choose and change their working time so as to improve the quality of their lives. Workers are typically faced with a choice over how to allocate the given physical hours ("universal" individual entitlements). Their choice will be made among the set of feasible, alternative combinations of working time and personal activities ("vectors of functionings"). It should be noted that working time in the capability set refers to both the length (e.g., daily hours) and arrangement (e.g., unsocial hours) of working time. Thus, as is illustrated in figure 3.1, the current working time pattern would be the outcome of a worker's choice over this functionings set.

It is typically assumed in economic theory that this choice is utility maximizing and that the labour market will function effectively so as to realize workers' preferences. The common assumption is that workers' preferred hours of work correspond to their actual hours, thanks to the presence of an effective adjustment function in the labour market that ultimately resolves any mismatches (Ghez and Becker, 1975). What differentiates the capabilities approach from this kind of an economic approach is the explicit recognition of the conversion factors that tend to make individual capacity sets much smaller than is assumed in mainstream economic theory. For example, different working time capacity can be

---

[1] "For example, a person who is disabled may have a larger basket of primary goods and yet have less chance to lead a normal life . . . than an able-bodied person with a smaller basket of primary goods" (Sen, 1999, p. 74).

Figure 3.1   Working time capability

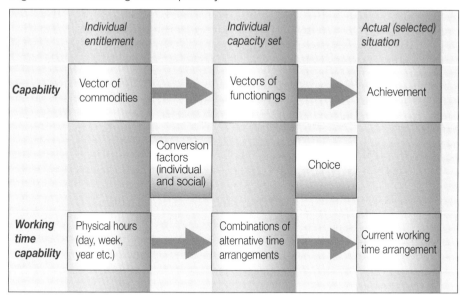

gauged from the differing views of the charwoman and the Fordist worker identified at the outset of this chapter. It is also clear that women's working time capability is dramatically reduced in the presence of the traditional gender division of childcare and domestic work. At the same time, the long working hours of professional women workers in industrialized countries, while often the outcome of restricted choice, cannot be considered to be comparable to those of poverty-stricken women workers in the informal economy of developing countries, although both work similarly long hours. While working time capability is constrained for both groups of workers, it is much more limited for the latter. Therefore, the capability approach captures the degree to which choice can be exercised (see figure 3.1).

Working time capability reflects the *substantive* freedom to adopt different working time patterns. From this perspective, attention needs to be paid not only to the hours that workers are working now, but also to the options from which they have had the opportunity to choose. Moreover, given that workers would often like to make different choices in changed circumstances, which is essential to the life-course perspective on working time (see Anxo et al., Chapter 4 in this volume), this approach captures the ability of an individual worker to change his or her working time preferences. For example, suppose that two workers currently "choose" to work on a part-time basis, but that one has the capability to change to full-time work, while the other does not. Similarly, suppose that two workers are working equally long overtime hours, but that one has the capability to refuse to work overtime, while the other does not. Under the working time capabilities approach, these part-time and long-hours workers cannot be viewed as enjoying the same capability, although their working time arrangements are both "voluntary". The capabilities approach to working time, therefore, requires the broadening of the information base from existing working time arrangements to the alternative patterns that are meaningfully available to the workers in question.

3.3   WORKING TIME PREFERENCES AND CAPABILITIES

As discussed in section 3.2, the capabilities approach to working time requires the broadening of the informational basis for research and policy decisions, including encompassing what workers would like to achieve. In this regard, the increasing interest in workers' preferences over their working time is a welcome development, to which this chapter is intended to contribute. It draws on and seeks to further advance the work of Anxo et al. in identifying the primary elements of working time policies that promote decent work, and, in particular, on their suggestion that these policies should advance individual choice and influence over working hours (see Anxo et al., 2004b).

A growing body of research is questioning the economic assumption concerning the redundancy of preferences: that working hours are *optimally* set while matching preferred and actual hours. Even when the income implications of adjusted working hours are taken into account, workers' ability to exercise choice over their working hours, or to realize their preferences, is to a large extent constrained. In other words, the evidence suggests that working time capabilities in contemporary market economies are constrained.

One important trend identified in various studies is what Drago (2000) calls the "working time divide": that workers would prefer not to work very short or very long hours, and that the gaps between their current and preferred hours of work are associated with their current working hours (Lee, 2004). This phenomenon is demonstrated in figure 3.2, which shows, for the EU-15 countries, the proportion of working hour surpluses (preferred hours are shorter than actual hours) and deficits (preferred hours are longer than actual hours) within each hour band. Longer hours are associated with a higher proportion of working hour surpluses, while shorter hours increase the probability of working hour deficits. From the perspective of working time capability, this implies that the set of working time capabilities (alternative functionings of working hours and incomes, which are the focus of most empirical studies) is more likely to be limited for individuals who work either very short or long hours.

Figure 3.2   Working hour gaps: Working hour surpluses and deficits in EU-15, 1998 (percentage within each working hour band)

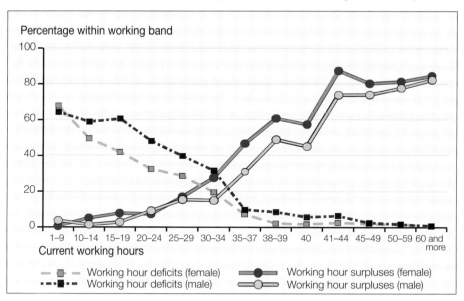

Source: Calculated from the Employment Options for the Future Survey (1998).

The role of conversion factors is also notable. As regards individual conversion factors, gender is of great significance. Women workers tend to prefer shorter work hours than their male counterparts. As figure 3.2 shows, they have a lower proportion of working hour deficits and a higher proportion of working hour surpluses in each hour band. This gender difference can, to a large extent, be attributed to the influence of the traditional gender division of domestic work, and therefore to the fact that women workers often have a "no paid work" option, which is not typically available to male workers. Gender factors, then, are not purely *individual* conversion factors, but are to a large extent shaped by *social* conversion factors. The interaction between these two and its implications have been subject to close scrutiny, as will be discussed later in this section.

Age also appears to play a role in shaping working time capabilities. There is evidence that, with age-related changes, such as the deterioration of mental and physical strength, and age-specific events, older workers tend to prefer shorter working hours. Instead, their actual working hours remain relatively stable (figure 3.3). Also interesting is that as the "no paid work" option is available for older workers, those with considerable working hour surpluses may withdraw from the labour market. As figure 3.3 indicates, inactive older workers tend to prefer much shorter working hours than younger age groups

Figure 3.3   Actual and preferred working hours by age in EU-15, 1998

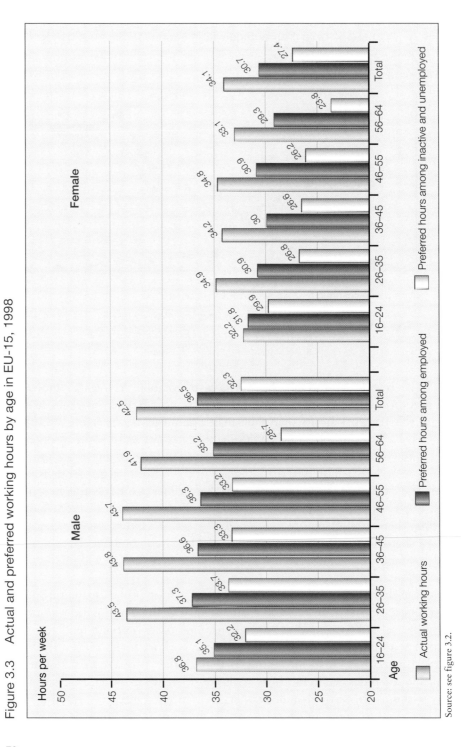

Source: see figure 3.2.

(see Jolivet and Lee, 2004 for a detailed discussion).[2] This forms part of a broader trend under which working hour preferences tend to change over time, depending on the different stages of working life (see Anxo et al., Chapter 4 in this volume; Clarkberg and Moen, 2001).

Social factors are also significant. With regard to labour market structure, one of the key findings of the empirical studies is that workers with working hour gaps are more likely than others to change their working hours, which means that these gaps could be a useful predictor of future working hour adjustments. From the perspective of the working time capabilities approach, however, it should be noted that this adjustment is normally effected through changing jobs or employers (Boeheim and Taylor, 2003; Clarkberg and Moen, 2001; Drago et al., 2004; Euwals, 2001; Altonji and Paxson, 1988; Fouarge and Baaijens, Chapter 6 in this volume). As many studies have demonstrated, the extent to which workers with working hour gaps are capable of achieving the required mobility is rather limited. More importantly, the fact that the difficulties and costs involved in job- or employer-change are considerable for many workers is often ignored.[3] Why, then, are employers reluctant to allow workers to change their working hours? It appears that, in contrast to typical economic assumptions, employers tend to provide "rigid" working hours, thus reducing workers' capability to change their working hours. Such rigidity is often suggested to be associated with the presence of fixed employment costs (Schor, 1992),[4] but the current understanding of this issue is not satisfactory. In this regard, recent interest in the presence of structural reasons for rigidity in working hours deserves more attention. Rebitzer and Taylor (1995), for example, have shown that the failure of the labour market in eliciting accurate preferences from workers may result in working hour surpluses, or, more specifically, in the underprovision of part-time work (see also Lang and Kahn, 2001).

Social norms and institutions as well as public policies are also important. In retrospect, it is clear that the recent interest in workers' choices and preferences regarding working time is related to various developments that have contributed to improving working time capability, most notably for women. One example is the combination of paid work and childcare, which used to be limited to a small group of women, but is a common feature among many more women today. However, great caution is required in evaluating the

---

[2] Other personal factors are also important. See, for example, Bell (2000) on the difference in working hour preferences between African-American and white workers in the United States.

[3] This point is illustrated in two recent popular works on low-paid workers in the United States and the United Kingdom: "Changing jobs means a week and possibly more without a pay check" (Ehrenreich, 2002, p. 116); "People tend to stick with the friends, routines and procedures they are familiar with because there might be worse out there" (Toynbee, 2003, p. 101).

[4] In the United States, for example, the probability of receiving fringe benefits, such as medical insurance, increases with the length of working time (Averett and Hotchkiss, 1995).

extent to which working time capability has been improved. For example, Hakim's preference theory is based on the assessment that recent changes in social conversion factors[5] have opened genuine choices to women, while "contextual and institutional" factors are less important (Hakim, 2000). This historical development, she argues, has also revealed the existence of heterogeneous preferences among women, who can be categorized into three groups: work-centred, adaptive and home-centred. For Hakim, then, the diversification of employment patterns among women workers should be seen as reflecting this heterogeneity. The upshot of her theory is the recognition of preferences as a crucial *independent* variable.

It should be noted that Hakim's discussion of preferences, rather than being concerned with the details of working hours scheduling, is more generic. Her concern is with three broad groupings: no employment, part-time employment and full-time employment. However, the way in which preferences are interpreted in her theory deserves particular attention. From the perspective of working time capability, preference theory implicitly assumes that these three groups of women have similar working time capability; otherwise, her assertion concerning "genuine" choice would be ungrounded. In other words, Hakim's theory requires the assumption that three alternative combinations of functionings are included as the capability set for all women. However, there are no convincing reasons to believe this is the case, even where the changes in conversion factors that Hakim identifies have occurred (see Nussbaum, 1999; Folbre and Nelson, 2000).[6] In adopting the working time capability approach, it is the nature of the preferences that is most important, and especially the presence of "adaptive preferences", which refers to the individual adjustments to circumstances that make life bearable in adverse situations (see Sen, 1992). As Sen (1999, p. 63) pointed out, "[D]eprived people tend to come to terms with their deprivation because of the sheer necessity of survival, and they may, as a result, lack the courage to demand any radical change, and may even adjust their desires and expectations to what they unambiguously see as feasible."

Such differences in understanding preferences are associated with different evaluative and policy directions. A good example is "voluntary" part-time work among women workers. Hakim (1997) is of the view that "part-time work is typically chosen voluntarily by women who prefer to give

---

[5] Hakim (2000, Ch. 1) refers to five such changes: the contraceptive revolution; the equal opportunities revolution; the expansion of white-collar occupations; the creation of jobs for secondary earners; and the increased importance of attitudes, values, and personal preferences in lifestyle choices.

[6] Interestingly, Folbre and Nelson (2000) note, concerning the dynamic development of female employment and care work, that "[t]he recent political shift (in the guise of 'welfare reform') to a belief that putting one's dependents in paid care and taking a job is financially and logistically feasible for all parents has likely worsened the standard of living for women with especially high personal caring responsibilities and low market wages" (p. 138).

priority to non-market activities and hence work not at all or only part-time" (pp. 44–45). This appears to be consistent with the fact that the overall proportion of involuntary part-time workers (i.e., those who have taken part-time jobs because they could not find a full-time job) is very low in the EU. However, labour statistics often define "voluntary part-time work" in ways that capture many workers who are arguably working on an involuntary basis. For example, part-timers who are considered "voluntary" include workers who have taken part-time jobs so as to look after children or adults.[7] In the United Kingdom, these workers accounted for 45.2 per cent of part-time workers in 2002, compared to 7.1 per cent in the Netherlands. It is interesting to note here that the lowest proportion of involuntary part-time work for women is found in the Netherlands (1.9 per cent) and the United Kingdom (6.3 per cent) – although there are substantial differences between these two countries in the quality of part-time work. Thus it is hard to infer whether and how those part-time workers who mentioned care responsibilities as a reason for working on a part-time basis see their preferences reflected in their working time arrangements (see, for example, Walsh, 1999).

From the perspective of working time capability, then, it is possible that statistical depictions of "voluntary" part-time work capture "adaptive" preferences (see Lee, 2004). Hakim's analysis lacks crucial information on whether those "voluntary" part-time workers were provided with a genuine opportunity to undertake full-time employment as well as to engage in full-time domestic labour. In this regard, great caution is called for in interpreting this type of preference data, taking into account the process of preference formation through social interaction.[8] As Fagan (2001, p. 244) has noted,

> [A] general feature of questions about preferences, satisfaction or other measures of desired change is that people are required – whether explicitly or implicitly – to draw comparisons between their current situation and an alternative in order to arrive at their answer. They formulate their answers by making comparisons on the basis of experience plus the amount and type of information they have access to about less familiar alternatives. This partial or "bounded" information is used by the individual to assess which arrangements are feasible or desirable in light of their existing domestic and workplace circumstances . . . people's satisfaction levels and preferences adapt in light of perceived alternatives.

---

[7] According to Eurostat, in 2002, about 13 per cent of part-time women workers were involuntary part-timers while 32 per cent did not want a full-time job. Another 32 per cent were working part-time due to childcare or elder care obligations (European Social Statistics: Labour force survey results, 2002).

[8] Sen treats this process in a more positive way, in order to emphasize the need for the sensitivity of social decisions to the *development* of individual preferences and norms (see Sen, 1999, p. 253). By contrast, this chapter is more interested in the conditioning effects of social decisions or interactions on workers' preferences.

It should also be noted that, despite the low incidence of involuntary part-time work, part-timers often encounter working hour deficits (see figure 3.2), which means that even many of the "happy" part-time workers are not really content with their current hours in their part-time jobs. In addition, full-time workers who prefer part-time work are often unable to realize their preference for various reasons, including the fear that their employers will not permit a change in their hours.

A similarly careful reading of preferences is required for the analysis of long working hours. Although it has already been shown that long hours are not normally preferred, there are workers who are working long hours apparently without resentment, despite their potentially negative health impacts (Spurgeon, 2003). The proportion of these workers is relatively low in many European countries (see figure 3.2), but tends to be higher in countries in which long working hours are more common (e.g., Australia, the United Kingdom and the United States; see Golden, Chapter 8 in this volume). Interestingly, the phenomenon of "happy overworking" is sometimes used as a caution against policy intervention to discourage long hours. In Australia, where "unreasonable" hours have been extensively debated, Wooden and Loundes (2001) found that the majority of those working more than 48 hours per week had relatively high job quality and would like to maintain or even increase their current hours. From this result, they concluded that "much of the high incidence of long-hours working is *supply generated*" (emphasis added).[9] The implication of this logic is that long hours can be attributed to workers' preferences, and therefore, social interventions will be ineffective.

Analyses based on preference or satisfaction data, however, are problematic from the perspective of working time capability. First, the relationship between capability and poverty and low income must be taken into account. When Keynes (1930) made the optimistic prediction that his grandchildren's generation (us!) would work 3-hour shifts or a 15-hour week, his point was really that working time capability would remain limited unless the "old Adam" (i.e., the "money incentive" or "economic necessity") was satisfied. The dramatic failure of his prediction can be explained by the fact that he was right for certain groups of workers, but not for all individuals. In other words, despite the economic success since achieved, low-paid workers for whom long working hours are a survival strategy still exist. As mentioned earlier, strong preferences for, or satisfaction with, long hours among these workers require careful analysis, especially in relation to the possibility of adaptive preferences. More importantly, while poverty should clearly be seen as capability deprivation (Sen, 1999), it should be noted that low income has

---

[9] See also Weston et al. (2004).

the same effect, in that the working time capability of low-paid workers is too small for them to be able to make a genuine choice over their hours.

In addition, workers' preferences can be influenced by the workplace dynamics of working time. Burawoy (1979) observed the "voluntary" intensification of work through the creation of an absorbing workplace game (termed "making out"), which resulted in relative satisfaction and more importantly the "consent" of employees. Subsequent research has shown that workers often participate in a workplace game under which working hours are used as a performance indicator, which workers accept as a "rule of the game".[10] For example, Landers et al. (1996) show that promotion criteria that favour long working hours result in a "rat race" towards long hours, and, at the same time, penalize workers who prefer shorter hours (see also Schor, 1992). The gender implications of this finding are demonstrated by Eastman (1998), who shows that because women tend to prefer shorter hours, this kind of workplace game is more likely to punish them. The point here is that where working hours are set by a competitive game, the working time capability of individual workers is reduced: changes in working hours, even where needs arise, are beyond them.[11] In addition, in the context of labour market segmentation, these studies show that such situations are more likely to occur in the primary sector, where there are relatively good employment conditions. The resulting shortage of part-time work, then, is more likely to occur in this sector, while most part-time jobs are created in the secondary sector and attract low wages (Rebitzer and Taylor, 1995). Therefore, it is entirely plausible that a labour market that tends to create working hour surpluses can also generate working hour deficits at the same time, thereby resulting in a polarization of working hours (see also Clarkberg and Moen, 2001).

The discussions thus far indicate that working time research and policies would benefit from shifting their focus to working time capability, and examining the alternative opportunities available for individual workers. In addition, there are good reasons to believe that working time capability is to a large extent determined by a broad range of social conversion factors, including incomes, gender, social norms and workplace practices. This calls for greater caution in interpreting preference information and evaluating the actual situation of working time, as any meaningful analysis requires a more careful investigation of working time capability. In a utilitarian world (invoking "freedom-invoking rhetoric"), in which market transactions are believed to achieve the fulfilment of preferences, it is tempting to believe that

---

[10] See also Sharone (2002), who discusses how engineers at a high-tech company worked long hours without resistance.

[11] This aspect needs to be taken into account in evaluating "high-performance" management practices. For example, see White et al. (2003).

workers are responsible for their current situations, and therefore that social interventions are neither necessary nor desirable. However, as Sen (1999, p. 284) has noted, "responsibility requires freedom . . . Without the substantive freedom and capability to do something, a person cannot be responsible for doing it."

3.4 WORKING TIME CAPABILITY, SOCIAL RIGHTS AND WORKER-CHOICE LAWS

As mentioned in section 3.2, the capabilities approach has recently been drawn on to reconceptualize social rights as conversion factors (Browne et al., 2002; Deakin, 2004; Deakin and Wilkinson, 2000). In this context, it has been suggested that there is a substantial role for legal regulation. As Browne et al. (2002) have argued,

> The Capabilities Approach justifies a wide range of legal relations or "social rights", which may require substantial policy intervention in the labour market and elsewhere in order to guarantee that externalities or market failures are corrected and individuals are equipped with largely equal "capability sets". (pp. 12–13)

From this perspective, social rights, rather than hindering the functioning of labour markets, constitute a central feature of those that facilitate the optimum realization of a society's resources (Deakin and Wilkinson, 2000). The capabilities approach, however, does not itself prescribe any specific substantive rights, instead offering a frame of reference from which to evaluate the range of potential policy approaches (Deakin, 2004). This embrace of social intervention, then, encourages speculation on the types of measures that can be adopted towards enhancing working time capability by offering workers genuine freedom to influence their working time arrangements.

As part of their suggestions for elaborating on decent work in the area of working time, Anxo et al. (2004b) have recommended a range of working time policy measures, a number of which can contribute towards advancing working time capability (see further Messenger, Conclusion, in this volume). It is apparent, for example, that traditional forms of regulation – of daily and weekly working hours, overtime work and unsocial hours – play a key role in the capability approach towards working time, by enabling the exercise of a certain degree of choice. Most obviously, strong limits on working hours can permit greater numbers of workers to realize their preferred hours by curbing excessive hours. Similarly, limitations on night work represent a strong form of protection for those who prefer to work during daylight hours. Indeed, although realizing the working time preferences of individual workers is not usually identified as among their policy goals, these traditional working time measures can be viewed as ensuring what Sen refers to as *basic* capabilities: "the ability to satisfy certain crucially important functionings up to certain minimally adequate levels" (Sen, 1992, p. 45). In other words, these laws form, at the very least, the necessary conditions for the minimum set of working time capabilities or for meaningfully defining working time capability (Peetz et al., 2003, p. 141).

However, in addition to these forms of regulation, social supports are also required to improve working time capacity beyond basic capability; towards allowing individual workers to influence working time in ways that cannot be comprehended by traditional collective regulatory approaches. As Fagan has noted about work/family measures:

> [W]hile a general reduction in hours sets an important upper limit on the work-place demands that can be made on people's time, it is too blunt a tool to resolve the complexity of work/life balance on its own. Rather, it is a foundation to support the efficacy of other measures tailored to accommodate the changing care responsibilities of workers at different stages in their lives (Fagan, 2004, p. 138).

Traditional forms of legislation are inevitably limited in the extent to which they can broaden the range of functionings by responding to the diversity of individual workers' preferences, even if they can capture their broad orientation, for example towards shorter hours. Policy suggestions for extending worker choice and influence over their working time that recognize preferences can differ and offer one way of responding to this diversity are of particular importance (Messenger (ed.), 2004). Thus, for example, in addition to the part played by conventional working time laws, the promotion of flexi-time and time-banking schemes can enhance working time capability by extending the number of available working time options that allow workers a choice over how they arrange their time within and outside of paid work (ibid.).

The focus of the remaining sections of this chapter, however, is another of the policy suggestions identified as having the potential to contribute towards worker choice and influence: legislation that provides individual workers with a degree of direct influence over their working time arrangements. Given the recent extension of this approach, and the role ascribed by the policy rhetoric to the potential of these measures to advance worker choice, our goal is to elaborate on this element of Anxo et al.'s work (Anxo et al., 2004b). Individual-choice measures also serve as a useful subject for a preliminary attempt to explore the policy implications of the working time capability approach. To this end, this section briefly indicates the range and extent of these laws, while section 3.5 applies the notion of working time capability in order to make a number of observations regarding the potential of these kinds of policies, and to suggest some policy considerations that could be taken into account in their future development.

Laws that offer individual workers the right to influence their working hours can be seen as embodying two coexisting approaches towards operationalizing individual worker preferences. The first, the "negative" approach, is reflected in rights to refuse to work in certain working time arrangements, and has emerged with respect to a number of different schedules. Most widespread is the entitlement to refuse to work at night. In a number of jurisdictions, this right is available only to specific categories of workers recognized as facing particularly acute risks to their health or well-being, or as needing to balance paid work with family or other caring responsibilities. Pregnant workers are one such group. The most recent international standard, the ILO's Night Work Convention, 1990 (No. 171), requires measures to ensure that an alternative to night work is available to women during pregnancy and after childbirth;[12] and most industrialized countries have enacted some kind of rules on the performance of night work by pregnant and breastfeeding workers, often in the form of a right for individual workers to request a transfer to day work. Rights to refuse to work at night that are available to all workers are less common, although one is in operation in Switzerland.[13]

Refusal rights can also be made available with respect to overtime hours. The strongest legislation in this regard appears to be that enacted in Finland, where the agreement of individual employees is required for any overtime work.[14] In other jurisdictions, this right tends to be more circumscribed. In the US state of Maine, for example, employers are prohibited from requiring their employees to work more than 80 hours of overtime in any consecutive 2-week period.[15] Elsewhere, the right to refuse to work overtime hours may cover only specific categories of workers, including in New South Wales, Australia, where employers cannot require part-timers who are party to a Part-Time Work Agreement under the Industrial Relations Act 1996 to work additional hours.[16] A more recent development relates to work performed on Sundays or on another day of rest, and is exemplified by legislation enacted in the Netherlands in 2003, which offers a right to refuse to work on Sundays, by requiring that the workers concerned must agree in each specific instance.[17]

In recent years, this trend in labour law towards refusal rights over working time has been accompanied by an increase in measures that offer a

---

[12] Article 7(1).
[13] *Loi sur le travail*, article 17(6).
[14] *Työaikalaki* No. 605/1996 (Working Hours Act), section 18.
[15] 26 MRSA §603.
[16] Industrial Relations Act 1966, section 80.
[17] *Arbeidstijdenwet* (Working Hours Act) article 5:4(1).

right not merely to refuse to work certain schedules, but to influence working time arrangements in more substantial ways. Again, these rights may cover only select groups of workers. In Norway, for example, workers are entitled to reduce their hours for health, social and welfare reasons.[18] A right to work part time can also be extended to older workers through progressive retirement schemes, which are in operation in a number of European countries, and have been introduced in legislation in Austria and Spain (see Jolivet and Lee, 2004). Rights to influence working hours, like those to refuse specified working time arrangements, can also be made available to pregnant and breastfeeding workers, most commonly in legislation that permits mothers to request breaks or hours reductions in order to breastfeed.

Rights to reduce hours are also increasingly being granted to parents. At the international level, this approach is reflected in the ILO's Part-Time Work Recommendation, 1994 (No. 182), which suggests that workers should be able to transfer to part-time work in specified circumstances, including during pregnancy or due to the need to care for a young child or a disabled or sick family member. At national level, the right for parents to change their working hours can be granted under parental leave schemes, by permitting the leave to be taken in the form of reduced working hours. These kinds of measures follow an approach that first emerged in the Swedish parental leave legislation in the 1970s. In some countries, the entitlement for parents to reduce their working hours can be available over a relatively long period. In Sweden, parents have a right to reduce their working hours up until their child is 8 years old;[19] and in the United Kingdom, a right to request "flexible working" – covering both reduced hours and working from home – extends to parents of children under 6 or disabled children to the age of 18.[20]

This trend towards legislating rights to working time adjustments has most recently been strengthened by the enactment of laws that are applicable to all workers. The softer version of such laws entitles part-time workers to priority in applying for full-time vacancies in their employers' firms and vice versa. In this vein, the EU's part-time work directive encourages employers to give consideration to requests from workers to transfer between full-time and part-time jobs, and to requests from part-timers to increase their hours,[21] a suggestion which has been adopted in a number of EU Member States. The most significant development in this trend, however, is the rights available to all workers not merely to transfer to available part-time or full-time positions,

---

[18] *Arbeidslivets lover* (Act No. 4 relating to worker protection and working environment), section 46A.

[19] *Föräldraledighetslag* (Parental Leave Act), section 7.

[20] Employment Rights Act 1996, Part 8A.

[21] Council Directive (EC) 97/81 concerning the Framework Agreement on part-time work concluded by UNICE, CEEP and the ETUC [1998] OJ L14/9, Clause 5(3).

but to change their working hours within their existing jobs. The Netherlands and Germany have both recently introduced such a universal right to working time adjustments. In the Netherlands, the *Wet Aanpassing Arbeidsduur* (Working Hours Adjustment Act), in force since July 2000, is part of a package of measures under its umbrella legislation on work and care. Building on similar provisions in collective agreements, the Act permits the adjustment of working hours, encompassing their reduction and extension, as well as the redistribution of existing hours. This legislation has been followed by the enactment of a similar measure in Germany, the *Gesetz über Teilzeitarbeit und befristete Arbeitsverträge* (Act on Part-time Work and Fixed-term Employment Contracts), which was partially modelled on its predecessor and came into force in January 2001. This Act permits both reductions and extensions of hours, although the right to adjust the distribution of working hours can only be claimed in conjunction with a request to change their duration.

3.5 TOWARDS ADVANCING WORKING TIME CAPABILITY THROUGH WORKER-CHOICE MEASURES: SOME POLICY CONSIDERATIONS

In addition to pointing towards the policy approach on which we have focused in this paper – the introduction of legal rights for individuals to influence their working hours – the capabilities approach provides the criterion for evaluating this form of intervention by demanding a focus on whether these legal rights are merely formal or whether they can in fact allow effective worker choice. The experience of individual-choice legislation is at a sufficiently advanced stage for the process of evaluation to have begun, and questions as to the effectiveness of these laws are being raised (Fouarge and Baaijens, Chapter 6 in this volume; Holt and Granger, 2005; Munz, 2004; Palmer, 2004). In this section, we hope to contribute to this process by relying on the working time capability approach to raise questions about the potential of these laws and to make a number of suggestions for their future development.

First, we would suggest that by providing support for workers to realize their working time preferences, the kinds of choice-rights over working time discussed in section 3.4 have the potential to play a role in generating and sustaining working time capability. Perhaps most significantly, these measures mark a response to the risk, highlighted in section 3.3, that workers who would prefer to reduce their hours will be compelled to find another job that is offered on a part-time basis, often one of a lower status (O'Reilly and Fagan, 1998; Drago et al., 2004). By allowing workers to remain in their existing jobs while altering their hours, these laws have the potential, when enacted together with a right to equal treatment of part-timers under labour law and social protection regimes, to broaden the range of occupations in which part-time work is available, in particular by extending it to managerial and professional jobs. On this basis, worker-choice laws can be viewed as an institutional support for individual capabilities (see Deakin, 2004). Where women are forced to downgrade jobs in order to work on a part-time basis, there is no incentive for either employers or the workers themselves to invest in skills and training, to the detriment of the economy and society as a whole. In contrast, where women can choose part-time work, there is an incentive for employers to provide training and for women to take it up.[22]

These laws also have the potential to help workers realize another form of preference: that over how they care for their children. Anxo et al. (2004b) have stressed the importance of this element of choice: for individual workers to decide for themselves not only how to balance work with childcare, but also on the form the childcare will take – whether it will be carried out by the parents themselves, outsourced, or arranged through a combination of both (ibid.). Rights to refuse certain working hours, or to influence how they are arranged, have the potential to operationalize this choice by preventing parents from being compelled to rely entirely on outsourced childcare and allowing them to help structure the relationship between their work and domestic lives, for example through synchronizing their work days with the availability of childcare. By doing so, they would extend the combination of functionings available to individuals, in both work and non-work time.

However, the working time capability approach also raises a number of concerns about the potential of legislated rights-to-change to advance real choice. The concern here is whether individual-choice laws, rather than offering a genuine opportunity for individuals to pursue their desired objectives, instead could operate as an infringement on working time capability by closing down avenues of choice. The reliance on individual rights as an element of working time regulation must inevitably be subject to certain constraints. The goal is to ensure that they do not reflect the form of market fundamentalism, mentioned at the outset of the chapter, which tends to detract from policy interventions in the field of working time by undermining collective limits on working hours. Most significantly, it is not being suggested that individual-choice rights be extended into the regulation of hours limits. It is notable that the evidence of the relationship between weak working time regulatory regimes and long hours encompasses both the United Kingdom[23] and New Zealand,[24] both of which permit "individual opt-outs" from their

---

[22] See Deakin's analysis of pregnancy discrimination legislation (2004, pp. 48–50).

[23] Working Time Regulations 1998, regulation 4(1).

[24] Minimum Wage Act 1983, section 11B.

weekly working hours limits (Anxo and O'Reilly, 2000; Lee, 2004). Although individual-choice rights would represent an advance in jurisdictions in which the traditional forms of regulation are weak or absent, and may even pave the way for stronger measures, they are clearly optimally situated in regimes in which firm hours limits are in place.

A related concern about the direction of modern working time law stems from the desire to preserve those times and days traditionally reserved for the entire community. The Supiot report is particularly forceful on this point, stressing that the individualization of working time, while welcome, may, if not carefully designed, have the potential to undermine what the report terms "community time patterns" – such as night-time and Sunday rest periods and midday breaks – and the social institutions that they support, including both families and trade unions (Supiot, 2001). From the perspective of working time capability, the risk is that enhancing the working time capability of some workers, by allowing work to be performed on Sundays, limits the capability of others to fully enjoy non-work time. This concern usually arises with respect to liberalizing Sunday work, rather than to individual-choice rights, and calls for a comprehensive approach to working time regulation that recognizes the value of both allowing a degree of individual control over work schedules and preserving time devoted to community life. However, individual rights over working hours can contribute towards the community time approach, which provides a rationale for measures like the Dutch law discussed in section 3.4 that allow individual workers to refuse to work on Sundays. In sectors or jobs in which work is carried out on the weekly rest day, then, the individual worker's right to refuse to work, coupled with the necessary supportive measures prohibiting discrimination on this basis, has the potential to ensure that workers' religious beliefs, family obligations, and/or preference for the customary day of rest cannot be disregarded.

On the other hand, the imposition of limits on work on the weekly rest day – and, more broadly, the community time approach towards working time regulation – can be viewed as a limitation on the working time capability of those workers who would prefer to work on Sundays. This highlights the need to consider whether there should be *external* limits on working time capability, introduced for reasons independent of the desire to enhance worker choice. Indeed, the collective regulation of working hours limits, on the basis that it is more effective than an individual or voluntary approach, could itself be seen as one such external limitation, as could the policy goal of ensuring that working time schedules preserve workers' health. The latter can be considered to justify curbing the working time capability of even those workers able to exercise a genuine choice to work longer hours, on the grounds, for example, of reducing the related medical costs or preventing accidents resulting from worker fatigue. Alternatively, the notion of social rights can be expanded in line with the reasoning of Deakin and Wilkinson, who have suggested that one of the primary purposes of social rights is to empower individual workers to realize their potential in a sustainable way that enhances their well-being (Deakin and Wilkinson, 2000). From this perspective, the choice to work detrimentally long hours would be unacceptable, due to its impact on the worker's health.

An additional policy consideration relates to the role of regulatory measures beyond the field of working time. It has been pointed out that the traditional forms of working time regulation facilitate basic working time capabilities by operating as the framework of fundamental entitlements within which individual choices are made. Limits on daily and weekly hours, overtime work, and evening, weekend and night work ensure that certain periods of the day and week are beyond the reach of paid labour, and therefore are available for family life, leisure interests and community responsibilities. In doing so, they lend meaning to the choice to spend time in these pursuits, by ensuring that there is no pressure to go to paid work during these times. However, other kinds of labour law rights can also support and enhance refusal rights, implying the need for attention to be directed to whether the overall structure of labour law is likely to advance working time capability. Most obviously, it is clear that minimum wage laws lend meaning to the right not to work overtime hours, by preventing workers from being compelled to work additional hours in order to earn a decent income.

If the findings on the impact of regulatory regimes on hours' distributions apply with respect to other forms of regulation, it would appear that achieving equality of capabilities requires social intervention. Golden's analysis of the availability of flexible working hours in the United States, for example, confirms that voluntary measures cannot evenly spread the availability of worker choice across the working population, with already disadvantaged groups being at particular risk of exclusion (Golden, 2004). It cannot be assumed, however, that regulatory measures alone are capable of fully realizing worker preferences over working time. A range of external factors contributes to the potential of legal measures to promote decent working time arrangements and working time capability. We discussed in section 3.3 the influence of social norms and institutions in structuring working time. The kinds of workplace "games" alluded to there are an element of workplace and national cultures that value long hours as a sign of commitment and productivity, and which are inevitably resistant to part-time work. The need to implement the goal of allowing hours adjustments can, then, be expected to circumscribe to some degree an employer's freedom to organize working time. As Schmidt has noted, the German choice legislation has required an adjustment of the traditional legal doctrine that the decision as to whether employees are hired on a full-time or part-time basis belongs solely to the employer (Schmidt, 2001). Worker-choice rights, then, may require the revision of some traditional notions of entrepreneurial freedom. Moreover, it can be expected that measures directed towards reshaping workplace cultures would be a primary element in the effectiveness of worker-choice laws, given the reluctance of many workers to request changes in their working hours (Fouarge and Baaijens, Chapter 6 in this volume; Fagan, 2004).

In addition to the need to address social norms and workplace cultures, the role of collective actors and mechanisms in advancing individual choice is crucial. Indeed, facilitating individual choice necessarily requires a broader focus than one confined to individual workers and legislative measures. It is clear that collective negotiations can also allow individuals to exercise choice over their working time. Indeed, although our discussion has been centred on legislated rights to influence working hours, the individual-choice approach was pioneered in Dutch collective agreements, and this form of regulation continues to generally be preferred to legislation for introducing flexi-time and time-banking arrangements, at least in addressing the detailed design of these schemes. It is also apparent that the kind of individual entitlements offered by worker-choice laws are likely to be best effected in circumstances of collective strength, since workers with limited bargaining power are susceptible to being compelled to forgo their employment rights. The implication that can be drawn for policies on the regulation of working time is that laws that strengthen collective actors have the potential to promote worker influence in collective agreements, and to strengthen legislated rights to choose.

Within this broader framework, we would also suggest that the needs of two particular groups of workers need specific consideration. First, workers with family and other caring responsibilities require special attention. A key factor in structuring parents' work/family-related working time needs, for example, is the availability of childcare during working hours, whether that of quality professional childcare or of a relative who cares for the child, or the working time patterns of the worker's partner. In countries in which professional childcare is scarce, the juggling act involved in synchronizing the different actors involved can be challenging. These difficulties imply, then, that an element of choice over distribution of hours, rather than being secondary to those on their reduction and extension, can be crucial. In a recent decision on the Dutch worker-choice legislation mentioned in section 3.4, for example, an office manager who requested to have her hours distributed over 3 days in a week was granted instead the same number of hours worked over a 4-day period.[25] It can be suggested, however, that the arrangement of hours over this longer period may hamper her ability to take care of her family responsibilities (Burri et al., 2003).

Individual-choice laws also raise particularly complex issues for the working time capability of women. The legal entitlement to work part time is intended as one method of encouraging men to play a more significant role in family and domestic work, and can be hoped to at least create the conditions in which this kind of role could be possible. However, if it is to contribute towards enabling a redistribution of paid and household labour, workplace cultures and complementary policy supports are of central importance. Otherwise, worker-choice laws could operate merely as a conduit for reinforcing the kinds of "adaptive preferences" discussed in section 3.3, by enabling women to achieve the hours they require due to the impact of the domestic division of labour. Instead, the working time capability approach requires a vital role for childcare, leave and gender equality policies, if it is to be able to fully extend to women workers.

This kind of interaction between various forms of labour market interventions is essential, since the ultimate aim is not an isolated legal instrument, but the creation of a social norm supporting flexibility in working time that is "self-enforcing in a way which is independent of the law itself"[26] (Deakin, 2004, pp. 49–50). Individual-choice rights can be viewed as an element in the shift from a substantive towards a procedural approach in the regulation of working time, in that they do not impose specific standards, but rather enable the identification and promotion of the substantive outcomes that individual workers need or prefer. As such, they have the potential to reshape workers' preferences, playing a part in the process of preference formation through social interaction, by involving individual workers in an ongoing process of influencing decision-making on working time. It can be suggested, then, that their procedural nature may advance the "seeding" process,[27] although this question deserves more attention and is an avenue for future research.

---

[25] *Ktr. Haarlem* 17 May 2001, *JAR*, 2001, p. 117, discussed in Burri et al. (2003), p. 334.

[26] Deakin makes this point with respect to pregnancy discrimination legislation.

[27] Browne et al. describe the aim of public intervention as being to "seed" social conventions "to the extent that they are 'taken for granted' in the way that conventions of property and contract currently are" (Browne et al., 2002, pp. 13–14).

References

Aglietta, M. 1979. *A theory of capitalist regulation* (London, Verso).

Altonji, J.; Paxson, C. 1988. "Labor supply preferences, hours constraints, and hour-wage trade-offs", in *Journal of Labor Economics*, Vol. 6, No. 2, pp. 254–76.

Anxo, D.; O'Reilly, J. 2000. "Working time regimes and transitions in comparative perspective", in J. O'Reilly, I. Cebrian and M. Lallement (eds.): *Working time changes: Social integration through transitional labour markets* (Cheltenham, Edward Elgar).

—; Fagan, C.; Lee, S.; McCann, D.; Messenger, J. 2004a. "Introduction: Working time in industrialized countries", in J. Messenger (ed.), 2004, pp. 1–9.

—; —; —; —. 2004b. "Implications for working time policies", in J. Messenger (ed.), 2004, pp. 195–211.

Averett, S.; Hotchkiss, J. 1995. "The probability of receiving benefits at different hours of work", in *AEA Papers and Proceedings*, Vol. 85, No. 2, pp. 276–80.

Bell, L. 2000. "The incentive to work hard: Differences in black and white workers' hours and preferences", in L. Golden and D. Figart (eds.): *Working time: International trends, theory, and policy perspectives* (London, Routledge), pp. 106–26.

Boeheim, R.; Taylor, M. 2003. "Option or obligation? The determinants of labour supply preferences in Britain", in *Manchester School*, Vol. 71, No. 2, pp. 113–31.

Browne, J.; Deakin, S.; Wilkinson, F. 2002. *Capabilities, social rights and European market integration*, ESRC Centre for Business Research Working Paper 253 (Cambridge, University of Cambridge).

Burawoy, M. 1979. *Manufacturing consent* (Chicago, University of Chicago Press).

Burri, S.; Opitz, H.; Veldman, A. 2003. "Work–family policies on working time in practice: A comparison of Dutch and German case law on working-time adjustment", in *International Journal of Comparative Labour Law and Industrial Relations*, Vol. 19, No. 3, pp. 321–46.

Clarkberg, M.; Moen, P. 2001. "Understanding the time-squeeze: Married couples' preferred and actual work-hour strategies", in *American Behavioral Scientist*, Vol. 44, No. 7, pp. 1115–36.

Deakin, S. 2003. "Social rights and the market: An evolutionary perspective", in B. Burchell, S. Deakin, J. Michie and J. Rubery (eds.): *Systems of production: Markets, organizations and performance* (London, Routledge), pp. 74–88.

—. 2004. *Renewing labour market institutions* (Geneva, International Institute for Labour Studies).

—; Wilkinson, F. 2000. *Capabilities, spontaneous order and social rights*, ESRC Centre for Business Research Working Paper No. 174 (Cambridge, University of Cambridge).

Drago, R. 2000. "Trends in working time in the US: A policy perspective", in *Labor Law Journal*, Winter, pp. 212–18.

—; Black, D.; Wooden, M. 2004. "Gender and work hours transitions in Australia: Drop ceilings and trap-door floors", Melbourne Institute Working Paper No. 11/04 (University of Melbourne).

Eastman, W. 1998. "Working for position: Women, men and managerial work hours", in *Industrial Relations*, Vol. 37, No. 1, pp. 51–66.

Ehrenreich, B. 2002. *Nickel and dimed: Undercover in low-wage America* (New York, Granta Books).

Euwals, R. 2001. "Female labour supply, flexibility of working hours, and job mobility", in *Economic Journal*, Vol. 111, pp. C120–C147.

Fagan, C. 2001. "Time, money and the gender order: Work orientations and working time preferences in Britain", in *Gender, Work and Organization*, Vol. 8, No. 3, pp. 239–66.

—. 2004. "Gender and working time in industrialized countries", in J. Messenger (ed.), 2004, pp. 108–46.

Folbre, N.; Nelson, J. 2000. "For love or money – or both?", in *Journal of Economic Perspectives*, Vol. 14, No. 4, pp. 123–40.

Ford, H. 1926. "Why do I favor five days' work with six days' pay?" (interview with S. Crowther), in *World's Work*, October, pp. 613–16.

Ghez, G.; Becker, G. 1975. *Allocation of time and goods over the life cycle* (New York, NBER).

Golden, L. 2004. "The flexibility gap: Employee access to flexibility in work schedules", mimeo.

Hakim, C. 1997. "A sociological perspective on part-time work", in H. Blossfeld and C. Hakim (eds.): *Between equalization and marginalization: Women part-time workers in Europe and the USA* (Oxford, Oxford University Press), pp. 20–79.

—. 2000. *Work lifestyle choices in the 21st century: Preference theory* (Oxford, Oxford University Press).

Holt, H.; Grainger, H. 2005. *Results of the second flexible working employee survey*, Employment Relations Research Series No. 39 (London, Department of Trade and Industry).

Jolivet, A.; Lee, S. 2004. *Employment conditions in an ageing world: Meeting the working time challenge*, Conditions of Work and Employment Series No. 9 (Geneva, ILO).

Keynes, J. 1930. "Economic possibilities for our grandchildren", in *Essays in persuasion* (New York, W.W. Norton & Co.), pp. 358–73.

Landers, R.; Rebitzer, J.; Taylor, L. 1996. "Rat race redux: Adverse selection in the determination of work hours in law firms", in *American Economic Review*, Vol. 86, No. 3, pp. 329–48.

Lang, K.; Kahn, S. 2001. "Hours constraints: Theory, evidence, and policy implications", in G. Wong and G. Picot (eds.): *Working time in comparative perspective (I): Patterns, trends, and the policy implications for earnings inequality and unemployment* (Kalamazoo, Michigan, W. E. Upjohn Institute for Employment Research), pp. 261–87.

Lee, S. 2004. "Working hour gaps: Trends and issues", in J. Messenger (ed.) 2004, pp. 29–59.

Messenger, J. (ed.). 2004. *Working time and workers' preferences in industrialized countries: Finding the balance* (London, Routledge).

Munz, S. 2004. "Flexibility of working hours and job mobility in Germany: The role of the Part-time and Fixed-term Act", Paper presented to the TLM.NET Conference "Quality in labour market transitions: a European challenge", Amsterdam, 25–26 Nov. 2004.

Nussbaum, M. 1999. "Women and equality: The capabilities approach", in *International Labour Review*, Vol. 138, No. 3, pp. 227–45.

O'Reilly, J.; Fagan, C. (eds.). 1998. *Part-time prospects: An international comparison of part-time work in Europe, North America and the Pacific Rim* (London, Routledge).

Palmer, T. 2004. *Results of the first flexible working employee survey* (London, Department of Trade and Industry).

Peetz, D.; Townsend, K.; Russell, B.; Houghton, C.; Allan, C.; Fox, A. 2003. "Race against time: extended hours in Australia", in *Australian Bulletin of Labour*, Vol. 29, No. 2, pp. 126–42.

Rebitzer, J.; Taylor, L. 1995. "Do labor markets provide enough short-hour jobs?: An analysis of work hours and work incentives", in *Economic Inquiry*, Vol. 33, pp. 257–73.

Schmidt, M. 2001. "The right to part-time work under German law: Progress in or a boomerang for equal employment opportunities?", in *Industrial Law Journal*, Vol. 30, No. 4, pp. 335–51.

Schor, J. 1992. *The overworked American: The unexpected decline of leisure* (New York, Basic Books).

Sen, A. 1992. *Inequality reexamined* (Oxford, Clarendon Press).

—. 1999. *Development as freedom* (Oxford, Oxford University Press).

Sharone, O. 2002. *Engineering consent: Overwork and anxiety at a high-tech firm*, Center for Working Families Working Paper No. 36 (Berkeley, University of California).

Spurgeon, A. 2003. *Working time: Its impact on safety and health* (Seoul, ILO and Korea Occupational Safety and Health Agency).

Supiot, A. 2001. *Beyond employment: Changes in work and the future of labour law in Europe* (Oxford, Oxford University Press).

Thompson, E. 1967. "Time, work-discipline, and industrial capitalism", in *Past and Present*, Vol. 38, pp. 56–97.

Toynbee, P. 2003. *Hard work: Life in low-pay Britain* (London, Bloomsbury).

Walsh, J. 1999. "Myths and counter-myths: An analysis of part-time female employees and their orientations to work and working hours", in *Work, Employment & Society*, Vol. 13, No. 2, pp. 179–203.

Weston, R.; Gray, M.; Qu, L.; Standton, D. 2004. *Long work hours and the well-being of fathers and their families*, Australian Institute of Family Studies Research Paper No. 35 (Melbourne, Australian Institute of Family Studies).

White, M.; Hill, S.; McGovern, P.; Mills, C.; Smeaton, D. 2003. "'High-performance' management practices, working hours and work-life balance", in *British Journal of Industrial Relations*, Vol. 41, No. 2, pp. 175–95.

Wooden, M.; Loundes, J. 2001. *How unreasonable are long working hours?*, Melbourne Institute Working Paper No. 1/02 (Melbourne, University of Melbourne).

DECENT WORKING TIME IN A LIFE-COURSE PERSPECTIVE[1]

4

Dominique Anxo,* Jean-Yves Boulin and Colette Fagan**

4.1   INTRODUCTION

Over the last century, the regulation of working time has changed its focus, encompassing longer and longer time frames: initially the single working day (the 8-hour-day reform), then the week (free weekends), then the year (paid holidays), and finally the entire life course (retirement age). However, the regulation of working time implied the establishment of homogeneous standards that did not give individuals any real autonomy in the organization of their working time schedules or the possibility to adapt periods of work and non-work during their life course. On the contrary, the regulation of working time contributed to a segmentation of individuals' lives into three major and fairly strictly watertight sequences: initial education, market work and, finally, retirement. Until recently, this tripartite division of the life course has not been called into question, even if the timing of transitions between these three sequences has changed over time, principally through longer schooling and earlier withdrawal from the labour market.

Stimulated by economic, social and cultural changes, life-course arrangements are becoming more diverse, more self-directed and subject to

* Economist and Professor at the School of Management and Economics, Department of Economics and Statistics, Växjo, Sweden.

** Sociologist at the School of Social Sciences, University of Manchester, United Kingdom.

[1] The present chapter summarizes part of a recent project funded by the European Foundation for the Improvement of Living and Working Conditions and coordinated by D. Anxo and J.-Y. Boulin (2005, 2006). The overall objective of this project was to provide new empirical evidence concerning the current state and development of time options, time arrangements and income over the life course and to examine the disparities between demographic groups and also across EU Member States. The researchers involved in this project were Inma Cebrian (Alcala University), Colette Fagan (University of Manchester), Ute Klammer (Hans Boeckler Stiftung), Kristina Klenner (Hans Boeckler Stiftung), Saskia Keuzenkamp (Sociaal en Cultureel Planbureau, the Netherlands), Gloria Moreno (Alcala University) and Luis Toharia (Alcala University).

negotiations (Krüger, 2003). Most people do not expect to be doing the same type of work all their lives, as was usually the case for the majority of the population in traditional cultures (Giddens, 1993). Citizens' living conditions and approach to life courses are becoming increasingly varied. Hence, extended possibilities to adjust working time to the changing needs of workers during their lifetime appear to be in line with the growing heterogeneity of households' preferences. As stressed by Heinz (2003), if individuals consider their life course as a project in which they perform paid work with varying intensity depending on their circumstances and preferences, then a new social system would have to offer citizens the opportunity to design their own projects.

Currently, combinations of and transitions between different social activities are not always facilitated. This is clearly illustrated by those women who want to combine employment with raising young children: the high cost and/or low availability of childcare might well constrain their labour supply following childbirth. A second example is the lack or inadequacy of training institutions for promoting investment in knowledge and skills over the entire job career, while societal interest in expanding knowledge is steadily increasing (Leijnse et al., 2002). As stressed in a Dutch governmental report, the division between paid work and other activities and the allocation of income over the life course are far from ideal. The generation between the ages of 30 and 45 is currently experiencing a great deal of time pressure as a result of having many obligations and aspirations. During this life phase, most people want to pursue a job career, take care of children (or others), participate in training and invest in social contacts and networks. In the Netherlands, for example, this time pressure has led to an increasing number of individuals suffering from stress and an increasing incidence of premature cessation of employment due to disability (ibid.).

The concept of a new organization of time and income over the life course implies that individuals are better equipped to adapt their time allocation between paid work and other social activities in relation for example to changes in their working life (investment in human capital, job mobility, etc.) and/or to changes in preferences or circumstances regarding activities outside the labour market (child-rearing and other family commitments, voluntary work, leisure, etc.). From this perspective, the concept of a new organization of time becomes part of a strategy to develop and implement work–life balance policies.

Several forms of employment and/or working time patterns allow – at least theoretically – employees to influence their time and income allocation over the life course: part-time work, progressive early retirement schemes, working time accounts and different forms of leave arrangements. However, the conditions and environment which generally surround these systems – e.g., the tax and social protection structures, the employment situation (high unemployment rates) – restrict the possibilities for individuals to adjust their working time over the life course. The growing volatility of employment patterns (periods of unemployment, successive short-term contracts or interim missions with periods of inactivity, etc.) are generally more endured than desired, often being imposed either as a result of employment policies developed by governments and/or the social partners, or due to firms' strategies for increasing productive efficiency. In short, these discontinuities are more often associated with the words "precariousness" and "insecurity" than with freely assumed choice. On top of this, some of these time and income arrangements may promote age and gender discrimination. Therefore, policy measures aiming at enhancing the range of options to adapt working time patterns over the life course appear to be of high relevance in societies where men and women tend to participate in a wider range of social activities and where life expectancy is increasing in a context of declining fertility.

In our view, this kind of policy echoes the five significant dimensions of "decent working time" as suggested by the International Labour Office (ILO) Conditions of Work and Employment Programme (Anxo et al., 2004; Messenger, Conclusion in this volume). In order to be "decent", working time patterns should be *healthy*, and there is reason to believe that a new organization of working time over the life course might be a way to secure workers' health – especially in a period of the intensification of working time, of increased complexity in coordinating competing demands during certain life phases, and of the lengthening of their working lives as promoted by the European Employment Strategy. A second dimension of decent working time is to allow workers to better balance work and family (*family-friendly*), one of the main fields of application for life-course policies both at the institutional and firm level. We argue in the following discussion that the lack of family-friendly working time arrangements (and more substantially for better balancing work and life) is an obstacle to the implementation of *gender equal opportunity*, which is another dimension of decent working time. We assume that working time options such as working time accounts, sabbaticals or lifelong training schemes could play a crucial role in the enhancement of firms' competitiveness and *productivity* (the fourth dimension of decent working time) via an increase in human capital, together with an improvement of the social capabilities of their employees. As illustrated by some Swedish firms encouraging fathers to take parental leave, the workers become more flexible in their work behaviour after such an experience (Den Dulk, 2001). Regarding the fifth dimension of decent working time, working time options designed from a life-course perspective entail *greater choice for workers*, if we assume that in post-industrial societies there is an increasing emphasis upon individual decisions and responsibility in the shaping of life trajectories (Heinz, 2003). Obviously these five dimensions are interrelated since, for example, workers with extended possibilities to better adapt market work to social and family commitments will be more involved in their work, leading to an increase in productive efficiency (Osterman, 1995). But it is worth noticing that existing working time options designed in a life-course perspective do not automatically entail possibilities for all to shape their biographies. It is important to stress that a new organization of time over the life course also necessitates policy measures that prevent individuals from incurring a large income loss over the life course or negative path dependencies that may entail gender discrimination or a dramatic decrease of pension rights. Universal rights might also suffer from drawbacks, such as for example variations in the take-up rates between different social categories due to large differences in their working time capabilities (see Lee and McCann, Chapter 3 in this volume). As stressed by Hörning et al. (1995, p. 167): "Without support of a reflexive visualization of the conception of life, greater latitude to shape lifestyle organization is of no value . . .".

4.2 THE RELEVANCE OF A NEW ORGANIZATION OF WORK THROUGHOUT THE LIFE COURSE

Reviewing the major theoretical developments in the literature on the life course, the relevance of the life-course perspective for understanding the major changes experienced by contemporary societies appears to be of prominent importance. In *The handbook of the life course* (2003), "life course" is defined as "interdependent sequences of age-related social roles across life domains (family, education, work, health, leisure). In this sense it is a product of the linkages among state (welfare), market and familial (gender) institutions and demographic behaviours across the life span" (O'Rand, 2003, p. 693). Helga Krüger identifies the major markers of life-course dynamics: "historical or personal events in biographical time and their effects in accordance with ageing . . . transitions between specific life stages . . . the duration of life stages; changes in participation patterns and status configuration over the life span" (Krüger, 2003, pp. 33–56). Furthermore, she identifies the coexistence of three quite distinct units of life-course structuration: the *attainment logic* which emphasizes status attainment (rests on the serial programme of successfully progressing through education, labour market positioning and corresponding retirement benefits); the *tandem logic* of the labour market and the family in the period of adulthood; and the *back-up logic* of private and public costs and benefits in intergenerational life-course settings, which results from the rules of sharing care and reproductive work between the state and the family (Krüger, ibid.).

Another important issue in our understanding of life trajectories concerns the ways of analytically disentangling the impact of individual behaviour, e.g. *agency* (choices and actions), from the influence of the social structure in a broad sense and the dynamic of social changes. Obviously, the institutional environment (social protection systems, labour market policies, regulatory framework concerning working time options, tax and transfer systems related to the different life phases and household categories, etc.) plays a crucial role in the patterns of households' time and income allocation over the life course. For instance, the educational system, labour market institutions and the social protection system channel individuals and organize their life courses around the employment system. But social structures are also influenced by the changing values and the evolving representation attached, for instance, to different social activities (paid work, family, leisure, social commitments, etc.) and the ways in which individuals and different social categories support and implement them. There is a complex and interrelated relationship between social structure and individual agency over the life course.

An important dimension of the life-course approach is its attempt to take a holistic view, in that the analysis no longer focuses on isolated specific events, phases or demographic groups as being discrete and fixed, but rather considers the entire life as the basic framework for empirical analysis and policy evaluation. Considering the life course as a whole is also a way to acknowledge the importance and consequences of early transitions for later experiences and events. Hence focusing on these early events and transitions such as educational attainment, the extent of labour market participation (part time/full time, continuous or erratic labour market entry and job career), and family formation (union formation, parenting, separation) is a way to recognize that these early events might have large consequences in the later years of life. In other words, the present situation of individuals is not independent of the choices, transitions, opportunities and constraints encountered in the past. To some extent we may observe that some form of path dependency and past experience matters, and may restrict an individual's options in the future. The social implications and consequences of early transitions and choices will obviously differ depending on the historical and societal context. The availability for example of public lifelong training systems or active labour market policy programmes may reduce the "social" costs of early drop-out from the educational system. Hence if time is irreversible,[2] life trajectories may be reversible and the social implications of early "negative" choices in life could, depending on the institutional context and options, be "corrected" later on in life. This appears particularly important in a context in which "the tasks of life planning are being increasingly assigned to individuals, who are compelled to

---

[2] "Even God could not change the past" (Aristotle).

intensify the thematization of the course of their lives" (Hörning et al., 1995, p. 140). Alain Supiot has directly related this individualization tendency to the issue of working time regulation: "the new principle governing working time is self-regulation of time . . . ultimately by individuals themselves, now responsible for the organisation of their own time providing they commit themselves to their employer's objectives" (Supiot, 2001, p. 83).

4.2.1 Changes that foster the need for a new organization of time throughout the life course

Individuals nowadays change roles more often during their life course than previously. This is partly the result of individual decisions, and partly due to the fact that jobs and relationships, for example, offer less long-term security than was previously the case. Changes are also occurring in the relationships between employers and employees, some of which are conflicting: employers demand strong commitment and flexibility, while employees strive for autonomy and security. As stressed by Heinz:

> There is cross-national evidence that economic and social change has modified both cultural standards and persons' biographical timing, which in turn has led to a more flexible sequencing of male and female work life courses. Instead of relying on age as the major indicator of the individual life course, the timing, kind and duration of a person's involvement with labour market institutions are more useful as a focus of career analysis. A career then can be analysed as a sequence of life events and movements in education, work and family life, a sequence which is co-constructed by institutional gate keeping and personal decisions. (Heinz, 2003, p. 194)

During recent decades, major changes in the *timing of transitions* over the life course have occurred. Globally, the industrialized countries have experienced a postponement of entry into the labour market due to later exit from the educational system, combined with earlier exit from the labour market due to early retirement schemes and a lowering of the pension age. Simultaneously, the trends toward individualization, the emergence of new lifestyles and changes in values and norms have largely modified the traditional family life-cycle model of marriage, parenthood, followed by retirement within a stable marriage, which was still prevalent during the 1950s and 1960s (Beck, 1992; Giddens, 1990). The overall reduction in marriage rates, increased rates of divorce, consensual unions, lone parenthood, the decrease of family size, the postponement of family formation (average age at first child), the rising rates of childlessness and the increase in life expectancy, coupled with the growing instability in the labour market, have certainly modified individuals' expectations and options over the life course. Hence, if the traditional tripartite sequencing of work history (education–employment–retirement) or the sequencing of critical life phases (singleness, marriage/cohabitation, children, empty nest, etc.) remains predominant in many industrialized countries, most advanced economies have experienced a *rescheduling* of traditional critical events, an increase of instability and risks (separation/divorce, unemployment), and therefore a growing heterogeneity of life trajectories.

The significant changes in the timing of transitions at the two ends of the age distribution have shortened the period of "active working life". The various reforms aiming at reducing weekly and yearly working time have also reinforced the diminution of time spent on paid work. If we take into account the large increase in life expectancy, the time devoted to market work has dramatically decreased during the last decades. Thus there has been both an absolute reduction in the amount of time devoted to market work over the life course, as well as a proportionate reduction relative to life expectancy. This trend applies particularly to men, for, as discussed above, in recent decades the time allocated to paid employment during the lifetime has increased for women, partly offsetting the reduction for men.

Time devoted to housework has also decreased due to the growing availability of household goods and services offered in the market and/or provided by the public sector (outsourcing). Technological progress and increased capital intensity in home-produced goods and services have also contributed to a huge increase in productivity in the home sector and the reduction of time spent on household activities. Households contain fewer children, and so the total time devoted to child-raising has fallen (even if the time-intensity per child is higher than in earlier historical periods). Hence, globally, recent decades have seen a large increase of "leisure time" over the whole life course. However, gender inequalities in time-use persist. At the household level, the reduction of men's paid working time has been partially compensated by the increase of female labour supply, but the bulk of unpaid housework and care activities are still predominantly performed by women – even though in many countries the male share of household production has increased (see Anxo et al., 2002; Gershuny, 2000). The resilience of a traditional gender division of labour also has dynamic implications in terms of career prospects, expected life-cycle earnings and welfare development over the life course.

4.2.2 *The emergence of life-course policies in Europe*

In this context, it is not surprising that one of the major objectives of the European Employment Strategy is to augment the overall employment rate, which is critically dependent upon a further integration of women and the retention of older workers in the labour market. This employment goal therefore requires the implementation of pro-active policies making it possible for both men and women to better reconcile work and other social commitments over the life course. Hence policy reforms aimed at increasing individuals' working time options and ensuring the reversibility of individual choices over the life course might be a good policy instrument for fostering a time and income allocation conducive to an increase in the overall employment rates supporting the sustainability of the social protection system.

The idea of a new organization of time and income over working life is not new. The pioneering works of Jean Fourastié (1965) and his concept of "the 40,000 hours", as well as Gösta Rehn's free choice society (1972, 1977), are two illustrations of early attempts to conceptualize time and income allocation over the life course that depart from the traditional tripartite division between education, continuous employment and retirement.[3] More recently, and in a totally different economic, social and cultural context, the transitional labour market approach has focused on determinants of various transitions over the life course (Gazier, 2003; Schmid and Gazier, 2002), while Alain Supiot has made a plea for the recognition of the social utility of time devoted to care activities and social commitments such as human assistance (Supiot, 2001).

At the European Union level, the idea of promoting flexibility in working life has been a key issue in efforts to improve the employment content of economic growth. In order to promote a more modern labour organization, the social partners have been exhorted to negotiate agreements (at the appropriate level) to introduce flexible and innovative methods of labour organization reconciling firms' competitive constraints and employees' preferences regarding working time patterns (Social Protocol of the Maastricht Treaty and Luxembourg's four pillars). From 2000 onwards, the European Strategy for Employment has stressed the need to foster the development of a knowledge-based society (Lisbon Summit, 2000) and to increase the overall employment rate by implementing employment policies aimed at increasing the labour market participation of women and older individuals (Barcelona Summit, 2001). This quest for new forms of negotiated flexibility has taken the form of agreements on the reduction of working time, the "annualization" of working hours, the development of part-time work, "lifelong" education and career breaks. Even though these EU-level efforts to promote the emergence of negotiated flexibility and the development of new time policies are partly in line with the idea of increasing the variability of

---

[3] The political awareness, at that time, of the necessity of implementing new patterns of time allocation over the life course can also be illustrated by an OECD report from 1973: "Both the economic aim of using the whole potential labour force and the social aim of meeting each individual's preferences do demand that people can choose their working time – its length and its allocation per day, per year and per life – with as few constraints as possible" (Evans, 1973, quoted in Boulin and Hoffman, 1999, p. 17).

working time over the life course, they are still piecemeal measures and not part of an integrated model combining reforms of social protection and the allocation of time. Thus they are not in a position to challenge the major influence of the institutional framework upon the life-course trajectories of men and women, as can be shown by a cross-country comparison of the gender disparities in the patterns of labour market integration and working time arrangements over the life course (Anxo and Boulin (eds.) 2006).

4.3 LIFE-COURSE PROFILES: A CROSS-NATIONAL COMPARISON

Life-course research has emphasized the emergence of more flexible and individualized ways of integrating work and other social commitments over the life course: job entries, employment spells and exits from the labour market across the life course are becoming increasingly more diversified. Employment, family and intergenerational arrangements are being transformed (Heinz, 2003). These transformations are mediated by social institutions in the labour market and in the educational, family and the welfare systems influencing the way individuals shape their working and life trajectories. They provide guidelines and resources for individuals who are constructing their careers through decisions and self-reflexive actions in the context of interrelated biographies (ibid.).

When looking at the role of institutional contexts in the framing of individual biographies, analyses differ in the extent to which they accentuate the standardization of modern life-course patterns or their deregulation (Krüger, 2003). Some countries (Germany, for example) have strong life-course regimes due to structural linkages between social background and educational attainment, between education credentials and labour market entry, and between employment careers and retirement benefits (ibid.). For instance, comparing Germany and the United Kingdom, Heinz (2003) shows that in the United Kingdom, 15- to 20-year-olds exhibit a higher employment rate, mainly in the casual labour market segment, whereas in Germany most of the teenagers are either still at school or in apprenticeship training. Conversely, labour market exits occur relatively early in Germany, where employment rates start to decline by age 55, and just 43 per cent of men and 15 per cent of women older than 60 are still in the labour force. This contrasts with the United Kingdom, where more than half of men and 18 per cent of women are still employed, or Norway where almost three-quarters of men and 60 per cent of women in the same age group remain in employment. These results show that entry into paid work and career prospects hinge on the linkage between educational and labour market institutions: formal and connected pathways create less variability in the transition and less uncertainty in the work life course compared with more market-driven and flexible arrangements in the United States or the United Kingdom (ibid.).

4.3.1 Gender disparities in the patterns of labour market integration and working time arrangements over the life course

One of the most salient features and persistent trends in advanced economies is the increased feminization of the labour force; the related shift from the single male breadwinner household towards dual-earner households; and the increased diversification of household structures. Despite these common trends implying a significant reduction of the gender employment gap, there are still large differences in the patterns of household labour market integration over the life course. In a previous study (Anxo and Boulin (eds.) 2006,) we have shown that this pattern and the magnitude of gender differences differ considerably between European countries. Four broad patterns of labour market integration and working time arrangements over the life course are identified in figures 4.1–4.8.[4]

The Nordic "universal breadwinner" model of high and continuous labour market participation over the life course involving long part-time or full-time hours, portrayed here by Sweden, is characterized by high employment rates (in particular at the two ends of the age distribution); high employment continuity (sustainability) over the life course; and relatively low gender disparities in labour market integration (figures 4.1 and 4.2). In Sweden, neither marriage/cohabitation nor family formation significantly affects women's employment rates. The main impact of family formation is a temporary reduction of working hours to long part-time hours while children are young. Compared with other European countries, the large opportunities to adjust working time over the life course – through various forms of income-compensated "legal absenteeism" (e.g., parental leave, leave for sick child or relatives) with a complete employment guarantee and a reversible reduction in working time – allow a more flexible management of work and family constraints. More globally, this strategy appears to be an efficient tool to secure women's labour market integration, foster employment continuity, and improve gender-equal opportunities.

---

[4] In order to visualize life-course profiles of labour market integration and working time arrangements, we have selected a range of household categories coinciding with different transitions and phases in the life course: transition out of the parental home and entry into the labour market (young singles without children), union formation (cohabiting couples without children), parenting (differentiating couples according to the age of children); the midlife "empty nest" period (middle-aged couples without cohabiting children); and lastly the elderly phase and exit out of the labour market (couples older than 60 years). See Anxo and Boulin (2006) for a more detailed discussion of our methodology and also an extension of the analysis to seven European Member States.

Figure 4.1   Employment rates, Sweden, 1998

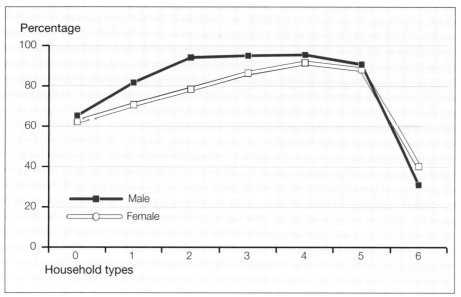

Figure 4.2   Weekly working time, employed, Sweden, 1998

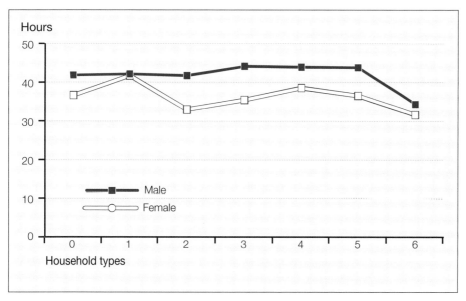

0. Young singles without children
1. Young couples without children
2. Couples with pre-school children
3. Couples with children less than 13 years old

4. Couples with children more than 13 years old
5. Couples without children, female more than 45 years old
6. Older couples without children (spouses more than 60 years old)

Figure 4.3   Employment rates, France, 2000

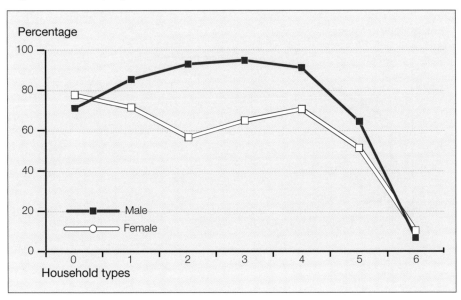

Figure 4.4   Weekly working time, employed, France, 2000

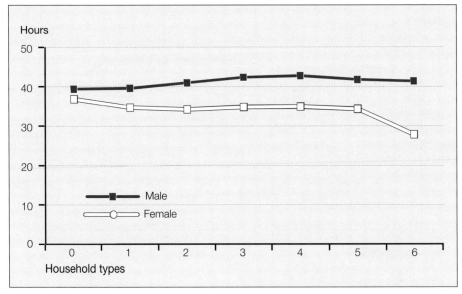

0. Young singles without children
1. Young couples without children
2. Couples with pre-school children
3. Couples with children less than 13 years old

4. Couples with children more than 13 years old
5. Couples without children, female more than 45 years old
6. Older couples without children (spouses more than 60 years old)

Figure 4.5   Employment rates, Spain, 2000

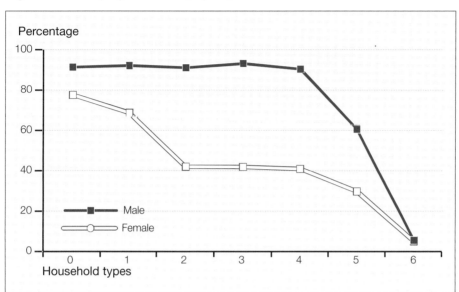

Figure 4.6   Weekly working time, employed, Spain, 2000

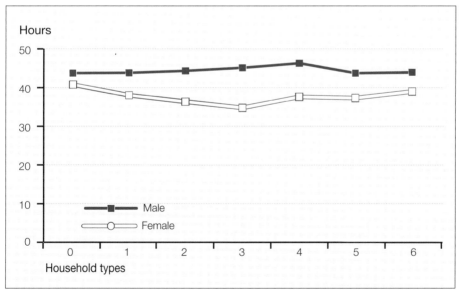

0. Young singles without children
1. Young couples without children
2. Couples with pre-school children
3. Couples with children less than 13 years old

4. Couples with children more than 13 years old
5. Couples without children, female more than 45 years old
6. Older couples without children (spouses more than 60 years old)

Figure 4.7   Employment rates, United Kingdom, 2000

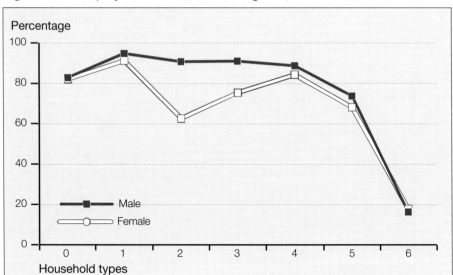

Figure 4.8   Weekly working time, employed, United Kingdom, 2000

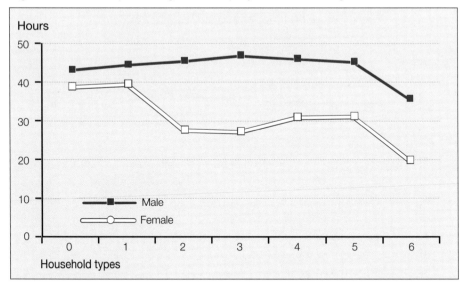

0. Young singles without children
1. Young couples without children
2. Couples with pre-school children
3. Couples with children less than 13 years old

4. Couples with children more than 13 years old
5. Couples without children, female more than 45 years old
6. Older couples without children (spouses more than 60 years old)

Source: ECHP and HUS for Sweden, own calculations; Anxo and Boulin (2006), Chs. 2 and 6.

In the *"modified breadwinner" model*, illustrated here by France (see figures 4.3 and 4.4), some women exit the labour market when they have young children, while the majority work full time or long part-time hours. Hence, in contrast to the situation in the Nordic countries, family formation and motherhood are still associated with withdrawal from the labour market for some groups of women. Most mothers who are employed work full time or long part-time hours in "reduced-hour" arrangements. This life-course pattern for French mothers is supported by the high coverage rate and low cost of public childcare, as in Sweden, but high levels of unemployment undermine the ability of women with low levels of qualifications to follow this route. Even though the activity rate of French prime age adult women started to rise for generations from the mid-1950s onwards, the trend is still that younger generations of mothers have more continuous participation profiles across their working lives than their predecessors. When the younger generations enter these older age groups, we might expect them to maintain higher levels of labour market integration than are observed for the current cohort of older women, which will operate to reduce the gender gap in working time among older age groups.

The Mediterranean "exit or full-time" model, illustrated here by Spain, in which women's employment rates are low but largely involve full-time work. As shown by figures 4.5 and 4.6, family formation and the presence of children have a clearly negative impact on female labour market integration, but essentially in terms of lower labour force participation despite rising participation rates as younger cohorts of women move through their working lives. Fewer women are employed, but when they are employed they generally work full time. The relatively low public provision of childcare facilities for young pre-school children, the low income replacement rate, and the weakness of subsequent employment guarantees for parental leave still constitute a barrier to women's labour market integration and support the "housewife" system of childcare and the "male breadwinner" system of family provisioning. The prevailing working time rigidities, in particular the low availability of part-time jobs, constitute a barrier to women's labour market integration and encourage a traditional gender division of labour. As in France there is a strong cohort trend of higher labour market participation profiles emerging for younger and better-educated generations of women across the period of family formation and into the older age groups. However, in Spain as in Italy, the difficulty of combining employment with motherhood has contributed to an accompanying sharp decline in fertility rates. Younger generations of women defer or avoid motherhood in order to become established in the labour market, particularly in the context of high unemployment – compounded in the case of Spain with a high incidence of temporary contracts.

In the *"maternal part-time" work model*, illustrated here by the United Kingdom, the onset of motherhood is associated with a reduction in the employment rate that is less than that found in France or in Spain, but where part-time hours are the norm for mothers and generally remain the norm even when children are older (see figures 4.7 and 4.8). Furthermore, the hours worked by part-timers are typically shorter than the more substantial part-time hours that prevail in Sweden and to a lesser extent in France. This "maternal part-time" model is also underwritten in the British welfare state regime. While childcare is now expanding, it still falls short of that found in France and the Nordic countries. By comparison to other countries with a high incidence of female part-time work, like Germany or the Netherlands, the United Kingdom part-time model is also characterized by a predominance of very poor quality part-time work (see Fagan, 2001).

Two main conclusions might be drawn from this evidence. First, this comparative analysis emphasizes the predominant role of the institutional context in shaping the patterns of labour market integration of men and women over the life course. The cross-country comparison clearly shows the impact of legal options allowing employees to vary the extent of their labour market commitment (e.g., by taking temporary leave), and thereby adapt their working hours during different life phases. They highlight not only the role of these legal provisions, but moreover the importance of their conditions of implementation: employment guarantees, income compensation and the maintenance of social protection coverage. In this sense they illustrate the linkages and interrelated effects of various institutions, such as the educational and care systems, the labour market and the social protection system in shaping individual life trajectories:

> When these linkages are tightly coupled and universally salient in a population, their coherence and normative strength lead to a more highly institutionalized, age-graded life course. When they are loosely coupled, variability (de-institutionalization) in the life-course increases: the relationship of age to role transitions weakens and the synchronization of roles across life domains becomes less standardized. (O'Rand, 2003, p. 693)

Second, our analysis shows also that the gender division of labour varies according to social and cultural contexts. As stressed by Helga Krüger, this tends to elevate gender to a pivotal mechanism of resilience in dealing with contradictions between the institutional demands of status attainment and interdependencies between life courses (Krüger, 2003).

Despite its crucial relevance in the framing of gender discrepancies in the profile of labour market integration over the life course, the gender division of labour is not the focus of this chapter. The following section analyses the changes in the institutional framework and firms' practices aiming to enhance individuals' possibilities to influence their work–life balance. It is worth noticing that in flexible and weakly regulated labour markets individuals must, to a larger extent than in other regimes, bear the cost of transitions between different status and time arrangements (such as investment in human capital) and act as the producers of self-constructed pathways through the employment system (Heinz, 2003). However, the extent to which there is individual autonomy in time and income allocation depends on the institutional set-up of labour market transitions and the nature of welfare policy. The balance between regulation of the labour market and welfare state provisions[5] differs between neo-liberal, conservative and social-democratic regimes, creating a range of new opportunities as well as substantial risks and uncertainty over the life course.

4.4 EMPIRICAL EVIDENCE OF THE EMERGENCE OF A LIFE-COURSE PERSPECTIVE IN TIME POLICIES

A recent study from the European Foundation reported a large, untapped preference for part-time *working hours* (not necessarily part-time *jobs*)[6] among men as well as women across the EU, among both the employed and those wanting employment (Fagan, 2001; see also Bielenski et al., 2002). Overall, 19 per cent of employed men and 23 per cent of employed women are employed full time and would prefer part-time hours. This preference for part-time hours is mostly for a finite period (typically between 1 and 4 years) at particular stages in the life course (notably when parents have young children, when they approach retirement, or when they have elder care responsibilities). There are also important national differences in the extent of this untapped preference for an expansion of part-time work, and it can coexist with high levels of involuntary part-time work, such as in France and Sweden. The study also recorded widespread support for a number of other measures that would increase options for individuals to vary their working time over the life course; notably, sabbaticals (including unpaid ones) were considered attractive by a large share of the workforce, as was time banking among those working overtime. Finally, these preferences coexisted with a widespread awareness among the workforce of the obstacles to and penalties of trying to secure

---

[5] In which we include measures favouring the variation of working time duration and organization throughout the life course.

[6] The distinction made here is that working hours are only one dimension of a job, and *part-time jobs* can be viewed negatively, and as something to avoid, in labour markets where such employment is concentrated in poor-quality and low-paid parts of the economy. Hence someone might prefer to reduce their working hours to part-time if they could remain in their current "job" (such as under the Swedish parental leave system or the Dutch working time legislation), but would not want to change jobs to obtain this working time adjustment.

part-time hours, in terms of inferior social protection entitlements, employers' reluctance to permit such working time adjustments in their current post, or career penalties if they did secure this adjustment. In other words, the desire or capability to translate working time preferences into the preferred arrangements was institutionally constrained by national policy and workplace features. We now turn to highlighting what are the main trends in this field.

4.4.1 Trends at the institutional level

In our research for the European Foundation (Anxo and Boulin (eds.), 2005), we have identified a clear trend towards the emergence of life-course-oriented "working time options" (WTOs). When looking at the institutional developments, several working time options allow – at least theoretically – individuals to influence their time allocation over their life course: reversible working time reductions (from part time to full time and conversely), maternity and paternity leaves, parental leaves, care leaves, sabbaticals and career breaks, educational leaves, working time accounts and flexible retirement schemes.

The regulatory framework, in particular the level of regulation, for these WTOs varies significantly among European Member States.[7] These national disparities in the nature of working time regulations, particularly the extent and scope of legal rights regarding working time reductions or various forms of leaves of absence, appear to have significant implications for employees' opportunities to adapt working time over the life course, and therefore on their ability to combine market work with other social activities. Our analysis shows that significant differences exist between, on the one hand, countries with a regulatory regime mainly based on statutory regulation (universal citizen rights) and/or collective agreements covering a large portion of employees, and, on the other, countries in which working time options are mainly regulated through company agreements or through individual employment contracts. In countries such as Sweden, Germany and the Netherlands, the regulation of WTOs results from negotiated compromises in which both the public authorities and the social partners play a crucial role in shaping households' and companies' time management. At the other end of the spectrum we find more liberal and market-oriented countries, such as the United Kingdom, where both the Government and social partners are less involved in developing WTOs and where these options are mostly initiated and regulated at the company level.

---

[7] Six countries have been surveyed in this report in order to assess the trends in the institutional frameworks: France, Germany, the Netherlands, Spain, Sweden and the United Kingdom.

Another important difference among the European countries analysed here relates to the conditions linked to these different working time options. Taking parental leave as an example, the gap is wide between Sweden, where the duration of the leave is 15 months and the income replacement rate is up to 80 per cent, and most of the other countries discussed here, in which the leave duration is the basic EU norm (3 months) and is unpaid (most of the countries) or is paid at the lowest rates (a lump sum), e.g. in France or Germany. One of the main conclusions of our survey is that, seen from a life-course perspective, the Swedish working time options provide the most support for different stages in the life course.

Making a distinction between *specific life-phase/events-oriented WTOs* and *life-course-oriented WTOs*, some conclusions may be drawn from our cross-country analysis of the national regulatory frameworks:

1. Concerning the *specific life-phase/events-oriented WTOs*, we may observe the following:

   (a) most of the countries surveyed have implemented mainly WTOs corresponding to specific life phases, such as parenting and retirement;

   (b) the most common trend during the last 20 years concerning these life-phase-oriented WTOs has been a shift from short periods of leave (maternity leave periods are generally up to 16 weeks) towards longer leaves of absence. To illustrate, parental leave that covers longer periods has recently been introduced among Member States. If parental leave provisions tend to be generalized due to the existence of an EU directive, the main differentiation lies in the rules concerning their duration, the flexibility in the use of such leave (e.g., the possibility to take it on a part-time basis and to extend its use until the eighth birthday of the child), and the extent of income replacement;

   (c) another difference lies in the possibility to return to the same or a similar job (Sweden, Germany) and/or the sustainability of the employment contract (Sweden versus the United Kingdom) when taking up this kind of leave;

   (d) concerning exit from the labour market, a shift can also be observed towards a more dynamic approach – away from early retirement schemes through which employees used to retire permanently from the labour market before the legal retirement age and towards more flexible retirement schemes (before or after the standard retirement age).

2. *Life-course-oriented WTOs* are less common and have appeared more recently. Our survey also provides some information concerning these WTOs:

    (a) although all the countries studied have regulations on part-time work, the right to temporarily reduce or increase working hours (which is one of the main preferences of the European people) is statutorily regulated only in the Netherlands, while in Germany there is a right only to reduce working hours. Moreover, the right to reduce working hours must be appraised while keeping in mind the conditions that surround part-time contracts, which are different from one country to another;

    (b) during recent years some countries have introduced regulations on working time accounts (Germany, the Netherlands and France). This is a mechanism for financing sabbaticals, lifelong learning periods or other career breaks that until now were barely paid (even though there are statutory provisions for them in most of the countries surveyed). From a life-course perspective, a distinction should be made between short-term and long-term working time accounts. The latter allow for more controlled, flexible, destandardized life-course profiles, while the former are generally the result of a compromise between firms' economic needs (annual production cycles) and employees' preferences, embedded in a standardized conception of the life course. Consequently, in countries in which working time accounts are regulated, one should also look at the scope and limits of how the working time accounts can be filled and at their conditions of use (after how much time or up to which amount of accumulated leave; limitations concerning the ways of using the working time accounts; limitations imposed by employers; transferability between companies, etc.);

    (c) individual lifelong learning schemes which aim to overcome the problems of financing training courses that are not directly linked to the job have also appeared recently (this has spread in all the countries studied except the United Kingdom).

As a general conclusion concerning the institutional framework, we would like to highlight three marked trends:

1. The first trend refers to the regulation of more life-course-oriented working time options which (theoretically) allow for the construction of individual biographies linked to the differentiated needs and lifestyles of employees.

2. The second trend acknowledges the increasing orientation towards working time options that allow for longer leave periods that facilitate deviations from the standard working time regimes.

3. The third trend concerns the level and mode of regulation of these working time options. Although during the last 25 years there has been a trend towards the decentralization of working time regulation in Europe (from legislation and/or national collective agreements or industry-level agreements towards firm or unit agreements), the regulation of working time options designed in a life-course perspective tends to be, in its general principles (to provide a right to use them that is a question of social equity), regulated at the national level, mainly by law, even in those countries in which working regulations used to be ruled primarily by collective agreements (the Netherlands constitutes a good example). Conversely, conditions and modes of enforcement tend to be regulated through industry- or firm-level agreements.

4.4.2 Firms tend to limit the use of WTOs to parenthood and exit from the labour market

A publication by the *Harvard Business Review* (2000) foresees that a growing number of companies will be compelled to implement time policies in order to reconcile their economic needs with the increasing demands of their employees to better balance work and life. The management of the relationship between the working sphere and the personal and social sphere of employees constitutes, in their view, one of the most important levers for change in organizations which have to take account of environmental, social and societal evolutions.

Evidence from different surveys shows that a growing number of firms are implementing working time arrangements that depart from the standard organization of working time. This is not new since, for more than 20 years, companies have implemented flexible working time schedules in order to improve their economic efficiency. What appears to be new is the implementation of working time arrangements that reconcile both employees' and employers' needs and that allow employees more leeway in their life-course profiles. If it is difficult to assess the extent of such developments at the company level due to the lack of surveys in many countries,[8] several social,

---

[8] The United Kingdom is an exception, and company survey data on working time developments are available from a number of sources, including the government's new regular "work-life balance" survey, as well as from the periodic Workplace Employee Relations Survey.

economic, cultural and institutional trends that tend to constitute a favourable context for these kinds of developments have been identified: higher educational attainment, changes in aspirations and lifestyles, greater integration of women into the labour force, the development of information technologies, new values attached to the different social times, etc.

A growing economy may favour such developments because employers are more willing to create employment conditions that fit the needs of their workforce than in a declining economy. Economic and employment growth, moreover, favour a more diverse workforce because many workers are needed. And the more heterogeneous the workforce, the greater the pressure on employers to provide facilities that support the reconciliation of work and life. The above-cited publication by the *Harvard Business Review* concludes that firms that react positively to the wishes of their employees are generally more productive.

However, the life-course perspective (long-term working time accounts, possibilities of reducing/increasing working hours, lifelong learning schemes) is less developed; it is more likely to be found in large firms and in certain industries (finance, high technology). At the firm level, we have identified the prominent place of work/family arrangements, and more generally of working time arrangements that fit with specific phases in the life course. This clear tendency to focus on specific life phases, essentially parenting and the transition towards retirement, can be partly related to the European strategy aiming to enhance gender-equal opportunity, and also to major changes in the composition of the workforce (feminization) and the demographic context (e.g., the ageing of the population). In certain industries these kinds of policies are also related to the necessity of attracting and retaining employees in the context of tighter labour markets.

Our analysis has also highlighted a recent tendency towards the implementation of more dynamic working time arrangements, such as working time accounts or lifelong learning policies. Here also we might yield to the temptation of making a correlation with the European Employment Strategy as designed in Lisbon and Barcelona, and with a trend towards the implementation of statutory regulations related to these working time options in some European countries. Another study (Seifert, 2004) stresses the fact that companies play an ever more prominent role in regulating working hours, and the key question concerns the extent to which they are really willing to do so. Employers certainly tend to prefer the ability to decide for themselves which working time arrangements they will provide and to which employees they should offer certain options. From the company perspective this makes human resource management easier, but it can lead to a situation in which not all employees are offered the option to take advantage of life-course-specific working time options. It is not the biographical situation of the individual –

for example the necessity to provide care or a desire for professional reori-entation – which determines the option, but the position of the employee in the company or similar factors. Some employers tend to use schemes designed at the institutional level (parental leave, working time accounts, (progressive) early retirement schemes, lifelong learning schemes) for purposes other than those for which they were originally adopted.

It seems to us that there is a major risk of inequity if there are no basic principles defining the conditions of access to working time options defined at the statutory level that afford rights to individuals. The main conclusion of our analysis of firms' practices in the area of life-course policies that are based on both the principle of employee autonomy in the design of their life-course profile and the need for the firm to adjust its working time regimes to the economic evolution is that there is a need for an institutional framework (at European and/or national levels through the "subsidiarity principle") that might provide for collectively agreed regulation of individual choices.

4.5 CONDITIONS FOR IMPLEMENTING A NEW ORGANIZATION OF TIME OVER THE LIFE COURSE

From a life-course and a comparative perspective, we have shown that the Nordic working time regimes, portrayed here by Sweden, constitute the more integrated and coherent system of time and income management over the life course. Family formation is positively related to female labour market participation, and the impact of young children on female labour supply remains limited to very young children. Actually, the broad "palette" of individual working time options in Sweden – backed by a complete employment guarantee and extended childcare facilities – provides large opportunities for households to adapt their working time to various situations and commitments over the life course without significant income losses. Sweden constitutes a good illustration of a regime of *negotiated flexibility*, in which the social partners are largely involved in the shaping of working time options, thus ensuring their social legitimacy. In Sweden the working time options over the life course also seem to be better adapted to both companies' productive requirements and employees' needs and preferences. In other words, Sweden appears to meet most of the criteria of the decent working time concept. In the other European countries surveyed in our study, the legal opportunities to adjust working time over the life course appear to be much more limited, fragmented and often restricted to specific life phases, specific bargaining areas or certain companies. These legal options are furthermore associated with a weaker employment guarantee and often entail a larger income reduction compared with the Nordic countries.

However, even in Sweden, working time adjustments typically incur penalties in terms of reduced career and earnings development in subsequent working life. In all countries, it is largely women who make these adjustments, and in part the penalty incurred in career and wage evolution is because it is a gender "signal" of women's deviation from the standard employment relationship. Men incur these penalties when they deviate too, presenting a further obstacle for those men who would prefer to deviate from the standard employment relationship at different stages in their life course. Men's take-up rates of various types of extended leave are almost universally low, although progress has been made in some areas, such as the Swedish parental leave system[9] and with the proportion of male part-timers in the Netherlands. The question of how to raise men's take-up rates of extended leave and other working time adjustments is a key consideration if such adjustments over the life course are to be promoted as a policy instrument for reducing gender inequality in employment and care work. This means that conditions should be fulfilled in order to favour an organization of working time over the life course that is not limited to certain categories such as women, low-skilled workers, ethnic groups, etc.

4.5.1 Conditions related to the social protection system

In a comparative perspective, one crucial issue is to identify to what extent the national design of the social protection system establishes different incentives or disincentives for households' patterns of labour market integration and working time profiles over the life course. An analysis of the relationships between the patterns of labour market integration over the life course and social protection has to consider the interrelated and intricate relationships between the nature of the welfare state regime, the broad range of working time options and the individual and collective implications of different time options/arrangements on social security.

An assessment of the impact of time options/arrangements on the household's social protection needs to differentiate between "career interruptions" and systems that allow a flexible distribution of working time over the life course (reversible part-time working for instance). The right to take leave does not automatically guarantee some form of income compensation. In fact many prevailing parental leave schemes in the EU countries do not provide the right to a "decent" income replacement, except in the Nordic countries. Sabbaticals are generally unpaid unless they are linked to

---

[9] Around 80 per cent of Swedish fathers use their right to parental leave. On average their relative share of the total number of compensated days amounted to 20 per cent (80 days) in 2004.

active labour market policies, such as in Denmark during the 1990s[10] or implemented in order to limit sickness absenteeism and to improve employees' health.[11] In most countries training leave is financed through employers' social contributions, state subsidies and/or individually through subsidized loans, such as in Sweden. More recently companies have introduced time credits that can be used for personal development through training leaves.[12] The principle is the same as for working time accounts that are based on an intertemporal redistribution of time and income by the user. This gives people some options while the continuation of the employment contract ensures that social protection is granted. However, as far as social security protection is concerned, such arrangements contain some risks. One serious shortcoming is that many of the time credits earned in working time accounts are (to date) not insured against the insolvency of the employer.

Long-lasting periods of part-time work, even in the Dutch context where its reversibility is statutorily regulated, still contain an additional risk of poverty. From a life-course perspective, the total duration of part-time spells is a decisive factor for subsequent income development later in life and for later pension claims. Special social risks are also connected with "marginal" part-time jobs. In order to avoid these drawbacks in the case of temporary shifts towards part-time work, there is a necessity to "bridge" this right to vary the number of working hours with working time accounts.

Independent of the existing rights to interrupt working life or to adjust the number of working hours over the life course, universalistic and individualized social security schemes – e.g., health-care systems or pension systems based on citizenship or residence – give people some room for manoeuvre to use different time schemes and options. In this respect the Scandinavian countries, as well as the Netherlands, provide a better institu-tional environment for a flexible allocation of time and income over the life course than some of the continental/conservative or Mediterranean countries.

Another crucial issue is to identify to what extent the different time options and their take-up rates have an impact on the expenditures and the financial *sustainability of the social security and social protection systems*. In principle all leave systems that provide income replacement or cash benefits

---

[10] In 1992–94 the Danish Government implemented long periods of paid leave (parental, training, sabbatical), in order to reduce the unemployment rate through a job rotation system. This country has registered a drop in the unemployment rate from around 12 per cent down to 4 per cent between 1992 and 2000.

[11] After an experiment in 12 local authorities, Sweden has recently (1 January 2005) implemented a system of sabbaticals that allow employees to have a break when they feel they need one, instead of being compelled later to be on sick leave. Beyond preventing the "burn-out" syndrome, the scheme also aims at a job rotation with priority given to unemployed persons to replace the worker on sabbatical.

[12] For instance, a French national collective agreement (2003) confirmed by the law has endowed employees with a time credit of 20 hours per year over 6 years to be used for educational leave (*Droit Individuel à la Formation*).

cause direct social expenditures. However, the prevailing leave schemes so far have not contributed much to the financial imbalance of most welfare states. First, many leave schemes (e.g. several European parental leave schemes) are unpaid or subject to a low level of income replacement such as in France. Second, many leave schemes (e.g. sabbatical leave schemes) have had, up until now, low take-up rates. Third, public expenditures on certain leave schemes can in the long run lead to savings in social security expenditures. The Danish job rotation programmes or some Swedish active labour market policy schemes, in which training or sabbatical leaves are combined with employment opportunities for unemployed persons, can serve as examples of this situation. It is worth noticing that other kinds of work interruptions (in particular unemployment and "inactivity") threaten the financial sustainability of many social security systems to a much larger extent. Working time accounts based on an intertemporal redistribution of time and income do not affect the financial sustainability of social security systems, particularly if they are linked to job rotation schemes in countries with high unemployment rates.

4.5.2 The new organization of time over the life course as part of the employment dynamic and as a device for enhancing social cohesion

We may assume that the current reforms related to the life course will have contrasting impacts depending upon the position of people in the life course. To illustrate this point, we may expect that the current reforms concerning pension systems will not only affect older workers' labour market/retirement behaviour, but will also impact on the time allocation decisions of younger cohorts. Put differently, in terms of social justice and equity, we may assume that the consequences of such reforms may affect individuals' earnings development over the life course quite differently depending on the distribution of risks concerning career and employment disruptions among socio-economic groups. Hence the reforms of the social protection systems ought to consider the diversity in the patterns of labour market integration over the life course and the uneven distribution of risks by limiting the cost of necessary work interruptions linked to parenting, care activities, or involun-tary employment disruptions such as unemployment, disability or sickness.

Several conditions for the implementation of such new schemes can be derived from these remarks:

•   All leave systems must be associated with a subsequent employment guarantee – i.e., the right to return to the former job or a similar one. If this employment guarantee is not granted, a period of leave can turn out to be detrimental to any future career, and this fact may well have a negative influence on the take-up rate. Moreover, as has recently been decided in France for those who are on parental leave, such leave must not constitute an obstacle to the career progression of the taker and must not entail a decrease in their social protection entitlements. This means that the person on leave has the possibility to be involved in the firm's training courses and to contribute to the social security and pension funds, etc. These are also preconditions for encouraging more men to ask for such schemes, and thus reducing the gender bias in the current take-up patterns.

• These conditions are difficult for a firm alone to fulfil – particularly a small or medium-sized company. That is why a distinction should be introduced between leave that is subject to universal rights which grant each employee an entitlement to take it due to their societal (e.g. collective) status, and other types of leave which are more correctly related to the personal life and development of the individual. Alain Supiot (2001) supported the idea that some time allocation (devoted to care for children or the elderly, to human assistance or other voluntary involvement) ought to be assimilated into working time and subjected to similar entitlements as working time periods. It is up to society to decide what kinds of leave ought to be included in this category. Other types of leave related to the personal trade-off between work and leisure should be financed by individuals through an intertemporal redistribution of their time and income.

• The intertemporal allocation of time and income also has a collective dimension, at the firm level or at the local level. Consequently, savings for leave and training will have to be further developed and promoted. The social partners may elaborate integrated and collective working time accounts in order to avoid the risk of insolvency of the firm and to give the possibility to (younger) employees who have not accumulated sufficient time credits to benefit from their existence. The level of integration could be the firm, but preferably the sector in order to secure the transfer of time credits from one firm to another and to build a unified, comprehensive and coordinated system for financing periods of leave. Existing savings schemes in the area of leave and training will have to be combined wherever possible to provide transparency and a more integrated approach. Leave schemes will also have to adopt a more generic character, i.e., a reduced distinction between the various forms of leave.

4.6 CONCLUSION

The basic assumption of this chapter is that embedding working time policies in a life-course perspective might give substance to the notion of "decent working time". While statutory limitations on long working hours or a general reduction of standard working time may, for countries with a high incidence of long hours, be a means for curbing excessive hours, the need for working time flexibility over the life course cannot be satisfied only by standardized or statutory regulations giving little room for individual differentiation. Moreover there is a conflict between the short-term time horizon of firms and the life-course perspective. The current trend towards the development of short-term contracts and precarious employment is in conflict with the emergence of sustainable life-course career options. In this context of growing uncertainty, there is a need to find collective solutions that secure sustainable life-course trajectories. If we add the current trend towards the growing heterogeneity in household needs and preferences, there is scope for introducing legal options making it possible to adapt working time over the life course, thus favouring a better reconciliation between paid work and other social activities. Therefore policy measures have to be undertaken to extend and secure the range of working time options – in order to better adjust working time to various events and risks over the life course. Some national initiatives to secure, through statutory provision, the individual right to *modulate* working time over the life course, such as recently in the Netherlands, appear promising and largely in line with the European Employment Strategy. In our view, an increased individual freedom in time and income allocation over the life course not only has to be guaranteed through the application of a universal citizens' right, such as in the Netherlands, but also has to be complemented by an integrated system of income redistribution and income transfers, such as in Sweden. Removing rigidities in the prevailing working time regimes – in particular by increasing the range of statutory and/or negotiated options to adapt working time over the life course without large income losses – appears, therefore, crucial not only in terms of gender-equal opportunities and better work–life balance, but also in order to secure a better and more efficient allocation of time and resources over the life course.

Hence it is necessary to favour a holistic approach and recommend the implementation of a unified, comprehensive and coordinated system for financing all periods of non-paid time (Anxo et al., 2001; Supiot, 2001). Individual freedom and sovereignty in time allocation over the life course could be guaranteed through the application of a universal citizens' right, complemented by an integrated system of income transfers that could be implemented through industry and/or local agreements. Along these lines, the introduction of an income insurance fund with access to individual drawing rights could provide a high degree of flexibility in the allocation of time and income over the life course (Rehn, 1972, 1977). Besides an inter-temporal allocation of time and income implemented through working time accounts, we could also imagine an inter-individual redistribution through a mutualization of working time accounts at the industry or inter-industry levels and an active labour market policy through the implementation of job rotation schemes.

References

Anxo, D. 2004. "Working time patterns among industrialized countries: A household perspective", in J. Messenger (ed.): *Working time and workers' preferences in industrialised countries: Finding the balance* (London, Routledge).

—; Boulin, J.-Y. (coordinators). 2005. *Working time options over the life course: Changing social security structures* (European Foundation for the Improvement of Living and Working Conditions, Luxembourg, Office for Official Publications of the European Communities).

—; —. (coordinators). 2006. *Working time options over the life course: New work patterns and company strategies* (European Foundation for the Improvement of Living and Working Conditions, Luxembourg, Office for Official Publications of the European Communities).

—; Brossier, C.; Gazier, B. 2001. "Assessing the influence of Gösta Rehn in France", in H. Milner and E. Wadensjö (eds.): *Gösta Rehn and the Swedish model at home and abroad* (Aldershot, Ashgate).

—; Fagan, C.; Lee, S.; McCann, D.; Messenger, J. 2004. "Implications for working time policies", in J. Messenger (ed.): *Working time and workers' preferences in industrialised countries: Finding the balance* (London, Routledge).

—; Flood, L.; Kocoglu, Y. 2002. "Offre de travail et répartition des activités domestiques et parentales au sein du couple: Une comparaison entre la France et la Suède", in *Economie et Statistique*, Vol. 352–353, No. 2, pp. 127–50.

Beck, U. 1992. *Risk society: Towards a new modernity* (London, Sage Publications).

Bielenski, H.; Bosch, G.; Wagner, A. 2002. *Working time preferences in sixteen European countries* (Dublin, European Foundation for the Improvement of Living and Working Conditions).

Boulin, J.-Y.; Hoffmann, R. 1999. *New paths in working time policy* (Brussels, European Trade Union Institute).

Den Dulk, L. 2001. "Work–family arrangements in organisations: A cross-national study in the Netherlands, Italy, the United Kingdom and Sweden", in *International Journal of Cross Cultural Management*, Vol. 3, pp. 329–46.

European Foundation for the Improvement of Living and Working Conditions. 2003. *Working-time preferences and work–life balance in the EU: Some policy considerations for enhancing the quality of life* (Dublin).

Eurostat. 2003. *European Community Household Panel 2000* (Luxembourg, Office for Official Publications of the European Communities).

Fagan, C. 2001. *Gender, employment and working-time preferences in Europe* (Luxembourg, Office for Official Publications of the European Communities).

Fourastié, J. 1965. *Les 40 000 heures* (Paris, Laffont-Gonthier).

Gazier, B. 2003. *Tous sublimes: Vers un nouveau plein emploi* (Paris, Flammarion).

Gershuny, J. 2000. *Changing times: Work and leisure in post industrial societies* (Oxford, Oxford University Press).

Giddens, A. 1990. *Modernity and self-identity. Self and society in the late modern age* (Cambridge, Cambridge Polity Press).

—. 1993. *Sociology* (Cambridge, Cambridge Polity Press).

Glick, P.C. 1947. "The family cycle", in *American Sociological Review*, Vol. 12, No. 2, pp. 164–74.

Harvard Business Review. 2000. *Harvard Business Review on work and life balance* (Boston, Harvard Business School Press).

Heinz, W.R. 2003. "From work trajectories to negotiated careers: The contingent work life course", in J.T. Mortimer and M.J. Shanahan (eds.): *The handbook of the life course* (New York, Kluwer Academic/Plenum Publishers).

Hörning, K.; Gerhardt, A; Michailow, M. 1995. *Time pioneers: Flexible working time and new lifestyles* (Cambridge, Cambridge Polity Press).

Household Market and Non-Market Activities (HUS). 2004. Department of Economics, (Göteborg, Sweden, University of Goteborg).

Krüger, H. 2003. "The life-course regime: Ambiguities between interrelatedness and individualization", in W.R. Heinz and V.W. Marshall (eds.): *Social dynamics of the life course: Transitions, institutions and interrelations* (New York, Aldine de Gruyter).

Leijnse, F.; Goudswaard, K.; Plantenga, J.; van den Toren, J.P. 2002. *A different attitude to security: Life course, risk and responsibility*, report for the Netherlands Minister of Social Affairs and Employment (The Hague, Ministry of Social Affairs and Employment).

O'Rand, A.M. 2003. "The future of the life course: Late modernity and life course risks", in J.T. Mortimer and M.J. Shanahan (eds.): *The handbook of the life course* (New York, Kluwer Academic/Plenum Publishers).

Osterman, P. 1995. "Work/family programs and the employment relationship", in *Administrative Science Quarterly*, Vol. 40, pp. 681–700.

Rehn, G. 1972. *Prospective views on patterns of working time*, Manpower and Social Affairs Directorate (Paris, OECD).

—. 1977. *Towards a society of free choice* (Stockholm, Swedish Institute for Social Research).

Schmid, G.; Gazier, B. (eds.). 2002. *The dynamics of full employment: Social integration by transitional labour markets* (Cheltenham, UK, Edward Elgar).

Seifert, H. 2004. "A change of model: From uniform to variable distribution of working time", paper presented at the Ninth International Symposium on Working Time (ISWT), Paris, 26–28 February.

Supiot, A. 2001. *Beyond employment: Changes in work and the future of labour law in Europe* (Oxford, Oxford University Press)

TIME, WORK AND PAY: UNDERSTANDING THE NEW RELATIONSHIPS[1] 5

Jill Rubery,* Kevin Ward** and Damian Grimshaw*

5.1 INTRODUCTION

The organization and management of working time is at the heart of the employment relationship. The employment relationship has been defined by the agreement to work under the direction of an employer for a specified time: "what the worker sells, and what the capitalist buys, it is not an agreed amount of labour, but the power to control labour over an agreed period of time" (Braverman, 1974, p. 54). Working time is taken as fixed and continuous; it is the effort level and the reward that remain in contention. The argument to be made here, drawing on the analysis found in the influential Supiot (2001) report and in complementary empirical research recently undertaken in United Kingdom employer organizations, is that time is being made to take on new roles in shaping employment relations. For some employees, it is the period of time that is neither agreed nor specified; instead the employment relationship is moving from a clear contract of service based on time, to contract for services related to outputs or results. For others, the agreed period of time is becoming fragmented into shorter, discontinuous periods and is being scheduled across the week or the year to match the requirements of employers. The scheduling of time becomes part of the process through

* European Work and Employment Research Centre and the Manchester Business School, The University of Manchester, United Kingdom.

** European Work and Employment Research Centre and the School of Environment and Development, The University of Manchester, United Kingdom.

[1] This chapter draws on joint work with a large number of other academic researchers who have participated in the projects conducted within the European Work and Employment Research Centre, including Marilyn Carroll, Phil Almond, Gail Hebson, Fang Lee Cooke, Jill Earnshaw, Mick Marchington, Mark Smith, Colette Fagan, Darren Nixon, Hugh Willmott, Steve Vincent, Irena Grugulis and Huw Beynon.

which employers manage the amount of labour provided under a time-based contract, as periods of slack demand are eliminated from schedules. Thus, as a contribution to debates about "decent working time", this chapter argues for the need to understand the role of the demand side – that is, the changing objectives of, and pressures upon, employers – in transforming the rules and norms of the organization of time at work.

These arguments are made, and supported by empirical evidence at the organization level, for the United Kingdom labour market. However, while it might be argued that these developments are specific to the United Kingdom social, economic and institutional context, the evidence we have found of changing employment relationships around the issue of time management certainly suggests what might happen in other countries were their systems of working time and employment regulation to be changed in a similar manner.

5.2 RECONSTITUTING THE EMPLOYMENT RELATIONSHIP: THE IMPACT OF WORKING TIME CHANGES

Under the standard employment relationship, the benefits for employers can be identified as the bringing of labour under the direct control of the employer or his or her agent so that the effort expended may be directly monitored, thereby ensuring that the benefits of changes in technology and work organization may be captured by the organization (Marglin, 1974), and so that employers are able to change, within limits, the composition of tasks to be performed without recontracting (Williamson, 1985). The guarantee of continuous employment over a standard working week should be interpreted as the price that employers have to pay for the right to exercise that direct control. Indeed the establishment of rights to continuous employment and guaranteed earnings has been a major plank of trade unions' efforts to regulate the standard employment relationship and to ensure that it offers protection to workers and does not simply act to subject workers to the discipline of the employer. Marsden (1999) has made the argument that for employers, this trade-off – whereby the employer provides regular and guaranteed work in return for opportunities to directly influence the labour process and to respecify tasks without recontracting – has proved to be a price well worth paying. Indeed, the relatively slow move away from the internalized employment relationship, despite the claims over the emergence of the network firm, is taken as an indication of the superiority of this relationship and indeed the potential for a win-win solution for both employers and employees. However, this argument perhaps overlooks the ways in which the internal employment contract is being restructured through the use of new approaches to time management among other factors, thereby enabling employers to change the basis of the trade-off and to reduce the costs of the standard relationship. The relevant comparison is, therefore, not simply between internalized contracts of service and external contracts for services, but between different approaches to the management of the internalized contract.

The Supiot report (2001) on how the employment relationship is changing has argued that we have witnessed the spread of two main types of working time principles in opposition to the standard time-based employment relationship, namely the increasing move from a means-based time-regulated employment relationship to a results-based system; and the increasing tendency within time-based employment relationship to adopt a more fragmented approach to time. These divided logics correspond to the increasing promotion in the management literature of targeted human resource practices, aimed at workers with different types of skills and located in different segments of the production process (Lepak and Snell, 1999). These two tendencies in human resource practice have been identified as part of the change from a Fordist to a post-Fordist employment regime.

> The new principle governing working time is self-regulation of time: . . . ultimately, by individuals themselves, now responsible for the organization of their own time providing they commit themselves to their employer's objectives. In the light of this trend, the surrender of their time ceases to be the primary purpose of the obligation of employees, which moves from being means- to being results-based. (Supiot, 2001, p. 83)

This new system, in replacing for some groups of employees the clock-based control of the Fordist model, could potentially, if combined with employee representation and more democratic control, provide a basis for a more autonomous system of working that restores discretion and responsibility back to the workers. However, this is by no means an automatic or likely outcome, and instead workers may be required to surrender not just time but also "their hearts and minds" to the organization (Thompson, 2003). The second logic of the post-Fordist system – the intensification of work within time-based systems through the move to fragmented time – has a similar double-edged impact as "flexible working hours hold out both the promise of freedom and the threat of greater subordination" (Supiot, 2001, p. 223).

While the two human resource strategies appear to have opposing logics, they both impact upon two fundamental elements of the standard or Fordist time-based employment relationship: first, both challenge the standard time-based system of allowing some customary "paid on the job inactivity", a practice that is associated with the notion of purchasing labour in chunks of standard time, whatever the work flow. The development of the notion of standard and regular working hours led to the principle that employers should pay for all time when the employee was "at the employer's disposal at the workplace" (as defined in French labour code, for example) (Supiot, 2001, p. 65). Employers needed to develop a regular and reliable workforce, and, as a consequence, were willing to accept these variations in productivity in return for securing the commitment of the workforce to regular employment. However, issues of rights to lay off workers for short or longer periods of time with or without notice are a major area of contention in industrial relations, and while employers benefit from internalized systems, they have only reluctantly accepted the fixed or overhead element embedded in the standard employment relationship (Jacoby, 1984).

Fragmented time is explicitly aimed at removing "paid on the job in-activity", or the porosity of the working day, while a results-based system is aimed instead at removing the cost to employers of unproductive time at work. Employers can distribute tasks in a way that assumes no unproductive time and if staff cannot always work at full productivity they may have to complete their tasks outside standard or contractual hours without additional payment. There may be limits to the extent to which extra, unpaid hours are acceptable to employees (even to those in managerial/supervisory positions), but the employer may not be identified as the primary cause of the overload. This is because results-based systems are being developed in the contexts of more self-regulated work systems, where the individual or the team is held responsible for managing workloads (Sewell, 1998), or where staff are being asked to respond directly to customer demands. Such developments may not only reduce opportunities for shirking that have traditionally been associated with management-directed systems, but may also distract attention from the employer as the prime source of the additional demand and extended working time, with instead the "customer" or the "client" being constructed as to blame for the need to work longer, harder, or both (Beynon et al., 2002).

The changes taking place in the organization of working time may therefore contribute to multifaceted pressures towards work intensification. Where working time is fragmented or individualized, the opportunities for staff to develop customary norms relating to reasonable effort levels are reduced. For results-based workers, the impact may be to increase either work intensity or the length of working hours or both; for those on fragmented time, the impact is to increase work intensity during paid hours but also potentially to extend the time boundary, or the length of time, over which an individual may be called in to work.

These two approaches to human resource management also call into question collective aspects of the organization of work and life by challenging

Table 5.1   The impact of three different working time principles
            underpinning the employment relationship

Working time principle	"Paid on-the-job inactivity"	Standard or community time
Standard time-based employment relationship	Paid for standard hours when at the disposal of employer at workplace; activity levels dependent on provision of work by employer	Shared communal leisure/ break times; compensation for disruption to division between work and community/private time
Results-based employment relationship	Self- or customer-driven activity levels; performance- not time-related pay	Requirement to work whenever and for however long to complete tasks/meet performance targets
Fragmented, time-based employment relationship	Work scheduled by employers to maximize activity levels, minimize paid on-the-job inactivity	Work time fragmentation leads to scheduling of work across standard and community time borders

"the community time patterns that have governed life on and off the job (night-time rests, Sunday rests, midday break) and bring about the collapse of solidarities based on such patterns (trade union, family, neighbourhood)" (Supiot, 2001, p. 84). Results-based employment relationships blur the boundaries between work time and free time while fragmented time relationships often explicitly facilitate the scheduling of work in parts of the day or week that would previously have been considered "community time". One factor in permitting this scheduling across borders is the diversification of social and family relations that may be rendering previous notions of community time patterns outdated. However, while institutions become outdated and need renewal, new community time patterns more in tune with the new gender divisions and capable of sustaining balance across the different aspects of life are unlikely to spontaneously emerge through a process of primarily individualized and employer-driven change in working time arrangements (Perrons et al., forthcoming). For a summary of the impact of the different principles, see table 5.1.

5.3   EXPLORING THE PROCESSES OF WORKING TIME CHANGE

Now that we have established that there are changes taking place in the management of time, with significant consequences for the employment relationship, we need both to provide some evidence in support of this hypothesis and to begin to explore the conditions under which these changes are taking place. The evidence of change will be limited to the United Kingdom and primarily to case studies of organizations carried out within the research programme of the European Work and Employment Research Centre (EWERC) at the University of Manchester with which the authors are associated.[2] We would argue, however, that the framework that we will use to explore the conditions associated with these changes has more general applicability and might identify the conditions under which similar changes may occur in other industrial nations.

The framework we use draws upon that developed by Karston and Leopold (2003), who see time management as shaped by interactions between employment relations (here the main social actors are the social partners and government), the organizational sphere (involving the system of competition and cooperation between firms), and the domestic sphere (involving both the social division of labour and time constraints at the household level). These spheres are also all influenced by pan-national legislation, in the shape of European-level regulation.

This framework is a general one; the main actors shaping employment relations are the social partners including government, but while in many European countries these actors are mainly active at the societal and sectoral levels, in the United Kingdom the shaping of employment relations takes place primarily at the level of the organization (except in the public sector where there are still national-level negotiations). This means that there is potentially even more interaction in the United Kingdom between the organizational sphere and the employment relations sphere. Indeed, in contrast to accounts that focus on the lack of social regulation of working time in the United Kingdom (for example Supiot, 2001, p. 72), the argument made here is that this approach underestimates the influence of the particular form of industrial relations and collective bargaining in the United Kingdom (Rubery, 1998; Rubery et al., 2005). The United Kingdom industrial relations system has historically promoted working long hours as a means of generating higher guaranteed earnings and created strong notions of custom and practice at the workplace that provide the basis for claims for higher earnings for additional and unsocial hours working. This organization-level regulation of working time has been identified as a major means of regulating the wage–effort relationship in the United Kingdom (Blyton, 1992; 1995); consequently changes to working time arrangements, including, for example, experiments with annualized hours working, need to be interpreted not as

---

[2] For more information on the European Work and Employment Research Centre (EWERC), see www.mbs.ac.United Kingdom/ewerc

mainly or only aimed at introducing more variable working time, but rather as a means to change the wage–effort relationship, through eliminating expensive paid overtime and promoting work intensification (Heyes, 1997; Bacon and Storey, 1996; Gall, 1996). Thus the organizational drivers towards working time changes are rooted not only in the systems of competition, but also in managerial efforts to challenge the traditional system of industrial or professional relations (Beynon et al., 2002).

While stressing the interactions between the three spheres, we address each sphere in turn. First, we look at changes in working time management associated with changes in employment relations, and with developments in collective bargaining and regulation. Second, we examine the changes taking place in the organization of work and employment within companies. Third, we consider explanations for workforce compliance in working time arrangements that appear to be incompatible with private and family life. Much of the argument we develop here is based on detailed case studies of a wide range of organizations that we have been engaged in in the United Kingdom since the mid-to-late 1990s. The research involves in-depth inter-views with both managers and employees, including in several cases follow-up interviews to identify the pattern of change over a 2- to 3-year period (see Appendix, table 5A.1 for summary details of projects). We do not present the detailed evidence here (for further information on the case studies see Marchington et al., 2005; Beynon et al., 2002; Bosch and Lehndorff, 2005), and provide only a small "taste" of the detailed interview material (again see Beynon et al., 2002; Marchington et al., 2005).[3] Instead, summary tables in the Appendix show the main examples of changes that we identified in the movements towards results-based or fragmented time systems. We also draw on other secondary source material on changes in United Kingdom working time, including other case studies and more general information on the pattern of and regulation of working time in the United Kingdom to situate our findings in a broader context.

5.3.1 Employment relations and new working time arrangements

To consider the role of changing employment relations in the reshaping of time management we discuss changes in collective regulation and in legal regulation. In the case of legal regulation of hours, this is a new development in the United Kingdom and indeed was implemented after many of the case studies we report on here were completed.

---

[3] Fictitious company names are used when presenting the case study material.

In the United Kingdom, collective regulation now only applies to a minority of employees – particularly in the private sector. Sectoral- and national-level bargaining outside the public sector is rare – although some research has identified a legacy of such arrangements with respect to working time in sectors where sectoral bargaining on those issues was particularly strong (Arrowsmith and Sisson, 1999). Here we discuss the changes that have taken place within those sectors that are still covered by collective bargaining – although the existence of many organizations outside of collective regulation is of course one factor promoting change within the regulated sectors.

Traditionally in the United Kingdom working time standards – including standard working weeks, days, overtime and unsocial hours premia – were set in considerable detail by sectoral- or national-level agreements. These standards in turn provided a framework for the development at the workplace of systems of work organization which shaped the wage–effort relationship and where informal or local methods of regulation and control took on particular significance. The guarantees with respect to overtime and unsocial hours premia provided incentives at the workplace level for employees to promote systems of work organization that spread the work over a longer period to generate overtime opportunities and to shift the wage–effort relationship more in favour of employees.[4] Such systems included, for example, the effective enforcement of customary job demarcations (so that the shortage of one type of labour could lead to overtime opportunities for all); the systematic use of absenteeism to generate overtime opportunities for fellow workers (Heyes, 1997); and controls over the pace of work to maximize overtime opportunities (Noon and Blyton, 1997, ch. 4). The study by Heyes (1997) of a chemical company introducing annualized hours is illustrative. Here the main motivation from management was to reduce the incentives to create overtime opportunities. Before the new hours system, craft mainten-ance workers had ensured that machine problems were not dealt with until late in the working day, thereby creating overtime opportunities for themselves and potentially other shop-floor workers. There was also, according to management, a systematic use of absenteeism so that other shop-floor workers were offered the opportunity to work a double shift at a premium rate when a fellow worker called in sick. Annualized hours systems reduced these incentives as additional hours were worked out of the allowance of "stand-by" hours, and thereby inconvenienced fellow workers by requiring them to work hours that had already been paid for and which would not have to be worked if no one were absent and/or the work were done on time.

---

[4] These strategies were used in the United Kingdom by employees and the unions that represented them as a means of increasing what were often relatively low wages, in a way of making up a living wage.

It is in this context that the role of employment relations in shaping recent changes in time management in the United Kingdom needs to be understood. While there has been a major decline in the sectoral and national regulation of working time, there are still some forms of workplace control over working time, based on both informal custom and practice, as well as more formal current collective agreements and contractual employment conditions. Our case study work suggests that one of the main motivations for employers to change working time arrangements in this context is to reassert control over work organization and the wage–effort relationship.

The main evidence of change in employment relations as a factor in the trend towards results-based and fragmented time employment relations is found in the following changes in the employment relations framework:

- removal of, or evasion of, premia prices for unsocial hours or extra hours;

- reduction in union/employee influence on the implementation of working time systems and the organization of work at the workplace level;

- removal of union influence through derecognition of unions or contracting out, where unions are less likely to be in a position to represent the demands of employees.

The distinction between standard and non-standard hours has been a hallmark of the United Kingdom employment relations systems, but in almost all the organizations we studied (see Appendix tables 5A.2a and 5A.2b), there had been either direct changes to the premia rates system or increased opportunities for employers to evade these higher rates, despite, at the same time, the increases in the need for flexible scheduling. This blurring of the standard /non-standard hours divide, which provides the basis for less costly systems of flexible scheduling, was achieved through a range of different processes, as we now outline:

- the cutting or removing of the supplements (for example in a large media company Mediaco – a newspaper group – where unions were derecognized, and in a large supermarket company Retailco which still recognized unions but cut premia in line with other large retail companies);

- the negotiation of new supplements, but at lower levels than the previous rates (a large bank – Bankco – had established a new call centre without any premia but had kept the traditional premia for its staff who had previously worked at one of its now closed branches; however, when operating two systems created barriers for staff movement, a new harmonized system was introduced, with premia set at lower levels than the older branch rates);

- the extending of standard days from, for example, 8 a.m. to 6 p.m. to 8 a.m. to 8 p.m. (for example at a large telecommunications company – Telecomco – and a large bank, Bankco);

- the transferring of staff to new companies which did not pay for overtime, at least for higher-grade staff (a large customer services firm – TCS-L – and a computer services firm, Futuretech);

- the varying of rights to overtime pay according to the wishes of clients – in the case of a multi-client call centre set up by the customer services organization TCS-NW;

- the use of more flexible scheduling for standard hours (flexible days, start and finish times) (in the case of Bankco, Telecomco, Retailco, Mediaco, and a large council – Councilco); and

- simple evasion by using part-timers and direct-hire and agency-placed temporary staff who were not eligible for the payments (found particularly in public sector organizations such as Councilco and a large hospital – Healthco – still subject in principle to national agreements setting premia rates).

This removal of extra payment increases the incentives both to extend hours and to schedule hours whenever required, as the cost of each hour becomes the same. In some cases union acceptance of the changes was obtained as part of an apparent package of benefits to the workforce or to the union. In Bankco and Retailco the changes were introduced as part of the consolidation or establishment, respectively, of union partnership agreements; and in the public sector, the evasion of the rates through the hiring of more part-timers and temporary workers was seen as the price to be paid for advantageous collective agreements negotiated at the national level for those on permanent contracts.

The change made to the premia rates, or their implementation, is already symptomatic of the second change – that is, the reduction in the power of unions to influence the pattern of work organization and associated working time workplace arrangements. Mediaco and TCS-NW were the only cases in our studies where there was no union presence, meaning that much of the change we found was taking place in apparently collectively regulated environments. Nevertheless, we found very few examples of collective resistance – and even these proved to be short-lived. At Councilco the union did try to resist a decision to activate a longer standard working day from 8 a.m. to 8 p.m. for homecare workers who had been accustomed to working more standard days. Complaints were made to employment tribunals, but after some modifications (in particular the agreement that the family circumstances of individual workers would be taken into account but monitored on an annual basis), the longer working days were agreed upon and the complaints dropped. At CouncilA a similar change in contracts was planned, with some increase in basic pay offered in return for flexible scheduling, but at the time of our study the council was anticipating fierce resistance and possibly a strike.

The airport – Airportco – provided a further, and arguably more extreme, example of a successful erosion of union workplace power by the employer. At this airport, which was collectively owned by the local authorities, the baggage handlers had been able to control both rates of pay and employment policies (reducing the share of seasonal and temporary staff to deal with fluctuations in demand, thereby allowing for more on-the-job paid inactivity). Government competition policy forced the airport to put baggage handling out to tender, and in order to be competitive with the private sector, Airportco formed a new wholly owned subsidiary which employed staff on new lower rates of pay and on more flexible and temporary staffing contracts, often guaranteeing only part-time hours to manage the variations in demand over the seasons. The new company was still unionized by the same union but was not able to resist the employer's introduction of "market rates" and core/periphery employment policies.

The weakening of union control was more common than derecognition: the main example of derecognition among our cases was the newspaper Mediaco, which had not only derecognized the union in the 1990s, but had also, at the same time, introduced a new set of terms and conditions that ended paid overtime and introduced compulsory unsocial hours working, with time off in lieu as the only compensation available for extra hours. This "bold" move to change the whole basis of the employment relationship followed on from the severe weakening of the previously strong print unions when they lost a major strike in the 1980s to stop Rupert Murdoch from sacking all the Fleet Street printers. While these changes to collective bargaining took place in the early to mid-1990s, they provided a framework in which it was easier to introduce new shifts requiring more weekend working without additional compensation. An example of Mediaco exercising its new-found political muscle occurred while we were researching the organization, when in 2001–2 the company introduced a new, free newspaper to counter competition from a rival new, free newspaper, and oversaw this introduction by changing the working times of most of its employees.

Another means of removing union influence was through the transfer of staff to companies with only a weak or, indeed, no union presence. The promotion of contracting out within the United Kingdom public sector is particularly noteworthy here, although it parallels developments in manufacturing in the United Kingdom where research has shown employers to be reviewing continually the decision whether or not to keep an activity inhouse or subcontract it out of house (Ackroyd and Proctor, 1998). This contract culture reduces the power of unions at the workplace to control the wage–effort bargain. In the case studies we have undertaken, contracting out to private companies has been important in bringing in a results-based approach to the employment contract for professional, supervisory and lower-level managerial staff previously employed under time-based contracts in the public sector. Both of the private sector organizations – one a large American IT company (Futuretech) and the other a customer services organization (TCS-L) – in practice expected staff to work whatever hours were required to complete a job. This was explicit at Futuretech, in which there was no provision in the contracts of employees for paid overtime or time off in lieu, and where staff who opted to retain civil service employment conditions, where extra hours could be taken as flexitime, were effectively disadvantaged in their career prospects. At TCS-L the right to claim overtime existed in principle, but the workplace ethos was such that staff found it difficult to claim in practice.

While collective regulation of working time has declined, legal regulation of working time was introduced into the United Kingdom for the first time in 1998, implementing the European Union's Working Time Directive. Some of the case studies we are reporting on here were conducted before this legislation had been fully implemented, but the likelihood of regulation was already widely known. Nevertheless, for the most part the regulation of working time did not feature as a major factor in our case studies. Almost no one reported changes (or planned changes) as a result of the EU Working Time Directive, possibly because of the widespread knowledge that a voluntary opt-out from the regulations would be in place. Where changes were planned – for example to reduce the length of part-timers' shifts in the case of Telecomco – the primary aim of employers was to evade the legislation by ensuring that they did not have to provide paid breaks for part-timers. There was no expectation among managers whom we interviewed that regulation would enforce a move away from the emergent results-based employment culture for higher-level staff. The hospital – Healthco – was adjusting to interim national measures to limit doctors' working hours to 56 as a means of implementing a gradual and long-term adjustment to a possible 48 hours limit in the future. Nurses' hours were also being affected by this 56-hour limit and this was requiring management to consider more effective ways of maintaining nurses' hours; while full-time staff only worked 37.5 hours, they were free to contract to work extra hours through nursing agencies both at their own hospital and elsewhere; thus extra hours were not recorded. Hence, in some

Table 5.2   Changes to employment relations and regulation

Protection of standard time-based work contract	Erosion of source of protection and move to results-oriented employment relationship	Erosion of standard time and move to fragmented time
Collective agreements – pay related to standard time – compensation for extra and unsocial hours or time off in lieu (TOIL)	Decline in coverage of agreements – excluded workers more likely to be found on results-based contracts	Reduction and removal of unsocial hours/additional hours premia in non-union environments or under "modern" collective agreements or local implementation of agreements – fragmentation to pay for overall improvements
Legal regulation	Voluntary opt-out plus exclusion of managerial staff from regulation permits the continued development of a results-based system	Regulation of rest periods may encourage fragmentation of work time

cases, managers could not assume that nurses were only working the hours they worked for them when seeking to manage the consequences of the reduction in the working hours of doctors.

The changes to employment relations and regulation are summarized in table 5.2.

5.3.2 Organizational and workplace drivers for new working time arrangements.

Interrelated changes in the management of work and performance have contributed in our case study organizations both to the tendency towards a results-based employment system, and to a more fragmented time-based system (see table 5.3). We discuss these tendencies in turn.

Results-based employment system

Results-based employment systems are dependent upon employees feeling either obliged or incentivized to work whatever hours are required, or a mixture of both. Feelings of obligation are associated with more devolved or responsible autonomy systems of work organization (Sewell, 1998); while incentives derive from discretionary systems of job and pay promotion, based on fewer permanent vacancies (as a consequence of, for example, delayering

Table 5.3 Managing working time and the employment relationship at the workplace: Three approaches

Standard time-based work contract	Results-oriented employment relationship	Fragmented time
Direct control of labour process in consolidated blocks of standard time – in return work is time limited and low activity periods are paid – at least at minimum rates. Productivity level by custom and practice. Work organization in standard teams – variable work flows	"Responsible autonomy" – devolution of task responsibility and/or responsibility for generating business; productivity also promoted by more direct engagement with demands of customers, more use of technology to ensure flow of work. Job demarcations relaxed to promote work intensification. Individual responsibility for tasks breaks link between hours and workloads; allows for vacancies to be left unfilled. High work-load barrier to taking time off in lieu (TOIL)	Monitoring of productivity/performance within labour process through external contracts or internal monitoring system; use of time measurement/targets and/or technology to promote work intensification/productivity. Adjustment of hours/team size to meet variations in workload
Regulated and incremental promotion	Discretionary promotion/more limited opportunities and bigger "steps" associated with delayering – pressure to produce results, accept "acting-up" positions	Fragmented time jobs means of access to organization – first step on "promotion" to permanent/full-time
Standard time for both managers and supervised staff. Non-standard hours within standard hours	Decoupling of work time of managers and supervised staff	Non-standard hours outside standard hours rather than within standard hours
Pay related to "standard days"	Pay related to tasks/results/performance	Pay related to hours of activity
Work responsibilities limited to scheduled time at workplace	Mobile technology/emails/on call extend responsibilities outside of standard hours	Scheduling across work/community time borders plus short notice leads to extension of work time commitments

and downsizing), and on the demonstration of performance in the job with reference to specified criteria. Evidence from national surveys in the United Kingdom suggests that there has been an increase in unpaid overtime hours accounting for long hours of work; over two-thirds of those in managerial and professional jobs working long hours (over 48 per week) were not provided with any compensation in pay or time off in lieu, and even among associate professionals and clerical and related workers, the shares not receiving compensation were around 30 per cent and 20 per cent, respectively (see Kodz et al., 2003, figure 3.10, based on Workplace Employee Relations Survey data for 1998). It should also be noted that the overwhelming majority of those working long hours as a consequence of unpaid overtime reported that the main reasons were "to get all my work done" or because "it's required as part of my job" (Kodz et al., 2003, figure 4.1).

At their most extreme, results-based systems require employees not only to simply carry out their tasks, but also to take responsibility for generating new and repeat business through their actions. Within our case studies we found such requirements were very much part of the work culture at two software companies (Largeco and Smallco). Such requirements reduce the distinction between those in direct employment and the self-employed, who are responsible not only for their assigned tasks, but for generating the contracts that pay their wages, thereby adding to the pressure to work whatever hours are required.

In other cases the pressures came from managing too high a volume of work or from work responsibilities that spread over a long period of the week, rather than from concerns about generating new work. In particular, the extension of organizations' operating and opening hours was often not accompanied by increases in supervisory staffing levels. As a result, the hours of supervisors and staff were decoupled, leading to an increase in pressure on supervisory and managerial staff to cover extra and unsocial hours. A Retailco supervisor at a store that stayed open 24 hours a day explained that "my staff start at six o'clock in the morning, and the last ones don't finish until eleven o'clock at night, so to be able to see those people means that . . . sometimes I will work from seven o'clock till eight o'clock at night just so that I can see my own staff". And a Bankco team manager at a debt management centre reported how she had been working in "an 8:30 till 5 o'clock environment and we've now extended that from 7:30 to 7:30, again and we're looking towards changing it to an 8:30 finish . . . It has [affected me] as part of being a Team Manager to have open the area up to 7:30."

Another common factor placing pressure on staff to work extra and longer hours was the non-filling of staff vacancies, while retained staff still had to meet targets related to the "customer" or "client" demands, or meet the specified staffing levels laid down by companies or by regulation. In Retailco, the company required a fresh-food manager to be present at all times, but had not replaced a manager when she went on maternity leave and did not return, as the one manager on duty in the city-centre store explained: "I did it temporary while one of them was on maternity leave – they said – for six months. It's nearly two years down the line, and they've not replaced her. It's the wage cost, the wage budget." In the case of a local council – Councilco – the responsibility for resolving the dilemma of how to meet the new government targets to meet care needs in the community in a context of a chronic shortage of homecare workers was effectively devolved to homecare organizers, who would have to stay at work until they had ensured that the vulnerable older people would receive some care the next morning. This management strategy was premised on the strong sense of responsibility that employees felt for their clients.

Promotion opportunities were also directly linked with pressure to accept long hours of work, this pressure often accompanying even a minor promotion. For example at Retailco, those shop-floor staff who were accepted on to the training programmes that could lead to future promotion were expected to demonstrate commitment before advancement. As one employee in the city-centre store remarked, "You get no extra pay going on this Options, and you've got to work longer hours, more responsibility – I don't want to go on it because . . . they're getting you to do all the dirty work with no extra pay, no incentive. There's not even a guaranteed job at the end of 12 months." Even more common was the practice of offering temporary promotions – opportunities that were known as "acting up" at the next grade – with confirmation in the higher grade being dependent, at an uncertain date in the future, on performance. As an employee at Telecomco's repairs call centre explained, "All the team coaches at the moment are 'acting'. There's no substantive team coaches out there."

Even when promoted, many of the staff we interviewed appeared to accept the obligation to work whatever hours were necessary, on the grounds that this was the price they had to pay for having a higher-paid or a more responsible job. As an IT worker at Futuretech contrasted the old time-based employment system in the government department to the new approach at Futuretech, "You're paid this much a year to finish the job, and although they don't use those words, that's the way". This approach could also rule out the possibility of compressed working weeks, so that even though more than contractual hours were worked within the first four days at work, anyone with management responsibilities might have to be present the whole working week, as a manager at Bankco's debt management department explained, "When I started I did look to do four long days a week, which was a shift that a lot of my Team Managers were doing. But unfortunately I then had to get called into so many different meetings every day that I couldn't afford to be in four days. So that was a little bit irritating, but I really just wanted my cake and eat it. I appreciate it goes with the job. It goes with the money. It's reflected in the salary so it's no issue."

This expectation that supervisory or managerial staff would work whatever hours were required of them to fulfil their own tasks was in some cases explicitly built in to the system of pay and rewards: thus as one manager at a Bankco call centre explained, "If they're missing a team manager at a weekend for instance, because they're on holiday, then I would be able to apply for paid overtime to cover that missing team manager. But if I had more tasks in my own area that I couldn't fit in on a working day that needed to be completed, then that overtime would have to be unpaid." Furthermore, pressures for managerial and supervisory staff to work with and motivate their staff could also lead to pressures to work outside standard hours to fulfil basic managerial tasks. As one Telecomco manager at a repairs centre explained, "I see myself as a team member, although I have a different job, and because of that I don't have enough time to sit quietly doing all the paperwork . . . those are the kind of things I tend to take home and do . . . I suppose it's a choice because I want to be available to the staff and I can't do two things."

Despite these findings, it is important to recognize that results-based systems do not necessarily lead to a long-hours culture. Avoidance of long hours is only likely, however, if employers are obliged to adjust staffing levels to meet workload requirements. Otherwise, and in the absence of institutional restrictions, the temptation may be too strong for employers to allow the staff to absorb any additional workload without more resources. Working time, under these conditions, may spiral upwards, with numerous "knock-on effects" in terms of health, job satisfaction, stress levels and well-being, both inside and outside of the workplace (Burchell et al., 1999; Green, 2001).

Fragmented time employment systems

Fragmented time systems are frequently associated not simply with changes to the length or pattern of working time, but also to changes in the mode of monitoring and rewarding work. While the extension of operating and opening hours may provide for some fragmented time jobs simply to cover additional hours, in general the introduction of fragmented time jobs has provided employers with an opportunity to rethink their commitments to purchasing labour in continuous and regular chunks of time which usually also implies some acceptance of some paid on-the-job inactivity. Fragmented time systems tend to be introduced in a context of much closer monitoring of productivity and performance within labour processes and it may indeed be the monitoring of effort levels and/or customer demand that leads to the planning of labour demand on a fragmented time basis.

This hypothesis was borne out in a number of our cases where we found evidence of the more sophisticated planning of time schedules against demand (see Appendix table 5A.2c. In particular, these were being increasingly used in contexts where employment and therefore labour costs remained time dependent – and where there appeared to be scope for enhanced productivity and/or responsiveness to demands through such detailed tailoring. Evidence was found not just in retailing, where IT-based sales information has long been used to implement detailed staffing schedules based on variations in demand measured by 15-minute intervals or less, but also in call centres and in councils, where, for example, permanent staffing levels were fixed to the low point of demand (such as in the school dinner service to the few weeks in the summer when some students have left after examinations), and during the rest or main part of the year extra hours were added according to demand. At the TCS-NW multi-client call centre one client, Gambleco, wanted labour supply to be matched to its racing/betting schedule: temporary staff in particular were brought in for very short bursts of activity – sometimes for no more than two hours. Even in more stable industries, clients wanted to retain maximum flexibility, so that staff at TCS-NW working for a truck rental company still did not receive their schedules for the next week until just a few days beforehand. In part, the need to schedule working hours to meet these variations in client demand arose because of the use of dedicated staff for each client; this separation of contracts was based in part on variations in client-specific demands and in particular on the need for the subcontract staff to identify with the client so as to represent the client image to the external customers.[5]

Fragmented time systems could be used to manage workloads and productivity during all working hours, but this process may lead to ever more demands for more fragmented schedules: in homecare, the time needed to visit each client was increasingly counted in minutes rather than halves or quarters of an hour, so that the more precise monitoring of work effort levels and the more flexible scheduling of working hours went hand in hand. In some cases this time monitoring led to "multiskilling" to reduce paid on-the-job inactivity. In the post office low-paid hybrid post office/retail staff workers were replacing higher-paid, specialized post office staff, a move stimulated by concerns about variations in work flows for the post office section of integrated retail and post office stores. Nor was this time accounting limited to lower-skilled jobs: in the IT companies we studied (Largeco, Smallco),

---

[5] This is increasingly a rare occurrence: there is growing evidence in the United Kingdom of multi-client call centres, where operators will answer the calls for more than one client, changing their on-the-phone greeting and engagement on the basis of the information provided to them by the caller when they enter their needs in the form of keyed-in numbers.

individual staff had the responsibility to ensure that all work time was chargeable project time. In the case of Smallco the company had become, for want of a better word, "obsessed" with time accounting, such that it became increasingly hard to find time for activities such as training, as this could not easily be "valued" and there was no account code to which it could be charged. In this case, a time accounting system is combined with full-time employment that had eliminated "paid on-the-job inactivity" by introducing results-based performance criteria into the employment relationship (Smith, 2001).

For professional workers, such tight scheduling may result in their personally working additional unpaid hours outside of standard hours to ensure that a system works smoothly. In other examples, it is the supervisory and lower managerial staff who have to work extra hours to manage a system of work organization for the supervised staff based on tight time scheduling: for example when a local authority first contracted out housing benefit work to TCS-L, the performance indicators were set too tight, with the result that supervisory and managerial staff had to work additional hours to keep the system going as the estimated staffing levels relative to work volumes proved to be far too low. Alternatively, the over-tight scheduling may lead to unplanned overtime: at the airport the airlines tended to pay for too few handling agent staff to cover the check-in, despite the strict on-time departure goals set by both the airlines and the airport. In practice additional labour often had to be found, so that there was frequent use of "on-the-day stay-backs" – that is, unplanned overtime to cover staffing shortages. This points to some of the differences between policies in principle and the situation in practice.

5.3.3 Employee compliance: How employers succeeded in implementing the new working time practices

The organization of the domestic sphere – or the fit between working time demands and personal and family life commitments – could be anticipated (Karston and Leopold, 2003) to represent a third set of factors shaping working time. The United Kingdom is a country with a high level of dual-earner households and also a reasonably high birth rate. However, neither of the systems we have described appears to provide a very good fit with United Kingdom domestic life, even though their emergence may not be unrelated to the growth in one-and-a-half and two-income households: the results-based system often involves not only long, but unpredictable hours, and while fragmented time systems do facilitate the development of part-time working, they may also involve acquiescence in the flexible scheduling of work. The issue, therefore, is not so much how working time has adjusted to family life but how and why "family-unfriendly" working time arrangements have been allowed to develop in the United Kingdom, while at the same time more family members are now performing paid work.[6] Our projects were mainly concerned with the workplace rather than the domestic sphere, such that we will primarily address this issue from the perspective of what we found from our interviews about the reasons for individual compliance at the workplace.

There is a range of factors that explain these developments. Some of these can be located in the employment relations sphere, such as the weak collective regulation and the lack, until recently, of legal regulation. One of the major factors that may explain compliance at both the individual level and by trade unions is the changes taking place in employment security. Certainly in the public sector individual security has been eroded as a consequence of the widespread system of contracting out services to the private sector, leaving most public sector workers exposed to potential threats of either a change of employer or actual employment loss. To avoid the threat of transfer, staff faced with having to tender for their own jobs are willing to break the link between pay and hours of work: as one catering supervisor put it after a retendering process which reduced the time allocation for meal production, "My actual contracted hours have not increased, my actual time that I actually am in this kitchen and work in this kitchen has increased because I can't get through the job any other way . . . We used to have 13 staff here and now we've got nine. But we've still got to do the work of 13 staff" (Councilco). We found many lower-level managerial and supervisory staff working in the public sector, either for the public employer or contracted private sector organizations, where, as a TCS IT manager put it, it was "not an option for me to do my job within 37 hours". While in the past pressure exerted on individuals to work long and flexible hours might have been resisted through job quits and other individualized strategies, many of the staff we interviewed felt that these changes were not specific to their organizations, but would be found wherever they moved; in particular for many managers and supervisory staff it was simply felt that "it goes with the territory". Acceptance of these arrangements among our interviewees also seemed to be reflective of a perception that the new results-based employment relationship was now to be found in most workplaces – and that the public sector might simply be catching up with private sector practices. For some of our interviewees the change to working time arrangements had been incremental and not fully in place when they had first moved on to supervisory or results-based-types systems. We found some remarkable examples of stoicism in the face of clearly

---

[6] We are not suggesting that all working time arrangements in the United Kingdom are currently following these "family-unfriendly patterns"; many part-timers do for example work fixed hours that have been chosen to fit their family arrangements. However, in some of our case studies the rights to hours arrangements to fit with domestic conditions were being challenged as employers increased pressure for more extended or more flexible working.

extremely inconvenient schedules: a team manager at Bankco, who was also a lone parent, described a new requirement to work late occasionally as "fitting in with her lifestyle", as she was "fortunate enough" to have a free evening once in a while when her ex-husband took the kids, and on these free evenings she could take her turn to cover the extended working hours.

Acceptance of fragmented time systems appears to be largely based on two different and to some extent alternative functions of these types of employment arrangements. For some part-time or temporary employees there was no alternative to working more weekends than permanent full-timers, having to take an early evening shift or miss out on break times. It was the price that had to be paid either for an opportunity to better reconcile their work and family arrangements or to enable them to get a first foot on the employment ladder. In some cases – for example at CouncilB – the requirement for flexible working was explicitly restricted to new recruits, with existing staff not required for the moment to change their hours. However, evidence from other case studies might suggest that once the share of staff working flexible hours moved towards the majority, additional pressure would be placed on those on "old" terms and conditions to comply or to leave. Where the main motivation for taking a fragmented-time job was reconciliation, there were often limits to the extent to which these staff would be compliant with employer demands, but this was resolved in part by systems of offering the least favourable shifts to the new recruits often on temporary contracts. Alternatively unsocial hours work was contracted out as in the case of home-care work for CouncilA. However, some very unsocial hours were still acceptable to those with domestic commitments as they enabled partners to share in the childcare. As one part-time evening and night-shift worker at Retailco's 24-hours store put it, "I would love to work during the day. I would love to have a proper job again, but it's just a case of, who'd have the kids?"

While these new working time systems were by no means costless for employers, with particular problems emerging in turnover rates among those workers on fragmented time contracts, there was little evidence in follow-up interviews of any major move away from these new principles for managing both working time and the employment relationship. Only one example was found of an employer reversing the results-based system – at Telecomco, where new shift arrangements had been put in place to stabilize the hours of managerial/supervisory staff, through the employment of part–time supervisors to cover the additional unsocial hours in the evening. Over the period that we undertook the case studies (1997–2002), and despite the issue of work–life balance becoming more widely debated in political circles and in the national press, we found little evidence of it changing or modifying these trends towards more employer-driven working time schedules.

5.4   CONCLUSION

The evidence from this extensive body of case studies in the United Kingdom is that the move towards new employment relations, based around both results-based and fragmented time systems, is both widespread and ongoing. These findings are supported by a recent United Kingdom survey of employees that has found a major deterioration in satisfaction with working hours: the share of male employees satisfied with their working hours was found to have dropped from 35 per cent to 20 per cent between 1992 and 2000, and an even more dramatic fall was recorded for women – from 54 per cent to 26 per cent (White et al., 2003). The research also identified "long working hours as the dominant issue for employees", and found that the implementation of new systems of work organization associated with so-called high-commitment workplaces was intensifying problems of work–life balance.

While the dissatisfaction with working time arrangements frequently surfaced in our interviews, this dissatisfaction could be often considered more evidence of reluctant compliance. For higher-level staff there was the view that extended working hours was the price that had to be paid for even a minor step up to a supervisory role, say to school dinners supervisor. In other cases, the extra responsibility did come with a much larger pay packet, but there were few opportunities in our case study examples for staff to trade a smaller pay packet for more limited hours; it was an all-or-nothing trade of higher pay for longer hours, with few opportunities to tailor the package to suit personal circumstances. Another factor that may help explain compliance is that the United Kingdom could be said to have a rather fragmented and individual-ized social and family system with a weak and declining tradition of shared community time. The lack of strong social norms around, for example, the free Sunday to spend with families and friends may assist employers in seeking "compliant" workers for weekend working, and may even give a somewhat strange twist to what might be considered "family-friendly working arrangements" in the United Kingdom. Many mothers take "fragmented time jobs during unsocial hours, precisely so as to economise on childcare that can be provided by their partners during their 'free time'" (Harkness, 2002). However, while many mothers do take on these fragmented jobs, this is often on the basis of very tightly constrained arrangements, where the individual or the family is trying to find a means of reconciling the effectively irreconcilable – due to the lack of childcare and transport infrastructure, the instability and complexity of family set-ups, and the demand by employers for highly flexible or long hours of work (Jarvis, 2005; Jarvis et al., 2001). Such complexity illustrates the interrelatedness of supply-side changes (e.g. household structure, lifestyle choices) and demand-side pressures (e.g. employer policies to fragment working time schedules) in transforming time at work. What is clear from our evidence, however, is that employer pressures regarding working time have had a transformative impact on the work environment in a range of sectors of the economy. There has been much attention focused on the upward pressures on working time faced by "knowledge workers" – for whom longer hours are needed to process more information (ILO, 2001) – but this chapter demonstrates the more widespread nature of change.

Despite problems of low worker morale and motivation, and difficulties in recruitment and retention, the managers at the organizations we studied appeared to have little interest in investing effort in moving back to a more regular time-based system. The notion that work should be fitted into standard hours where possible had all but disappeared from the managerial rhetoric; managers stressed that hours schedules needed to fit with the interests of the employer and/or the clients and customers. To achieve this, a major objective was to regard all hours as equivalent, with no additional costs associated with unsocial or extra hours. Where recruitment problems were encountered, the problem was often passed to temporary work agencies to fill the most unpopular shifts. The subcontracting of the problem to these agencies may have encouraged managers to believe that workers' preferences and personal circumstances no longer had to be taken into account by employers. It was also the case that individual managers, struggling to match the demands placed on them by private and public sector employers alike, are not necessarily in a position to offer any simple alternative. In the short term they are reliant on systems that require staff to work whenever and for however long is necessary to process the volume of work coming into the organization. They are not necessarily able to contemplate longer-term strategies to bring work and life back into better balance. All of these explanations point to the need for the reinstitutionalization of working time by involving social actors at the regional, industry and national level. The promotion of "decent working time" will not be effective if it is believed that a better work–life balance can be forged either through negotiations with individual workers, or even through actions and policies introduced in single organizations or workplaces.

APPENDIX

Table 5A.1 Summary of the case study projects

Project	Title	Sectors/sites (brackets used to indicate sectors/sites not referred to in this chapter)	Companies cited	Methods	Themes
Leverhulme Project 1997–2000	Managing Employment Change (for full details see Beynon et al., 2002)	Banking, local government, healthcare, media, retailing, telecommunications (pharmaceuticals)	Bankco, Councilco, Healthco, Mediaco, Retailco, Telecomco	Two sets of semi-structured interviews with employees and managers	Staffing issues, skills and training, working time
Fourth Framework NESY Project 1999–2001	New forms of work and working time	Information technology, homecare (healthcare)	Largeco Smallco CouncilA CouncilB	One set of interviews with managers	Work organization and working time, interrelationships
ESRC Future of Work Project 1999–2002	Changing organizational forms and the reshaping of work	Airport Customer services company Post Office and franchises IT outsourcing (public sector) Hospital trust private finance initiative (Ceramics industrial district, chemical company supply chain, teacher supply agency)	Airportco, FHL and BH TCS-L and TCS-NW Post Office and Cornerco, Localco Futuretech PFI	One set of interviews with employees and managers	The human resource implications of inter-organizational relations

Table 5A.2a Examples of methods of reducing costs of additional and/or
           extra hours

Methods	Examples from case studies
Reductions in or elimination of premia	Leverhulme: Bankco, Councilco, Healthco, Mediaco, Retailco, Telecomco FOW: Airportco, PFI NESY: Largeco, Smallco, CouncilA, CouncilB
Use of part-time or temporary staff to evade overtime/unsocial hours premia	Leverhulme: Bankco, Councilco, Healthco, Retailco, Telecomco FOW; Airportco, FI, TCS-NW
Use of staff grades where no eligibility for premia or for claiming overtime	Leverhulme: Telecomco, Councilco, Retailco, Healthco
Transferring staff to new organizations where no premia or overtime paid (in principle and/or in practice)	FOW: Futuretech, TCS-L
Extending time deemed to be standard hours	Leverhulme: Bankco, Councilco, Healthco, Mediaco, Retailco, Telecomco FOW: Post Office, TCS-NW NESY: CouncilA, CouncilB
New consolidated salaries to include premia for weekend working, etc.	Leverhulme: Councilco, Healthco NESY: CouncilA
Variations in premia according to client	FOW: TCS-NW – for agency staff

Table 5A.2b Examples of methods of reducing paid on-the-job inactivity

	Methods	Examples from case studies
Results-based	Increased workloads/reduced staffing levels or unfilled vacancies	Leverhulme: Healthco, Retailco FOW: TCS-L, Futuretech
	Temporary promotions/ "acting" up – pressure on performance	Leverhulme: Telecomco
	Increased use of targets and/or time auditing	Leverhulme: Councilco NESY: Largeco, Smallco
Fragmented time	Time scheduling according to customer demands	Leverhulme: Telecomco, Retailco, Bankco FOW: TCS-NW
	Time measurement of tasks – used for flexible scheduling of hours and/or for increased multiskilling to reduce inactivity	Leverhulme: Healthco, Councilco FOW: Post Office/Cornerco NESY: CouncilA, CouncilB
	Minimization of core staff – use of part-time, temporary, overtime to match with variations in demand	Leverhulme: Councilco, Telecomco, Retailco FOW: TCS-NW, Airport-BH, FHL NESY: CouncilA, CouncilB, Largeco

Table 5A.2c Examples of erosion of standard working time/community leisure time

	Methods	Examples from case studies
Results-based	Extended opening and operating hours – supervisors/managers on call	Leverhulme: Bankco, Councilco, Healthco, Mediaco, Retailco, Telecomco
	Difficulties in taking time off in lieu	Leverhulme. Bankco, Councilco, Healthco, Mediaco, Retailco, Telecomco
	Devolved responsibilities for tasks/functions	FOW: TCS-L, Futuretech Leverhulme: Bankco, Councilco, Healthco, Retailco, Telecomco
	Requirements to generate new business/keep clients happy	FOW: Futuretech, TCS-L FOW: Futuretech, Airport-BH, FHL
Fragmented time	Scheduling across extended days	NESY: Largeco, Smallco Leverhulme: Bankco, Councilco, Retailco, Telecomco FOW: TCS-NW, Post Office – Cornerco, Localco NESY: CouncilA, CouncilB
	Scheduling across week/weekend	Leverhulme: Bankco, Councilco, Healthco, Retailco, Telecomco FOW: TCS-NW, Post Office – Cornerco, Localco NESY: CouncilA, CouncilB
	Variable scheduled hours at short notice	Leverhulme: Retailco FOW: TCS-NW
	Variable extra hours at short notice	Leverhulme: Retailco, Councilco FOW: Airport-FHL

References

Ackroyd, S.; Proctor, S. 1998. "British manufacturing organization and workplace industrial relations: Some attributes of the new flexible firm", in *British Journal of Industrial Relations*, Vol. 36, No. 2, pp. 163–183.

Arrowsmith, J.; Sisson, K. 1999. "Pay and working time: towards organization-based systems?", in *British Journal of Industrial Relations*, Vol. 37, No. 1, pp. 51–76.

Bacon, N. and Storey, J. 1996. "Unilever. Flexible working: Introducing annualised hours and 24-hour working", in J. Storey (ed.): *Blackwell cases in human resource and change management* (Oxford, Blackwell).

Beynon, H.; Grimshaw, D.; Rubery, J.; Ward, K. 2002. *Managing employment change: The new realities of work* (Oxford, Oxford University Press).

Blyton, P. 1992. "Learning from each other: The shorter working week campaigns in Germany and Britain", in *Economic and Industrial Democracy*, Vol. 13, No. 3, pp. 417–430.

—. 1995. "United Kingdom: The case of the metal manufacturing industry", in *OECD flexible working time* (Paris, OECD).

Bosch, G.; Lehndorff, S. (eds.). 2005. *Working in the service sector – a tale from different worlds* (London, Routledge).

Braverman, H. 1974. *Labour and monopoly capital* (New York, Monthly Review Press).

Burchell, B.; Day, D.; Hudson, M.; Ladipo, D.; Mankelow, R.; Nolan, J.; Reed, H.; Wichert, I.; Wilkinson, F. 1999. *Job insecurity and work intensification: Flexibility and the changing boundaries of work* (York, England, Joseph Rowntree Foundation).

Gall, G. 1996. "All year round: The growth of annual hours in Britain", in *Personnel Review*, Vol. 25, No. 3, pp. 35–52.

Green, F. 2001. "It's been a hard day's night: The concentration and intensification of work in late twentieth-century Britain", in *British Journal of Industrial Relations*, Vol. 39, No. 1, pp. 53–80.

Harkness, S. 2002. *Low pay, times of work and gender*, Equal Opportunities Commission Research Discussion and Working Paper Series (Manchester, EOC).

Heyes, J. 1997. "Annualised hours and the 'knock': The organization of working time in a chemicals plant", in *Work, Employment and Society*, Vol. 11, No. 1, pp. 65–81.

ILO. 2001. *World employment report: Life at work in the information economy* (Geneva, ILO).

Jacoby, S.M. 1984. "The development of internal labour markets in American manufacturing firms", in P. Osterman (ed.): *Internal labour markets* (Cambridge, Massachusetts, MIT Press).

Jarvis, H. 2005. "Moving to London time: Household co-ordination and the infrastructure of everyday life", in *Time & Society*, Vol. 14, No. 1, pp. 133–54.

—; Pratt, A.; Cheng Chong Wu, P. 2001. *The secret life of cities: The social reproduction of everyday life* (Harlow, Prentice-Hall).

Karston, L.; Leopold, J. 2003. "Time and management: The need for hora management", in *Personnel Review*, Vol. 32, No. 4, pp. 405–21.

Kodz, J.; Davis, S.; Lain, D.; Strebler, M.; Rick, J.; Bates, P.; Cummings, J.; Meager, N. 2003. *Working long hours: A review of the evidence*, Department of Trade and Industry Employment Relations Research Series No. 16.

Lepak, D.; Snell, S. 1999. "The human resource architecture: Towards a theory of human capital allocation and development", in *Academy of Management Review*, Vol. 24, No. 1, pp. 31–48.

Marchington, M.; Grimshaw, D.; Rubery, J.; Willmott, H. (eds.). 2005. *Fragmenting work: Blurring organizational boundaries and disordering hierarchies* (Oxford, Oxford University Press).

Marglin, S. 1974. "What do bosses do?", in A. Gorz (ed.): *The division of labour: The labour process and class struggle in modern capitalism* (Brighton, Harvester Press).

Marsden, D. 1999. *A theory of employment systems: Microfoundations of societal diversity* (Oxford, Oxford University Press).

Noon, M.; Blyton, P. 1997. *The realities of work* (Basingstoke, Macmillan Business).

Perrons, D.; Fagan, C.; McDowell, L.; Ray, K.; Ward, K. (eds.). Forthcoming. *Gender divisions and working time in the new economy: Public policy and changing patterns of work in Europe and North America* (Cheltenham, Edward Elgar).

Rubery, J. 1998. "Working time in the United Kingdom", in *TRANSFER, European Review of Labour and Research*, Vol. 4, No. 4, pp. 657–77.

—; Ward, K.; Grimshaw, D.; Beynon, H. 2005. "Working time, industrial relations and the employment relationship", in *Time and Society*, Vol. 14, No. 4, pp. 89–111.

Sewell, G. 1998. "The discipline of teams: The control of team-based industrial work through electronic and peer surveillance", in *Administrative Science Quarterly*, Vol. 43, No. 2, pp. 397–429.

Smith, M. 2001. *IT services in the United Kingdom*, Report for the NESY Project, April.

Supiot, A. 2001. *Beyond employment: Changes in work and the future of labour law in Europe* (Oxford, Oxford University Press).

Thompson, P. 2003. "Disconnected capitalism: Or why employers can't keep their side of the bargain", in *Work, Employment and Society*, Vol. 17, No. 2, pp. 359–78.

White, M.; Hill, S.; McGovern, P.; Mills, C.; Smeaton, D. 2003. "High-performance management practices, working hours and work-life balance", in *British Journal of Industrial Relations*, Vol. 41, No. 1, pp. 175–97.

Williamson, O. 1985. *The economic institutions of capitalism* (New York, The Free Press).

PART II

INDIVIDUAL CHOICES AND COLLECTIVE OPTIONS

LABOUR SUPPLY PREFERENCES AND JOB MOBILITY OF DUTCH EMPLOYEES 6

Didier Fouarge* and Christine Baaijens**

6.1 INTRODUCTION

In the Netherlands, annual average working hours per job – incorporating full-time, part-time and flexible jobs, but no overtime – have decreased 39 per cent between 1950 and 2001 (Baaijens and Schippers, 2003). This decline can primarily be explained by a shortening of the full-time working week and a rapid growth in the number of part-time jobs. The latter has mainly taken place among women, while most men are still in full-time employment. Even though the working week has become shorter and more diverse over the last decades, still not all employees' preferences with respect to the length of the working week seem to be fulfilled. Our research shows that in the year 2002 about a quarter of all employees reported a desire to change their number of working hours.

The existing discrepancy between preferred and contractual working hours has been deemed undesirable by the Dutch Government. In order to facilitate employees' adjustment of working hours, the Government has recently introduced the Adjustment of Working Hours Act. The Act states that employers must honour employees' requests for either upward or downward adjustment of working hours, unless precluded by conflicting business interests.

The ILO identifies five guiding principles that contribute to decent working time (Messenger, ed., 2004): healthy working time, family-friendly

* Institute for Labour Studies (OSA) and Tilburg Institute of Social and Socio-Economic Research (TISSER), Tilburg University, The Netherlands.
** Utrecht School of Economics, Utrecht University, The Netherlands.

working time, gender equality through working time, productive working time, and choice and influence regarding working time. This study investigates the discrepancy between preferred and contractual working hours of Dutch employees and whether they succeed in realizing an adjustment of working hours. Therefore our focus on the possibilities to adapt working hours to life events and preferences fits well within the concept of decent working time.

Adjustment of working hours is often studied in the context of job mobility. In other studies this has been defined as a change of employer. A novelty in this chapter is that we make a distinction between job mobility in terms of a change of employer and within-firm mobility. A second novelty is that we investigate whether or not the introduction of the aforementioned Act has led to behavioural changes among employees.

We find that only a small portion of Dutch employees who are not satisfied with the length of their working week successfully adjust their hours. We further find that changes in working hours often coincide with either a change of employer or within-firm mobility. New Dutch legislation in the area has thus had no effect on these patterns to date.

6.2 THE DUTCH LABOUR MARKET IN INTERNATIONAL PERSPECTIVE

Since the beginning of the 1970s, most European Union (EU) countries have seen a marked growth in the proportion of part-timers in the total labour force. Exceptions include the southern European countries, where the incidence of part-time employment has remained low. Figure 6.1 shows the relative growth in part-time employment in both the Netherlands and the EU as a whole.[1,2] Between the mid-1980s and today part-time employment rose relatively faster among male workers than female workers, both in the Netherlands and the EU. However, since initial levels of male part-time employment were very low, the share of male part-time employment in total part-time employment remains low. Moreover, at least in the Netherlands, male part-time jobs are often held by students. Part-time work remains, therefore, a predominant feature of female employment. The gender imbalance not only exists in countries in which part-time employment is a rare phenomenon, but also in those countries where part-time employment is common, as figure 6.2 shows. The "femaleness" of part-time employment is

---

[1] Note that Eurostat bases the distinction between full-time and part-time work upon a spontaneous response by the respondent.

[2] Note that the ten new countries that joined the European Union in 2004 have not been taken into account.

Figure 6.1   Share of part-timers in total employment in the Netherlands and the European Union (EU), 1985–2001 (percentages)

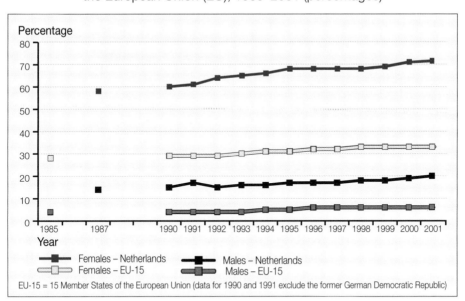

Source: European Commission (2002, pp. 173–188; 2000, p. 85, 95; 1996, p. 47).

often associated with women's roles as housewives and mothers. However, the impact of motherhood on women's working patterns is found to differ among countries (Fagan and Rubery, 1996, pp. 231–235).

In no other EU country is part-time employment as widespread as it is in the Netherlands. Its unique position is illustrated in figure 6.2, showing that, on the basis of harmonized European data, the Dutch incidence of part-time employment is much higher than in any other EU Member State. The large share of part-timers in the Netherlands today is the result of a combination of labour demand and supply factors. On the demand side, the advance in part-time employment can be explained by a changing attitude among employers who started to see its advantages in a context of extending operating hours and a growing service sector (Lomwel, 2000). On the supply side, the entry of married women into the labour force has contributed greatly (Baaijens, 1999).

Dutch labour market policy has contributed to a large degree toward the normalization of part-time employment by introducing, in the last decade, various measures to improve the legal position of part-timers. In 1993, existing thresholds that related to the number of hours worked were removed from entitlements to the statutory minimum wage and the minimum holiday allowance. Legislation in 1996 elaborated on the subject by prohibiting discrimination between employees based upon the number of working hours.

Figure 6.2   Proportion of part-time employment in total employment, EU countries, 2001 (percentages)

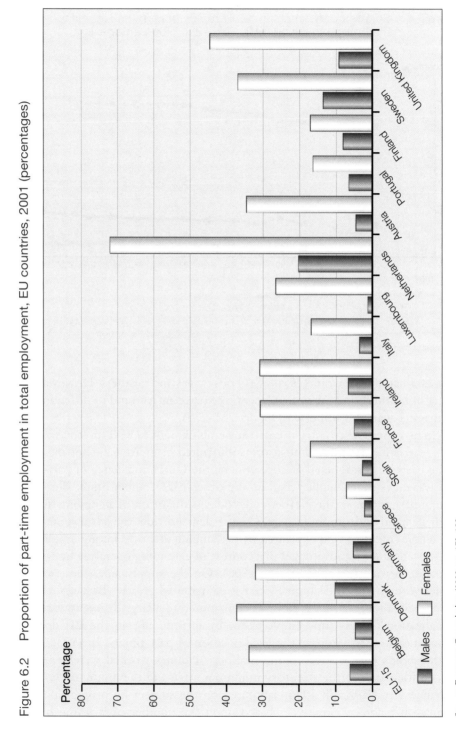

Source: European Commission (2002, pp. 173–188).

The Act awards part-time employees an explicit right to equal treatment – pro rata – in areas negotiated by the social partners, such as wages, holiday pay and entitlements, bonuses and training. As a result, part-timers and full-timers today enjoy similar conditions of employment in the Netherlands. Moreover, in many branches of industry – such as healthcare, the public sector, education and services – and in many organizations part-time work has become a normal and accepted phenomenon. In this respect the Dutch situation sharply contrasts with the situation in countries such as the United States, the United Kingdom, France and Germany, where part-time employment is often a form of *marginal* employment (Visser, 1999). Nevertheless, even in the Netherlands, part-timers seem to have less career development and fewer chances to enter management jobs than full-timers. In addition, part-time employment seems to be more accepted among women than among men.

6.2.1 A right to change the number of working hours

With the legal position of part-timers secured, the Dutch Government turned its attention towards increasing the number of part-time jobs. One of the reasons for this is that part-time employment is seen as a means for both men and women to combine work and caring activities. It is in this context that the Adjustment of Working Hours Act (Wet Aanpassing Arbeidsduur) was introduced in July 2000. According to this Act, employees have a right to request an upward or downward adjustment of working hours in their current job. In principle, employers have to honour such requests unless precluded by pressing conflicting business interests. Although this does not imply that all requests have to be honoured, it does imply that employers have to justify refusals. Employees, however, are under no obligation to specify the motivation for their request. This different treatment of employers and employees shows in particular that the legislators have taken sides with workers in their struggle to realize their desired working hours.

Within the European Union only Germany has a somewhat comparable law. This law came into force in January 2001, and is called the Part-time Work and Fixed-term Contracts Act (Gesetz über Teilzeitarbeit und befristete Arbeitsverträge). Although this is the subject of ongoing debate, it has been argued that, contrary to its name, the Act also grants workers the right to extend their working week (Jacobs and Schmidt, 2001). The German Act does not apply to workers in organizations with fewer than 15 employees, nor does it apply to civil servants. The Dutch Act also excludes organizations of fewer than 10 employees. However, according to the Dutch Act these companies have to make their own arrangements. The Dutch Act is equally applicable to the market sector and the public sector.

We have shown in this section that one key feature of the Dutch labour market is its large part-time segment. On top of that the Adjustment of Working Hours Act was introduced to facilitate the transition from working full time to working part time. In the rest of this chapter, we turn to the investigation of the processes by which employees adapt their working hours. We examine to what extent changes in working hours are associated with job mobility. Then we question whether legislation in the area has contributed to behavioural changes of Dutch employees.

6.3 PREVIOUS RESEARCH

The question of working hours preferences has been the subject of several studies over the past decades. These studies, mostly descriptive, reveal that although a majority of Dutch employees are satisfied with their contractual working hours, some groups of employees report a discrepancy between preferred and current working hours (for an overview, see Baaijens, 2000).[3] In general women more often than men state a desire to either increase or reduce their working hours. What we see in the Netherlands is that women in general, when staying in the labour market, reduce their working hours after the birth of their first child (Steenhof, 2000; Groot and Maassen van den Brink, 1997; Kragt 1997; Portegijs et al., 2004). For men a connection between having (young) children at home and a desire to work fewer hours does not seem to exist.

The fact that employees state that they would like to adjust their working hours does not mean that they make attempts actually to do so. Various Dutch studies reveal that a minority of the employees who would like to adjust their working hours make such a request to their employer. In addition, these studies show that not every request put forward is honoured. In a study among male workers more than half of the employees with a desire to reduce hours did not follow through (Spaans, 1997). Most of the employees did not make attempts because they thought that it would not be possible in their position. Of those who did request a change in working hours, 59 per cent were successful.

Research by Statistics Netherlands shows that only 22 per cent of men and 37 per cent of women undertake action when they desire to work fewer hours. However, these attempts are reasonably successful: of the men and women who did request a reduction of working time to their employer, 60 and 74 per cent, respectively, were successful (Boelens, 1997). Employees seem to be *less* hesitant to submit requests to *extend* contractual working hours. The

---

[3] Variations in the results of these studies depend highly upon differences in the phrasing of the relevant questions and by characteristics of the group of employees under investigation.

same study reveals that 38 per cent of men and 51 per cent of women with a desire to work more hours undertook steps to increase their working hours, with respectively 61 and 58 per cent of the attempts being successful. Since women are less hesitant to undertake steps than men, they more often experience a change in working hours. For example, between 1996 and 1997, 32 per cent of women changed working hours as opposed to 10 per cent of men (Schobben, 1998).[4]

Using the Dutch Socio-Economic Panel, Euwals (2001) finds that flexibility of working hours within jobs is low among female employees. As a result, women who stay with the same employer have a much smaller chance of adjusting their working hours than women who change jobs. In addition, Baaijens and Schippers (2003) – using the OSA Labour Supply Panel; see below – find that employees who change jobs succeed significantly more often in realizing a desired adjustment of the working week.

How do the Dutch findings compare with those in other countries? According to a study covering 15 EU Member States plus Norway (Bielenski et al., 2002, p. 43), half of the workforces surveyed preferred fewer hours and 11 per cent preferred more hours. However, almost two-thirds of full-timers assume that their current employer would not agree to let them work part time (ranging from 71 per cent in Austria to 44 per cent in Finland), while almost half of them say that working part time would harm their career prospects (ranging from 55 per cent in Germany to 31 per cent in Denmark) (Bielenski et al., 2002, p. 57).

In their seminal contributions, Altonji and Paxson (1986, 1988, 1992) have studied the adjustment of working hours of married women in the United States. They distinguish between women who stay in their job and women who change employers and conclude – using the US Panel Study of Income Dynamics – that the working hours of married women are two to four times more variable when changing employers than when staying in the same job. Based upon the US National Longitudinal Survey of Youth, Martinez-Granado (2003) finds that for prime-aged males the variance of the change in hours is more than six times higher across jobs (defined as a change of employer) than within jobs. Both findings suggest that in the United States both male and female employees have substantial difficulties in adjusting their working hours without changing employers. In addition, Böheim and Taylor (2004) find – using the British Household Panel Survey – that job changers in the United Kingdom are more able to adjust working hours in line with their preferences than those who stay in the same job.

---

[4] A 4-hour cut-off was used in this study to eliminate changes to weekly working hours due to a collective reduction of the work-week.

6.4 MODEL AND DATA

From previous research it seems that restrictions (or perceived restrictions) on the labour demand side play an important role in the process of adjustment towards the desired number of hours: when an adjustment is taking place, it will generally involve a job change. The question is whether this relationship between job mobility and changes in working hours also holds in a "part-time economy" such as the Dutch economy and, if it does, whether legislation in the area leads to behavioural changes. To provide answers to these questions, longitudinal information is required on actual and preferred working hours of individual employees, as well as on job mobility. Such longitudinal information is available in the OSA Labour Supply Panel, a panel of Dutch persons (aged 16 to 64) that started in 1985. As of 1986, data are collected every other year among some 4,500 persons in more than 2,000 households. In this chapter, we use nine waves of the panel covering the period 1986–2002. The data include information on demographic characteristics on the level of the individual (gender, age, marital status) and the household (household composition), socio-economic characteristics (labour market status, income), job characteristics (sector of activity, contract type) and human capital indicators (educational level, health status).

The data also include information on actual and preferred working hours, which is crucial for this research. We use information on contractual working hours, which are the hours that employers and employees have agreed upon. The data account for arrangements for collective working time reductions, which are common in the Netherlands. Contractual working hours exclude overtime hours. We do this because we want to test the effects of working time legislation, which only applies to contractual working hours; however, overtime hours are used as an explanatory variable in the analyses. We have computed contractual working hours in a way that is consistent over the years. Between 1986 and 1998 preferences for working hours were assessed by asking employees for their preferred number of working hours. A comparison of contractual and preferred working hours revealed whether employees were satisfied with their working week or not. However, in 2000 and 2002 respondents were asked directly whether they wanted to work more or fewer hours.[5] This change in the questionnaire has had no effect on the proportion of employees reporting that they want to work fewer hours: the proportion fits well within the trend-series. However, the change in the questionnaire has resulted in a reduction of the proportion of employees

---

[5] It is important to note that, in all years, respondents had to assume that their hourly wage and the labour supply of other household members remained unchanged when reporting their preferred number of working hours. It was made explicit that working fewer (more) hours implied a reduction (increase) in income.

who report that they want to work more hours (see Fouarge and Baaijens, 2003, pp. 38, 52–53). Therefore, one should be cautious when comparing the information concerning preferences for more hours before and after the change in questionnaire.

6.4.1 Modelling the effect of the Adjustment of Working Hours Act

We have a biennial measure of contractual working hours for the employees in the dataset in the 1986–2002 period and estimate the probability – using a probit model (see Appendix 6.1) – that an employee (we have excluded the self-employed) will *reduce* his or her working hours between two years. In a second model, we estimate the probability that an employee will *increase* his or her working hours between two years. The models, which are estimated separately for male and female workers, include a number of explanatory variables measuring personal and household characteristics as well as job and firm characteristics.

Among the explanatory variables, we include a set of dummy variables to measure job mobility (within-firm mobility or change of employer), preferences for working hours (preference for more or fewer hours) and time (1986–1992, 1992–2000, 2000–2002) as well as interactions of time with job mobility and preferences. The time dummy for changes in the working hours between 2000 and 2002 indicates the period following introduction of the Adjustment of Working Hours Act.[6] On the basis of the existing literature (see section 6.3), we expect changes in the number of working hours to be positively correlated with job mobility, and we expect working time preferences to be good predictors of actual changes in working time. However, we anticipate these associations to have *changed* after the introduction of the Act. In particular, we expect increases or decreases in the number of working hours to be *less* associated with job mobility in the post-Act period (i.e. we expect a negative sign for the cross-term between job mobility and the post-Act time dummy 2000–2002). In addition, we expect that it should be easier for employees who are dissatisfied with their working hours to change their hours after the introduction of the Act (i.e. we expect a positive sign for the cross-term between dissatisfaction and the post-Act time dummy 2000–2002). We take both measures as empirical tests for the effect of the Act and discuss the results of the estimations in section 6.7. Although it is probably true that being unsatisfied with one's number of working hours is not the only reason

---

[6] The Dutch economy showed an economic downturn in the 1992–93 period, and a strong growth of labour market participation in the period thereafter. Therefore, the 1986–92 dummy reflects the pre-downturn period; the 1992–2000 dummy the growth period; and the 2000–2002 dummy the post-Act period.

why people change jobs,[7] additional analyses on our data do show that individuals who would like to work more or fewer hours are indeed significantly more likely to change jobs.[8]

6.5   WORKING HOURS PREFERENCES

Are Dutch employees satisfied with the number of hours they work? Not all of them. In 2002, as many as 16 per cent of Dutch employees would have preferred to work fewer hours (at least half a day) than their current contractual number of hours and 6 per cent would have liked to extend their working hours (table 6.1). These percentages vary strongly between males and females. Fifteen per cent of male employees want to work fewer hours and 10 per cent want to work more hours, whereas the respective percentages

Table 6.1   Preferences for working fewer or more hours, Dutch employees, 2002 (percentages)

	Desire to work fewer hours	Satisfied with current number of hours[1]	Desire to work more hours
Total (N=3,361)	17	77	6
Male employees (N=1,803)	20	77	3
Female employees (N=1,558)	14	77	9
Male employees by educational level			
Primary school or lower	24	72	4
Lower secondary	19	77	4
Higher secondary	19	78	3
Higher education	16	82	2
University	22	74	4
Female employees by educational level			
Primary school or lower	17	72	11
Lower secondary	8	80	12
Higher secondary	12	80	8
Higher education	19	73	8
University	32	62	6

Note: [1] Desired change is less than 4 hours.

Source: OSA Labour Supply Panel 2002.

---

[7] Career motives or the desire to do something new are important factors as well.

[8] The analyses are not shown but are available on request.

Table 6.2   Extent to which Dutch employees think they will be able to
achieve their desired change in working hours within one year,
2002 (percentages)

	Possible within one year	Not possible within one year because of employer or job[1]	Not possible within one year for other reasons[2]	Does not know
Male employees (N=432)				
Desire to work fewer hours	20	52	21	7
Desire to work more hours	58	19	16	7
Female employees (N=390)				
Desire to work fewer hours	41	29	16	14
Desire to work more hours	50	17	16	17

Notes: [1]"Job does not allow a change" or "employer does not allow change". [2]"Health does not allow change", "childcare activities do not allow change" or other reason.

Source: OSA Labour Supply Panel 2002.

among females are 18 per cent and 13 per cent. Higher-educated workers especially wish to reduce their working week. If all Dutch employees were to act upon their preferences, this would potentially result in a sharp reduction of the total labour supply.

Over the years 1986–2002, an increasing number of male workers wanted to reduce their working hours, but the reverse holds for female workers. Despite this trend, as we saw in figure 6.2, the incidence of male part-time employment has remained low in the Netherlands. It seems that male workers cannot, do not dare, or do not wish to realize their latent preferences. Our data offer information on the extent to which employees with a desire to change their working hours think they will be able to do so within one year and, if not, the reasons why. The results for 2002 are displayed in table 6.2. Males who want to reduce their number of hours worked are less confident than females that they will be able to do so within a year. They are, however, more confident than females that they will be able to increase their hours. In the majority of cases, when employees think they will not be able to change their hours, they state that this is because of their employer or their job. In particular, male employees who want to work fewer hours see their employer or their job as the main impediment. However, whether this perception is correct can be questioned. As has been elaborated above, previous research has shown that although employees are reluctant to address the issue of adjusting working hours to their employer, those employees who do so are often successful (Boelens, 1997).

Of course, at the individual level, some employees do succeed in adjusting their working hours in accordance with their preferences. But to what extent is

Table 6.3   Desired working hours and change of contractual working hours, Dutch employees, 1986–2002 (rows add up to 100 per cent)

Desired working hours	Change of working hours between t and $t + 2$		
	Fewer hours	No change[1]	More hours
Male employees (N=8,107)			
Fewer hours	10	87	3
No change[1]	5	92	3
More hours	4	82	14
Total	**6**	**90**	**4**
Female employees (N=4,785)			
Fewer hours	33	62	5
No change[1]	13	73	14
More hours	6	50	44
Total	**16**	**67**	**17**

Note: [1] Desired or realized change is less than 4 hours.

Source: OSA Labour Supply Panel 1986–2002.

this taking place? Table 6.3 depicts the changes in contractual working hours between two years in the period 1986–2002. Three main conclusions can be drawn from the table. First, most workers who are dissatisfied with their working hours in one year – they would like to adjust hours either upward or downward – have not changed their hours two years later. Second, given employees' preferences, it seems easier to increase working hours than to reduce them. Third, male employees have a more stable employment pattern than female employees. Male employees work full time and tend to keep on doing so, irrespective of their preferences. Female workers, however, tend to be more flexible and adjust their working hours more often in accordance with their preferences. Presumably, there is a relationship between male and female behaviour: because they are flexible in adjusting their working hours, female workers render it possible for males to remain inflexible. This, however, should be the subject of further investigation.

6.6   CHANGES IN WORKING HOURS

6.1.1   *Reducing labour supply*

Working hours changes are driven by four sets of factors: individual pre-ferences for working hours, individual and household characteristics, job characteristics, and labour demand and institutional factors.[9] It has been shown that a preference for a different number of working hours is a strong determinant of changes in actual working hours: individuals with a preference for fewer (more) hours are more likely to reduce (extend) their labour supply (Euwals et al., 1998; Böheim and Taylor, 2004; Baaijens and Schippers, 2003; Fouarge and Baaijens, 2003).

In table 6.4, we present model estimates for the probability of reducing the number of hours worked between two years. It appears that the household context – having a partner, having children – plays a crucial role in the case of female workers. This tends to confirm Becker's specialization hypothesis according to which individuals will specialize in activities where they yield the highest return (Becker, 1985). Although the household context is of less importance to male workers with a preference for fewer working hours, similar to their female counterparts, they tend to reduce their labour supply following the birth of a child. The effect for female workers is, however, much stronger. Given that one has a partner, the longer the working hours of the partner, the lower the likelihood that female workers reduce their labour supply. However, we find the opposite effect for males. One explanation could be that there exists a "homogamy of working hours": the more often employees search for and find a partner with an equal educational level, the greater the probability that both partners will want to work the same number of hours. Thus, given the fact that female employees in the Netherlands often work part time, it could be argued that female employees do not reduce their hours if their partner is working long hours, but male employees do.

Female managers are less likely to reduce their working hours. Although we found the same sign for this effect for male managers, for them it is insignificant. The fear of negative future career consequences is probably the main reason for this, especially since it is still more difficult for female workers to get into higher management levels than it is for male workers. It is, however, also possible that it is the organizational culture that makes it difficult for female managers to reduce their working hours when they prefer to do so. Male workers engaged in manual labour or who are dissatisfied with their current job are more likely to reduce their working time. Male part-time workers are also found to be more likely to reduce their working time further, while the opposite effect is found for females. The difference is most probably due to the fact that male part-time workers are engaged in "substantial hours" part-time work, while female part-timers work, on average, in jobs with an

---

[9] Preferences are influenced by individual and household characteristics on the one hand, and job characteristics on the other, but such characteristics also have a direct effect on the probability that an individual will change his or her labour supply.

already small number of hours. Females working full time are especially likely to reduce their labour supply.

Changes in labour time are also driven by individual preferences. Employees with a preference for a shorter working week are indeed more likely to reduce their working hours. The Adjustment of Working Hours Act should make it easier for employees to adjust working hours to their preferences. Hence we would expect dissatisfied workers to be more likely to adapt their working time after the introduction of the Act; that is, we would expect a positive sign for the cross-term between dissatisfaction and the dummy variable 2000–2002 (indicating the period after the introduction of the Act). Yet we find no such effect.

Individual preferences, however, are not the only determinant of changes in working hours. Labour demand and institutional constraints also play an important role in shaping working hours. Earlier, we referred to the demand side as a major contributor to the growth of part-time employment in the Netherlands. However, the incidence of part-time employment still varies strongly among firms. Moreover, as previous research has shown, there are labour demand constraints on the labour market (Altonji and Paxson, 1992). As a consequence, it is not always possible for employees freely to change their number of working hours in accordance with their preferences. Therefore, changes in the number of hours worked often coincide with job mobility. In the model, labour demand factors are accounted for through the inclusion of a set of sector dummies and firm size dummies (see table 6.4). In addition, dummy variables for change of employer and within-firm mobility have been introduced. The sector of activity plays no role in female working hour changes. However, male employees in the sector "education" or "health care" have a higher probability of reducing their number of hours. This is probably because these sectors offer a large number of part-time jobs.

Our analyses confirm that changes in working hours often coincide with job mobility, be it a change of position with the same employer or a change of employer. As table 6.2 shows, most employees who do not think they will be able to adapt their working hours in accordance with their preferences attribute this to the unwillingness of the employer or the impossibility to do so within their current job. Additional analyses have shown that such constraints indeed affect the probability of adapting the number of hours worked. Employees who report that their job or their employer do not allow for changes in working hours are less likely to adapt their working hours in accordance to their preferences and are more likely to change their job (Fouarge and Baaijens, 2003, pp. 82–84).

As explained above, the new Adjustment of Working Hours Act was introduced with the aim to facilitate working hours changes within the

Table 6.4   Parameters for the probability of working fewer hours between t and t + 2, male and female workers, 1986–2002

	Males	Females
Individual and household characteristics		
Age	0.029	0.032
Age squared (/100)	−0.025	−0.037
Educational level (ref: primary school or lower)		
Lower secondary	0.031	0.037
Higher secondary	0.091	0.022
Higher education	0.161	0.258[1]
University	0.202	0.502[2]
Household type (ref: couple without child)		
Couple with child	−0.004	−0.023
Divorced/widowed	0.208	−0.385[3]
Single	0.176[1]	−0.416[3]
Birth of a child	0.182[1]	0.937[3]
Number of hours worked by partner	0.006[3]	−0.005[3]
Job characteristics		
Ln(hourly wage)	−0.209[2]	−0.535[3]
Permanent contract	−0.173[1]	−0.099
Manager	−0.062	−0.204[3]
Heavy work	0.204[3]	0.046
Dissatisfied with work	0.135[1]	0.079
Part-time job	0.316[3]	−0.179[2]
Overtime work	−0.04	0.086
Labour demand factors		
Sector (ref: commerce, catering, transport)		
Industry or agriculture	0.011	−0.09
Financial business services	0.074	−0.159
Other services	0.138	0.054
Public sector	0.044	−0.007
Education	0.718[3]	0.063
Healthcare	0.246[2]	0.102
Firm size: (ref: 100 or more employees)		
11–99 employees	0.026	0.147[2]
1–10 employees	0.025	0.052
Time (ref: 1992–2000)		
1986–1992	0.201[2]	−0.114
2000–2002	0.405[3]	0.374[3]

/cont'd

Table 6.4 (/cont'd)

	Males	Females
Job mobility		
Change of employer	0.572[3]	0.839[3]
Within-firm mobility	0.152	0.360[3]
Time and job mobility		
Change of employer 1986–1992	0.054	−0.16
Change of employer 2000–2002	0.08	−0.092
Within firm mobility 1986–1992	0.286[1]	0.404[2]
Within firm mobility 2000–2002	0.296	0.143
Preferences		
Prefers fewer hours	0.288[2]	0.665[3]
Prefers more hours	−0.165	−0.265
Preferences and time		
Prefers fewer hours 1986–1992	0.029	−0.14
Prefers fewer hours 2000–2002	0.038	−0.094
Prefers more hours 1986–1992	0.123	0.323
Prefers more hours 2000–2002	0.224	−0.265
Selection (lambda)		
for selection equation, see table 6A.1 in Appendix 6.2	−2.743[3]	−0.584
Constant term	1.642[3]	0.562
N=	6 813	3 518
Pseudo-R^2	0.123	0.167

Notes: [1] Significant at 10%; [2] significant at 5%; significant at 1%; robust estimator of variance for clustered data.

Source: OSA Labour Supply Panel 1986–2002.

present job. The institutional change is captured in the model through the inclusion of three dummy variables: one dummy indicating the period following the introduction of the Act, and two dummies indicating job mobility (within-firm mobility or change of employer) after the introduction of the Act (i.e. a cross-term between mobility and the post-Act time dummy 2000–2002). If the downward adjustment of working hours were *less* associated with job mobility in the post-Act period, we would expect in our model estimates a significant negative sign for the cross-term between job mobility and the post-Act time dummy 2000–2002. However, our model estimates show no such results. This means that working hours reductions are no less often associated with job mobility after the introduction of the Act than they were prior to the Act. Summarizing, both measures we have used as empirical tests for the effect of the Act turn out to be insignificant.

6.6.2 *Increasing labour supply*

The results of the model estimates for the probability of increasing the labour supply are presented in table 6.5. The hourly wage affects the probability of increasing labour supply positively. This means that employees in high positions, and therefore earning a high wage, are better able to increase their labour supply. For male and female employees, having a permanent contract reduces the probability of increasing labour supply. It must be noted, however, that most male workers on permanent contracts already work full time, and that, in this case, it is almost impossible to increase the number of contractual working hours. Mothers of young children are less likely to increase their labour supply, supposedly because of the caring activities involved.

As in the previous model, labour demand factors do affect male labour supply, but have little effect on female labour supply. Males working in non-commercial services and in the education sector are more likely to increase their labour supply. Both males and females are more likely to increase their hours when working in firms of average size (11–99 employees).

Again, working hours preferences are found to be a strong determinant of working time changes: male and female employees with a preference for longer working weeks are more likely to increase their working hours than employees without such preferences. For males, this association between their preferences and working time changes has changed after the introduction of the Adjustment of Working Hours Act: after the introduction of the Act male employees with a preference for working more hours are *less* likely to actually change their hours. However, it is possible that this effect is due to changes in the questionnaire (see section 6.4).

To what extent are increases in the number of hours worked associated with job mobility? Both male and female employees are more likely to change working hours when changing employers. In addition, female employees are also more likely to increase working hours when changing jobs with the same employer. Thus we can deduce that hours restrictions do play a role, especially for female employees. Turning to the effect of the Adjustment of Working Hours Act, if the upward adjustment of working hours were *less* associated with job mobility in the post-Act period, we would expect in our model estimates a significant negative sign for the cross-term between job mobility and the post-Act time dummy 2000–2002. The empirical results are mixed. For female employees we can conclude that the association between mobility and working hours increases has not changed after the introduction of the Adjustment of Working Hours Act. However, for males we find that they are less likely to change job in order to increase working hours after the year 2000 than they were in the period prior to the introduction of the Act. Again it is possible that this effect is due to a different phrasing of the relevant questions (see section 6.4).

Table 6.5   Parameters for the probability of working more hours between t and t + 2, male and female workers, 1986–2002

	Males	Females
Individual and household characteristics		
Age	−0.025	0.071[2]
Age squared (/100)	0.009	−0.113[3]
Educational level (ref: primary school or lower)		
Lower secondary	−0.027	−0.068
Higher secondary	−0.136	−0.064
Higher education	−0.111	0.005
University	−0.24	−0.365[1]
Household type (ref: couple without child)		
Couple with child	−0.023	−0.353[3]
Divorced/widowed	0.189	0.158
Single	0.122	0.226[1]
Birth of a child	0.011	−0.218
Number of hours worked by partner	0.002	−0.003
Job characteristics		
Ln(hourly wage)	0.400[3]	0.311[3]
Permanent contract	−0.307[3]	−0.391[3]
Manager	−0.12	−0.225[3]
Heavy work	0.071	−0.047
Dissatisfied with work	0.08	0.173[1]
Part-time job	1.601[3]	1.260[3]
Overtime work	0.045	0.043
Labour demand factors		
Sector (ref: commerce, catering, transport)		
Industry or agriculture	0.125	0.088
Financial business services	−0.047	−0.142
Other services	0.449[3]	0.135
Public sector	0.006	0.008
Education	0.527[3]	0.109
Healthcare	0.04	−0.008
Firm size: (ref: 100 or more employees)		
11–99 employees	0.174	0.230[3]
1–10 employees	0.16	0.129
Time (ref: 1992–2000)		
1986–1992	0.299[2]	0.143
2000–2002	1.242[3]	0.358[2]

Job mobility		
Change of employer	0.708[3]	1.072[3]
Within-firm mobility	0.226	0.820[3]
Time and job mobility		
Change of employer * 1986–1992	-0.364[2]	-0.278[1]
Change of employer * 2000–2002	-0.515[2]	-0.122
Within-firm mobility * 1986–1992	-0.091	-0.006
Within-firm mobility * 2000–2002	-0.343	0.107
Preferences		
Prefers fewer hours	-0.008	-0.26
Prefers more hours	0.722[3]	0.623[3]
Preferences and time		
Prefers fewer hours * 1986–1992	0.212	0.06
Prefers fewer hours * 2000–2002	0.104	0.149
Prefers more hours * 1986–1992	0.009	0.044
Prefers more hours * 2000–2002	-0.942[2]	-0.127
Selection (lambda)		
for selection equation, see Table 6A.1 in Appendix 6.2	0.682	1.367[2]
Constant term	-3.141[3]	-4.392[3]
N=	6 699	3 472
Pseudo-R[2]	0.3796	0.263

Notes: [1] Significant at 10%; [2] significant at 5%; [3] significant at 1%; robust estimator of variance for clustered data.

Source: OSA Labour Supply Panel 1986–2002.

6.7 CONCLUSION

Our main focus in this chapter has been on the adjustment of working hours to workers' preferences, which fits well within the concept of "decent working time" developed by the ILO (Messenger, ed., 2004). We have questioned whether or not legislation can improve this adjustment process and henceforth contribute to more decent working times. We have shown that a quarter of Dutch employees are dissatisfied with the number of hours they currently work. They would prefer to work either more or fewer hours. However, from our analyses of the OSA Labour Supply Panel it turns out that, even in the Dutch part-time economy, only a small portion of employees that would like to adjust working hours is actually doing so. Between 1986 and 2002, only 15 to 27 per cent of employees with a desire to work fewer hours, and 22 to 35 per cent of employees with a desire to work more hours, have adjusted their working hours accordingly two years later. One of the main conclusions of this chapter is that it is easier to realize an upward adjustment of working hours than it is to realize a downward adjustment. We also found large differences between male and female workers. Male employees show more stable working hours patterns, whereas women show more flexible patterns.

Although it is possible to adjust working hours within the same job and with the same employer, our analyses show that changes in working hours often coincide with job mobility, be it changes of position with the same employer or a change of employer. Employees who report that their job or their employer does not allow for changes in working hours are indeed not only less likely to adapt their working hours in accordance with their preferences but also more likely to change jobs. With the introduction of the Adjustment of Working Hours Act in 2000, Dutch policy-makers were expecting to smooth away such labour demand constraints. We therefore expected adjustments in working hours to be realized less often by means of job mobility after its introduction. However, we found no significant effect. In addition, we did not find the expected result that it should be easier for employees who are dissatisfied with their working hours to change their hours after the introduction of the Act.

6.7.1 Policy implications

What lessons can we learn from the Dutch experience to date? First of all we need to give a word of caution. In our study, the period following the introduction of the new Adjustment of Working Hours Act is relatively short (2 years). It is possible that the positive effects of such policy measures will only materialize in the longer run. For example, it could be the case that this policy measure allows more female workers to remain in the labour market (be it on a part-time basis) when they become mothers. It is also possible that the new legislation will induce a further "normalization" of part-time employment, and thus lead to more transitions between full-time and part-time jobs over the life course. However, it is difficult to evaluate such long-term effects because they can also flow from all sorts of contextual changes that one cannot control for.

Apart from the official evaluation of the Act by the Dutch Ministry of Social Affairs and Employment (MuConsult, 2003) there is, to our knowledge, no other evaluation of the effects of this new legislation available in the Netherlands. The official evaluation is, contrary to ours, positive about the Act. However, this is primarily based on the *potential* use of the legal framework – it is argued that the large number of employees dissatisfied with their working hours justifies the legal framework – and much *less* on its *actual* effect on generating greater working hours flexibility. With respect to the German Part-time Work and Fixed-term Contracts Act, an evaluation using methods similar to ours also comes to the conclusion that job mobility is a means of adjustment in working hours, and that the German Act has had no effect on this relationship (Munz, 2004). Thus the results are in line with our findings for the Netherlands.

Many employees with a desire to adjust working hours are reluctant to put forward such requests. Our results show that particularly male employees think that their employers or their jobs are important obstacles in realizing a preference for working fewer hours. They seem to fear that their employer will not approve or to think that it is not possible in their job, although this may not objectively be the case. Fear of possible negative consequences for their careers is also likely to play a role. Employees may be justified in fearing such effects. As a recent Dutch study shows, part-time employees who switch back to full-time jobs display lower wage rates and lower wage growth even after some years of full-time employment – although there is a slow recovery for male workers (Román et al., 2004).

Over the years employers in the Netherlands have realized the advantages of part-time employment as a form of flexible labour and as a way of increasing labour supply in a situation of shortages in the labour market. After all, part-time employment makes it possible to combine paid employment with care activities. From this perspective it is plausible that employers will grant changes in working hours if requested by employees. Previous research has indeed shown that although employees are reluctant to request adjustment of working hours, their attempts are reasonably successful. Nevertheless, both employer and employee behaviour is likely to be different in the various phases of the business cycle. When the labour market is tight, an employer will be more willing to grant an employee's request for working hours change rather than see him or her leave the firm for another job with the preferred number of hours. Under these conditions employers and employees will work out a solution that benefits both, and thus there is no need for legislation. In an economic downturn, however, employees can be expected to be reluctant to address the issue of changes in working hours: on the one hand, there is little scope for increases in working hours and, on the other hand, requesting a reduction in working hours would send the wrong signal to one's employer. From that perspective as well, whether or not employees have legal back-up for such a request would not seem to make much of a difference.

APPENDIX 6.1   PROBIT MODELS FOR THE DECREASE AND INCREASE IN WORKING HOURS

Contractual working hours are measured for $i = 1, ..., N$ individuals over $t = 1, ..., 9$ time periods. Since these time periods are 2 years apart, we can measure the change in contractual working hours between t and $t + 2$. We estimate two probit models: one for the probability that an employee reduces his or her working hours between 2 years (model A) and the other for the probability that he or she increases them (model B). The models, estimated separately for male and female workers, are specified as follows:[10]

$$[y^* = \beta X + \delta_1 M + \tau_1 P + \gamma T + \delta_2 M^* T + \tau_2 P^* T + v,]$$

with

$y = 1$ if $y^* = H_{G2} - H_C \le 4$, and $y = 0$ if $y^* = |H_{G2} - H_C| < 4$ in model A;

and

$y = 1$ if $y^* = H_{G2} - H_C \ge 4$, and $y = 0$ if $y^* = |H_{G2} - H_C| < 4$ in model B.

In both models, H_t^C represents the number of contractual hours per week, X is a set of individual, household and job characteristics (such as age, marital status, household composition, sector of activity, etc.), M indicates whether job mobility has taken place between t and $t + 2$, P represents a preference for working fewer or more hours at time t, and the Ts are time dummies, one of which indicates the period after the introduction of the Adjustment of Working Hours Act. In both models, the reference group is composed of those who did not change their labour supply.

In both models, we use a 4-hour cut-off regarding preferences to change working hours and changes of working hours. Thus an employee is said to have a preference for working fewer (more) hours when his or her preferred number of working hours is at least 4 hours less (more) than his or her contractual working hours. Likewise, an employee is said to have reduced (increased) working hours when his or her current working hours are at least 4 hours less (more) than his or her working hours 2 years before. This is not only done in order to account for small measurement errors, but also because it is assumed that small adjustments in working hours are easily negotiable with the employer.

Selective attrition in the panel is likely to bias the coefficients estimated. In addition, the coefficients will also be biased when the probability of

---

[10] We have estimated random effects probit panel models. However, as in Böheim and Taylor (2001), the individual effects turned out to be insignificant. Hence, probit models estimated on the pooled person-year data perform equally well. Standard errors are corrected to account for the fact that the observations are not independent.

remaining in paid employment is selective. To account for that, we estimated the following selection equation (see Heckman, 1979) and included a selection term in our main equation (two-step procedure):

$$[\, z^s = (\beta^s X^s + u > 0)]$$

In other words, we only observe y when $z^s > 0$. $z^s > 0$ if the respondent is employed in two consecutive years. It is equal to 0 if the respondent has left either the panel or paid employment between two consecutive years. The explanatory variables in the selection equation (X^s) include age, household status, time dummies and, in order to identify the model, a dummy variable for new respondents. The idea is that being a new entrant to the panel influences the probability of remaining in the panel, but not the probability of changing working hours.

APPENDIX 6.2   SELECTION EQUATION

Table 6A.1   Results from the selection equations for the probability of remaining in paid employment between t and $t + 2$

		Males	Females
Age		0.132[3]	0.066[3]
Age squared (/100)		−0.193[3]	−0.094
Household type (ref: couple without child)			
Couple with child		−0.120[2]	−0.267[3]
Divorced/widowed		−0.207[1]	0.012
Single		−0.052	0.167[2]
New respondent		0.014	0.013
Time (ref: 1986)			
	1988	0.024	−0.061
	1990	0.146[2]	0.231[3]
	1992	−0.005	0.068
	1994	0.058	0.174[2]
	1996	−0.563[3]	−0.190[2]
	1998	−0.586[3]	−0.111
	2000	0.255[3]	0.396[3]
Constant term		−0.774[3]	−0.318
N		9 467	5 972

Notes: [1] Significant at 10%; [2] significant at 5%; [3] significant at 1%; robust estimator of variance for clustered data.

References

Altonji, J.G.; Paxson, C.H. 1986. "Job characteristics and hours of work", in R.G. Ehrenberg (ed.): *Research in labor economics* (Greenwich, Connecticut, Westview Press), pp. 1–55.

—; —; 1988. "Labor supply preferences, hours constraints and hours-wage trade offs", in *Journal of Labor Economics*, Vol.6, No. 2, pp. 254–76.

—; —. 1992. "Labor supply, hours constraints and job mobility", in *The Journal of Human Resources*, Vol. 27, No. 2, pp. 256–78.

Baaijens, C. 1999. "Deeltijdarbeid in Nederland", in *Tijdschrift voor Arbeidsvraagstukken*, Vol. 15, No. 1, pp. 6–18.

—. (2000). "Werkgevers en de wensen rond arbeidstijden bij werknemers in Nederland", in *Sociale Wetenschappen*, Vol. 43, No. 1, pp. 73–96.

—; Schippers, J.J. 2003. *The unfulfilled preference for working fewer hours in the Netherlands*, Paper presented at the ESPE conference, 13–15 June, New York.

Becker, G. 1985. "Human capital, effort and the sexual division of labour", in *Journal of Labour Economics*, Vol. 3, No. 1, pp. s33–s58.

Bielenski, H.; Bosch, G.; Wagner, A. 2002. *Working time preferences in sixteen European countries* (Dublin, European Foundation for the Improvement of Living and Working Conditions).

Boelens, A.M.S. 1997. "Meer en minder willen werken", in *Sociaal Economisch Maandstatistiek*, Vol. 4, No. 5, pp. 26–28.

Böheim, R.; Taylor, M. 2004. "Actual and preferred working hours", in *British Journal of Industrial Relations*, Vol. 42, No. 1, pp. 149–66.

European Commission. 1996. *Employment in Europe 1996* (Luxembourg, Office for Official Publications of the European Communities).

—. 2000. *Employment in Europe 2000* (Luxembourg, Office for Official Publications of the European Communities).

—. 2002. *Employment in Europe 2002: Recent trends and prospects* (Luxembourg, Office for Official Publications of the European Communities).

Euwals, R. 2001. "Female labour supply, flexibility of working hours, and job mobility", in *The Economic Journal*, Vol. 111, May, pp. c120–c134.

—; Melenberg, B.; van Soest, A. 1998. "Testing the predictive value of subjective labour supply data", in *Journal of Applied Econometrics*, Vol. 13, No. 5, pp. 567–85.

Fagan, C.; Rubery, J. 1996. "The salience of the part-time divide in the European Union", in *European Sociological Review*, Vol. 12, No. 3, pp. 227–50.

Fouarge, D.; Baaijens, C. 2003. *Veranderende arbeidstijden. Slagen werknemers er in hun voorkeuren te realiseren?* (Tilburg, OSA-publicatie A199).

Groot, W.; Maassen van den Brink, H. 1997. *Verlate uittreding: Oorzaken van uittreding uit het arbeidsproces ruim na de geboorte van het eerste kind* (Den Haag, VUGA).

Heckman, J. 1979. "Sample selection bias as a specification error", in *Econometrica*, Vol. 47, No. 1, pp. 153–61.

Jacobs, A.; Schmidt, M. 2001. "The right to part-time work: The Netherlands and Germany compared", in *The International Journal of Comparative Labour Law and Industrial Relations*, Vol. 17, No. 3, pp. 371–84.

Kragt, C.M. 1997. "Arbeidsdeelname van jonge ouders", in CBS: *Sociaal-economische dynamiek 1997* (Den Haag, Sdu).

Lomwel, G. van. 2000. *Essays on labour economics* (Amsterdam, Thela Thesis).

Martinez-Granado, M. 2003. *Testing labour supply and hours constraints* (University of Madrid, CEMFI, October).

Messenger, J. (ed.). 2004. *Working time and workers' preferences in industrialized countries: Finding the balance* (Abingdon/New York, Routledge).

MuConsult. 2003. *Onderzoek ten behoeve van de evaluatie Waa en Woa* (Amersfoort, MuConsult).

Munz, S. 2004. *Flexibility of working hours and job mobility in Germany: the role of the Part-time and Fixed-term Act*, Paper for the TLM.NET Conference "Quality in labour market transitions: a European challenge", Amsterdam, 25–26 November 2004.

Portegijs, W.; Boelens, A.; Olsthoorn, L. (eds.). 2004. *Emancipatiemonitor 2004* (Den Haag, Sociaal en Cultureel Planbureau/Centraal Bureau voor de Statistiek).

Román, A.; Fouarge, D.; Luijkx, R. 2004. *Career consequences of part-time work: Results from Dutch panel data 1990–2001* (Tilburg, OSA-publicatie A206).

Schobben, C.L.E. 1998. "Meer of minder uren werken", in CBS: *Sociaal-economische dynamiek 1998* (Den Haag, Sdu), pp. 29–33.

Spaans, J. 1997. *Tussen wens en realiteit: Onderzoek naar de wijze waarop mannelijke werknemers hun deeltijdwens en/of wens tot calamiteitenverlof realiseren en de belemmeringen daarbij* (Den Haag, VUGA).

Steenhof, L. 2000. "Werkende moeders", in *Maandstatistiek van de Bevolking*, Vol. 48, No. 4, pp. 17–23.

Visser, J. 1999. *De sociologie van het halve werk*, Oratie uitgesproken ter gelegenheid van de aanvaarding van de benoeming tot hoogleraar empirische sociologie aan de Universiteit van Amsterdam op 20 mei 1999.

THE FRENCH 35-HOUR WEEK: A DECENT WORKING TIME PATTERN? LESSONS FROM CASE STUDIES

7

Pascal Charpentier,* Michel Lallement, Florence Lefresne**
and Jocelyne Loos-Baroin***

7.1   INTRODUCTION

7.1.1   *Reduction of working time – a lever for improving decent working time?*

Can the reduction of working time act as a lever for improving employees' working, employment and living conditions, while at the same time meeting companies' demands in terms of economic performance? It is precisely because French legislators answered this question in the affirmative – until the second Aubry law (Aubry II) – that they insisted on intervening in the area of the organization of working time. Thus, from the 1982 ordinance on reducing the working week from 40 to 39 hours until Aubry II in 2000, which brought the legal standard down to 35 hours, the authorities introduced a set of measures encouraging industrial and professional sectors and/or companies to reduce and reorganize their employees' working time (see box 7. 1). The permanent role of the State regarding a topic that is dealt with elsewhere in Europe via collective bargaining can be explained by the special attention given to the reduction and organization of working time in French public employment policies.

Debates on these policies have often been heated, but in fact the issues have hardly changed over the past 20 years. The only real change concerns the gradual weakening of the link between the reduction of working time and

---

* Laboratoire Interdisciplinaire pour la Sociologie Économique (LISE) – Centre National de la Recherche Scientifique (CNRS) and Conservatoire National des Arts et des Métiers (CNAM), Paris.

** Institut de Recherches Économiques et Sociales (IRES).

*** Université de Marne la Vallée, LATTS–CNRS.

employment, which had been postulated *a priori*. Thus there was talk of "sharing employment and income" and then, more recently, of "win-win" agreements. The latter imply that collective bargaining on working time could not only lead to satisfactory compromises for all actors involved, but also contribute to corporate competitiveness and thus, indirectly, to job creation. During this period, a number of companies were regularly identified as having reached agreements which were considered exemplary, in that they harmoniously link the various dimensions that are at the heart of reducing working time, namely, employment, work and production organization, working and living conditions and productive efficiency.

In theory – and many examples provide evidence of this – an approach to organizing working time that is based on consultations and negotiations can thus contribute to regulating the employment market, while at the same time maintaining both corporate competitiveness and the quality of employees' working, pay and living conditions. In other words, organizing and reducing working time makes it possible – in certain situations – to reconcile economic and social aspects or, to use more recent terminology, to fit "decent working time"[1] and "productive working time" into the same mould (Messenger, ed., 2004). However, is it still possible to verify – under the conditions of Aubry II, according to which the reduction of working time becomes a legal obligation, whatever the particular situation in each company – what action could be taken at the level of a company in the context of incentive measures?

7.1.2 The Aubry laws – public controversy and corporate compromise

This question has greatly structured our thinking throughout the survey, whose main results are presented here.[2] It seemed essential to understand – via longitudinal observation of several firms – the kinds of compromises that are negotiated when moving from a situation that is well marked out by incentives to reduce working time to one in which the switch to the 35-hour work-week is imposed. The hypothesis at the outset was that a concern for competitiveness – which was that much stronger given that the economic situation had deteriorated since the implementation of the law – could lead to a deterioration of working and employment conditions for employees: increased flexibility, intensified work, stagnating or even lower pay, etc. In other words, to what extent does an

---

[1] The notion of "decent working time" incorporates several complementary components: health, work–life balance, gender equality, productive efficiency and employees' ability to influence their working time.

[2] This text expands on research that was carried out for DARES (Ministry of Labour). The final report was submitted in December 2003: *Pilotage du changement, gestion des temps et action collective: Les incidences de la loi Aubry II sur l'organisation*.

Box 7.1   The Aubry laws

Following on from the Robien law (11 June 1996), the first Aubry law (13 June 1998), called Aubry I, introduced a system of incentives for reducing working time and constituted the first stage before changing the legal length of the working week. This was set at 35 hours on 1 January 2000 for companies with more than 20 employees and on 1 January 2002 for the others by the second Aubry law (19 January 2000), called Aubry II.

More precisely, Aubry I enabled companies to benefit from "financial incentives" if they reduced working time before 1 January 2000. In order to qualify for this financial aid, working time of all or some employees had to be reduced by at least 10 per cent; this gave the employer a right to a reduction of their social security contributions for 5 years. The obligation to preserve employment for 2 years was the same as in the Robien law, but the required level of job creation for the proactive component was not proportional to the reduction of working time (commitment to 6 per cent job creation or preservation for a 10 per cent reduction of working time). Receipt of financial incentives was subject to negotiation of a company agreement.

Aubry II set the legal duration of working time at 1,600 hours per annum and thus introduced – for the first time since 1936 in a general way – an annual standard. This standard provides for "variable working time" (*modulation*), namely variations in weekly working hours in line with economic fluctuations. The term "annualization" is used when the reference period is a year. With Aubry II, financial incentives were abolished and replaced by "long-term subsidies", which merge with reduced employers' social security contributions for low- to medium-pay levels. This measure is no longer subject to the condition of creating or preserving jobs, nor to a fixed mode of calculating working time, thus enabling companies to exclude from actual working time certain breaks, training time and public holidays, which were previously included. Aubry II is also innovative regarding conditions for accessing long-term subsidies. Access thus depends on negotiating an agreement that is accepted by the majority at the level of the company or establishment, or on applying an extended sector-level agreement. This possibility of "direct access" concerns companies with fewer than 50 employees. As was the case with the Robien law and Aubry I, Aubry II confirms the possibility of negotiating a company or establishment agreement with an employee who is authorized by a representative trade union, and provides for organizing a referendum of employees, which is also required when the unions which sign an agreement do not represent the majority of the employees concerned. There are specific provisions for companies with 20 or fewer employees.

imposed major reduction of working time run the risk of leading to a deterioration of certain components of "decent working time"?

Following on from assessments of previous measures on the organization and reduction of working time, there is a series of recurring questions regarding the nature and balance of negotiated compromises and, therefore, the conditions for compatibility – as mentioned earlier – between different kinds of social time. Therefore, the issues raised here are not really new – they have been widely discussed over the past 20 years in a context of increasing flexibility and gradual challenging of the weekly framework for calculating working time. However, they are sharper now, not only because of the size of the reduction in hours and the generalized nature of the measure, but also because fierce debates regarding their appropriateness have resumed. Several firms have recently negotiated a "rearrangement" of initial compromises (SEB and Bosch, etc.) and the challenging of the legal standard of a 35-hour week encourages political jousting with the prospect of possible "relaxation" of the rules. Opponents of the law consider that it puts French firms in a "disadvantaged position regarding competition" and also "devalues work". However, during current debates on the draft law relaxing the 35-hour week, it is clear that the 35-hour week is a social gain to which the majority of employees are attached, and many companies are not in a hurry to negotiate again. Even if one puts to one side the ideological nature of the debates between those in favour of and those against the Aubry laws, it is difficult for outside observers to have a clear opinion of what is at stake and the real implications of the 35-hour week (see box 7.1), because of the controversy they have stirred up and still arouse.

The difficulty of making a precise assessment of the impact of the law is related to the size of the reduction in working time: by exacerbating tensions inherent in any negotiations on this topic, the issue of the 35-hour week has reminded us how difficult it is to reach compromises that are both satisfactory and lasting among the various kinds of (economic, organizational and social) logics concerned, which are difficult to reconcile because they are partially contradictory. Moreover, what is perhaps new is that the reduction in working time has been able to contribute gradually to changing the perception that the actors concerned – companies and employees – have of decent work: the 35-hour week shows that, besides obvious difficulties of combining economic and social aspects, the various social dimensions at the basis of traditional employment relationships are subject to arbitration, which is also sometimes problematic. Those directly concerned do not always think that the results of such arbitration are satisfactory, but they can be considered acceptable given resulting advantages and disadvantages. Thus the contradiction between the feeling of some employees that their working conditions have deteriorated (flexibility, pay moderation and intensified work, etc.) and their attachment to the 35-hour week is only apparent.

7.1.3 Reduced time and combining the components of decent working time

It is now easier to see why it is of interest to consider the components of working time, their relationship, and the conditions for optimizing them. One cannot deny the existence of potentially conflicting logics between the various dimensions of decent work, nor the fact that the intensity of such conflicts and the arbitration that they lead to vary from country to country – women's night work and part-time working are good examples of such logics. Standards also vary depending on the structure of production, occupational categories and socio-demographic features of employees. So it is no longer a matter of knowing whether the components of decent working time are independent of each other, but rather of examining what combinations are possible and on the basis of what criteria and particular circumstances they can develop. If, instead of wondering about their degree of independence, one accepts the hypothesis that the components can constitute a system, one can then reason in terms of possible patterns of decent working time. This has the disadvantage of distancing one from the normative aim of optimizing the various components, but it has the advantage of reflecting in a more relevant way real, observed situations. It also has the merit, among other things, of explaining how agreements on organizing and reducing working time, which are negotiated in conditions that are not optimal and increase the demands of production, can produce compromises that are relatively stable over time.

The results of this survey of four companies should, therefore, be analysed in the context of the above general problem area (box 7.2). The general idea was not to pass normative judgement on the impact of the law, but to understand how it has been implemented and why the negotiated agreements appear to be stable, even though the main actors involved – both management and employees – sometimes have strong reservations about them. The small number of companies covered by the survey means that it cannot claim to be representative; however, it is sufficient to validate the hypothesis referred to above concerning the essentially contingent nature of the compromises that have been negotiated regarding the organization and reduction of working time, as well as the notion of decent working time itself. Three main components have been chosen for analysing the latter notion: ability of employees to intervene in the definition of their organization (measured by the role and procedures of collective bargaining), productive efficiency (assessed in terms of the nature of organizational compromises and the development of management methods) and working conditions and work–life balance (analysed on the basis of employees' perceptions of the reduction in working time, which are sometimes contradictory).

Box 7.2   The method

The survey combines qualitative and quantitative approaches. It draws on monographs of establishments, based on interviews with actors concerned with the organization and reduction of working time: management, human resources directors, trade union representatives, line managers (a category that plays a pivotal role in work and time management) and employees. A closed-ended questionnaire concerning key analytical variables was submitted to all employees in each establishment. The interviews and questionnaires were carried out in two phases (the first from September to December 2002 and the second from August to November 2003). This made it possible to observe any changes and adjustments made since the signature of the agreements and their implementation and, thus, to assess short- and medium-term experimentation.

The sample is made up of four companies,[1] which are specialized in the production of intermediate goods and the production of services with high added value for companies or individuals. Plastic and Conserve produce respectively components for the car industry and packaging for preserving agricultural and food products. PF1/PF2 and PM are three call centres, created by Banque, within the framework of rationalizing working time in its branches (by outsourcing telephone work). SI provides consultancy services to companies and sends out its IT experts. The way in which they each organize work varies greatly. At Conserve and Plastic, there is shift work. In the call centres, there are overlapping and rotating working hours. For some SI employees, working time and organization depend on the client for whom they are working. At SI – as in the call centres – work is carried out at a distance from colleagues and, therefore, requires coordination with intermediaries (at SI, with the technical assistant or head of project, and at Banque, with tele-assistants and sales staff in the branches).

Another feature of our sample is that – apart from the call centres, which are decentralized services of a banking group – we are dealing with small structures, even if some of them are controlled by a major company. They experience the traditional difficulties of small and medium-sized companies, especially regarding their restricted situation in the sector (dependence on a partner up or downstream and attachment to the local fabric, etc.), which leaves little room for manoeuvre and exposes them greatly to competition and economic setbacks. The companies that were analysed have existed for varying lengths of time, and their markets and corporate activities are more or less dynamic: growth for Banque, stability for Plastic, maturity and even decline for Conserve. SI's situation is more complicated because of the highly cyclical nature of IT services. The staff of each company were also varied: on the one hand, low-skilled employees and a gendered distribution of positions (Plastic and Conserve) and, on the other, higher-skilled staff in services (SI and Banque). In our sample, women were present, above all, in banking, but less so in industry, where they occupy the most insecure jobs. At SI, employees are mainly young men with diplomas (up to baccalaureate + 5 years of study), mostly at the beginning of their careers, whereas at Conserve, production staff were older and often at the end of their careers (with many between 45 and 55 years old).

Note: [1]Fictitious names are used when presenting interview data from the four companies.

7.2 IMPERFECT BARGAINING CONDITIONS

Both institutionalized representation of employees' interests (trade union freedom) and minimum industrial relations regulation (normative system, which provides a framework for disputes and their regulation) are important components of decent work. France has already complied with this twofold imperative for a long time – at least in legal terms. However, in many areas – especially as far as small companies are concerned – actual labour relations are not in line with the legislation, notably because trade unions are absent. Relatively recent institutional innovations, e.g. the "mandating" mechanism,[3] have definitely contributed to improving regulation. But there is still a big gap between practice and legal rules: for example, negotiations often become informal and individual arrangements often take priority over collective agreements.

Our survey highlights some salient features of the shortcomings that still have to be overcome in order to achieve a social dialogue that fully involves all the stakeholders concerned by the 35-hour week. It is true that company-level bargaining is not traditional in French industrial relations. Until the 1980s, some observers had noted that when it occurs officially, it is more like a kind of protest and non-dialogue than real discussion leading to reciprocal compromises (Morel, 1981). The trend towards decentralized collective bargaining, which started in the mid-1980s, changed the situation somewhat. The Aubry laws greatly encouraged social actors to negotiate at the level of companies and establishments, which revealed difficulties in producing satisfactory forms of regulation for all the actors concerned. The negotiating conditions in the establishments covered by our survey are outlined in table 7.1.

---

[3] The "mandating" mechanism was rendered legal by Aubry I and makes it possible for an employee who is not a union member and who is willing to be mandated by a representative trade union (Confédération Générale du Travail (CGT), Confédération Française Démocratique du Travail (CFDT), Confédération Française des Travailleurs Chrétiens (CFTC), Confédération Général des Cadres (CGC) or Force Ouvrière (FO), to sign a company agreement with the employer. Sixty-four per cent of Aubry I agreements were ratified using this type of procedure.

Table 7.1 Negotiating conditions in the establishments covered by the survey

	Date of the Aubry II agreement	Actor who initiated the process	Collective agreement sector	Reasons referred to for "late" entry into negotiations	Management's partner[1]	Form of ratification	Problematic points of the negotiations	Employees concerned	Monitoring of the agreement
Plastic	02/2002	Company management	Plastics	Risks of organizational destabilization	CFDT (staff rep)	Referendum	Possibility of the shift system being jeopardized	All	None
PF1 PF2 PM	09/2000	Company management	Banking	Cost of switching to the 35-hour week; Lack of stability of sector agreement	CGT and CFDT (union reps.)	Negotiation with the unions	Working, pay and career development conditions	Tele-advisors, supervisors, tele-assistants	None
Conserve	06/2001 and adoption of amendment in 06/2002	Group – and then company – management	Metal industry in Finistère	Time necessary for negotiation of agreement at level of the group	CFDT (staff rep.)	Referendum	Conditions of variable working time and number of "reduction of working time" (RWT) days obtained in compensation	Manual workers and clerical workers	Monitoring commission
SI	10/2001 and an amendment in 11/2002	Company management	Syntec (IT and consultancy, etc.)	Company's economic difficulties	CGT (union rep.) and CFE-CGC (mandate)	Referendum	Relationship between reduction of working time and periods between contracts	All	Monitoring commission which is not very dynamic

[1] Translator's note: staff representative = délégué du personnel; union representative = délégué syndical; mandate – see footnote 3 above.

7.2.1   Negotiations on the employers' initiative

Our first observation is a traditional one, namely that in all the companies we studied, employers initiated negotiations, whether at the enterprise or overall group level; in the latter case implementing their decisions throughout the companies they own. This situation is not surprising, as it is in line with predominant practice in France regarding negotiations on working time and other topics (pay and qualifications, etc.). It can be explained by the fact that French trade unions do not have a management culture and are rarely equipped for taking initiatives in the area of organizational reform, and also because unions are weak or even virtually absent from companies, as was, broadly speaking, the case in our survey.

When we asked a trade union member who had been the main partner during the introduction of the 35-hour week in one of the companies in our sample which union he was a member of, he was unable to answer. Although one cannot generalize, this anecdote says much about the French paradox concerning negotiations on the 35-hour week. On the one hand, the State invited companies to carry out decentralized negotiations, while on the other, trade unions did not have enough representatives and skills to be able to initiate them – they were thus sometimes reduced to the simple formality of accepting choices made by management. It is, therefore, not surprising that in order to validate new working time standards, three of the four companies opted for a referendum, rather than an agreement.

7.2.2   Negotiations with numerous constraints

Another observation is that, in all the cases we analysed, the companies concerned started negotiations both late and reluctantly, with the feeling that they were doing so in a situation riddled with numerous constraints, whether economic (the cost of reducing working time), organizational (the effect on productivity and work organization) or linked to agreements (combining rules which had been negotiated or were in the process of being negotiated at sector level). First, economic constraints: for reasons related to the general situation, which was hardly favourable, or to their specific situation (the development of a new activity), all our companies were on a "knife edge" – at least according to the people we spoke to. Thus, in all cases, management felt that the obligation to switch to the 35-hour week was particularly dangerous, as they had to deal with a relatively depressed economic situation. Even though they did not have all the accounting tools they needed in order to optimize their decision, they worked out new time arrangements on the basis of economic considerations – they refused to award too big a quota of "reduction of working time days"[4] (henceforth RWT days) in order to avoid falling below the break-even point, and introduced a system of variable working time in order to avoid using such expensive measures as short-time working, etc.

Organizational constraints – or at least as seen by management – also influenced decisions. Companies procrastinated regarding collective bargaining on the 35-hour week because they anticipated a series of major difficulties, such as having to manage employees working on the same site but with very different statuses, as some were already working according to measures introduced by the Robien and Aubry I laws (see box 7.1), some were working 4 days and others 5, some were part-time and others agency workers. However, other companies were able to turn constraints into opportunities, such as at Plastic, where the 35-hour week was used to negotiate – or at least undertake – both reform of working time and reorganization of work with the aim, among others, of improving quality procedures, developing multiskilling and reducing the number of levels of management.

Finally, one should not underestimate the role of what was seen by company-level actors as constraints related to collective agreements, i.e., framework directives coming from the parent company or sectoral-level agreements. From this point of view, the case of the bank that manages three call centres is particularly interesting. Sectoral-level bargaining had been marked by many twists and turns, and especially by the challenging of the 4 January 1999 agreement (Aubry I) by the unions that had not signed it (CGT, CFDT, FO and CFTC),[5] which explains why the company started negotiations quite late. What is particularly interesting is that there is no automatic relationship between the sector and the company. It very quickly becomes clear that in the context of standards which have been negotiated by sectoral-level employer and employee organizations, local actors put a set of issues on the bargaining table whose implications go beyond the narrow field of working time. The first is inseparable from the creation in December 2001 of the first call centre for "diverted incoming calls".[6] Unions were originally not in favour of this initiative because of the risks that the work might be very strenuous. The issue of work pace is still at the heart of collective bargaining on the organization and reduction of working time. Unions object to the

---

[4] Most agreements provide for a reduction of the number of working days, only some of which can be chosen by employees.

[5] Confédération Générale du Travail, Confédération Française Démocratique du Travail, Force Ouvrière and Confédération Française des Travailleurs Chrétiens. Only one union (the Syndicat National de la Banque et du Crédit (SNB-CGC)) signed this agreement.

[6] In this case, clients think they are calling their branch, but in fact their call is diverted to a tele-adviser, who is working in a call centre.

option of a 4-day week; however, the majority of employees who are given the choice of a 4- or 5-day week opt for it. Negotiations also make it possible to make decisions about breaks, recording conversations, calculating time and forms of remuneration. Career development is also on the agenda. The agreement limits time in call centres to between 18 and 36 months – or up to 4 years, if employees so wish. This compromise hides union questioning about the job of tele-operator, as to whether it is a real occupation or an "interlude during a career".

7.2.3 Negotiating issues: Work rather than employment

The last observation brings us to a third common feature of regulating working time at company level. Even though it may seem that negotiations have had little impact on working conditions (attendance time, how time is calculated, and forms of remuneration), in fact, they – rather than jobs – have been at the heart of negotiations. One has to remember that the main aim of the Aubry laws was to stimulate job creation and – unlike in the 1970s – not to contribute to changing employees' working and living conditions. However, in fact, the latter issues were at the centre of discussions.

At Conserve, for example, management said they wanted to increase flexibility by using a new system of variable working hours, which would not only avoid using short-time working (work-sharing), but also loosen constraints imposed by existing rules concerning prior notice required before changes in work schedules. Employees, however, wanted to have 23 RWT days. Calculations of the real impact of switching to the 35-hour week (which notably incorporates breaks) led to a possible reduction of only 9 days. On this basis, 70 per cent of employees rejected the proposed agreement. Management then agreed to add an extra day off. In all, increased flexibility (annualization with individual monitoring of hours worked) led to 10 RWT days, half of which could be freely chosen by employees. Such transactions clearly not only involve opposition between management and employees, but can also lead to disagreement among employees.

Focusing on working conditions – not on employment – also manifests itself in a concern often expressed by employees, namely their attachment to relative stability of compromises concerning their working hours. At Plastic, for example, management used a firm of consultants to propose various scenarios regarding the switch to the 35-hour week. In the end, they came up with two proposals: either introducing a system of five alternating shifts or opting for a number of RWT days. During the referendum, employees chose the latter proposal. The reason for this is simple: those who work day shifts do not want to change their work schedules, whereas those who work nights and weekends do not want to lose their financial benefits. On this basis, an agreement was concluded and ratified with a union representative. A reduction of 30 minutes per day was awarded to administrative staff and 20 minutes to production staff. The former also have 10 RWT days per annum, while the latter have 12 days. The involvement of the trade union representative served, above all, to legalize the process, because he played a very discreet role in the discussions.[7]

To conclude on the issue of negotiations, we should note the weak impact of the adoption of the 35-hour week on the industrial relations dynamic of all the companies. This is significant, given that one of the parallel objectives of Aubry I was to render industrial relations more dynamic by making financial incentives for companies depend on reaching a company-level agreement. Aubry II did not keep this measure. In any case, the results regarding our companies are somewhat ambiguous, given that, on the one hand, negotiations were either of a purely formal nature or mobilized few people and, on the other hand, both commissions, which were created at Conserve and SI to monitor the agreements, only play a minor role in the life of these companies. The only outcome was the signing of an additional clause at SI – at the request of the CGT representative – aimed at clarifying the situation of executives and explicitly designating those who are considered to be autonomous, and at Conserve aimed at fighting absenteeism by reducing RWT days.

In short, despite a legal framework that is quite favourable from an industrial relations point of view to promoting decent working time, it has to be noted that practice has not always been in line with the letter and spirit of the Aubry laws. This deficit is particularly marked in the case of our companies, as they started negotiating late. It is, therefore, possible to put forward the hypothesis that the relative dynamism of negotiations observed in the wake of the Aubry laws – at both sector and company levels – does not prejudge the "decent" nature of the negotiated regulations that result.

7.3   FROM RULES TO PRACTICE

Is it possible to reconcile the search for productive efficiency and decent working time in actual working practice? In order to assess the degree of cohesion between these notions – and even the gap which can exist between them – in companies that have signed Aubry II agreements, we have chosen two approaches: first, analysis of the content of the organizational compromises that were made at the time of negotiating agreements on the 35-hour week, and then the adjustments

---

[7] In this company, we recorded the greatest criticisms by employees – especially manual workers – of the effects of the switch to the 35-hour week on pay. In all the companies, bargaining led, at best, to a pay freeze and, at worst, to lower pay resulting from less overtime.

that were rendered necessary after a year of experimenting with these rules; and second, analysis of management methods and "management measures"[8] that were implemented in order to regulate the 35-hour week and that also influence employees' working conditions.

7.3.1 Compromises and adjustments of standards, negotiated in conditions of economic uncertainty

At the beginning of this study, we hypothesized that the procrastination of companies that did not introduce the 35-hour week before it was legally imposed – and, therefore, did not apply for financial incentives – can be explained by the absence of an "associated project for change", which could have harmoniously combined the various components of decent working time: work and production organization, productive efficiency and working and living conditions. These companies' concern was rather to benefit economically in one way or another – in terms of flexibility or productivity – from a social constraint, if only to limit its costs. We observed this logic in three of the companies in our sample, which did not have an *ex-ante* or concomitant project. The one exception to this rule was Banque, whose project was to make the reduction of working time coincide with a new strategy (the agreement came at the same time as – and in support of – the large-scale introduction of a new service activity). All three companies that did not link bargaining on the 35-hour week to an economic project have little market power for various reasons: they are small in mature markets, which are highly competitive; they are service providers or subcontractors in areas in which their clients have significant negotiating power; and they are highly exposed to short-term risks. In short, all three have little control over their medium- and long-term development policies. Thus they can be compared with small companies, which experience similar difficulties (Charpentier and Lepley, 2003, p. 100): "the ability of companies to anticipate the 35-hour week and draw up a project associated with the reduction of working time is greater if they are in a phase of growth and/or have significant market power. The main discriminating variable in this context is not so much company size as their strategic situation."

There is no doubt that the search for productive flexibility has become – in this context and for all four of our companies – a shared regulating ideal. As a subcontractor in the car industry, Plastic has to manage very unpredictable flows of corporate activity. Peaks are absorbed in a system that is already

---

[8] In line with the work of Berry (1983) and Pezet (2004), we are interested in social "nanotechnology" and "invisible technology", in order to "reveal effects, other than those related to their supposed efficiency and performance".

organized on the basis of continuous production by using temporary agency staff. At Conserve, annualized working time replaced the old system of variable working hours. This makes it possible to be more in line with flows of corporate activity by avoiding short-time working in periods of low production and extending work to Saturdays in periods of high production. At SI (staff sent out to work in client companies' offices), employees depend on clients' pace of work. Closures imposed by clients and periods in between contracts constitute expensive slack time. In order to absorb such losses, the company has placed 50 per cent of RWT days during such slack periods. As far as Banque is concerned, the search for flexibility operates on the basis of the two-way link-up between the branch (an increase of 13 per cent in sales and marketing time freed up) and the call centres, which take on board clients' calls, using standardized treatment of their requests and longer opening hours.

A year later, the economic situation had deteriorated: 2003 was disastrous for Conserve because of competition and also because of the heat wave, which led to a huge drop in vegetable production. Short-time working and transfers of staff between two sites were organized and employees were forced to take annual leave and RWT days. Both Plastic and SI suffered a great deal in 2003 – the former from clients' increased demands and the latter from significantly reduced corporate activity in markets for IT services (many corporate customers reduced their budgets). These difficulties, which were partly short term, contributed to maintaining or even reinforcing demands in terms of productivity and, in the case of SI, led to reducing the workforce.

More than ever before – and given this particularly depressed economic situation – working time seems to have become a major adjustment variable for adapting the time when people are present to variations in corporate activity. With the Aubry II agreements, the regulation of RWT days has gradually been introduced as a tool for optimizing work flows. Thus, at Conserve, Plastic and SI, such specific days off, which were sometimes freely chosen by employees during the first year of implementing Aubry II, are increasingly regulated by management. They are now used to absorb periods of short-time working, deal with peaks of activity and absorb periods of inactivity between contracts. With the Aubry II agreements, sources of flexibility also extend to training periods. At Plastic, for example, a training programme has been developed to help operators to carry out new functions in the context of the ongoing reorganization, but the training has been organized entirely outside working time, because of the requirements of continuous production. Time in training is paid as additional hours, not as overtime, so there is little incentive for employees to attend (absenteeism is as high as 40 per cent). The 35-hour week led to recruiting ten young technicians at Conserve, but also, when they arrived, to an abrupt end to training for assembly line operators. Finally, it should be noted that more or less agreed "clandestine" forms of flexibility emerge here and there: thus at SI, time which overruns working hours is not billed, but leads to informal arrangements between IT engineers and client companies. It is not rare to hear some administrative staff or line managers in more traditional industrial activities (notably at Plastic) talk about agreed, uncounted time, which overruns allotted working time, in order to finish urgent work. Moreover, such company practices are part of management measures and methods which consecrate the search for productive efficiency.

7.3.2 Managerial logic and management measures as sources of tension for employees

Following Pezet (2004, p. 2), we use the term "management measure" "because it covers the idea of an arrangement and assemblage of techniques and also of ideals and positions (for example, efficiency and performance), social customs and power games". We examine each of the four components of such arrangements: the degree of subjugation of all types of time to productive time; forms of control; the measurement of time; and planning functions.

These arrangements seem specific and determined by the nature of the productive activities involved: thus in traditional industries with continuous or semi-continuous production (Plastic and Conserve), individual working time is more subjected to productive time (functioning of machinery), to the detriment of social time (elimination of idle time and collective breaks). Such pressure on time is evident at several levels: breaks taken in turn by one-third of employees at a time and the rule of mutual replacement for shift workers; time for passing instructions on to the next shift cut by a half for assembly line mechanics and technicians at Conserve. At Plastic, control by the immediate hierarchy has been tightened (even including more authoritarian regulation of breaks for smoking); administrative staff say they are working as much in less time and those in charge of work schedules say that coordinating all the various kinds of absence (sick leave, annual leave and RWT days, etc.) has become more complicated. In both companies, the social climate has deteriorated: a high rate of absenteeism and an increase in the number of those declared unfit for work at Conserve; a drop in pay because of the abolition of overtime, lower productivity and increasing absenteeism at Plastic. All these factors led the company to introduce a new kind of work organization and management that promotes employees' initiative (reduced management structures and control by results).

However, the 35-hour week does not seem to have led to the same tensions in companies where control by results prevails. At SI, controlling daily working time does not make sense as the client company's time predominates, rather than that of one's own company. Nevertheless, monitoring time is of strategic importance, as the notion of "person-days" is the measurement used for billing the service provided. Monitoring one's own time is at the heart of assessing individual performance and employees who invest a great deal in their career and are mostly fairly indifferent to the 35-hour week (where necessary, when time is overrun, informal arrangements with the client prevail). In the call centres, employees monitor themselves at their work station when they log in.[9] Time also structures their direct relationship with clients, as does the position of each person in the team. Time and performance measurements are closely linked and subjected to new rules: monitoring one's own working time is now guided by national standards (which are always displayed in the call centre) as the call centres are interconnected. This makes it possible to regulate calls centrally and adjust the workload of tele-advisers (it is also possible to divert calls to the other call centres if there is a problem). However, there is still also more traditional control via direct supervision; supervisors monitor conversations in real time, which is used to determine pay, and they are also responsible for daily management of their team on the basis of each person's performance in terms of time (they also train tele-advisers, solve problems between tele-advisers and clients, and schedule break times).

Within a year, planning time and workloads became essential functions in three of the companies in our sample. They have generally been given to line managers, who are not necessarily well prepared or equipped to carry them out with ease. Thus, at Banque, planners have become central in the call centres, where work is organized on the basis of overlapping and rotating working hours. They plan shifts on the basis of the relationship between the volume of calls and resources of the call centre. At Plastic, combining freely chosen RWT days with annual leave and sick leave made management of absences too complicated. At the same time, the unpredictable nature of orders makes the task of planning workloads more complicated for line managers, who complain of increased stress.

Adjustments have been made since (much more restricted choice of RWT days for employees and training organized outside working time), which are not unanimously supported. Such adjustments have led to monitoring tools: in industries with continuous and semi-continuous production, clocking in is still the rule; however, SI has innovated – it has perfected a system of "activity reports", which are used to count the number of hours

---

[9] The internal clock of tele-advisers' computers makes it possible to record employees' presence (in terms of both timing and number of hours) and also the length of calls, the time taken transcribing them, training and breaks, etc.

worked by engineers out on jobs for clients. The engineers mark the number of hours they have worked on the report, as well as the type of service provided: before paying, clients ask for the report of the number of hours devoted to the particular service – signed by the person in charge – as well as the bill. Unlike both of the previous cases, at SI, client companies plan time and deal with tensions, not the line managers. They also make informal arrangements to resolve disputes when planned time budgets are overrun.

7.3.3 The contingent nature of decent working time practices and patterns

On completing this study of company practices, we must emphasize the extent to which they remain contingent. We have shown how a law (in this case, Aubry II), which *a priori* is designed to promote certain aspects of decent working time, is taken on board in very different ways, and thus leads to company agreements, management measures and working conditions that may be more or less "decent" in reality. Even though the companies in our sample have little market power and are in a fragile state because of the particularly depressed economic situation, they do not interpret their difficulties in the same way.

Thus interviews showed that none of the three most fragile companies identified switching to the 35-hour week as being the direct cause of their difficulties. However – and this phenomenon had already been identified in previous surveys – greater economic constraints and the management of the 35-hour week in client companies increase pressure on firms that are suppliers and subcontractors. This is especially clear at Plastic, which observed a strategy of increasing some in-house activities and relocating others (which management attributed to the 35-hour week). Pressure is clearly of a very different kind in a company like Banque, which is also indirectly experiencing the consequences of the 35-hour week in the changing behaviour of its clients, who are themselves mainly employees and now have more free time. This can even lead to increasing margins for organizational manoeuvre given that clients can now adapt more easily.

Nor do the same causes produce the same effects. Thus the negative impact of the particular ways in which the 35-hour week was implemented, which has been identified here and there (reduced motivation, increased absenteeism and work accidents, increased proportion of products which do not comply with standards, etc.), as well as reduced performance in relation to competition, led one of our companies (Plastic) to adopt a plan for a proactive reorganization; this strategy was aimed at reducing the number of hierarchical levels and giving operators more autonomy, as well as training and incentives in order to be more productive (the introduction of partly variable pay linked to team and quality performance). Thus the 35-hour week imposed "with constraints" has, in this case, resulted in organizational learning (Argyris and Schön, 1978), which encouraged the company to make the most of it and explore the possibility of more ambitious organizational changes.

Finally, an analysis of company practices makes it possible to identify more or less optimal patterns of decent working time. Thus in services, management measures that combine time management, performance management and career development management seem to be a source of satisfaction for employees; in contrast, in traditional industries with continuous or semi-continuous production, where the margins for manoeuvre are the smallest, combinations of time management, tightened control and the lack of career development prospects are sources of tension. It was on the basis of this implicit observation – and in order to escape this negative spiral – that Plastic decided to embark upon a reorganization that makes it possible to incorporate time optimization within a management system that is more favourable to developing employees' skills, encouraging them to take on responsibility, and promoting team performance. However, employees' subjective preferences regarding working time are difficult to interpret, and understanding them requires an appropriate survey methodology and an analysis of the results, which we now present.

7.4   SUBJECTIVE WORKING TIME PREFERENCES: A COMPLEX INTERPRETATION

Face-to-face interviews and questionnaires made it possible to collect the opinions of employees in all four companies. This was done in two phases – the first after the signing of the agreements and the second a year later, thus making it possible to observe any changes made to the agreements, as well as medium-term effects. Without claiming to be representative, the survey involved more than 200 people in service companies in urban areas and industrial companies in rural areas. It therefore provides a relatively diversified and significant picture of the effects of Aubry II on working time (box 7.3). An initial observation can be made: the perception of working time depends greatly on the organization of production, strategic choices and the contents of the negotiated agreement – therefore each company is a specific case. Nevertheless, the study suggests a more common reflection about the perception employees have of the factors of decent working time, on the one hand, and on the other, of some of the compromises that the reduction of working time can imply.

Box 7.3   Structure of the sample and variables of decent
           working time

Analysis of results focuses on the second phase of the survey, for which there were
responses from 213 employees in four companies (six establishments). In order to
analyse the answers statistically, weighting was used, which makes it possible to find
in each company distributions by gender, age and qualifications that are similar to
those of the populations of the different establishments and which also gives equal
importance to each company. The population of the weighted sample was 54 per
cent male, which is very close to the proportion of men in the economically active
population in France. However, the weighted sample somewhat overrepresents the
extremes concerning the situation observed in the economically active population,
whether in terms of age:

	Percentage
Under 29 years	35
30–49 years	43
50 years and above	22

or in terms of socio-occupational categories:

Manual workers	39
Clerical workers	23
Technicians and supervisors	10
Executives	28

Variables of employees' perception of time:

- impression of doing the same work in less time (since the agreement on the
  reduction of working time);

- adapting the workload to the reduction of working time;

- recuperating from fatigue;

- freedom to take breaks;

- free choice of using RWT days;

- degree of control of working time by line managers;

- possibility of having prior knowledge of one's work schedules;

- commuting time.

7.4.1 Perceptions of working time in the four companies: A situational perspective

The interviews carried out in each company make it possible to identify four types of employee perceptions regarding working time.

1. *Unchanged time.* At Plastic – where the agreement reduced daily working time by 20 minutes – operators did not notice any real change. During the first phase of interviews, time pressure was hardly discernible, whereas a year later, it was referred to by line managers, who have to deal directly with clients' demands, but operators do not seem to suffer from this pressure. Even though the latter have to work on several machines, instead of only one, they say that the 35-hour week has hardly changed their daily work. Demotivation is a good way to describe manual workers' reactions, resulting from a pay freeze and uncertain career development prospects. "Unchanged time" thus also reflects the effects of inertia: demotivation and a lack of career prospects have led to manual workers' reluctance to become involved in the new organizational and training system proposed by management.

2. *Compressed time.* At Conserve, where daily working time has not changed, perceptions of time have crystallized around tensions created by replacing absent staff. Moving from one work station to another (an operator can, for example, monitor flows and intervene on two lines at a time) increases the fatigue of this firm's employees, whose average age is high. This phenomenon is greater because breaks are now staggered. As breaks are now taken in small groups, they no longer allow recuperation or chatting with colleagues, and are even sources of new forms of tension. "Compressed time" involves keeping an eye on one's watch, in order not to miss out on breaks, and has also increased the pace of work. Employees do not put this process down to the reduction of working time, but rather to new production demands and a chronic lack of staff. Their feelings of discontent are related to the fact that the number of RWT days is not sufficient compensation for the imposed increases in productivity (multiskilling and staggered breaks).

3. *Incompressible time.* At SI, the effect of reducing working time is perceived in yet another way. The bone of contention also concerns the small number of RWT days (8 in all); however, the feeling of injustice is even greater, as it is impossible for engineers effectively to reduce their working time. There are two reasons for this "incompressible time": the prevalent in-house logic (small structure, climate of confidence, possibility of making arrangements

The French 35-hour week

with management, etc.), which means time is not calculated, and the desire of "colleagues" to show their personal investment in the company, by claiming not to know how many hours they really work. Thus the availability of SI's employees comes up against problems related to the availability of employees in some of the client companies, whose RWT days can be almost three times as many as those in force at SI.

4. *Freely chosen time*. In the call centres, the latitude that the majority of employees have for fixing their working week (4 or 5 days) and, above all, when they work (work is organized by relays of shifts throughout the day and on a rotating basis during a 6-day week) explains employees' relative satisfaction. However, "freely chosen time" should not mislead; worries crystallize elsewhere, for example concerning the lack of recruitment in a situation of increased workload, and the intensified work that could result. The latter is far from being perceived in an equally acute way by all employees. Those staff who come from the back office dread the pressure of time, whereas those who come from the front office recognize that they are under less pressure than when working in the branch itself – where clients are physically present, files pile up, and it is impossible to "divert" work elsewhere.

7.4.2 Aspects of decent working time

Besides this initial observation of the contingent nature of perceptions of time, is it possible to take the first steps towards a more general representation of decent working time? In order to answer this question, we put a direct question to each employee in our sample, namely, has the implementation of the agreements led to intensified work? The aim was not so much to obtain an objective measure of work intensification as to identify precisely how the situation is felt by employees. The hypothesis that we are testing is that the perception of work intensity is not formally the result of the impression of doing the same work in less time, but rather the result of a set of variables which confer greater or lesser "density" on working time. These variables constitute decisive parameters of decent working time.

Only one-third of those involved in the survey have the impression of doing the same work in less time since the implementation of the agreement (i.e., a year later). And, above all, when it does exist, this perception is generally not directly linked to the reduction of working time: 40 per cent of employees who say they are doing the same work in less time attribute this to the reduction of working time; therefore, in all, only 13 per cent think that the reduction in working time has led to work intensification. As we have already seen, this is very clearly the case of employees at Conserve, who suffer greatly from the pressure of the pace of work, but clearly link it to production demands and lack of staff. This result also reflects the limits of the effectiveness of reducing working time, as already emphasized in SI's case.

Given the difficulty of identifying work intensification, our approach sought to differentiate between what we called the heart of intensity (the impression of doing the same amount of work in less time) and how it is felt by employees. It is both the convergence and compatibility of a set of constraints that indicate an increase in the strenuous nature of work: only one-third of the population studied considers that the planning of the workload has been adapted well to the reduction of working time, and 40 per cent think that the latter makes it possible to recuperate better from work fatigue (the proportion is the same in both phases of the survey).

Assessments vary significantly between the different companies and thus diverge between employees at Plastic – where the reorganization that was embarked upon has not been completed (only 11 per cent of employees consider that the workload has been adapted well and 13 per cent say that they manage to recuperate from fatigue) – and those at Banque, where new activity has been planned precisely (the proportions are 57 per cent and 71 per cent respectively). Differing statuses partly explain the differing perceptions: manual workers were significantly more negative about both of these questions than clerical workers.

Commuting time between home and work also plays an important role – only 12 per cent of employees who live less than half an hour away from work say that planning is poorly adapted to the reduction of working time; 20 per cent of those who live between half an hour and an hour away say so; and 40 per cent of those who live over an hour away hold this opinion. Likewise, 88 per cent of those who live near their workplace think that the reduction in working time makes it possible to recuperate from work-related fatigue. The proportion drops as commuting time increases – only 40 per cent of those with more than an hour's commuting time are of the same opinion.

When seeking to summarize these perceptions, two central themes seem to play a structuring role. The first concerns the possibilities of recuperating from work-related fatigue by reducing working time. On the one hand, there are those who say they are able to recuperate more easily and for whom planning of the workload has often been adapted well to the reduction of working time (this is the case of the call centre employees). On the other hand, there are those who do not feel that they can recuperate better following the reduction of working time and who say that the latter has led to sacrificing breaks (typically employees at Conserve). The situation seems better for staff in both of the service companies in urban settings than for manual workers in industrial plants in the countryside.

The second theme concerns the degree of freedom and control of time. It contrasts those who can choose their RWT days freely and say they are not subjected to control of their working hours with those who feel an increased lack of control and difficulties in having prior notice of when they must work and who also cannot freely choose their RWT days. Such differences are again affected by the status of the respondents. For example, executives at SI have autonomy in their work. Paradoxically, in both of the companies in which negotiations on the reduction of working time were also used as an opportunity for reorganizing work, the feeling of time constraints is strongest (i.e., at Banque, where the agreement created the possibility of developing call centres, and at Plastic, which sought to reorganize work).

Thus the judgements that employees make about their working time do not just depend on the amount of time worked, but on a set of variables that constitute the perceived bases of decent working time in this case, namely: the freedom of having proper breaks and discussing matters with colleagues; the forms and degrees of control of working time; the ways in which the workload is adapted; the ability to recuperate from fatigue; and prior information about programming of working hours. These are all interrelated factors that determine employees' ability to take action within the time framework fixed by the agreements.

7.4.3 The conditions of decent working time

Employees' perceptions of decent working time can be broadened out to that of compromises, of which negotiations on working time are a part. Such perceptions probably play a role in the actual development of such compromises. Our introductory comments show that the latter have significantly changed over time: from seeking win-win agreements, based on a harmonious relationship between corporate performance, employment and employees' well-being, to more bitter and unstable compromises in which freed-up time is increasingly subject to productive constraints, if it is not quite simply jeopardized. Our study, which is set in a twofold context – on the one hand, an unfavourable economic situation and, on the other, political delegitimization of the Aubry laws – highlights certain key factors of imbalance in the terms of this exchange and, at the same time, poses some possible conditions for implementing decent working time.

7.4.4 Decent working time and decent pay

Responses to the questionnaire highlight a clear judgement: three-quarters of the employees in our sample put life outside work at the top of the list of improvements resulting from the reduction of working time. This point is fundamental, because it explains that, in spite of deteriorating working conditions referred to above, the reduction of working time continues to be acclaimed by the great majority of employees. Nevertheless, one factor tempers this significant result – shorter working time has led to a drop in income for a quarter of those surveyed. At Plastic, as many as half of the employees have lost out financially. In all the sites, one-third of all women employees estimate that their pay has dropped compared with only one-sixth of men. One-third of manual workers and technicians say the same thing, compared with one-sixth of executives and clerical workers. Those categories of employees who consider that they have lost out financially more than others are also those who are the least inclined to say that their quality of life has improved: 61 per cent of women – compared with 81 per cent of men – put life outside work at the top of improvements resulting from the reduction of working time.[10] In a similar manner, employees in the service sector who live more than an hour away from their workplace are also less likely (64 per cent) than those with shorter commuting times to put life outside work at the top of the list of improvements. In other words, insufficient pay, on the one hand, and commuting time, on the other, are both elements that temper improvements in life outside work. Manual workers at Plastic, who have even calculated exactly how much they have lost financially because of the loss of overtime (between 20 per cent and 30 per cent of previous pay), describe their situation clearly – free time without financial means is hardly attractive. As they mainly do home building and repair work, free time "without money" is synonymous with lost time. It should be said that this point of view is not that of the majority, but it identifies definite limits to compromises concerning working time, especially for manual workers.

7.4.5 Decent working time and staff cohesion

The second factor of imbalance is related to certain tensions among the staff. This is clear in the case of Conserve, where employees' disappointment with the reduction of working time was increased by a feeling of inequality. During the referendum on the establishment's agreement, solidarity that developed during the strike did not continue: "at the beginning, we fought for the same thing" and "some got more compensation (13 RWT days, financial compensation and additional recruitment for mechanics), but we, 'minor

---

[10] Studies by DARES also show that life outside work is the item that is most acclaimed by employees when they are asked to put the positive effects of the reduction of working time in order of preference. However, these studies conclude that women are generally more satisfied than men. This result differs from ours because of the structure of our population, which includes few women executives, whereas DARES's surveys show that executives in general, and women executives in particular, are those who gained the most, in terms of declared satisfaction, from switching to the 35-hour week.

figures', got less (operators only have 10 RWT days)". As a result of Aubry II, supervisors at Conserve were promoted to executive grade. Another symptomatic case is the differing situations of production, administrative and temporary agency workers at Plastic. The first group benefited from a greater range of tasks; the second was subjected to a cut in income; and the third was quite simply left out of the agreement. At Plastic and SI, another division emerged – between those employees who are in direct contact with clients and suppliers and the rest of the staff. The former – production quality control staff, sales and marketing staff and those who are sent out to work for other companies – mention more often than the latter increased difficulties in being able to work efficiently because of an increased lack of synchronization between their working hours and those of their external contacts.

7.4.6 Decent working time and stable rules

Perceptible tensions concerning the 35-hour week are greater today, as the reduction of working time can be negotiated with infinitely variable compromises. In small companies that have introduced a reduction of weekly working time, the switch to the 35-hour week has been relatively neutral in terms of its effects, provided they have been able to quickly stabilize their new way of operating and impose rules that have been negotiated – sometimes with difficulty – but have become accepted benchmarks. This has not been the case as far as the four companies analysed. They have been subjected much more than others to the whims of the market and competitive pressures and have, therefore, not been able to reach such a balanced state of affairs. The interviews and results of the questionnaires show this very clearly. Employees say they don't appreciate situations where a social advantage (the 35-hour week) – which they did not necessarily seek out, but to which most are now strongly attached – is offset by management-related factors, over which they have no control and which can also change over time. This could explain the preference – which *a priori* might appear to be a paradoxical one – that some of them have for a real reduction of weekly hours rather than RWT days, over which they feel they have less and less control.

7.5 CONCLUSION

The results of our survey emphasize a surprising feature of the laws on the 35-hour week. A major reduction of working time was not desired by companies because of the constraints involved, nor did it correspond with a strong aspiration among employees, who saw it also as a threat regarding pay, intensified work and worsened working conditions. However, the current proposed legislation aimed at relaxing the Aubry laws has led to hostile reactions from employees and has been less than enthusiastically welcomed by employers. This situation leads us to draw three main conclusions.

First, it confirms that the introduction of agreements on the organization and reduction of working time involves prior collective bargaining, which, by definition, can at best lead to a satisfactory compromise for all actors concerned. And even when the compromise is contested by management or employees, it is most often only marginally changed. But a return to the previous situation is rarely desired, because of the cost – in both financial and human terms – of the changes that would be involved. The equilibrium made possible by negotiations is thus, most often, preferable to a head-on challenge of the initial compromise.

Second, and following on from the first remark, changes introduced as a result of a new way of organizing time concern many aspects of the notion of "decent working time", some of which are improved (such as increased free time for employees) while others may deteriorate (such as intensified work and a relative worsening of pay conditions). Therefore an overall assessment of the agreements cannot be reduced, as was traditionally the case, to an appraisal of observed advantages and disadvantages for the different categories of actors involved. It is also the result of individual perceptions, which themselves are compromises created by each person depending on their personal characteristics and on changes made to the various components of working time. One thus realizes with Aubry II that previous assessments of measures concerning the organization and reduction of working time implicitly contrasted the employees' point of view with that of the company, as represented by its management and executives. However, today there is a new situation, because executives themselves are concerned by the reduction of working time. This makes it easier to understand why it is so difficult to make a normative judgement of the impact of the Aubry laws, because the latter have meant that the actors concerned – executives, manual workers and clerical workers – have had to choose between pressures that are sometimes of a contradictory nature (e.g., free time, constraints of corporate activity, and intensified work). As such choice is also related to individual constructions, combining the working, family and social spheres for each person, it becomes clear that employees prefer the *status quo* and have a pronounced loathing for change and uncertainty. In this context, one can see that challenges to the 35-hour week run the risk of being seen as coming only from employers, and not including those – of whom there are many both in big and small companies, as our own surveys showed – who prefer the current compromise to an improbable renegotiation of the organization of working time. This is perhaps also the opportunity for us to point out that the idea of the stability of the patterns that have been produced by negotiated compromises can also be an aspect of the notion of "decent working time".

Third, and more generally, new patterns of the organization of working time that have resulted from negotiations on the 35-hour week also reflect a fundamental change in individuals' perceptions of what "decent working time" would mean for them, because this notion is, as we have seen, an essentially subjective and contingent one, and is deeply affected by the mental images that structure employees' perceptions. It should be emphasized that even if the principle of annualization of working time, which was consecrated by the Aubry laws, remains a controversial issue for unions, it is nevertheless something that exists and that individuals at work are gradually learning to come to terms with. Exchanging free time for flexibility is now too long-standing and commonplace to lead to the same kind of opposition as at the beginning of the 1980s, when the first measures breaking with the principles introduced by the 1936 laws were introduced. The stacks of legal derogations which have been introduced since the 1982 ordinance on the 39-hour week find a kind of logical outcome in the Aubry laws: collective working hours (i.e. the same for everyone), assessed on a weekly basis, have now been replaced by other criteria that are based on an annual standard and are, above all, increasingly varied. Initial texts contributed to developing flexibility by emphasizing the differences between the situation of stable employees and that of those with insecure jobs. It would seem that the new segmentations, which are reinforced by the introduction of the 35-hour week, now affect even core employees, depending on the economic situation of their companies and also on the different categories of employees within the same company – i.e., executives and non-executives, manual workers and clerical workers, and also according to age and personal situation, etc. Without always saying so explicitly, those who defend the Aubry laws seek to limit this trend, which these laws have nevertheless accentuated, towards even more individualized management of work relationships and a more contractual and bilateral approach to employment relationships.

References

Argyris, C.; Schön, A. 1978. *Organizational learning: A theory of action perspective* (Reading, MA, Addison-Wesley Publishing).

Berry, M. 1983. "Une technologie invisible? L'impact des instruments de gestion sur l'évolution des systèmes humains" (CRG Ecole Polytechnique, non publié).

Commissariat Général du Plan. 2001. *Réduction du temps de travail: Les enseignements de l'observation* (Paris, La Documentation Française).

Charpentier, P.; Lepley, B. 2003. "Développement et dialogue social: les TPE face aux 35 heures", DARES, document d'étude No. 65.

DARES. 2003. *Pilotage du changement, gestion des temps et action collective: Les incidences de la loi Aubry II sur l'organization* (Paris, DARES).

Dayan, J.L. 2002. *35 heures, des ambitions aux réalités* (Paris, La Découverte).

IRES. 2003. "La réduction du temps de travail: négociations et transformations des normes", in *La Revue de l'IRES*, Special issue coordinated by F. Michon, Vol. 2, No. 42.

Lallement, M. 2003. *Temps, travail et modes de vie* (Paris, PUF).

Loos-Baroin, J. 2000a. "La loi Aubry I: Contrainte ou opportunité pour les entreprises?", in Groupement d'Etudes Interdisciplinaires sur les Sciences du Travail, *Temps de travail et temps de vie* (Strasbourg, Presses Universitaires de Strasbourg).

—. 2000b. "35 heures: Le triangle d'or de la performance au niveau des enterprises", in *Revue Française de Gestion*, No. 128, mars–avril–mai.

Messenger, J.C. (ed.). 2004. *Working time and workers' preferences in industrialized countries: Finding the balance* (London and New York, Routledge).

Morel, C. 1981. *La grève froide* (Paris, éditions d'organization).

Pezet, A. 2004. "Comment les dispositifs de gestion créent des mondes singuliers, le cas de l'investissement" (Université de Marne la Vallée, mimeo).

Pham, H. 2002. "Les modalités de passage à 35 heures en 2000", in *Premières informations, premières synthèses*, DARES, février, No. 06.

OVEREMPLOYMENT IN THE UNITED STATES: WHICH WORKERS ARE WILLING TO REDUCE THEIR WORK-HOURS AND INCOME[1]?

8

*Lonnie Golden**

8.1 INTRODUCTION

Achieving "decent working time" requires that employees have at least some discretion, if not control, over the duration of their work-hours, in order to close or eliminate gaps between their actual and preferred working hours. If hours worked are longer than those preferred by a worker, other aspects of decent working time may be undermined as well – if the additional hours lead to health risks associated with overwork, diminished per hour productivity, greater time conflict with executing family responsibilities and such imbalances fall relatively more heavily on one gender. In the United States, there is only a smattering of information concerning how many, which and by how much workers may be employed beyond their preferred number of work-hours. By their nature, hours preferences are not directly observable, precise or stable, and may be influenced by constraints, either real or perceived. Nevertheless, constraints in a given job or workplace or restrictions on individuals' choice of hours of work are widely acknowledged as a central feature of the labour market in many conventional economic studies of labour supply (e.g., Idson and Robbins, 1991; Dunn, 1996; Kaufman, 1999; Euwals and van Soest, 1999; Feather and Shaw, 2000; Altonji and Oldham, 2003; Böheim and Taylor, 2004; Hart, 2004). This chapter focuses on the state of "overemployment", defined as workers' inability to obtain reduced hours despite a willingness to proportionately sacrifice income.

* Penn State University, Abington College, Abington PA, USA 19001. Lmg5@psu.edu

[1] Acknowledgements: Alfred P. Sloan Foundation, Workplace, Workforce and Working Families for support, Grant #2004-5-32; Tesfayi Gebreselassie and Valen Costello for valuable research assistance and Eileen Appelbaum and Mark Montgomery for comments on preliminary segments of this research.

The May 2001 Supplement to the Current Population Survey (CPS) is the main data source because it queried United States households directly, for the first time since 1985, regarding a hypothetical choice between more income with more hours, fewer hours for less income or the same hours and income. Section 8.2 of this chapter generates estimates of the "rate of overemployment" in the United States workforce, which can be contrasted to previous estimates using identical instruments (Shank, 1986), different instruments or samples (e.g., Bell and Freeman, 1995; Kahn and Lang, 1995; Bond, 2003; Merola and Clarkberg, 2003; Reynolds, 2004), as well as to the volume or rate of overemployment observed in comparable countries (Fagan, 2001; Bielenski et al., 2002; Sousa-Poza and Henneberger, 2002; Tijdens, 2002; Merz, 2002; Stier and Lewin-Epstein, 2003; Böheim and Taylor, 2003). Consistent, accurate estimates of the level of over-employment have proven elusive, largely because they are highly sensitive to question wording and the range of options presented in surveys. Section 8.3 explores the potential theoretical reasons underlying observed changes in the rate of overemployment, including a dynamic process of endogenous preference formation. Section 8.4 – the crux of the chapter – uses the CPS data to establish empirically the determinants of overemployment according to workers' personal and job characteristics. The extent and actual concentrated locations of overemployment in the United States labour market should be used by policy-makers as a guide to better target legislative and regulatory reforms that would promote more decent working time. By facilitating more reduced-hours options for workers, this would indirectly help promote the decent working time attributes of healthier work, more family-friendly working conditions, greater equality between the genders and all those employed. Overemployment, no matter how common, represents a key, often neglected, threat to decent working time arrangements, especially those directly affected, but also those indirectly burdened, such as the underemployed.

8.2   MEASURING OVEREMPLOYMENT

Overemployment is considered herein to exist when there are workers employed who are willing but unable to reduce their hours of paid work at their current (or comparable) job if they are prepared to accept (proportionately) lower current or future income. Estimates of the volume or rate of overemployment vary considerably, in the United States as elsewhere. Estimates depend heavily on the type of sample, instrument, wording and context of the question from which it can be derived. Table 8.1 summarizes the various available estimates from a wide range of relevant studies, both in the United States and elsewhere, considering the technical aspects of the survey attempting to measure hours preferences and the existence (or size) of a discrepancy with actual hours. The overemployment rate represents the volume of overemployment as a ratio of those employed or a measure of overutilization of labour resources (which is not strictly comparable with the rate of volume of underemployment, see Simic, 2002; Pierce, 2003). The relevant survey questions are those querying the employed regarding who is willing but unable to reduce hours (at either their current or in another comparable job) in exchange for lower income. The rates of overemployment are higher in most EU states than in the United States (OECD, 2004). However, there is considerable variation between EU Member States.[2]

The Panel Survey of Income Dynamics (PSID) and General Social Survey (GSS) yield estimates ranging from 6 to 10 per cent (Bell and Freeman, 1995; Kahn and Lang, 1995; Reynolds, 2003) in the United States. Other surveys find much higher proportions. Even plausible estimates vary in large part because the question posed regarding the willingness to trade income for time varies so much. First, it is generally the case that if the set of survey questions includes an alternative option of obtaining higher income, especially when the survey adds that this would involve more hours of work, the proportions of respondents indicating a preference for fewer hours are typically lower. When presented simultaneously with the alluring "more money" option, choosing fewer hours may lose its relative appeal, even if such hours are not available at their current job.[3] In contrast, if workers are presented only with various hours and pay reduction options, proportions indicating overemployment are higher. For example, among those wage and salary workers on a fixed hour schedule (not free to choose when or how long they work), over 50 per cent were willing to work fewer hours for proportionately lower income in order to have more free time (Feather and Shaw, 2000). A recent survey found that as much as 27 per cent of unionized and 39 per cent of non-union employees were willing to reduce their incomes (progressively, by either 10 per cent, 20 per cent, etc.) in order to get proportionately shorter weekly hours (Friedman and Casner-Lotto, 2003). Another survey revealed that over 28 per cent of respondents would give up a day's pay for one fewer days of work per week (Galinsky and Bond, 1998). Another 1998 survey found that 17 per cent would accept a

---

[2] By way of contrast, in the United Kingdom, almost 11 per cent of the employed indicate overemployment (Simic, 2002), although estimates range as high as 34 per cent (Fagan, 2001). The overemployment hours gap among male industrial workers is 4.3 hours (Stewart and Swaffield, 1997). For reasons including a higher level of income inequality, the ratio of those preferring more hours to those preferring fewer is higher in the United States, see Bell and Freeman (1995) and Osberg (2002).

[3] There are exceptions. The Heldrich Center *Work Trends* survey found that 30 per cent in 1999 (up from 28 per cent in 1998) prefer fewer hours (for less income), given the choice, about twice as many who prefer more hours. A Roper-ASW (a market research firm's) poll consistently finds somewhat stronger general preference for money over time, but a sizeable proportion valuing time. In 2003, 34 per cent of North Americans "would prefer more time to more money" (only slightly lower than the 40 per cent observed globally and about the same as the 35 per cent found in 2001 and 37 per cent found in 2000).

Table 8.1 Overemployment estimates

Source	Year	Data source	Sample size	Overemployment rate	Satisfied with current hours	Question wording
Friedman and Casner-Lotto (2003)	2002	Phone survey	815	27% union 39% non-union		• Answered "yes" to: Suppose you could choose among the following work schedules. Which would you probably select at this point in your life? Your current work schedule, OR 90% of a FT schedule with 90% pay and benefits, 80% of a FT schedule with 80% of pay and benefits and so on through 70%, 60%… etc.
				33% union 36% non-union		• If you had more high quality (decent wages, benefits and job security) part-time options available to you right now, how likely do you think you would be to use them and reduce your schedule? Very likely plus somewhat likely vs. not too likely plus not likely at all?
Clarkberg and Moen (2001)	2001	National Study of Families and Households (NSFH) 1987/8 & 1993/4	9 108	36% of husbands in dual-career couples; 39% of neo-traditional couple husbands	41% of wives; 44% of husbands	• (If employed) Would you prefer to work more or less than your present work schedule? • (If married) Does your spouse work full-time, part-time or not at all? • Would you prefer your spouse to work or yourself?

Source	Year	Survey	Sample	Percentage	Percentage	Question
www.NewDream.org	2003	Center for the New American Dream and Take Back Your Time			52%	• Would you be willing to trade one day off a week for an equivalent pay reduction?
Reynolds (2003)	1997	International Social Survey Program (ISSP) & The General Social Survey (1998)[1]	1 228	42%	37%	• Suppose you could change the way you spend your time, spending more time on some things and less time on others. Which of the things on the following list would you like to spend more time on, which would you like to spend less time on, and which would you like to spend the same amount of time on as now?
USA Today, 10 Apr. 1995, p. 2A	1995	USA Today		55%	14%	• Would you prefer to work more hours and receive increased income, fewer hours with less income or would you prefer your hours and pay to remain the same?
Schor (1994)	1994				51%–10% cut 19%–20% cut 37%–time off	• (Would you) take the option of a four-day week, for a 10% pay cut? 20% pay cut? • (Do you) prefer a raise or more time off?
Feather and Shaw (2000)	1992	National Survey of Recreation (NSRE), phone survey	860		25% of hourly wage workers	• Those on a fixed schedule (not free to choose when or how long you work), were asked: Would you be willing to work fewer hours in order to have more free time?
Heldrich Center (1999), p. 16	1999	Work Trends Survey Center for Survey Research and Analysis		56%	30%	• Would you like to work more hours than you currently work, the same number of hours as you currently work, or fewer hours than you currently work?

Note: [1] Work hours not designed for familial obligations; ISSP lacks certain questions (ref. 1181), 5 per cent of part-time workers feel they are forcibly overworked.

20 per cent pay cut to get a 4-day work-week while over 50 per cent would accept a 10 per cent cut in their pay to get it (Schor, 2001). Estimates are higher when there is greater precision in the trade-off offered, such as "one day off per week," "4-day work-week" or "more time to spend with family members" or "more free time" (Schor, 1995).

Another factor that will suppress the rate of overemployment is that it will vary inversely with the extent to which respondents inherently believe they are unable in practice to change their own hours to their truly preferred hours. Workers may perceive that hours reduction is infeasible or penalized (no quality part-time or shorter standard work-week options) or not permissible (e.g., mandatory overtime). Third, respondent openness to hours reduction is typically greatest when surveys do not explicitly state any direct trade-off of lower income. For example, in the National Study of the Changing Work Force (NSCW), over 60 per cent of workers' "actual" exceeded their "ideal" work-week, rising from about 5 hours in 1992 to 11 hours in 1997 (Jacobs and Gerson, 2001; Galinsky and Bond, 1998). Estimates of the proportion overemployed also tend to be greater if individuals are also asked to specify how many hours they would have preferred to have worked in a given week, rather than just indicating fewer (or more) hours. But questions with hours preferences are challenging, not only because they are trickier to measure than actual working hours (Tijdens, 2002), but because it is often left unclear whether and how workers would get their "preferred" number of hours and whether they implicitly assume they would get a more (or less) than proportional reduction in compensation, such as access to employee benefit coverage or premium pay. For obvious reasons, more workers prefer fewer hours for no less pay than for less pay. In the United Kingdom, among the 12 million employed indicating a desire for fewer hours, about 3 million would accept less pay (Simic, 2002). Fourth, surveys tend to query only those employed, whereas it is conceivable that many of those who have been recently overemployed may be between jobs, via either lay-off or a voluntary quit, or outside the labour force. On the other hand, some analysts are sceptical whether workers' stated preferences would become revealed preferences. Fifth, fewer hours may not be desired if a worker anticipates a period of under-employment or unemployment in the future. Workers employed in cyclically sensitive, downsizing industries or insecure jobs may "prefer" longer hours as a hedge against anticipated future reduction of income or an "insurance" against future lay-off (Roche, 1987; Bell and Freeman, 1995; Bluestone and Rose, 1998).

Finally, willingness to sacrifice income for more time might be an issue of magnitude. Preferences are not necessarily linear with respect to the size of the hypothetical changes. More workers might prefer to spend "a bit less time" than "much less time" at work, and these combined are far greater proportions than indicated by the more general "work less" option (Bell and Freeman, 1995;

Schor, 1995). Moreover, because survey questions do not address the intensity of work, respondents may well be interpreting the "work less" question as implying not only less pay, but also greater work effort or pace. In sum, survey estimates of overemployment may be biased downward if a survey provokes certain implicit assumptions about the current income foregone, and the amount and dimensions of hours reduced and type of gains realized in time off.

8.3   REFINING THE CONCEPT OF OVEREMPLOYMENT

The conventional economic model of labour supply aptly identifies the initial sources of overemployment. However, the factors that increase individuals' desired labour supply are typically relegated to the status of "exogenous changes" in preferences or constraints. This is unfortunate, not only because these "shifters" are crucial to understanding recent trends in preferred work-hours and overemployment, but also because some of the "shifters" may become endogenous with actual hours. A richer way to conceive of over-employment would be as a dynamic process. This would explain why overemployment may either persist or dissipate over time despite its various spillover costs, and it would differentiate the microeconomic and macro-economic sources of overemployment.[4]

8.3.1   Overemployment at the microeconomic level

In the conventional microeconomic model of labour–leisure choice, it is assumed that workers form their desired number of work-hours and are assumed to adjust their hours of labour supply until the unique point where their relative preference for an hour of leisure vis-à-vis work exactly equals their market wage rate. Workers may face constraints, often binding, imposed by their employer, such as fixed shift lengths and minimum hours requirements for a job, resulting in overemployment. However, in the conventional model, it is assumed that in the long run, workers and firms sort themselves to match desired and required hours of work. If hours demanded exceeds hours desired, employers will not be able to retain labour, losing workers to other firms that offer shorter work hours in accordance with their preferences, or to non-labour force participation. That said, a "synthesis" view in the literature recognizes that hours mismatches can persist indefinitely, where optimizing employers regularly require longer hours than employees

---

[4] Overemployment may be more likely among employees who face pressure from their employer or supervisor to work overtime hours. This comprises from 16 to 28 per cent of the full-time employed (Ehrenberg and Schumann, 1984; Idson and Robbins, 1991; Cornell University Institute for Labour Studies, 1999; Golden and Wiens-Tuers, 2005), a level not inconsistent with those found elsewhere, such as in Australia (Campbell, 2002).

might prefer (Kahn and Lang, 1995; Rubin and Richardson, 1997; Contensou and Vranceanu, 2000; Maume and Bellas, 2001; Campbell, 2002). The labour market does not truly offer "diverse durations" of shift lengths; instead, it has a tendency to underprovide short-hour jobs (Rebitzer and Taylor, 1995). The distribution of hours within firms may reflect workers' personal character-istics and preferences within firms, but there is no tendency for workers to be sorted by hours preferences among firms (Bryan, 2004).[5] The main way in which workers seek actual hours of work that move towards their preferred hours is through job mobility. Changes in workers' hours take place mainly through their changing of jobs (Altonji and Paxson, 1992; Drago et al., 2004).

8.3.2 Overemployment at the macroeconomic level

Labour–leisure models portray overemployment as an individual or single labour market phenomenon; however, it can also be viewed from a macroeconomic perspective. Categorizing the contributing economic sources of overemployment can be treated as analogous to classifying the sources of unemployment. There are three distinct types: structural, cyclical and frictional. Structural overemployment occurs because of the presence of structural incentives inherent in labour-market-related institutions or work organization that lengthen hours demanded per worker. Such work organi-zation includes the growing use of mandatory (compulsory) overtime practices (Golden and Wiens-Tuers, 2005). Such labour market institutions include those that heighten the fixed costs of hiring employees, such as computerization (Hubler, 2000); required hiring and training costs (Contensou and Vranceanu, 2000; Glosser and Golden, 2004); and the escalating cost of premiums for employee health benefit coverage, structured in the United States as employer contributions per employee rather than pro-rated by hours worked.[6] Institutional practices include the degree of non-compliance with the Fair Labor Standards Act (FLSA) overtime regulations or the intensity of government enforcement of regulations (see Belman and Belzer, 1998; Golden, 1999). The introduction of the weekly overtime pay premia rules measurably restrains average work hours (Hamermesh and Trejo, 2000; Costa, 2000; Hart, 2004). Finally, the diminishing presence and weakening of labour unions in the United States undermines a traditional brake on overtime hours, as in Australia (Peetz et al., 2003). Cyclical factors may also alter the extent of overemployment. When demand (orders, customers) is surging, cyclical

---

[5] The main theoretical justification for the persistence of mismatches – compensating wage differentials for inconvenient hours – has to date received little empirical support (Ehrenberg and Schumann, 1984; Altonji and Paxson, 1992).

[6] A lack of quality part-time jobs is a source of hours restrictions faced by unmarried adults (Euwals and Van Soest, 1999).

overemployment is created when hours demanded per worker are rising faster than workers' desired hours (the latter induced by rising wage rates if the substitution effect on labour supply is dominant). Conversely, cyclical over-employment would tend to diminish when a weak macroeconomic climate leads employers to scale back (overtime) hours demanded, leading to greater underemployment (including involuntary part-time employment). Third and finally, frictional overemployment stems from the bundling of wages and hours in typical employment contracts and from incomplete markets and inform-ation. Frictions in the workplace and labour market exist when there are barriers to full, perfect information among employers about their employees' preferences and among worker applicants about job requirements and alternative jobs. Lags and asymmetries in the transmission of information about individuals' changing preferences and the typical hours (when not explicitly stipulated in contracts) in jobs lead to a greater incidence of mismatches.[7]

8.4 EXPLAINING THE RISE AND FALL OF OVER-EMPLOYMENT AS A DYNAMIC LABOUR SUPPLY PROCESS

Table 8.2 shows that estimates of the overemployment rate using the 2001 CPS question on the willingness to trade income for reduced hours has not increased since last measured in 1985 at 7.6 per cent (Shank, 1986). Given the widespread acceptance that hours of work have grown – at least among households if not individuals – it is perhaps surprising that this estimate of the proportion of workers that prefers the option of reducing their hours and income is no higher and even a bit lower than 16 years previously. Despite other surveys displaying contrary evidence of rising rates (such as the doubling in the rate from less than 6 per cent to over 10 per cent between 1989 and 1998 in the GSS), this deserves serious inspection.

There may be good theoretical reasons why the rate of overemployment may be no higher than reported in the year 1985. However, perhaps the relatively low rate observed in 2001 should be discounted, for a variety of legitimate reasons. The wedge between actual and desired hours may cease to grow if either average hours supplied per worker have become shorter or preferred hours per worker have lengthened. Regarding the former, actual average hours in the private sector (which includes all employees, full time and part time) are a full hour shorter in 2001 than they were in the second quarter of 1985, 33.9 versus 34.9 hours per week. In 1985, however, 20 per cent reported working longer than 40 hours per week whereas 29 per cent did so in 2001. Thus the slightly falling

---

[7] Like unemployment, the rate of overemployment can never reach a rate of zero, because there will always be some unavoidable frictional overemployment.

Table 8.2   Employed who prefer to work fewer hours, 2001 (percentages)

Demographic variables	Percentage
Usual full-time	6.3
Usual part-time	3.9
Female	8.2
Married	7.1
Divorced/widowed	5.0
Not married	3.8
Not a parent	4.3
No child	7.2
At least 1 in 0–2	7.7
At least 1 in 3–5	7.0
At least 1 in 6–13	6.2
At least 1 in 14–17	6.1
Union members	6.5

Source: US Current Population Survey, May 2001: Work Schedules and Work at Home Supplement.

average masks that there have been growing proportions of workers employed for longer than "standard" hours, and at shorter hours at the other end of the spectrum. In addition, average hours demanded per worker were probably shorter for cyclical reasons. In the second quarter of 2001 (including the survey date of May 2001), the economy was in the midst of a recession while in 1985 it was in rapid expansion. Thus cyclical overemployment was probably a larger factor in the earlier but not the later period. More likely, however, is that the wedge has not increased because workers' preferred hours are longer than they might have been in 1985, further closing the wedge. For one thing, as would be stressed in applying a conventional model of labour supply, real earnings of non-supervisory workers did not surpass the level in 1985 until the end of the 1990s. Especially among men, there might be a net income effect dominating opposing substitution effect pressures, increasing the preference for work-hours over leisure time, on balance.[8] A fuller theoretical consideration of overemployment determination would thus help illuminate why the rate of overemployment might stay constant across time periods.

Thus a three-step theoretical model describing the sequential dynamics of labour supply is needed to better account for the extent and trend in the mismatch between actual and preferred hours. Just as the state of unemployment may, in the long run, lead individuals to make adjustments that cause the

---

[8] Real hourly wage rates are found to have little impact on the quantity of labour supply (Bryan, 2004).

unemployment rate to subside, such as labour force withdrawal, overemployment may also rise and then abate on its own. Such endogeneity of hours preferences suggests that workers either maladapt to overly long hours or ratchet up their consumption level that solidifies their desire for income over time (Altman and Golden, 2004). Workers may tend to adjust their preferences upward towards their existing hours, an application of observational equivalence (Schor, 1995). Step one of a dynamic model presumes that individuals first assume a predominant identity or role (see Altman and Golden, 2004). This leads them to then desire a level of market work sufficient to support their pre-established goals regarding both consumption and non-market time. Their goals reflect a hierarchical ordering of their physiological and unsatisfied needs. For women, their desire for paid work time may reflect where their preferences currently lie along the continuum between home-centred and work-centred preferences (see Hakim, 2000). The majority are in the middle, wishing to combine work and home. However, women's preferences are far more heterogeneous in this regard than men's. Thus it is quite likely that they vary through time as well, perhaps going through sustained periods of increase. Let us suppose, as in the constrained labour supply model, that employers require or offer longer actual hours than the hours initially preferred by workers in many jobs or time periods.

The second step is that workers' higher income eventually raises individuals' target income. This may occur for at least four contributing reasons. First, the targeted amount of hours and income desired may be adjusted upward as attitudes associated with loss aversion are adopted (Dunn, 1996). If income foregone takes on proportionately greater value than income gained, then there will be an inherent bias against giving up income. Second, if individuals, particularly at higher income levels, are subject to interdependent utility, then working longer than one's initially preferred labour supply may make individuals or households become accustomed to the higher level of consumption facilitated by the additional income. In addition, if the higher consumption spending is financed in part by taking on higher household debt-to-income ratios, such as (virtually irreversible) higher mortgage or revolving credit expenses, preferred hours ratchet upward. Indeed, the observed increase in work hours in the United States is largely attributable to increased hours worked among dual-income households (Jacobs and Gerson, 2001; Osberg 2002). Thus, what may begin as predetermined wants may be changed (Altman, 2001) if higher income leads individuals to seek fulfilment of new, unsatisfied wants up the hierarchy of wants. A third reason is that higher income probably leads to greater exposure to the marketing and advertising that help create tastes for more and more market goods and services (see Fraser and Paton, 2003). In addition, to the extent that individuals and households may compete more for higher relative status by acquiring or accumulating social-status-conferring goods and services by emulating the consumption patterns of the rich, this requires that relatively less well-off individuals work more hours in order to sustain their relative position, especially among lower- and middle-income households (Schor, 1995; Altman, 2001). A fourth and final reason is that a period of overemployment creates time scarcity. This tends to shift household preferences from self-produced to market-produced goods and services. Workers alter their consumption preferences from time-*using* toward more time-*saving* goods and services (Rothschild, 1982), which requires a perpetuation of the flow of income. All four of these forces tend to ratchet up the individual's target consumption level and gradually dissipate the initial desire for shorter work hours, exemplifying endogenous labour supply preferences.

In the third step in the dynamic process, continuous employment may reinforce preferences for longer hours to the extent that employers enhance the reward for overemployment and/or penalize short hours. Employers might interpret "presenteeism" as an indication of an employee's level of effort and commitment, thus using longer hours as a signal of promotability. A greater dispersion among pay grades motivates workers to exceed the hours worked of their fellow workers, to engage in positive signalling tactics (Bell and Freeman, 1995). Among those who expect to be in managerial positions, there is a positive empirical association between the number of work-hours they "prefer" and the actual work-hours of their co-workers (Eastman, 1998). There is also a rising presence of professions that valorize long hours, which promote a "rat race" with workers increasing their own work-hours for reasons of relative status, such as jobs in law and consulting (Landers et al., 1996). Correspondingly, there are negative signalling effects for workers requesting shorter hours (Rebitzer and Taylor, 1995). Those expressing a wish to reduce work-hours may be passed up for hiring in an adverse selection model of hiring decisions. In addition, in a context of growing job or income insecurity, longer hours might be used by workers to build up an income to buffer against expected future job or income losses (Bluestone and Rose, 1998). If workers believe their employer is screening before a downsizing or reorganization, they may view longer hours as an inoculation against the risk of future job loss, income loss or demotion.[9] Moreover, if the amenities offered by the workplace outpace those associated with work in the household, from on-site day care to a more stimulating environment, time in the workplace becomes relatively more alluring

---

[9] Better matching or "congruence" between preferred and actual hours status is associated with employee performance. This suggests that overemployment may lead to work behaviours antithetical to productivity on the job (Holtom et al., 2002; Savery and Luks, 2000; Dollard and Winefield, 2002).

(Hochschild, 1997). To the extent work yields less disutility, by becoming more intrinsically rewarding, stimulating, safer or autonomous – over time or over one's life cycle – this will erode any resistance to long hours (Kaufman, 1999; LaJeunesse, 2004). For example, between 1985 and 2001, the proportion of the work force with flexible daily work schedules doubled, to over 28 per cent. They are more accessible to those who work longer than standard hours (see Golden, 2005). Thus, the advantage of working long hours has gained, to the extent workers can use the flexibility to shift some of their workload to different times of the day or locations, a means of easing some of the pressures that contributed to workers' past willingness to reduce hours. Indeed, workers who greatly value daily start- and end-time flexibility thus may even choose overemployment over standard hours. If the part-time compensation differential is sufficiently severe, workers may rationally prefer overemployment at standard hours over a part-time job at their desired, shorter hours. Thus, to the extent that the quality of part-time positions has improved over time, this might reduce the duration and incidence of overemployment. Full-time workers would become less reluctant to make transitions to part-time positions (see Drago et al., 2004).

In sum, individuals may eventually choose to work longer than initially preferred, not only because their own real wage, non-wage income or con- straints have changed, but because their hours preferences are not set purely exogenously in a static climate in isolation from their social reference groups or workplace incentives. A dynamic process occurs whereby an individual may start out working long hours involuntarily and later do so voluntarily. This suppresses any rise in the rate of overemployment even when average hours per week are lengthening. This is supported by a greater willingness among workers to forego future more than current income, such as a coming year's rise. Indeed, a recent survey reveals a much stronger preference for hours reduction in the more distant future than in the current period (Hart and Associates, 2003) – 15 per cent would prefer hours and income reduction now, but over 40 per cent favour this some time in the near future.

Who is more likely to be overemployed? Individuals whose actual hours (h) exceed desired hours (h^*) given their current wage and job:

$$h^* < h$$

This gap may occur so long as some employers are not induced to adjust h downward toward h^*. If

$$\lambda(h - h^*)^\theta \text{ given } \lambda > 0; \theta > 1$$

the gap can persist so long as:

(1) administrative costs (λ) associated with facilitating a constant adjustment of h toward each employee's h^* are large;

(2) the size of the gap between h and h^* is not overly large;

(3) long-term risks on the organization of overemployment are small or discounted (θ near one);

(4) employees lack bargaining leverage to impose adverse consequences (e.g., absences);

(5) employees are induced to tolerate or discount the (cumulative) consequences of overwork;

(6) it is relatively less costly for firms to induce employees to adjust upward their h^*, by internalizing the pressures from their reference groups in the workplace (or consumption targets).

8.5 HYPOTHESES

Not all workers are equally likely to experience a gap between desired and actual hours. Thus the distribution of decent working time may not be allocated evenly across types of sectors and workers. Some workers may be more prone to time surpluses and others to time deficits (see Messenger, ed., 2004). It is likely to be more prevalent among workers:

* with personal characteristics that on average tend to be associated with relatively shorter hours preferences because they have significant caregiving responsibilities, such as dual-earner parents with children present in the household (Merola and Clarkberg, 2003; Reynolds, 2004);

* whose preferences are more apt to shift towards shorter desired work-weeks after becoming employed at certain key intervals in their life cycle, such as approaching retirement;

* with personal characteristics associated with relatively higher relative wage rates and less apt to be underemployed, such as whites rather than minorities;

* with jobs whose hours are longer and/or growing for either cyclical or structural reasons;

* with jobs that make them face more structural constraints on reducing their hours at their current jobs or a paucity of job alternatives;

* whose bargaining leverage is insufficient for adjusting hours downward as needed when their preferences shift as such, such as younger or non-union members;

* in jobs with insufficient job autonomy to exert control over hours (Reynolds, 2004);

- in occupations and industries with relatively higher earnings per hour, if overemployment is positive in the real wage, particularly at high wage levels (and/or underemployment is negative in the real wage, particularly at relatively low wage levels); and

- in industries where there is at least some productivity per worker gained while the additional wage cost is negligible, such as jobs compensated with salary rather than hourly wages.

8.6 EMPIRICAL FINDINGS: DEMOGRAPHIC CHARACTERISTICS OF OVEREMPLOYMENT

The May 2001 CPS Supplement sample of households includes over 57,000 individuals, with information on their demographic and work characteristics. The distribution of overemployment by personal, occupation and industry characteristics appears in Tables 8.3 and 8.4. The sample collapsed responses into 52 detailed industry and 46 detailed occupational classifications. The key question asks households if individuals, "given the choice, [would] opt for more income and more hours, less income and fewer hours or the same income and hours?" The cross-tabulations presented in the tables show an incidence of overemployment noticeably higher for women, parents of young children and workers on relatively longer work-weeks. Tables 8.3 and 8.4 reveal discrepancies among occupations and industries of the employed. It appears to be higher in certain occupational classifications such as managers–administrators and in industries such as health care and utilities.

More rigorous empirical testing allows us to identify the personal and job status characteristics that contribute to the likelihood that an individual prefers "fewer hours and less income", controlling for all possible other factors. The three general sets of factors observable in the May 2001 CPS Supplement are: personal characteristics such as age, gender, race, marital status, and parental status; actual work-hours, such as usual full-time or part-time job or on a non-traditional shift; and job characteristics, such as their occupation and industry of employment, and flexibility of schedule in their job or workplace. The likelihood that an individual prefers the option of reducing both hours and income is determined by a probit regression on a comprehensive list of a given worker's personal and job characteristics.[10]

---

[10] The model estimates the probability of being overemployed as a function of personal (β) as well as job (δ) characteristics, including work hours, and the respective vectors of estimated coefficients, X and Y:

$$OVER_i = \alpha + X_i\beta + Y_i\delta + \varepsilon$$

The model is estimated using probit analysis. The dependent variable is bi-variate, taking on a value of one if the employed worker reports having a preference for fewer hours and less income over their current level. The coefficients represent the marginal probabilities that an individual possessing a given characteristic prefers fewer hours and less income.

Table 8.3   Overemployment rate by detailed occupation, full-time employed

Occupational classification	Percentage
Officials and administrators, public administration	6.5
Other executive, administrative and managerial	8.7
Management-related occupations	8.6
Engineers	8.2
Mathematical and computer scientists	7.6
Natural scientists	10.2
Health diagnosing occupations	12.2
Health assessment and treatment occupations	11.9
Teachers, college and university	9.8
Teachers, except college and university	7.8
Lawyers and judges	9.2
Other professional speciality occupations	6.8
Health technologists and technicians	9.1
Engineering and science technicians	5.8
Technicians, excluding health, engineering and science	7.8
Supervisors and proprietors, sales occupations	6.3
Sales representatives, finance and business services	6.6
Sales representatives, commodities, excluding retail	5.9
Sales workers, retail and personal services	4.6
Supervisors and proprietors, sales occupations	8.1
Computer equipment operators	8.1
Secretaries, stenographers and typists	7.8
Financial records processing	7.3
Mail and message distributing	6.5
Other administrative support, including clerical	7.1
Private household service occupations	4.2
Protective service	3.9
Food service	3.2
Health service	4.7
Cleaning and building service	4.1
Personal service	3.0
Mechanics and repairers	3.9
Construction trades	1.9
Other precision production, craft, and repair	5.2
Machine operators and tenders, excluding precision workers	3.4
Fabricators, assemblers, inspectors	3.0
Motor vehicle operators	4.8
Other transport and material moving occupations	4.0
Construction labourers	2.2
Freight, stock and materials handlers	3.1
Other handlers, equipment cleaners, labourers	2.4
Farm operators and managers	0.3
Farm workers and related occupations	3.1
Forestry and fishing occupations	1.1

Source: Author's calculations based on Current Population Survey, May 2001: Work Schedules and Work at Home Supplement.

Table 8 4   Overemployment rate by detailed industry, full-time employed

Industry	Percentage
Goods producing – agricultural services	4.3
Goods producing – other agricultural	1.7
Mining	3.6
Construction	3.0
Manufacturing – lumber and wood products, excluding furniture	4.1
Manufacturing – furniture and fixtures	3.8
Manufacturing – stone, clay, concrete, glass products	2.3
Manufacturing – primary metals	4.8
Manufacturing – fabricated metals	3.7
Manufacturing – machinery, excluding electrical	6.7
Manufacturing – electrical machinery, equipment supplies	6.3
Manufacturing – motor vehicles and equipment	5.7
Manufacturing – aircraft and parts	4.7
Manufacturing – other transportation equipment	5.5
Manufacturing – professional and photo equipment, watches	8.3
Manufacturing – toys, amusement and sporting goods	11.0
Manufacturing – miscellaneous manufacturing industries	6.8
Manufacturing – food and kindred products	4.8
Manufacturing – tobacco products	4.1
Manufacturing – textile mill products	6.6
Manufacturing – apparel and other finished textile products	4.2
Manufacturing – paper and allied products	8.5
Manufacturing – printing, publishing and allied industries	7.1
Manufacturing – chemicals and allied products	7.1
Manufacturing – rubber and miscellaneous plastic products	5.6
Manufacturing – leather and leather products	1.1
Transportation	5.9
Communications	7.3
Utilities and sanitary services	9.9
Wholesale trade	6.6
Eating and drinking places	4.3
Other retail trade	5.4
Banking and other finance	6.9
Insurance and real estate	7.7
Private household services	4.9
Business services	5.4
Automobile and repair services	3.9
Personal services excluding private households	4.6
Entertainment and recreation services	3.3
Hospitals	10.6
Health services, excluding hospitals	8.1
Educational services	8.0
Social services	5.2
Other professional services	7.6

/cont'd

Table 8.3   (/cont'd)

Industry	Percentage
Forestry and fisheries	9.9
Justice, public order and safety	3.9
Administration of human resource programmes	6.3
National security and internal affairs	4.6
Other public administration	7.5

Source: Author's calculations based on Current Population Survey, May 2001: Work Schedules and Work at Home Supplement.

The empirical tests find that female workers are more at risk of being overemployed than their male counterparts, all else constant. This cannot be attributed to the type of jobs they hold. In addition, as workers age, their preference for additional time over income grows, but this preference diminishes later in the life cycle. This is apparently attributable to getting their preferred work-hours length and shifts. Being married raises the likelihood of overemployment. Being divorced, separated or widowed, however, does not. Having children in the household (relative to having either no or fully grown children) is important, but with nuances. When the youngest child in the household is younger than 3 years old, this raises the likelihood of feeling overemployed. Having children aged 3 through 5, i.e., pre-school age, has a significant but weaker effect, about half the magnitude of the youngest children. Interestingly, when the youngest child present in the household reaches the age of 14, this reverses the effect of having children on the likelihood of overemployment. Thus it is apparent that when children first appear, there is a significantly greater demand for time. However, as they age, parents gradually shift their preference toward income, to the point where they actually prefer more income relative to time when their children are teenagers.

8.7   FINDINGS: WORK-HOURS AND JOB STATUS CHARACTERISTICS

As a full-time worker's average reported work-week lengthens, there is a progressively higher likelihood of being overemployed. Working a standard work-week of exactly 40 hours creates a higher likelihood of being overemployed relative to those who report usually working 35 to 39 hours. Working from 41 to 49 hours raises the probability of overemployment considerably, and working 50 or more raises it still further. Workers whose hours are "variable", in that they are not able to specify a usual work-week, have a reduced tendency to be overemployed, surprisingly. However, this may be attributable to the disproportionate share of workers in this category who are part-time workers. Part-time work (working 34 or fewer usual hours per week) tends to reduce the probability of experiencing overemployment. Thus part-time work provides workers with a good deal of (but not complete) relief from the risk of overemployment.

Those working on a regular daytime shift, the vast majority of US workers, have a slightly raised likelihood of being overemployed compared to those working the evening shift (the reference group). Those working on irregular shift times have the highest probability of being overemployed. This is traced entirely to men who work on a shift other than the regular day shift. Workers who have flexible schedules, some ability to vary their daily starting and ending times of work, have a somewhat reduced likelihood of over-employment. However, this is exclusively among those who have informal arrangements in the workplace to arrive later or leave work earlier (which represent almost two-thirds of all those with flexible schedules, see Golden, 2005). In contrast, formal flexi-time programmes do not reduce the chances of being overemployed. This dual face of flexibility suggests that the interference of work hours with work and family balancing is largely separate from flexibility of the daily schedule. Moreover, being able to perform some work at home actually exacerbates working longer hours than are preferred.

8.7.1 Job characteristics: Occupations and industries

There are several occupations that heighten the likelihood of wishing for fewer hours, and many that reduce it. The major occupational classifications that exhibit the greatest overemployment fall in the managerial and professional groups. In particular, by order of magnitude, these are engineers, health diagnosing occupations, natural scientists, mathematicians/computer scientists, health assessment and treatment, private (but not public) sector managers and administrators, lawyers/judges, and management-related occupations. There are two technicians' jobs – health and those other than health, science or engineering, and other administrative support (computer equipment operators is borderline) – in which overemployment is significantly higher. In general, it appears that the higher the general pay (skill or preparation) level of the job, the greater is the tendency towards overemployment. Several blue-collar occupations, notably construction trades and labourers, farm operators and fabricators/assemblers, and in-service jobs such as personal, health or food service occupations, are less likely to experience overemployment, indeed, they are more likely to experience underemployment.

Some industries stand out as creating a markedly greater likelihood of overemployment than others. Relative to production and service-type industries, being employed in public utilities raises the likelihood. Relative to other, non-service-type industries, the hospital sector raises the risk of overemployment. The communications and transportation and, to a weaker extent, wholesale trade, also raises the risk of overemployment, as do medical services other than hospitals. The latter is not surprising given the greater incidence of mandatory overtime work, and some high-profile labour disputes involving the level and distribution of overtime work in these tele-communications, public utilities and hospital sectors (Golden and Wiens-Tuers, 2005). The sole manufacturing industry producing greater overemployment is paper products. On the other hand, being employed in social services, construction, private household, justice/public order, stone/glass manu-facturing significantly reduces the likelihood of overemployment. This suggests that hours in these sectors' jobs may be more responsive to preferences for shorter hours. Alternatively, the workers employed there may be less apt to prefer shorter than actual hours.

In sum, overemployment is disproportionately concentrated among women, parents of young children, long-hours workers, and certain salaried positions, all else held constant.

8.8   SUMMARY AND IMPLICATIONS OF THE RESULTS: TOWARDS DECENT WORKING TIME POLICIES

Every post-industrial country places some sort of limitation on the duration of working hours. The extent of such regulation reflects a combination not only of working time preferences among men and women, but also the cultural, economic and institutional context of the affected domain (see Stier and Lewin-Epstein, 2003).[11] In the United States, the only institutional restraints on hours of work are: the Fair Labor Standard Act's (1938) overtime regulations enforced by the United States Department of Labor, requiring premium pay for hours worked in excess of 40 in a given one-week period, and the Hours of Service Regulations issued by the US Department of Transportation, limiting drivers' hours to no more than 60 per week and no more than 11 hours per 24-hour period. Sweeping changes have just been imposed in the rules that Department of Labor regulators will apply to determine FLSA coverage under the exemption for executive, administrative and professional jobs, which would potentially remove millions of occupational classifications with typically long-hours demands from the overtime pay premium requirement. Both houses of the Congress have proposed FLSA reforms that would permit employers who receive

---

[11] The greater are a country's GDP per capita, income equality and policies to mitigate market risks, the greater is the desire to reduce work-hours in that country.

written agreement from employees to substitute compensatory ("comp") time for premium pay for overtime work (H.R.1119) and a variable, 80-hour, two-week work-week (S.317).

Overemployment results from binding constraints on workers that create a persistent gap between actual and preferred hours. Overemployment persists despite an inherent tendency for overemployment to diminish on its own, to the extent that workers endogenously adopt the longer hours of the preferences of their workplace or national culture. Achieving the goals of decent working time requires minimizing the incidence of overemployment, its burden equitably distributed by gender and that the gap be closed by eliminating constraints that inhibit downward flexibility of hours rather than by upward escalating of hours preferences. Notwithstanding the conventional theory of perfect matching of desired and required hours in labour markets, the May 2001 CPS question yields conservative estimates of the rate of overemployment at 6 to 7 per cent of the workforce, but it is up to twice that rate in certain jobs, sectors and workers. The lower rate of overemployment in other sectors suggests that such constraints need not be considered inevitable. The relatively low rate of overemployment in the United States, at least as revealed in the CPS 2001 survey, should not lull policy-makers into a sense of complacency. Overemployment is significantly more likely among women and parents of young children, which poses a threat to gender equity. In addition, it is higher among long-work-week workers and selected occupational classifications such as managers–administrators, scientists, engineers and some technicians, and in industries such as healthcare, utilities and transportation. Although slightly lower in level, it is remarkably similar in distribution to the United Kingdom, where a preference for fewer hours is also higher among the older and managerial–professional workforce (see Pierce, 2003).

A key facet of "decent working time" is that there is value to workers in having a greater degree of choice and a larger array of reduced-hours options, even for those workers who do not necessarily need to exercise such a choice at the moment. This could ultimately help break the dynamic of constrained workers settling for longer hours than they may have initially preferred. This would also help avoid the currently socially wasteful reliance on workers either engaging in constant job mobility to attain their desired hours when their preferences change because of life-course or unexpected events, or alternatively, simply adapting upward their preferred hours toward those available or which they judge as feasible in their workplace. Furthermore, the considerably higher rates of underemployment in the United States could be somewhat reduced to the extent that the work performed by those relieved of their overemployment gap in hours was effectively transferred to those willing to work more hours – who are typically found in hourly paid, lower-wage occupations and industries. If a genuine goal of legislative reform is curbing the incidence, duration and effects of overemployment, the empirical results suggest that accomplishing that would be more likely if work-hours legislation and regulation were more precisely targeted toward the types of workers relatively more prone to overemployment.[12] For example, targeted limits on hours could be established in sectors in which the incidence of overemployment and mandatory overtime work is most concentrated (see Golden and Wiens-Tuers, 2005), such as telecommunications, hospitals, and transportation. Ultimately, some measure of new FLSA coverage would have to be extended to employees in those white-collar, salaried occupations (see Schor, 1995) displaying the longest work-weeks, and to workers at vulnerable points of their life cycle when time for caregiving responsibilities becomes most valuable, such as when a worker has a child younger than 3 years old. For example, adopting an American-style version of the individualized, "flexible employment" option now available in the United Kingdom for employees who request modifications to their standard work-hours and the adoption of "Reasonable Hours", as in Australia, would be important first steps. However, options alone in the United States may be insufficient because many workers may not avail themselves of existing opportunities unless they are accompanied by a change in a workplace culture that currently punishes the relative status of those choosing shorter-hours options.[13]

References

Altman, M. 2001. "Preferences and labor supply: Casting some light into the black box of income–leisure choice", in *Journal of Socio-Economics*, Vol. 30, pp. 199–219.

—; Golden, L. 2004. "Alternative economic approaches to analyzing hours of work regulation and reform", in M. Oppenheimer and N. Mercuro (eds.): *Economics: Alternative economic approaches to legal and regulatory issues* (New York, M.E. Sharpe).

Altonji, J.; Paxson, C. 1992. "Labor supply, hours constraints and job mobility", in *Journal of Human Resources*, Vol. 27, pp. 256–78.

—; Oldham, J. 2003. "Vacation laws and annual work hours", in *Economic Perspectives*, Vol. 28, 3Q, pp. 19–29.

Bell, L; Freeman, R. 1995. "Why do Americans and Germans work different hours?", in F. Butler, W. Shettkat and D. Soskice (eds.): *Institutional frameworks and labor market performance: Comparative views on the US and German economies*, pp. 101–31 (London and New York, Routledge).

---

[12] The 35-hours law in France was best accepted by employees (especially women) with children under 12 years old (Meda and Orain, 2002).

[13] See Drago et al. (2004); Berg et al. (2003); Maume and Bellas (2001); Hochschild (1997).

Belman, D.; Belzer M. 1998. "The regulation of labor markets: Balancing the benefits and costs of competition", in Bruce Kaufman (ed.): *Government regulation of the employment relationship* (Champaign, Illinois, Industrial Relations Research Association), pp. 178–219.

Berg, P.; Appelbaum, E.; Bailey, T.; Kalleberg, A. 2003. "Contesting time: International comparisons of employee control of working time", in *Industrial and Labor Relations Review*, Vol. 5, No. 3, pp. 331–49.

Bielenski, H.; Bosch, G. 2004. "Preferred working hours", in *British Journal of Industrial Relations*, Vol. 42, No. 1, pp. 149–66.

—; —; Wagner, A. 2002. *Europeans' work time preferences* (Dublin, European Foundation for the Improvement of Living and Working Conditions).

Bluestone, B.; Rose, S. 1998. "Macroeconomics of work time", in *Review of Social Economy*, Vol. 56, No. 4, pp. 425–41.

Böheim, R.; Taylor, M. 2003. "Option or obligation? The detriments of labour supply preferences in Britain", in *The Manchester School*, Vol. 71, Issue 2 (Mar.), pp. 113–218.

Bond, J.T. 2003. *Highlights of the 2002 National Study of the Changing Workforce*, No. 3.

Bryan, M. 2004. "Workers, workplaces and working hours", Institute for Social and Economic Research (Colchester, University of Essex).

Campbell, I. 2002. "Extended working hours in Australia", in *Labour and Industry*, Vol. 13, No. 1, pp. 91–110.

Clarkberg, M.; Moen P. 2001. "Understanding the time-squeeze: Married couples' preferred and actual work-hour strategies", in *The American Behavioral Scientist*, Vol. 44, pp. 1115–36.

Contensou, F.; Vranceanu, R. 2000. *Working time: Theory and policy implications* (Cheltenham, UK; Edward Elgar; American International Distribution Williston).

Cornell University Institute for Labour Studies. 1999. *Overtime and the American worker*. New York State School of Industrial and Labor Relations (Ithaca, New York, Cornell University Press).

Costa, D. 2000. "Hours of work and the Fair Labor Standards Act: A study of retail and wholesale trade, 1938–1950", in *Industrial and Labor Relations Review*, Vol. 53, July, pp. 648–64.

Dollard, M.; Winefield, A. 2002. "Mental health: Overemployment, underemployment, unemployment and healthy jobs", in *Australian e-Journal for Advancement of Mental Health*, Vol. 1, No. 3, pp. 1–26.

Drago, R.; Black, D.; Wooden, M. 2004. "Gender and work hours transitions in Australia: Drop ceilings and trap doors", Melbourne Institute of Applied Economic and Social Research, Working Paper No. 11/04, July.

Dunn, L.F. 1996. "Loss aversion and adaptation in the labor market: Empirical indifference functions and labor supply", in *Review of Economics and Statistics*, Vol. 78, No. 3, pp. 441–50.

Eastman, W. 1998. "Working for position: Women, men, and managerial work hours", in *Industrial Relations*, Vol. 37, pp. 51–66.

Ehrenberg, R.; Schumann, P. 1984. "Compensating wage differentials for mandatory overtime", in *Economic Inquiry*, Vol. 22, No. 4, pp. 460–78.

Euwals, R.; Van Soest, A. 1999. "Desired and actual labour supply of unmarried men and women in the Netherlands", in *Labour Economics*, Vol. 6, No. 1, pp. 95–118.

Fagan, C. 2001. "Time, money and the gender order: Work orientations and working time preferences in Britain", in *Gender, Work and Organization*, Vol. 8, No. 3, pp. 239–66.

Feather, P.; Shaw, D. 2000. "The demand for leisure time in the presence of constrained work hours", in *Economic Inquiry*, Vol. 38, No. 4, pp. 651–62.

Friedman, W.; Casner-Lotto, J. 2003. *Time is of the essence: New scheduling options for unionized employees* (Berkeley, California; Work in America Institute, Labor Project for Working Families).

Fraser, S.; Paton, D. 2003. "Does advertising increase labour supply? Time series evidence from the UK", in *Applied Economics*, Vol. 35, No. 11, pp. 1357–68.

Galinsky, E.; Bond, J.T. (eds.). 1998. *The national study of the changing work force, 1997* (New York, Families and Work Institute).

Glosser, S.; Golden, L. 2004. "The changing labor adjustment pattern in US manufacturing: The role of skill upgrades, nonwage labor costs and trade imbalance", in *International Journal of Manpower*, Vol. 25, No. 7, pp. 618–41.

Golden, L. 1999. "Projected labor market consequences of reforming the US overtime hours law", in G. De Geest, J. Siegers and R. Van den Bergh (eds.): *Law and economics and the labour market* (Cheltenham, UK, Edward Elgar), pp. 132–56.

—. 2005. "The flexibility gap: Employee access to flexibility in work schedules", Chapter 4 in I.U. Zeytinoglu (ed.): *Flexibility in workplaces: Effects on workers, work environment and the unions* (Geneva, IIRA/ILO).

—; Wiens-Tuers, B. 2005. "Mandatory overtime work: Who, what and where?", in *Labor Studies Journal*. Vol. 30, No. 1, pp. 1–23.

Hakim, C. 2000. *Work-lifestyle choices in the 21st century: Preference theory* (Oxford, Oxford Universtiy Press).

Hamermesh, D.; Trejo, S. 2000. "The demand for hours of labor: Direct evidence from California", in *Review of Economics and Statistics*, February, pp. 38–47.

Hart, Peter Research and Associates. 2003. *Imagining the future of work*. Alfred P. Sloan Foundation, February.

Hart, R. 2004. *The economics of overtime working* (Cambridge, Cambridge University Press).

Heldrich Center for Workforce Development. 1999. "Who will let the good times roll? A national survey on jobs, the economy, and the race for President", in *Work Trends Survey*, Vol. 1, p. 16.

Hochschild, A. 1997. *The time bind* (New York, Metropolitan Books).

Holtom, B.; Tidd, S; Lee, T. 2002. "The relationship between work status congruence and work-related behaviors", in *Journal of Applied Psychology*, Vol. 87, No. 5, pp. 903–23.

Hubler, O. 2000. "All goes faster but lasts longer: Computer use and overtime work", in *Ifo-Studien*, Vol. 46, pp. 49–71.

Idson, T.; Robbins, P. 1991. "Determinants of voluntary overtime decisions", in *Economic Inquiry*, Vol. 29, No. 1, pp. 79–91.

Jacobs, J.; Gerson, K. 2001. "Who are the overworked Americans?", in L. Golden and D. Figart (eds.): *Working time: International trends, theory and policy perspectives.* (New York, Routledge), pp. 89–105.

Kahn, S.; Lang, K. 1995. "The causes of hours constraints: Evidence from Canada", in *Canadian Journal of Economics*, No. 28, pp. 914–28.

Kaufman, B. 1999. "Expanding the behavioral foundations of labor economics", in *Industrial and Labor Relations Review*, Vol. 52, pp. 361–92.

LaJeunesse, R. 2004. "An institutionalist approach to work time", in D. Champlin and J. Knoedler (eds.): *The institutionalist tradition in labor economics* (Armonk, New York; M.E. Sharpe), pp. 159–74.

Landers, R.; Rebitzer, J.; Taylor, L. 1996. "Rat race redux: Adverse selection in the determination of work hours in law firms", in *American Economic Review*, Vol. 86, June, pp. 3229–48.

Lang, K.; Shulamit, K. 2001. "Hours constraints: Theory, evidence and policy implications", in G. Wong and G. Picot. (eds.): *Working time in a comparative perspective*, Vol.1 (Kalamazoo, Michigan; W.E. Upjohn Institute for Employment Research).

Maume, D.; Bellas, M. 2001. "The overworked American or the time bind? Assessing competing explanations for time spent in paid labor", in *The American Behavioral Scientist*, Vol. 44, No. 7, pp. 1137–57.

Meda, D.; Orain, R. 2002. "Changes in work and free time: Employees' opinion of the shorter working week", in *Travail et Emploi*, Vol. 90, Apr., pp. 23–38.

Merola, S.; Clarkberg, M. 2003. "Competing clocks: Work and leisure", in P. Moen (ed.): *It's about time: Couples and careers* (Ithaca, New York; Cornell University Press).

Merz, J. 2002. "Time and economic well-being – A panel analysis of desired versus actual working hours", in *The Review of Income and Wealth*, Vol. 48, No. 3, p. 317.

Messenger, J. (ed.). 2004. *Working time and workers' preferences in industrialised countries: Finding the balance* (London and New York, Routledge).

Organisation for Economic Co-operation and Development (OECD). 2004. *Clocking in and clocking out: Recent trends in working hours*, Policy Brief, *OECD Observer*, October.

Osberg, L. 2002. "Understanding growth and inequality trends: The role of labour supply in the U.S.A. and Germany", in *Canadian Public Policy*, Vol. 29, No. 2, pp. 126–43.

Peetz, D.; Townsend, K.; Russell, B.; Houghton, C.; Fox, A.; Allan, C. 2003. "Race against time: Extended hours in Australia", in *Australian Bulletin of Labour*, Vol. 29, No. 2, pp. 126–143.

Pierce, D. 2003. "Underemployment and overemployment in the labour market", in *British Economy Survey 2003*, Vol. 32, No. 2, pp. 24–27.

Rebitzer, J.; Taylor, L. 1995. "Do labor markets provide enough short-hour jobs? An analysis of work hours and work incentives", in *Economic Inquiry*, Vol. 33, April, pp. 257–73.

Reynolds, J. 2003. "You can't always get the hours you want: Mismatches between actual and preferred work hours in the United States", in *Social Forces*, Vol. 81, No. 4, pp. 1171–99.

— 2004. "When too much is not enough: Overwork and underwork in the U.S. and abroad", in *Sociological Forum*, Vol. 19, No. 1, pp. 89–120.

Roche, W. 1987. "Leisure, insecurity and union policy in Britain: A critical extension of Bienefeld's theory of hours rounds", in *British Journal of Industrial Relations*, Vol. 25. No. 1, pp. 1–17.

Rothschild, K. 1982. "A note on some economic and welfare aspects of working time regulations", in *Australian Economic Papers*, Vol. 21, pp. 214–18.

Rubin, M.; Richardson, R. 1997. *The microeconomics of the shorter working week* (Aldershot, UK, Brookfield, Vermont and Sydney, Ashgate, Avebury).

Savery, L.K.; Luks, J.A. 2000. "Long hours at work: Are they dangerous and do people consent to them?", in *Leadership and Organization Development Journal*, Vol. 21, No. 6, pp. 307–10.

Schor, J. 1994. "Worktime in a contemporary context: Amending the FLSA", in *Chicago-Kent Law*, Vol. 70, No. 1, pp. 157–72.

—. 1995. "Trading income for leisure time: Is there public support for escaping work-and-spend?", in V. Bhaskar and A. Glyn (eds.): *The North, the South and the environment, ecological constraints and the global economy* (London, Earthscan Publications Limited, United Nations University Press).

—. 2001. "The triple imperative: Global ecology, poverty and worktime reduction", *Berkeley Journal of Sociology*, Vol. 45, pp. 2–17.

Shank, S. 1986. "Preferred hours of work and corresponding earnings", in *Monthly Labor Review*, Vol. 109, pp. 40–44.

Simic, M. 2002. "Volume of underemployment and overemployment in the UK", *Labor Market Trends*, October, pp. 511–21.

Sousa-Poza, A.; Henneberger, F. 2002. "An empirical analysis of working hours constraints in twenty-one countries", in *Review of Social Economy*, Vol. 60, No. 2, pp. 209–42.

Stewart, M.B.; Swaffield, J.K. 1997. "Constraints on the desired hours of work of British men", in *The Economic Journal*, Vol. 107, March, pp. 520–35.

Stier, H.; Lewin-Epstein, N. 2003. "Time to work: A comparative analysis of preferences for working hours", in *Work and Occupations*, Vol. 30, No. 3, pp. 302–326.

Tijdens, K. 2002. *Employees' preferences for more or fewer working hours: The effects of usual, contractual and standard working time, family phase and household characteristics*, Research Report 02/15, December (Amsterdam, Universiteit Amsterdam, Institute of Advanced Labour Studies).

WOMEN'S PREFERENCES OR DELINEATED POLICIES? THE DEVELOPMENT OF PART-TIME WORK IN THE NETHERLANDS, GERMANY AND THE UNITED KINGDOM

9

Mara Yerkes and *Jelle Visser***

9.1   INTRODUCTION

In this chapter, we consider the phenomenal growth of part-time work and the emergence of the one-and-a-half earner model in the Netherlands, comparing this to the growth and the high levels of part-time work that are also evident in Germany and the United Kingdom. Despite cross-national differences in the development of part-time work, many working mothers, in all three countries, seem to accept part-time employment as a way to combine paid work and motherhood. In the Netherlands, part-time work is more widely diffused than elsewhere, among both men and women. This diffusion goes together with a pattern of "normalization" of part-time work also in terms of employee rights and entitlements, narrowing the differences between part-time and full-time work. Currently, involuntary part-time work is low in the Netherlands, with only a minor gap between women's preferred and actual working time (Yerkes, 2003). Another indicator is that the incidence of part-time work among Dutch men and women continued to rise in the 1990s, in spite of the large drop in unemployment rates, from 5.7 per cent in 1990 to 2.3 per cent in 2002 for men and from 10.9 per cent to 2.9 for women in the same period (OECD, 2004). While the initial rise of part-time employment in the Netherlands may have been shaped by the threat of unemployment, this is much less plausible for the 1990s. Hence we need to look at institutions and policies. While in a country like Denmark, the welfare state, job growth in public services and labour market and tax

---

* Amsterdam School for Social Science Research, University of Amsterdam, The Netherlands (M.A.Yerkes@uva.nl).
** Amsterdam Institute for Advanced Labour Studies, University of Amsterdam, The Netherlands (J.Visser@uva.nl).

regulations initially produced high levels of part-time employment among women, there has been a subsequent fall in the incidence of part-time work among women (Rasmussen et al., 2005). The Dutch situation, even in the 1990s, reflects a different history of women's work and motherhood, a path-dependent development that encouraged families, governments and social partners to see part-time work and shorter working hours as a model for balancing work-family pressures. In any case, the social partners and government supported the diffusion and normalization of part-time jobs towards a standard of "decent work" in terms of choice, rights, earnings and equality (ILO, 2004). Yet part-time work remains a highly gendered pheno-menon. In our comparison, we show that in Germany and the United Kingdom, which share a highly gendered employment pattern and a strong "breadwinner" welfare state tradition with the Netherlands, part-time work developed under different conditions that make it more difficult to overcome "marginalization". Recently governments in both countries, in response to European policies, particularly in the context of the European Employment Strategy, started to address issues related to part-time work, employee rights and reconciling work–family pressures.

Women's working patterns are not a new topic in sociology. Despite this, women's labour market participation patterns continue to receive a great deal of attention from scholars and policy-makers alike because many relevant questions regarding women's work remain insufficiently answered. Concerns abound regarding the proliferation of part-time work as well as care and leave arrangements within individual welfare states, which have more recently culminated in a body of research regarding women's ability to combine paid and domestic work (see Ackers, 2003; Crompton, 2002; Drew et al., 1998; Fagan, 2004; Hakim, 2000; Hantrais and Campling, 2000; Higgins et al., 2000; Kay, 2003; Kirby, 2003; O'Reilly and Fagan, 1998).

Women's participation in paid work varies across Europe. The Scandinavian countries are well known for high levels of female labour market participation, while southern European countries are often noted for having lower participation rates, with continental European countries exhibiting a female labour market participation rate generally near the European average. However, female labour force participation rates are only one part of the comparative puzzle. Levels of women's full-time and part-time work vary greatly across Europe, as do policies maintained by the various welfare states that affect women's working patterns. While most European countries have been moving away from the classic "male breadwinner" model during the most recent decades, remnants of these policies are still visible and continue to shape women's employment patterns and women's preferences and choices in combining paid and unpaid work.

It is with an eye on these employment patterns and preferences that we consider the dominant one-and-a-half earner model in the Netherlands. Is this model, as evident in the Netherlands, an example of decent work as understood by the ILO? Can it be a model for countries in which women have long remained outside the market for paid work (Visser, 2000)? With rising concerns about work intensity and pressures that make reconciling work and family aspirations difficult (OECD, 2001), can part-time employment offer a solution? What prevents the marginalization of part-time work? In this chapter we show that mothers in the Netherlands, Germany and the United Kingdom often prefer part-time work as a way of combining paid and unpaid work. Yet only in the Netherlands has this preference for part-time work been achieved in practice. Furthermore, levels of marginal work associated with very short working hours and flexible employment contracts lacking basic rights and entitlements are higher, especially in the United Kingdom. In both the United Kingdom and Germany, part-time employment is more often than not a highly constrained choice, its quality is poor, and also there are few meaningful alternatives for balancing work and family in these countries. Based on the Gender Role Modules in the ISSP[1] 2002, we observe that men and women in the United Kingdom experience much higher levels of work–family conflict and stress than in the Netherlands, which in international rankings scores the lowest stress levels. Germany takes a middle position. A plausible explanation for the high stress levels evident in the United Kingdom is that these are related to the rising number of people working very long or very short hours, and to the relative lack of control over working time. The low levels of regulation in the United Kingdom, even after the application of relevant EU law[2] by the Blair Governments, though often at the lowest possible level and with considerable "opt-out" possibilities for firms, are less conducive to making part-time work into "decent work".

In this chapter we consider with a degree of scepticism the increase of part-time work and the policies surrounding this development. On the one hand, and under conditions of conferring on part-time workers the same rights and pro rata earnings and benefits (sickness, unemployment, disability, old age pensions) as full-time workers, part-time work can be a promising alternative for remaining in the labour force. And it can be a way to address work–family issues related to having and raising children or caring for others, especially when the decision to work part time is free and reversible. Finally,

---

[1] International Social Survey Programme.

[2] The relevant EU law, in this case, comprises the directives on parental leave (Directive 96/34/EC (UK 97/75/EC)), part-time (Directive 97/81/EC (UK 98/23/EC)) and working time (Directive 93/104/EC). Two provisions in the last directive, and in particular the option for Member States not to apply art. 6 (which defines the maximum working week at 48 hours) if individual workers consent, were only used by the United Kingdom.

part-time work can be a way to enter or leave the labour force, combining education or retirement with paid work. In the Netherlands, since 2001, employees have had the right to request changes to their working hours. Similar legislation recently became effective in Germany and the United Kingdom. While legal disputes show that in the Netherlands employees usually find the law on their side, take-up rates have been very low, possibly reflecting that aspirations or preferences will not always be acted upon, as this may damage work relations and careers even in a context of overall low unemployment, as is the case in the Netherlands (Visser et al., 2004). Therefore, worker choice and influence over individual working hours should be questioned. Furthermore, part-time work remains women's work – while it is often promoted as a way for both mothers *and* fathers to achieve work–family balance, gender inequality in part-time work remains, reflecting differences in access to on-the-job training and career advantages (Evans et al., 2001).

9.2   GENERAL DEVELOPMENTS

Female labour force participation rates increased throughout the most recent decades across Europe, and there are a number of general explanations for this phenomenon. The introduction of the birth control pill was a foremost factor, as well as changes to household size, postponement of motherhood, and lessening of time spent on household chores. Economically, we also know that a number of factors increased the cost of remaining at home, making it more attractive for women to enter the labour market. Women's continued participation in higher education, rising wages and legislative changes in tax systems, and employment protection and wage setting aimed at reducing or ruling out the discrimination many women faced in the labour market, served to entice women to take part in paid labour. These developments were similar in the Netherlands, Germany and the United Kingdom, although the initial levels, timing and the nature of policies varied across countries, as did the resulting increase in female labour market participation.

Female labour market participation was slow to increase in the Netherlands, and it was not until the 1980s that women entered paid labour in large numbers. This development began in the 1960s in the United Kingdom and the 1970s in the former Federal Republic of Germany (West Germany).[3] In 2003, women's labour force participation rates were higher than the EU-15 average of 61.3 per cent in all three countries studied here (figure 9.1). The United Kingdom has the

---

[3] As will be discussed in section 9.4.1, due to the full employment policy in the former German Democratic Republic (East Germany), levels of female labour market participation were much higher there than in the former Federal Republic of Germany (West Germany). Even following reunification, the labour market participation rates of eastern German women remain higher than those of western German women.

Figure 9.1   Female labour force participation in the European Union, 2003 (percentages)

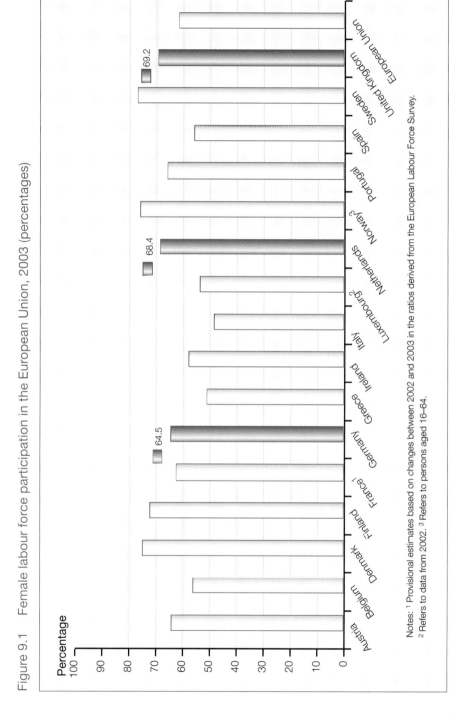

Notes: [1] Provisional estimates based on changes between 2002 and 2003 in the ratios derived from the European Labour Force Survey.
[2] Refers to data from 2002. [3] Refers to persons aged 16–64.

Source: OECD, 2004.

Table 9.1   Female labour force participation rates by age group, 2003

	15–24	25–54	55–64
Germany	44.9	78.9	34.3
Netherlands	72.7	76.5	32.9
United Kingdom[1]	63.9	76.6	47.3

Note: [1] Age group 15–24 refers to 16–24.

Source: OECD, 2004.

highest labour force participation of the three countries at 69.2 per cent, followed by the Netherlands at 68.4 per cent and Germany with 64.5 per cent. In the Netherlands female participation rates increased by 16 percentage points since 1990, in Germany by 9 percentage points, and in the United Kingdom by 2 percentage points (OECD, 2004).

The differences in female labour market participation across these three countries become more apparent when we consider selected age groups. As table 9.1 shows, all three countries have a relatively similar female activity level for women aged 25–54, yet Germany has a drastically lower participation rate for young women, and both Germany and the Netherlands have considerably lower participation rates for women over the age of 55.

Higher levels of labour market participation in the Netherlands and the United Kingdom among the young reflect the (increasing) cost of higher education. School enrolment rates are not very different, but students in the Netherlands and the United Kingdom are more likely to take part-time jobs to subsidize their studies. The cost of higher education is lower in Germany, making it often unnecessary for students to have a job on the side. The lower rates of participation for women over age 55 in all three countries are relatively common (also for men), given early retirement tendencies across western Europe, though this is more pronounced in the Netherlands and Germany than in the United Kingdom. Lower participation rates among women in older age cohorts also reflect lower participation rates in the past in both the Netherlands and Germany.

We should "correct" these patterns and trends with data on working hours and the division between full-time and part-time employment. All three countries exhibit high levels of part-time work, with the Netherlands in a record position (figure 9.2). A total of 59.6 per cent of all jobs held by women in the Netherlands are part-time jobs. The United Kingdom follows with 40.1 per cent, and Germany with 36.3 per cent; the three countries are the highest in the EU-15 (compared to 23.6 per cent for Italy, 22.8 per cent for France, 21.9 per cent for Denmark, 20.6 per cent for Sweden and 16.5 per cent in

Figure 9.2   Part-time employment in the Netherlands, United Kingdom and Germany, and the EU average, 1993–2003 (as a percentage of total employment in group)

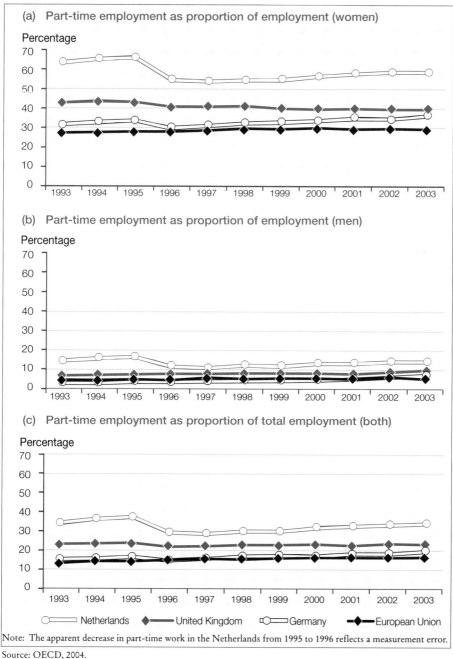

(a) Part-time employment as proportion of employment (women)

(b) Part-time employment as proportion of employment (men)

(c) Part-time employment as proportion of total employment (both)

Netherlands   United Kingdom   Germany   European Union

Note: The apparent decrease in part-time work in the Netherlands from 1995 to 1996 reflects a measurement error.

Source: OECD, 2004.

Spain) (OECD, 2004).[4] Although the incidence of part-time work is (slowly) rising among (younger and older) men, in combination with study and flexible retirement, part-time employment remains highly feminized. Three out of four part-time jobs are held by women in the United Kingdom and the Netherlands; in Germany women's share of part-time employment is even higher, at 83.3 per cent (OECD, 2004). Labour markets are far from gender neutral (see Beechey, 1988; Daly, 2000; Lewis, 1992; O'Reilly and Fagan, 1998; Pfau-Effinger, 1998; Tijdens et al., 1997; Tijdens, 1998; Tijdens, 2002). The Netherlands is an interesting case study, as it exhibits the highest level of part-time work among these three countries, as well as a seemingly strong female preference for this work form, shaped however in the context of a history of a strong "male breadwinner" model. The next section outlines how this development occurred.

9.3   THE NETHERLANDS

As indicated in the introduction, the Netherlands is an outlier in Europe with regard to part-time employment, but it was not until the 1980s that the Netherlands took over the first place occupied at that time by Sweden, Denmark and the United Kingdom. During the 1980s the growth of part-time employment accelerated in tandem with the rise in female and service employment. The initial diffusion of part-time employment was mostly the unintended consequence of the late entry of women into the labour force, following the rise in education and a shift in values, at a time of fewer employment opportunities, wage moderation and policy pressures towards the redistribution of work (Visser and Hemerijck, 1997; Visser, 2000). The absence of facilities and support for childcare made part-time employment the dominant coping solution for mothers. The part-time option was reinforced by the labour market adversity and by the wage moderation of the 1980s, stimulating the need for extra earnings in households. Employers saw part-time employment as a flexible, reversible and individual solution for work-sharing, and an alternative to the collective working time reduction desired by the trade unions. Public sector employers saw it as a way to save money without having to dismiss employees. Young women wanting or raising children, especially those working in the public sector, saw it as a way to hold on to their jobs and continue their careers, rather than retiring temporarily from the labour market as had been common for their mothers. Politicians, both left and right, saw it as a method of work-sharing in times of high (youth) unemployment and as an alternative to expensive public facilities for

---

[4] We define part-time jobs as those below 30 hours per week. See Lemaître et al. (1997).

childcare. After initial resistance to part-time work, associated with inferior working conditions, the Dutch trade unions came around in support of it, often under pressure from their female members. Towards the end of the 1980s, with collective working time reduction on the "back burner", Dutch trade unions began to encourage the "normalization" of part-time work, working towards equal rights and pay compared to full-time workers, the right of choice of employees, and similar levels of protection. They also pressed for better leave facilities for parents with young children and for public subsidies and employer investment in childcare. Several central agreements with employers in the 1990s tried to put these issues on the agenda of lower-level bargainers in sectors and firms.

The Netherlands comes from a deeply, socially and culturally, embedded model of housewifery (Knijn, 1994; Pfau-Effinger, 1998). In 1965, 84 per cent of the adult Dutch population expressed reservations concerning working mothers of school-going children. However, in 1970, this disapproval suddenly dropped to 44 per cent, decreasing to a mere 18 per cent in 1997 (SCP, 1998). It is useful to point out that this change in opinion preceded the improvement in services and conditions facilitating the combination of work and childcare. The same goes for institutional factors. Relative wages and returns from labour are influenced by institutional factors such as government and union wage policies, taxation and employment bans. All this changed, often under pressure from relevant EU laws. Until the early 1990s, minimum wage legislation excluded those working in "mini-jobs" (defined as under 15 hours per week), most of whom were women. The exclusion of part-time employees, again mostly women, from pension funds became illegal in 1994. Various smaller discriminations existing in collective agreements were successively removed during the 1990s.

In the 1990s, part-time jobs became common. Part-time jobs exist in two out of three firms with ten or more employees (StAr, 1997), and they can now be found in all sectors of the economy, as well as in all occupations – even at the managerial level (CBS-statline). However, short-hours part-time jobs remain an issue in the retail trade, hotels and catering, cleaning, nursing, teaching, and in personal services (in the last-mentioned branch, there also seems to be an issue of informal and undeclared work). In the 1990s, the Dutch labour market combined a *high incidence* of part-time work with a comparatively *small divergence* in occupational profiles between full-timers and part-timers (Fagan et al., 2000), which can be taken as one indicator of "acceptance" and "normalization" of part-time work. As noted in the introduction, levels of involuntary part-time work are now quite low in the Netherlands, and part-time jobs are, on the whole, not "marginal" – meaning that they are covered by the same rights and entitlements as those that apply to full-time workers. Legislation regarding the equal treatment of part-time workers became effective in 1996 (Wet Gelijke Behandeling), and the quality of part-time jobs in the Netherlands is comparatively high. Furthermore, the Working Hours Adjustment Act of 2000 (Wet Aanpassing Arbeidsduur) guarantees individual workers the right to request either an increase or decrease in their working hours. The reversibility of lengthening or shortening the individual work-week is a step towards part-time work as decent work. Yet part-time work is not gender neutral in the Netherlands, and despite policy efforts to increase men's participation in caring and household tasks (SZW, 2003), women are still more likely to perform caring and domestic duties. Also, part-time work does carry disadvantages: some in earnings (especially in the private sector and mostly in fringe benefits as opposed to wages), more in lower participation in job training, and also in career development prospects. And only the long-hours part-time jobs or those with higher earnings would seem to guarantee individual subsistence, outside of a household with additional income from earnings, benefits or rents. Yet panel data suggest that even among younger generations, mothers who have chosen to work part time when raising young children do not return to working full time when their children grow older. It is also relevant to note that the persistence of the part-time pattern continued when unemployment rates among women dropped significantly in recent years. All this points to part-time work as a choice above full-time work, in spite of some significant disadvantages but with the advantage of more disposable time for rest, care, education, travel or leisure. It goes without saying that such choices are made under constraints, such as individual and household earnings, the decisions and preferences of partners, a particular gendered division of household tasks, and job opportunities.

Concluding this section, we observe that part-time jobs in the Netherlands are *neither atypical nor flexible*, though the diffusion of part-time jobs is likely to have increased the aggregate flexibility of the Dutch labour market, bringing in more diversity in working time patterns. The "normalization" of part time is supported by the current process of "negotiated flexibility" in working time regimes, encouraged by various central, sectoral and company-level agreements. In recent times, these agreements offer a "choice" or "à la carte" menu to individual workers – supporting the possibilities of "working time" accounts or banks, the exchange of money for time, or time for money. Yet limited childcare facilities remain a crucial factor. Demand for childcare grew steadily, but it took until 1987 before unions, under pressure from their female members, began to negotiate childcare facilities in collective agreements (Tijdens et al., 2000). By its own admission, the Dutch welfare state does rather poorly, in comparison with other countries, in supporting young families (SZW, 2000). According to the Central Planning Bureau, the official

Dutch economic forecasting institute, the lack of – and the cost of – childcare facilities can become a constraint, limiting labour supply and putting pressure on wages (CPB, 1998). There is also the issue of falling birth rates and the high average age at which women give birth. Finally, although the Netherlands implemented relevant EU legislation on parental leave, in the private sector such leave is often unpaid. Like the absence of full-day schooling in some (rural) parts of the country, this structures the choice towards part time rather than continuing in a full-time job after a labour market interruption.

9.4   GERMANY AND THE UNITED KINGDOM

A high level of part-time work is not solely a Dutch phenomenon (O'Reilly and Fagan, 1998). While the Netherlands shows extremely high levels of part-time work, part-time work is also high in Germany and the United Kingdom in comparison to other EU countries (Fagan and Rubery, 1997; Killmann and Klein, 1997; OECD, 2004; Pfau-Effinger, 1998). Furthermore, part-time employment as a proportion of total employment continues to increase in Germany. Part-time employment has remained relatively stable in the United Kingdom over the last few years, although as a proportion of total employment, current levels reflect a growth of nearly 7 per cent in part-time work over the last three decades in both countries.

Germany presents an interesting research case because of the division between east and west. Despite unification in 1990, many differences still exist between eastern and western Germany when considering levels of part-time work. In unified Germany, part-time work levels are currently 19.6 per cent (OECD, 2004). This reflects a steady increase of 0.5 per cent per year since 1990 (OECD, 2004). The United Kingdom also has a tradition of high levels of part-time work. The current level of part-time work is 23.3 per cent, which is the second highest in the EU (after the Netherlands) and has been relatively stable since the early 1990s (OECD, 2004).

Part-time work remains a gendered phenomenon in Europe (Drew et al., 1998; O'Reilly and Fagan, 1998; Tijdens, 2002). Despite increases in male part-time working, women work decidedly more in part-time positions, and this is reflected in women's share in part-time employment, as well as in the proportion of part-time employment in women's total employment. Again, both Germany and the United Kingdom have lower levels of part-time work among women than in the Netherlands, but still higher than the EU-15 average of 30.1 per cent. Part-time levels among women are 36.3 per cent and 40.1 per cent in Germany and the United Kingdom in 2003 (OECD, 2004). Since 1990, these levels of part-time work among women have been constant in the United Kingdom and rising slightly in Germany. In both countries, the incidence of part-time work among males is increasing, albeit from very low levels. Male part-time work is most frequent in the Netherlands (14.8 per cent), followed by Denmark (10.5 per cent) and the United Kingdom (9.6 per cent), whereas it is below the EU-15 average (of 6.3 per cent) in Germany (5.9 per cent) (OECD, 2004). The share of women in part-time work is very high but slowly falling in both countries.

9.4.1 Germany

Taking a closer look at the development of part-time work in Germany, we see that part-time work evolved as more of a west German phenomenon. This is not surprising given the communist past of east Germany, where full employment, and hence *full-time* employment for both men and women, was the norm. Due to these differences, western Germany tends to have a lower female labour force participation rate. In eastern Germany, the activity rate for women is 14 percentage points higher, and this difference increases to 18 percentage points when married women are taken into account (Garhammer, 2000). However, while the level of labour market participation is higher in east Germany, this level has been decreasing since reunification in 1990, whereas the level of western German women entering and staying in the labour market continues to rise. This variation is also reflected in annual average working hours per person. Annual average working hours for both sexes have declined in the last 13 years in both eastern and western Germany, but annual average working hours continue to decline at a faster rate in eastern Germany than in western Germany (OECD, 2004).[5] Only in the last year did annual average working hours show a slight increase in both eastern and western Germany. However, while western Germany had a higher average of annual working hours at the time of reunification, the western Bundesländer have since maintained lower annual average working hours over the last five years in comparison with eastern Germany, and according to OECD figures, the gap between east and west is closing (figure 9.3).

Whether the differences in annual average working hours between the old and the new German states will dissipate over the next few years remains to be seen. Figures from EIRO (2002) suggest that average annual working hours declined at similar rates in both parts of the country. The dramatic decline in annual average working hours per person in western Germany in the early 1990s reflects reduced contractual working hours for full-time employees; in eastern Germany unions pressed in the same direction, but with considerably less success.

---

[5] Figures reflect annual average hours worked per person, both sexes. Figures on average annual hours worked in eastern Germany were calculated by the authors, based on OECD figures for unified and western Germany.

Figure 9.3   Annual average working hours per person, Germany 1990–2003

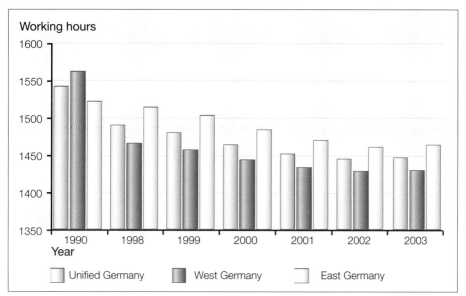

Source: OECD, 2004.

Women's part-time preferences

The development of part-time work in both eastern and western Germany cannot be attributed to a dominant preference among women. The male breadwinner model was a dominant factor in Germany during the development of high levels of part-time work among women; west Germany was a so-called "strong" male breadwinner state (Lewis, 1992). The "strong" male breadwinner model places an emphasis on the private responsibility of families for childcare and makes the employment of a second earner disadvantageous. In Germany, while the male breadwinner state actually created facilities and services for women with children, these policies served to push women out of the labour market. Opening times of schools and kindergartens, and the poor availability of childcare, also discouraged the active participation of mothers, especially those with young children (Killmann and Klein, 1997; Pfau-Effinger, 1998). Furthermore, the spouse-based joint tax-splitting system provided one of the highest levels of sole-earner relief, thereby supporting the male breadwinner model (Dingleday, 2001). In western Germany, part-time work provided an inroad into the labour market for many women, and in eastern Germany, part-time work was often involuntary as full-time work is the norm. Due to these limited options, as well as social norms regarding childcare, part-time work developed as a coping solution for many women looking to combine work and family life, rather similar to the Netherlands. However, this holds true only for western Germany. Part-time work has been forced onto many eastern German women after reunification, given the scarcity of available jobs and difficulties in maintaining their position in the labour market.

Remnants of this male breadwinner model still exist in Germany, allowing part-time work to remain an especially attractive option for mothers looking to combine paid and unpaid work. Although it is slowly disappearing, the male breadwinner model still predominates in policies as well as social and cultural norms. As Pfau-Effinger (1998) argues, the male breadwinner model in Germany is being updated or, as she calls it, "modernized". This is particularly true in western Germany, whereas in eastern Germany, part-time work is considered to be less prestigious, with lower incomes, resulting in fewer preferences for this form of working time (Garhammer, 2000). We see the effects of this development reflected in German women's working preferences today. Part-time work is now preferred by many western German mothers looking to combine work and family life, although many mothers of young children prefer to remain outside the labour market until their child is older (Garhammer, 2000; Killmann and Klein, 1997). The same cannot be said of eastern German women, who continue to prefer full-time work.

The role of government policy

The preferences of western German women for part-time work only played an indirect role in the strong development of part-time work in Germany, yet the initial growth and development of part-time work in Germany is not diectly attributable to government policy either. Part-time work was not directly supported by the government until late into the tenure of the centre-right Kohl Governments (1982–98), later continued by the centre-left coalition under Gerhard Schroeder (1998–2005). With rising unemployment and in an apparent move to counter collective work-sharing options of the German unions, the Kohl Government, and German employers, began to discover and praise the part-time job expansion of its small western neighbour. However, there were very few concrete policy proposals. In the mid-1990s there were only some job creation schemes, including some measures to reduce working hours to 80 per cent of the normal working time in the public sector (Killmann and Klein, 1997). Under the first Schroeder Government in 1998, support of part-time work, in the form of "mini-jobs" (with lower levels of wage costs and social protection), and legislation regarding employees' ability to work part time became more important. Some of the more recent efforts to support part-time work during the second Schroeder Government include the attempt to re-regulate "mini-jobs" and address work–family balance issues, also in response to European legislation and policies.

In 2001, the new law on part-time and fixed-term work came into effect, which gives employees the right to request a reduction in working time in companies with more than 15 employees and places restrictions on the use of fixed-term contracts (EIRO, 2002). While the long-term effects of this legislation are not yet visible, initial reports suggest that only a minority of employees is exercising their right to reduce working hours, less than 1 per cent in the year the new legislation came into force. Four out of five employees requesting a reduction in working hours are women (EIRO, 2003a). It is difficult to say whether greater numbers of employees will make use of this legislation, yet it theoretically provides many employees with the opportunity to have more influence over their individual working time.

The new focus on work–family balance could work to increase the popularity of reduced working hours, mostly in the form of part-time work. Legislation introduced in 2002 to promote work–family balance (EIRO, 2003a) intended to promote women's employment and increase equal employment opportunities for men and women. This legislation prompted mixed responses from the social partners and women's organizations. Social partners herald the legislation as much needed, yet employers' organizations remain sceptical about increased costs. Women's organizations feel the legislation is not far-reaching enough to create significant change. The current work–family balance campaign by the Ministry for Family, Seniors, Women and Youth, while recognizing problems such as a lack of childcare and the unwillingness of employers to address work–family issues, mainly recommends voluntary solutions, to be found in the context of collective bargaining (BFSFJ, 2003). German collective bargainers seem to have been less prominent in their attempt to raise the profile of part-time work and create a more sustainable balance of work and family life in comparison with their Dutch colleagues, possibly reflecting lower levels of cooperation between the social partners, and less coordination across sectors, using central agreements to recommend particular solutions or norms.

Furthermore, new regulations allowing employees to earn up to 400 euros monthly, exempt from payroll taxes and social security contributions, serve to increase the number of "mini-jobs" present in the German labour market. These jobs are mostly found in the service sector, typically performed by women, and hardly satisfy conditions of "decent work" in terms of earnings, social protection, and rights at work (EIRO, 2003a). This development is likely to reinforce the negative qualities of part-time work and contributes to a "marginalization" rather than a "normalization" of part-time work. By actively supporting the growth of short-hours jobs, the Government allows "marginal" part-time work to grow – i.e., those part-time jobs that are often precarious and poorly paid. And while new legislation allows employees to request a reduction in working hours, complementary legislation is necessary that secures the rights and position of people choosing to reduce their working hours.

The social partners

The growth of part-time work is not attributable to the policies of the social partners either. German trade unions responded similarly to Dutch unions, fighting the growth of part-time jobs, and unlike their Dutch counterparts, German unions were less in need of developing a part-time strategy. German unions were much stronger and more successful in pressing the collective solution to work-sharing by means of a reduction of working hours for all, and with fewer concessions on flexible working time. Before unification in 1990 and the economic crisis that followed, the economy performed better and unemployment was lower. Consequently, there was less pressure to create part-time jobs (for young people and women) as a "second-best" solution (compared with full-time work, but always better than unemployment). Other typical pressures, like wage moderation or an early central agreement in which employers adopted part-time work as a possible work-sharing solution in times of high unemployment, like the 1982 Wassenaar agreement in the Netherlands, were absent in Germany. Part-time work did not become a strategy for entry into the market for paid labour by women, but rather it became a tool for flexibility in the service sector for employers (Pfau-Effinger, 1998). This difference – whether part-time jobs result from the character of the labour supply or derive from the flexibility needs of employers – tends to have a big influence on the rights and conditions of part-time work, and on its image in society. Trade unions are slowly changing their perspective and have become supportive of government legislation allowing employees to request a reduction in working hours. Without specifically promoting part-time work, the German Federation of Trade Unions encourages a continued reduction of the working week as a means to achieve full employment (DGB, 2003). The reduction of the working week is seen primarily as a means of reducing the very high levels of unemployment, but also as a means of creating a better work–family balance.

Employers continue to resist the reduction in weekly working hours and have instead pressed for longer working hours as a means to raise competitiveness levels (EIRO, 2003a). Due to employer resistance, there have been relatively few changes to the collectively agreed work-week in the last two years of collective bargaining, and in 2003 the German unions in metal engineering lost a major strike on the issue. Many developments – towards both longer and shorter working hours – now take place in the context of special company arrangements, using hardship and opening clauses in sectoral agreements. Some of these, for instance at Volkswagen, Bayer and Deutsche

Bahn (the German railways), do address work–family balance issues, but it is impossible to say whether or not this is a general trend (BFSFJ, 2003).

Summing up, we see that the development of part-time work in Germany shares some parallels with the Netherlands, yet women's preferences for "soft" labour markets appear to be much less widely diffused and defended. The growth of the service sector, and with it part-time jobs, contributed significantly to the development of part-time work in Germany, although the pace of service sector growth was admittedly slower in Germany than in the Netherlands. Together with the development of "mini-jobs", this may have trapped part-time jobs in a pattern of marginalization, rather differently from developments in the Netherlands. Social and cultural attitudes regarding working mothers reinforced women's acceptance of part-time work as a coping solution in western Germany and the labour market difficulties following reunification limited eastern German women's labour market options. These developments were reinforced by job creation schemes throughout the 1990s and today, and current legislation strives to increase employees' flexibility regarding their working hours. While employers' organizations are hesitant to support these measures, some individual employers and trade unions are slowly coming round to the Government's call for promoting work–family balance. In the Netherlands, this change came earlier and, complemented by strong advocacy of women's groups in the unions and central agreements with employers, support for the "normalization" strategy was stronger. If this normalization process is to continue, allowing part-time work to develop into a "decent" working form, the negative qualities of part-time work in Germany, such as the promotion of short-hours "mini-jobs", must be addressed, as well as attempts to increase the gender neutrality of current individual adjustments to working hours.

9.4.2 United Kingdom

The development of part-time work in the United Kingdom differs from both Germany and the Netherlands mainly because it is shaped in a much less regulated labour market. The similarity lies in the heritage of a strong male breadwinner model (Lewis, 1992). Hence, in the United Kingdom, part-time work also developed mostly as a means for women wishing to combine paid labour and motherhood (Bruegel and Perrons, 1998). Nearly all of the post-war growth in married women's employment can be explained by the growth in part-time work (Lewis, 1992). However, there are two distinct differences in the way in which part-time work developed in the United Kingdom. First, while part-time work among women differs between the eastern and western parts of Germany, in the United Kingdom part-time work among women is divided along ethnic lines.

Full-time, not part-time, work seems to be the norm for minority ethnic women in the United Kingdom and ethnic minority women are more likely than white women to be working full time. This full-time pattern varies little based on occupation or the presence of children in the household (Dale and Holdsworth, 1998). Second, working hours are polarized in the United Kingdom, and part-time work often consists of "marginal" – i.e., very short – hours, which serves to increase the level of involuntary part-time work among women. Due to the short-hours nature of part-time work in Britain, workers are often excluded from social protection benefits, making their labour market position even more precarious (Bruegel and Perrons, 1998; Fagan and Rubery, 1997).

Women's part-time preferences

The growth in female part-time work in the United Kingdom is not reflective of female preferences for part-time work, but stems from the necessary practicalities of household and family organization and deeply entrenched social attitudes, a trend we see in Germany and the Netherlands as well (Fagan and Rubery, 1997). The largest preference for part-time work can once again be found among mothers looking to combine paid work with family responsibilities and childcare. Even with a slight increase in full-time jobs, most married mothers continue to work part-time (Dale and Holdsworth, 1998). As noted previously, it is more common for women of ethnic minorities to remain in full-time employment after having children. This is also true for highly educated women (Fagan and Rubery, 1997). Yet even this group of women is significantly smaller in comparison to other European countries due to long-held social beliefs regarding motherhood and paid work in the United Kingdom, a trend also visible in the Netherlands and Germany (Fagan and Rubery, 1997; Pfau-Effinger, 1998). However, the difficulty of combining paid work with motherhood does not deter all women from participating in the labour market. Despite a lack of childcare, young women with children have experienced the highest increase in the rate of labour market participation in the United Kingdom (Fagan and Rubery, 1997).

The largest inconsistency between the development of part-time work and women's working time preferences lies in the issue of hours. The precariousness of "marginal" part-time jobs in the United Kingdom is reflected in these preferences; very short working hours remain unpopular in the United Kingdom and longer hours are preferred by nearly one in five part-time workers (Fagan, 2000). In households where aggregate working hours are long, though, women do have a preference for shorter hours. The development of part-time work in the United Kingdom was not driven by women's preferences and their current preferences reflect the problem of undesirable hours in part-time work, creating serious obstacles to "decent" part-time work. This is in contrast to the Netherlands, where part-time work is more the outcome of what women want – admittedly conditioned by various constraints, but none-theless much less under direct influence of employers' need for flexibility. As is argued by Berg and colleagues (2003), in countries with little labour market regulation and low coverage of collective bargaining, as is the case in the United Kingdom (and the United States), employers have more power to shape when and how long people work, and employee autonomy is usually very low. This is, in the case of the United Kingdom, also reflected in higher levels of conflict and stress over work–family issues among both men and women, compared to Germany and, especially, the Netherlands (according to ISSP data of 2002). Fagan (2004) concurs that – apart from the length of working hours – it is the control of workers over their individual working hours that is crucial.

The role of government policy

This situation of extreme working hours in the United Kingdom stems partly from the laissez-faire government policies present until the Blair Administration. In contrast to Germany and the Netherlands, there was no explicit government policy concerning long working hours or promoting part-time work. Relevant EU legislation did not apply before 1997 and when it did, after the change in government, this legislation was applied in a minimalistic way. The expansion of part-time employment that did take place was market driven and hardly constrained by legal norms (Fagan et al., 2000). Many part-time jobs were marginal, without employment protection, and based on very short weekly hours (fewer than 16). While countries sometimes promote part-time work or reduced working hours to combat unemployment, this was not the case in the United Kingdom. The British Government maintained a policy of allowing firms to choose their own working time arrangements, both very long and very short hours.

Since the Blair Government took office in 1997, several changes to labour regulations have been made, including the introduction of a minimum wage in 1999; changes to maternity leave and the introduction of paternity leave arrangements in 2002; and, similar to Germany, a new effort has been launched to help employees reconcile work and family life (EIRO, 2003d). In 2000, the Government started a new campaign on the reconciliation of work and family life, asking employers to consider more "family-friendly" policies. This campaign culminated in the new Employment Act of 2002, which included the changes to maternity pay and maternity leave as well as introducing a paternity leave arrangement. However, the new legislation on Flexible Working Regulations, which allows working parents to reduce working hours under certain conditions, remains controversial (EIRO, 2003c). The change in legislation allows parents with children under the age of 6 (or a disabled child up to 18 years of age) to ask for changes in working hours and times and to request being able to work at home. These requests can only be applied for after 26 weeks of employment with one employer, and are restricted to those persons bearing responsibility for the raising of the child (EIRO, 2003c).

The new emphasis on family-friendly working time policies is popular among employees, but both unions and employers have responded with less enthusiasm. A recent government survey shows that nearly half of the respondents find flexible working hours more important than other company benefits: one-third of those employees surveyed would rather have flexible working hours than a moderate increase in annual earnings of one thousand pounds sterling (EIRO, 2003b). Currently, the Government is focused on three goals within the work–family balance campaign. These include focusing on sectors where the work–family balance is most critical, addressing the long-hours culture, as well as providing assistance and guidance as employers and employees adjust to the new policies and regulations. In the United Kingdom, about one-third of all men and close to 10 per cent of all women in employment work 48 hours (the EU maximum) or more; in Germany the percentages drop to 15 and 5 per cent, in the Netherlands to 10 and below 5 per cent respectively (data taken from the European Labour Force Survey of 2001, Eurostat). While a considerable part of the long-hours culture is associated with self-employment, it affects a very large number of the dependently employed as well. The current struggle between unions, employers and the Government, and with the European Commission, over the continuation of an "opt-out" for individual firms and employees, allowing longer working hours than those provided by relevant EU legislation, is directly related. It is the flip side of the unregulated development of part-time work as a special marginal segment of the British labour market. This certainly does not help to shape part-time work as a form of decent work, even though with its disadvantages part-time work has the benefit of allowing a reconciliation of work–family pressures during a particular phase in one's life.

The social partners

Just as there was no explicit government policy to promote the development of part-time work, the social partners did not actively endorse this work form either. The role of the British social partners differs from that in the Netherlands and Germany. During the 1990s in the United Kingdom, collective bargaining no longer took place on the national or sectoral level, and the coverage of employees under collective agreements dropped to half the levels in Germany and the Netherlands (EC, 2004). Only a minority of 35 per cent of all employees is covered by collective agreements in the United Kingdom. In terms of content, company-level collective agreements in the United Kingdom regulate matters of part-time rights distinctively less than even those in Germany, let alone the Netherlands. The lack of statutory or voluntary regulation, combined with the growth of the service sector, allowed British employers to cater to consumer-oriented services, contributing to the growth of part-time work, very short hours and very long hours, as well as unsocial hours – leaving employees with little control over their working times. Employers also often created low-skilled positions to restrict training costs, thereby increasing the number of low-skilled part-time jobs. British trade unions did little to halt these developments, and often remained supportive of overtime and unsocial hours working, with rendered extra pay (Fagan and Rubery, 1997). In the context of the recent activities of the Government to promote a better work–life balance, the social partners have been more vocal. The Trades Union Congress (TUC), the main organ for labour, representing 71 British unions, now focuses on work–family issues, with an entire section of its website dedicated to "changing times" (www.tuc.org.uk), and it is seeking a "partnership" on this issue with employers. While the TUC is enthusiastic about the new working time legislation, it is concerned that the legislation is not tough enough, providing employers with the means to reject employee requests.

The reaction of employers' organizations is mixed. While the Confederation of British Industry (CBI) responded favourably to the new working time legislation, the Institute of Directors (IoD) condemned the legislation as harmful to businesses, claiming that it will cause conflicts in the workplace (EIRO, 2003d). The CBI also expressed some concerns regarding the costs and consequences of such legislation on the preferences of those employees without children, many of whom may now want to have "flexible" working times as well.

Despite current similar campaigns to promote work–life balance, the development of part-time work in the United Kingdom differs from that in both Germany and the Netherlands in many respects. Precisely because of a lack of government labour market regulation, part-time work was allowed to expand and grow. Employers made use of this liberal labour market to promote consumer-oriented part-time jobs in the service sector and low-skilled part-time jobs. British part-time jobs lack the rights and quality often found in part-time jobs in the Netherlands. A working hours culture of extremes developed in the United Kingdom and consequently, part-time jobs are often short-hours positions with lower pay and poor benefits. All of this means that most part-time jobs are far from the aspirations and standards of "decent work". The gendered nature of part-time work reinforces that conclusion, although that is an issue in all three countries. However, in the United Kingdom, the issue of entrapment into low-skilled, low-paid and unprotected part-time jobs is mainly an issue for women, and is much more pervasive than in the other two countries. This is reinforced by the short supply of accessible and affordable childcare facilities and the very minimalistic application of relevant EU regulations on maximum working hours, paternal leave, irregular work and part-time employment.

9.5 CONCLUSION

This chapter attempts to explain the growth and high levels of part-time work in Germany and the United Kingdom by looking at which factors account for the phenomenal growth of part-time work and the existence of the one-and-a-half-earner model in the Netherlands. We show that while the growth in Dutch part-time work is attributable to women's preferences for "soft" labour markets, policies of the government and the social partners followed, rather than preceded, this development. However, the effect of such supportive policies was much stronger in the Netherlands than in the other two countries.

A number of similarities in the growth of part-time work are evident among the Netherlands, Germany and the United Kingdom. First, all three were strong breadwinner states, yet the effect of this on women's working times was differentiated within these countries. In Germany, there is a divergence between its eastern and western halves, with marked differences in labour market participation and part-time work levels both before and after reunification. The male breadwinner model present in west Germany discouraged the active participation of mothers of young children, making part-time work a more attractive solution. In contrast, until reunification in 1990, full-time work was the norm for women in east Germany, and the growth of part-time work among women in eastern Germany often remains involuntary. The presence of a strong breadwinner state also affected the growth of female part-time work in the United Kingdom, but here the effects of this model on working times differentiate themselves along ethnic lines. Part-time work developed as a norm for white women, whereas ethnic minority women are more likely to work full time. In the Netherlands, it seems as if levels of part-time work are homogeneous across all groups of women. Given the difference in size between the Netherlands and countries like Germany and the United Kingdom, this lack of variation in part-time work might be expected. However, despite the seemingly homogeneous nature of part-time work in the Netherlands, further research is needed to determine whether part-time working differences might exist along ethnic lines.

Within the Netherlands, but also in Germany and the United Kingdom, part-time work developed as a "second-best" option for many women, particularly working mothers. Part-time work was preferred to staying out of the labour market, or being unemployed (with few rights or benefits) – but not to a full-time job, with full rights, earnings and benefits. Therefore a danger of marginalization was present in all three countries, certainly in the initial stages of the growth of part-time work. We show that in the Netherlands this risk was reduced by an early and relatively effective strategy of "normalization" of part-time work, narrowing the differences in rights, benefits and earnings with full-time work, a strategy in which unions, employers and governments played a role. The successful diffusion of part-time work throughout all sectors and occupations in the Netherlands suggests some success of this development, although the heavily gendered nature of part-time work, as well as the lower training and career opportunities, signify some remaining obstacles and shortcomings on the road to fully defining part-time work in that country as "decent work". In Germany there are conditions for a similar strategy, though there appears to be more reluctance to accept this strategy, especially among the social partners, but perhaps also among German employees, both male and female. In the United Kingdom, however, part-time work developed in a far less regulated context and has, as a consequence, become heavily associated with marginal employment, low pay and little skill training. A qualitative strategy of normalization, upgrading the rights and attractions of part-time work, would require a much greater and most probably joint effort of the Government, unions and employers.

We conclude with some remaining questions regarding the growth of part-time work among women that are not answered in this chapter. Why did Dutch women continue to work in part-time jobs, despite more opportunities for full-time work and rapidly falling unemployment rates? Why did they not follow the road of Danish women? How decisive or important are leave rights in such developments and how do unemployment benefits rights factor in? Is the higher rate of full-time employment among Danish compared with Dutch women also reflective of higher divorce rates and more Danish women living on their own? How are norms concerning working hours and leisure, and full-time and part-time work, shaped and changed? Why is the take-up rate of leave rights among men so low, and why do only few women use their right to change working hours in all three countries? How do relative wage differences, education and training rights influence the gender structure of part-time and leave decisions? Finally, the issue of choice and control over when and how long one works – in a lifetime perspective – should be an issue high on the agenda for future research and in the search for decent work.

References

Ackers, P. 2003. "The work–life balance from the perspective of economic policy actors", in *Social Policy and Society*, Vol. 2, No. 3, pp. 221–29.

Beechey, V. 1988. "Rethinking the definition of work: Gender and work", in E. Hagen, J. Jenson and C. Reddy (eds.): *Feminization of the labour force: Paradoxes and promises* (Oxford, Polity Press).

Berg, P.; Appelbaum, E.; Baily, T.; Kalleberg, A.L. 2003. "Contesting time: International comparisons of employee control of working time", www.cww.rutgers.edu/data.

Bruegel, I.; Perrons, D. 1998. "Deregulation and women's employment: The diverse experiences of women in Britain", in *Feminist Economics*, Vol. 4, pp. 103–25.

Bundesministerium für Familie, Senioren, Frauen und Jugend (BFSFJ). 2003. "Familienleben und Arbeitswelt-für eine neue Balance. Wünsche und Realität junger Familien" (Berlin).

CPB. 1998. *Macroeconomische verkenningen 1998* (The Hague, Centraal Planbureau).

Crompton, R. 2002. "Employment, flexible working and the family", in *British Journal of Sociology*, Vol. 53, No. 4, pp. 537–58.

—; Harris, F. 1998. "Explaining women's employment patterns: 'Orientations to work' revisited", in *British Journal of Sociology*, Vol. 49, pp. 118–36.

Dale, A.; Holdsworth, C. 1998. "Why don't minority ethnic women in Britain work part-time?", in J. O'Reilly and F. Fagan (eds.): *Part-time prospects: An international comparison of part-time work in Europe, North America and the Pacific Rim* (London and New York, Routledge).

Daly, M. 2000. "A fine balance: Women's labour market participation in international comparison", in F.W. Scharpf and V.A. Smith (eds.): *Welfare and work in the open economy: Diverse responses to common challenges* (Oxford, Oxford University Press).

Deutscher Gewerkschaftsbund (DGB) (German Federation of Trade Unions). 2003. www.dgb.de (accessed 13 January 2004).

Dingleday, I. 2001. "European tax systems and their impact on family employment patterns", in *Journal of Social Policy*, Vol. 30, No. 4, pp. 653–72.

Drew, E.; Emereck, R.; Mahon, E. (eds.). 1998. *Women, work and the family in Europe* (London and New York, Routledge).

European Commission (EC). 2004. *Industrial relations in Europe in 2004*. Directorate General of Social Affairs and Employment (Luxembourg, Office of Official Publications of the European Community).

EIRO (European Industrial Relations Observatory Online). 2002. "2001 Annual review for Germany", www.eiro.eurofound.eu.int (accessed 4 January 2004).

—. 2003a. "2002 Annual review for Germany", www.eiro.eurofound.eu.int (accessed 4 January 2004).

—. 2003b. "Government survey shows strong employee preference for flexible working (UK)", www.eiro.eurofound.eu.int (accessed 4 January 2004).

—. 2003c. "New rules on flexible working come into force (UK)", www.eiro.eurofound.eu.int (accessed 4 January 2004).

—. 2003d. "Progress on work–life balance? (UK)", www.eiro.eurofound.eu.int (accessed 4 January 2004).

Evans, J.M.; Lippoldt, D.C.; Marianna, P. 2001. *Trends in working hours in OECD countries.* Labour Market and Social Policy Occasional Papers, No. 45 (Paris, Organisation for Economic Co-operation and Development).

Fagan, C. 2000. *Employment options of the future–actual and preferred working hours.* National working paper for the United Kingdom (Dublin, European Foundation for the Improvement of Living and Working Conditions).

—. 2004. "Gender and working time in industrialised countries", in J. Messenger (ed.): *Working time and workers' preferences in industrialized countries: Finding the balance* (London, Routledge).

—; Rubery, J. 1997. "Part-time work in Britain", in M. Klein (ed.): *Part-time work in Europe: Gender, jobs and opportunities* (Frankfurt and New York, Campus Verlag).

—; O'Reilly, J.; Rubery, J. 2000. "Challenging the 'breadwinner' gender contract: Part-time work in the Netherlands, Germany and the United Kingdom", in J. O'Reilly, I. Cebrian and M. Lallement (eds.): *Working time changes* (Cheltenham, United Kingdom, Edward Elgar).

Garhammer, M. 2000. *Employment options of the future – actual and preferred working hours.* National working paper for Germany (translated version) (Dublin, European Foundation for the Improvement of Living and Working Conditions).

Hakim, C. 2000. *Work–lifestyle choices in the 21st century. Preference theory* (Oxford, Oxford University Press).

Hantrais, L.; Campling, J. 2000. *Gendered policies in Europe: Reconciling employment and family life* (New York, St. Martin's Press).

Higgins, C.; Duxbury, L.; Johnson, K. 2000. "Part-time work for women: Does it really help balance work and family?", in *Human Resource Management*, Vol. 39, No. 1, pp. 17–32.

ILO. 2004. *A framework for implementing the decent work agenda.* Circular No. 598 Director-General (Geneva, ILO).

Kay, T. 2003. "The work–life balance in social practice", in *Social Policy and Society*, Vol. 2, No. 3, pp. 231–39.

Killmann, C.; Klein, M. 1997. "Part-time work in Germany: Gender-specific structures of working hours", in M. Klein (ed.): *Part-time work in Europe: Gender, jobs and opportunities* (Frankfurt and New York, Campus Verlag).

Kirby, J. 2003. *Choosing to be different: Women, work, and the family.* Policy paper (London, Centre for Policy Studies).

Knijn, T. 1994. "Social dilemmas in images of motherhood in the Netherlands", in *European Journal of Women's Studies*, Vol. 1, No. 1, pp. 183–206.

Lemaître, G.; Marianna, P.; Van Bastelaer, A. 1997. "International comparisons of part-time work", in *OECD Economic Studies*, Vol. 29, pp. 139–52.

Lewis, J. 1992. "Gender and the development of welfare regimes", in *Journal of European Social Policy*, Vol. 2, No. 3, pp. 159–73.

O'Reilly, J.; Fagan, C. 1998. "Conceptualising part-time work: The value of an integrated comparative perspective", in J. O'Reilly and C. Fagan (eds.): *Part-time prospects: An international comparison of part-time work in Europe, North America and the Pacific Rim* (London and New York, Routledge).

Organisation for Economic Co-operation and Development (OECD). 2001. *Employment outlook* (Paris).

—. 2004. *Employment outlook* (Paris).

Pfau-Effinger, B. 1998. "Culture or structure as explanations for differences in part-time work in Germany, Finland and the Netherlands", in J. O'Reilly and C. Fagan (eds.): *Part-time prospects: An international comparison of part-time work in Europe, North America and the Pacific Rim* (London and New York, Routledge).

Rasmussen, E.; Lind, J.; Visser, J. 2005. "Working-time arrangements: What can New Zealand learn from EU countries?", in *European Studies*, Vol. 21, pp. 53–74.

SCP. 1998. *Sociaal en cultureel rapport 1998: 25 jaar sociale verandering* (Social and cultural report 1998: 25 years of social change) (Rijswijk, Sociaal en Cultureel Planbureau).

StAr. 1997. *Evaluatie van de nota inzake deeltijdarbeid en differentiatie van arbeidsduurpatronen* (Evaluation of the report on part-time jobs and differentiating working hours) (The Hague, Stichting van de Arbeid).

SZW. 2000. *De Nederlandse verzorgingsstaat in vergelijkend perspectief* (The Dutch welfare state in comparative perspective) (The Hague: Ministerie van Sociale Zaken en Werkgelegenheid).

—. 2003. "Resultaten emancipatiemonitor 2000 (Results of the emancipation monitoring) (The Hague: Ministerie van Sociale Zaken en Werkgelegenheid).

Tijdens, K. 1998. "Gender and labour market flexibility: The case of working hours", in T. Wilthagen (ed.): *Advancing theory in labour law and industrial relations in a global context* (Amsterdam, North Holland Press).

—. 2002. "Gender roles and labor use strategies: Women's part-time work in the European Union", in *Feminist Economics*, Vol. 8, No. 1, pp. 1–29.

—; Doorne-Huiskes, A.V.; Willemsen, T. 1997. *Time allocation and gender: the relationship between paid labour and household work* (Tilburg, Tilburg University Press).

—; Van Der Lippe, T.; Ruyter, E. 2000. *Huishoudelijke arbeid en de zorg voor kinderen* (Household work and the care for children) (The Hague, Elsevier).

Visser, J. 2000. *The first part-time economy in the world: Does it work?* Working Paper No. 1 (Amsterdam, Amsterdam Institute for Advanced Labour Studies, Universiteit van Amsterdam).

—; Hemerijck A.C. 1997. *"A Dutch miracle": Job growth, welfare reform and corporatism in the Netherlands* (Amsterdam, Amsterdam University Press).

—; Wilthagen, T; Beltzer, R.; Van der Putte, E. 2004. "Part-time employment in the Netherlands: From atypical to a typicality", in S. Sciarra and M. Friedland (eds.): *New discourses in labour law: Employment policy and labour law in the EU* (Cambridge, Cambridge University Press).

Yerkes, M. 2003. "Actual versus preferred working times in the Netherlands: Part-time patterns or preferences?", Conference paper for the European Social Policy Analysis Network Conference, Copenhagen, Denmark, November.

PART III

FLEXIBILITIES AND CONDITIONS OF WORK

THE WORKING CONDITIONS OF BLUE-COLLAR AND WHITE-COLLAR WORKERS IN FRANCE COMPARED: A QUESTION OF TIME

10

*Nicole Gadrey, Florence Jany-Catrice and Martine Pernod-Lemattre**

10.1   INTRODUCTION

Unskilled jobs are not disappearing. Indeed, some types of unskilled jobs have recently increased in number. The premature declaration of the advent of the knowledge society has caused researchers to neglect the analysis of low-skill jobs, whether with regard to job content, competences, pay or working conditions. These jobs are located in industries (retailing, hotels and catering, personal and domiciliary services, among others) that lie beyond the borders of the information or knowledge society. They continue to provide large numbers of jobs in today's societies. In France, the available data even show an increase in the number of unskilled workers since the beginning of the 1990s, an increase due in particular to the very strong growth of white-collar unskilled jobs. More widely, these low-skill and, in many cases, low-paid jobs often reflect the choices societies make. Thus the majority of the jobs created in the last two decades have been in low-pay sectors. In the United States in particular, as many as 80 per cent of the jobs created between 1980 and 2000 were in low-pay sectors (Mishel et al., 1999).

Against this background, the analysis of working conditions takes on a particular significance and must be given fresh life. The available surveys in this area show that, despite mechanization and automation, physical arduousness in work has not disappeared. New risks and constraints emerged (see Gollac and Vokloff, 2000) in the final decades of the twentieth century, particularly, but not exclusively, as a result of the expansion of the service sector. However, the question of working conditions is usually raised with regard to blue-collar

* All three authors are researchers at CLERSE–IFRESI, University of Lille 1, France.

workers. Thus any proposal to compare the working conditions of these two broad occupational categories requires a critical re-examination of our understanding of white-collar employees' working conditions.

It is from this point of view that we investigate in this chapter the conditions under which work in the so-called "unskilled" occupational categories is carried out. What is happening with unskilled jobs in France? Can unskilled white-collar workers be said to work in bad conditions? Are there differences, in France at least, between unskilled white-collar and unskilled blue-collar workers? If there are, what are they?

At the international level, it is true that the analysis of working conditions has been enhanced by the development of various new concepts (decent work (ILO, 2001), job quality (OECD), suitable employment). Nevertheless, certain aspects have still not been thoroughly investigated, particularly the question of the temporal availability required of workers in the service sector.

In the French literature, Gollac and Volkoff talk of the "time constraints" that weigh increasingly heavily on workers (2001, p. 183). Others include indicators of working hours among the various aspects of work organization. However, most struggle to evaluate *temporal availability* in its full extent, quantitative or otherwise, as a constituent element of employees' working conditions. Three dimensions of time (duration, predictability and schedule) are included into the broad concept of temporal availability, as we regard it, following Devetter's contribution. Devetter (2004) legitimates this choice in the following manner: "First, employees and employers consider them as substitutable dimensions, as we can see in firms' agreements or in social legislation (exchange of reduced working time or greater time sovereignty for unsocial hours, for example). Secondly, consequences on workers' health are quite comparable. Finally, the combination of these three dimensions enables to determine the 'normal practices' linked with social rhythms."

In this chapter, we examine working conditions in several service industries, in particular those in which workers are in direct contact with customers or users. A high share of jobs in these industries is "involuntary" part-time jobs, and temporal availability lies at the heart of the question of working conditions. The findings presented here show that it is part-timers who suffer the greatest hardships linked to increased temporal availability. This will raise the question of whether involuntary part-time working can be considered as "decent working time" as defined by Messenger (2004) in his studies for the ILO – in which he considers working time as one of the elements that constitute "decent work".

In order to deal with these questions in their entirety, our analysis is divided into two stages. In the next section, we characterize, by means of statistical data, the unskilled white-collar category and the sectors in which unskilled jobs are concentrated, highlighting the fact that in France workers in this category are more likely than those in other categories to suffer poor employment conditions, low pay and poor working conditions. In the following section, we analyse in greater detail the specific characteristics of working conditions in the unskilled white-collar category against the background of the question of "decent working time" (Messenger, 2004). We will show, in particular, that temporal availability is an ambiguous concept.

10.2 EMPLOYMENT AND WORKING CONDITIONS OF UNSKILLED WHITE-COLLAR WORKERS IN FRANCE

10.2.1 Some methodological preliminaries

Defining and quantifying the unskilled white-collar category is a far from simple task, since there is no unanimous agreement as to its boundaries, either within the research community in France or in international debates. Should attention be focused on the low paid, the less educated or on low-skilled or unskilled workers? The notion of unskilled worker needs to be historically (and perhaps locally) defined, and international comparative findings are very sensitive to the definition adopted (box 10.1).

Depending on whether the main concern is with individuals' lack of skills, the unskilled nature of job content, or of employment, the emphasis will be on measuring the level of formal qualification or expertise, job content, or the level of pay. However, in France, for example, there has been an increasingly evident imbalance between these three dimensions of occupational grading (Méda and Vennat, 2004) and it would seem, to judge from international data, that this is true to varying degrees in other countries as well. Thus, whereas the United States and the United Kingdom have small shares of low-skill workers in employment compared with France, the share of low-paid workers is, on the contrary, higher in the English-speaking countries: 19.4 per cent in the United Kingdom and 19.7 per cent in Ireland, compared with 15.6 per cent in France – a figure close to the European Union (EU) average (European Commission, 2004, p. 122).

Furthermore, most of the comparative studies we have been able to review are concerned more particularly, indeed exclusively, with full-time employees, which enables them to avoid the measurement difficulties associated with national variations in working time and sub-national variations in the use of part-time employment. This is a genuine concern in the case of unskilled jobs, since it is known that many part-timers are employed in such

Box 10.1   Skilled, unskilled, less skilled

A distinction is fairly commonly made in the United States between skilled and less skilled employees. Formal educational qualifications are often the only distinguishing criterion used, with those workers having no more than a high-school education considered to be "less skilled" (Blank and Card, 2000).

We have adopted a more constructivist approach to the notion of "unskilled", one that takes account of the characteristics of both the individual and the job held. France's economic and social history shows, after all, that manual workers were placed in the unskilled categories on the basis of three criteria: a low level of educational qualifications, low pay, and relatively simple job content.

For the purposes of our statistical analysis, we had to choose a classification. We adopted that drawn up by Burnod and Chenu (2001), which uses pay levels as its main criterion. This is very similar to the international classifications of low-paid workers. In France, however, two other classifications are also frequently used. These are as follows:

* Bisault, Destival and Goux (1994) drew up a definition of an unskilled job based on the employment structure survey, which is used by employers and is based on institutional distinctions, and when possible, also on collective agreements. For occupations outside the scope of this survey, the authors used the twin criteria of level of educational qualification and level of vocational training.

* Chardon (2002) has drawn up a definition "based on the degree of specialized training individuals in the post require". Any occupation for which those starting out on their careers have to undergo a specific course of training is regarded as "skilled".

jobs. If such data are used, there is considerable risk that a significant share of the workforce will be ignored and, with them, the issues specific to that category, particularly when it comes to working conditions.

For these reasons, we decided to focus solely on the unskilled category in France, making comparative references, when possible, to the OECD countries. Thus our analysis will enable us to re-examine the practices of other countries.

Who are the unskilled white-collar workers?

As the service sector has expanded in the developed economies, the white-collar category has gradually supplanted the manual or blue-collar

Table 10.1 Evolution of the economically active population in employment from 1982 to 2002, white-collar and blue-collar workers (thousands)

	1982	1990	1999	2002	Growth over the period
White-collar	5 501	5 900	6 655	7 002	27.3%
Blue-collar	7 044	6 546	5 905	6 201	−12.0%

Sources: The data for 1982 to 1999 are taken from the population census, see Amossé, 2001. Those for 2002 are taken from the INSEE Labour Survey, 2002.

Table 10.2 Who are the unskilled white-collar workers in France? Comparisons with unskilled blue-collar workers, 2002 (percentages)

	Share of women	Share of young people	Share of foreigners	Share of graduates
Active population in employment (APE)	45.3	7.7	5.5	71
Unskilled white-collar workers (UWC)	78.2	12.7	8.2	51
Unskilled blue-collar workers (UBC)	36.4	19.3	12.3	40

Source: INSEE, Labour Survey, 2002.

category. In France, the number of workers in the white-collar category increased by a factor of 3.5 between 1954 and 2002. Today, there are 7 million white-collar workers in employment, compared with 6.2 million blue-collar workers, as table 10.1 shows. Within this dominant socio-occupational category, "unskilled" workers account for almost half of total white-collar employment in France (47 per cent, see box 10.1).

This white-collar category is characterized by a very high share of women (more than 78 per cent compared with 45 per cent across all categories), by a substantial share of graduates (51 per cent unskilled white-collar workers), by a not-insignificant share of young people (almost 13 per cent of unskilled white-collar workers are under 25) and by an extremely high part-time rate – over 40 per cent (table 10.2).

Where do unskilled white-collar employees work?

Unlike unskilled blue-collar workers, who are evenly distributed among the major sectors of the economy, unskilled white-collar workers are

Table 10.3   Where are unskilled white-collar workers employed?
Comparisons with unskilled blue-collar workers, 2002
(percentages)

	Agriculture	Manufacturing	Services
Active population in employment (APE)	4	24	72
Unskilled white-collar workers (UWC)	0	3	96
Unskilled blue-collar workers (UBC)	10	42	48

Source: INSEE, Labour Survey, 2002.

concentrated overwhelmingly in the service sector (table 10.3). Within that sector, retailing, hotels and catering and personal and domestic services account for half of all unskilled white-collar workers. This pattern of distribution is found in most western countries. Again, it is in these three industries that the rates of low-paid and/or low-skilled workers are highest: "within the service sector, there are remarkable differences, with 40 per cent and 26 per cent of low paid employees in hotels and restaurants and trade, respectively, as against around 12.8 per cent in public administration, education and health" (European Commission, 2004, p. 169).

It is for these reasons that we have focused in particular on these industries in the rest of this chapter.[1]

10.2.2   Employment conditions and pay

Employment conditions

Unskilled white-collar workers do not appear to be disadvantaged when their employment conditions are compared with those of unskilled blue-collar workers (table 10.4). Whereas 10 per cent of unskilled blue-collar workers are recruited on fixed-term contracts, only 6 per cent of unskilled white-collar workers are on contracts of this type. Unskilled blue-collar workers are also more likely to be on temporary contracts; this applies to more than 11 per cent of the category in France, compared with less than 1 per cent of unskilled white-collar workers. This reflects a fairly specific characteristic of the market for temporary workers in France, where such jobs are concentrated among the manual trades; in other European countries, in contrast, there are considerably more temporary workers in the service sector (Macaire and Michon, 2002).

---

[1] Our statistical data are drawn from the INSEE employment survey, the supplementary survey on working conditions carried out by DARES (French Ministry of Labour) and a qualitative survey during which some 50 individuals were interviewed. For further details on the methodology, see the report by Gadrey et al., 2003.

Table 10.4   Employment conditions of unskilled white-collar workers, 2002 (percentages)

	Part-time rate	Share of fixed-term contracts	Share of temporary contracts
Active population in employment (APE)	16	4	2.5
Unskilled white-collar workers (UWC)	41	6	0.5
Unskilled blue-collar workers (UBC)	17	10	11

Source: INSEE, Labour Survey, 2002.

However, and contrary to what the data suggest, many white-collar workers in France are also employed on various types of precarious contracts. In order to fully explain the reasons for this, we probably need to invoke the contradictions between work and employment that Margaret Maruani (1996) so rightly points to. In essence, the question she poses is the following: how can we explain why women are so active in the labour market when employment conditions for them are so unfavourable?

The degree of precariousness measured "objectively" by categories such as temporary employment or fixed-term contracts is no longer sufficient to measure precariousness in employment. There are various factors that help to explain this apparent paradox. The first is the state of the labour market which, in France more than elsewhere because of the high unemployment rate, creates reserves of labour and makes it vital for those in employment to cling to their jobs – on the principle that "any job is better than no job at all". Forced to work in order to survive, many employees, a high share of unskilled white-collar workers among them, take jobs despite the nature of the contract on offer. This is clearly illustrated by statements such as: "As soon as I can, I'm getting another job" and "I only stay because I need a job, otherwise I'd have been out of here a long time ago".

There are other factors at work as well. One is part-time working[2] and its "procession" of additional hours, as they are often described. This temporal availability shows that employees are the first victims of flexibility, which can affect both working time and pay. This latter aspect is reflected in variable monthly earnings, depending on the number of hours worked.[3] When the "smoothing" linked to annualization does not take place, the absence of any reference point as to the level of their future pay prevents

[2] This is usually for those workers on permanent contracts.

[3] In this respect, the annualization of working time, which has accelerated with the introduction of the 35-hour working week in France, has in many cases provided the justification for the annual "smoothing" of wages, although it has often also led to increased variability of work schedules.

workers from planning for the future and heightens their feelings of economic insecurity.

The last but by no means least of these factors is that, irrespective of the quality of their current employment contracts, workers often do not regard themselves as properly established in a job until they have obtained a full-time position. We will not examine this argument in any greater detail here, since it has been set out at length by Maruani and Nicole (1989). Thus the feeling of precariousness is significantly more complex than mere consideration of the contractual link to employment would suggest and is shot through with contradictions (Gollac and Volkoff, 2000, pp. 36 and 68; Maruani, 2000). It also brings into play the social valuation of jobs (and particularly pay), career prospects (the existence of internal markets) and working conditions.

The pay of unskilled workers

A comparison of average wages in the various occupational categories reveals, first, the strikingly high pay dispersion and, second, the low level of pay in the white-collar category (table 10.5). The average wage of unskilled white-collar workers is 40 per cent lower than the average wage of all workers in France.

These statements are, justifiably, subject to qualification on the grounds that these wages do not take account of working time, which is much lower among white-collar employees than among blue-collar workers because of the significantly higher part-time rates in the former category than in the latter.

Table 10.5   Average monthly pay by occupational and skill category, 2001

	Economy as a whole (euros)	Deviation from average wage (percentage)
Average wage	1 384	–
White-collar		
Unskilled	827	–40
Skilled	1 255	–9
Blue-collar		
Unskilled	943	–32
Skilled	1 254	–9

Field: Wages in bands expressed in euros, adjusted for non-responses (incl. bonuses imputed on a monthly pro-rata basis.

Source: INSEE, Labour Survey, 2001, authors' analysis.

Calculated on the basis of full-time or part-time wages, the pay differentials among blue-collar and white-collar workers are comparable. Thus the relatively low level of average pay in the unskilled white-collar category compared with the unskilled blue-collar category can be explained to a large extent by differences in the use of part-time work: 41 per cent of unskilled white-collar workers are part-timers, compared with only 17 per cent of un-skilled blue-collar workers. The low pay of unskilled white-collar workers is largely explained, therefore, by the extent of part-time employment. Thus in the collective consciousness, the duration of working time may seem to be a major factor in the social (de)valuation of work.

10.2.3   Working conditions characteristic of a changing labour market

Statistical surveys still inadequate to the task

The combined use of statistical data and field work results reveals that the difficulties experienced by employees in the workplace have not always been taken into account in surveys conducted by national statistical institutes.

Studies of working conditions and, more generally, of job quality carried out as part of international research projects have been enhanced in a number of ways in recent years.

Thus the OECD (2001), in its work on job quality in the service sector, used the European working conditions survey to investigate the working hours aspect of working conditions, including the constraints associated with working time and work schedules and the choice of break or holiday times (European Foundation for the Improvement of Living and Working Conditions, 2001). However, investigation of this time dimension remains ergonomic and industrialist in its approach, since only night or Sunday work, irregular schedules and rotating shift systems (3 x 8) are included in the "constraining" work schedules.

The European Commission, for its part, has proposed adopting a broader approach based on job quality. "Job quality is a relative concept regarding a job-worker relationship, which takes into account both objective character-istics related to the job and the match between worker characteristics, on the one hand, and job requirements, on the other" (European Commission, 2001, interviews conducted for this study). Working time, one of the ten aspects of job quality, includes both the number of hours worked and the organization of working time (working time arrangements). The analysis focuses on questions related to the number of hours habitually worked and additional hours, actual working hours and the number of hours worked outside core working time, the distribution of working time and flexible schedules. Little attention is paid to temporal availability and, even when it is investigated, it is mainly with reference to full-time employees.

A comparison of the quality of surveys of working conditions carried out in France in different periods (particularly between the mid-1980s and the present day) shows[4] that efforts have been made to obtain a better understanding of some of the hardships workers suffer, particularly in service occupations. For example, the question on tensions with supervisors appeared in 1998, when 30 per cent of employees in the service sector stated that such tensions existed; the question on tensions with members of the public appeared in 1991, and in 1998 half of respondents in the service sector said they were affected by such tensions. With regard to other aspects of working conditions, particularly temporal availability, the working conditions survey still concentrates more on concerns relating to rotating shift systems, to shift schedules and to night work. This is due in part to its industrialist focus. It struggles to capture in all their complexity the new forms of temporal availability that can be observed on the ground in some service activities, particularly those requiring a high level of contact with customers or users. As a result, we have to fall back on surveys that focus exclusively on time, such as Cottrell et al. (2002), for example.

10.2.4   A change in the nature of working conditions

Different working conditions for unskilled blue-collar and white-collar workers are characteristic of the changes taking place in the labour market. Far from being improved by the expansion of the service sector, working conditions for the unskilled categories have changed in nature. Analyses of the Taylorist work organization systems in which manual workers were employed frequently adopted an approach based on the alienation said to be a product of the division of labour, leading to the "fragmented work" of which Georges Friedmann spoke. The routinization of tasks, the separation of planning from execution and permanent supervision by management characterize situations in which working conditions (particularly the intensity and arduousness of work and the work environment itself) are harsh but where certain forms of recognition exist. For unskilled white-collar workers, it is the need for temporal availability and workplace relations (in the fullest sense of the term) that are the prime causes of the deterioration in their working conditions. As was noted in the introduction, these aspects of working conditions are less often adduced as indicators of difficult conditions in the workplace.

---

[4] As DARES (the French Ministry of Labour) itself notes in the introduction to its version of the 1998 survey.

Table 10.6 Working conditions of skilled and unskilled white-collar and blue-collar workers: Synthetic indicators

All sectors	Skilled white-collar workers (SWC)	Unskilled white-collar workers (UWC)	Difference UWC–SWC	Skilled blue-collar workers (SBC)	Unskilled blue-collar workers (UBC)	Difference UBC–SBC
Work environment	15	18	3	36	31	−5
Workplace relations	36	38	2	29	23	−5
Work intensity	25	24	−1	36	33	−3
Temporal availability	30	32	2	30	29	−1

Note on interpreting the data: the synthetic indicator of the physical work environment for skilled white-collar workers is 15, on a scale from 0 to 100. The closer the value of the index gets to 100, the more working conditions are regarded as bad from the workers' point of view.

Source: Gadrey et al., 2003.

Quantitative analysis of the working conditions of unskilled white-collar workers in France leads to the following observations.

• Across all sectors of the economy, the data indicate that working conditions are comparable in level and nature for skilled and unskilled white-collar workers, but are slightly more unfavourable for unskilled workers – contrary to what happens in the case of blue-collar workers. Among the latter, working conditions are more favourable for the unskilled category, and the differences between skilled and unskilled workers are slightly more pronounced than among white-collar workers (table 10.6). It is as if the "working conditions" variable played a considerably smaller role in the apprehension and evaluation of white-collar workers' occupational grading. In the case of manual workers, bad working conditions have been gradually offset, in part at least, by a higher positioning in the pay scales, achieved through bargaining and a favourable balance of power. This does not seem as evident when the data on white-collar workers are examined. In this category, bad working conditions tend to be more prevalent among the unskilled.

• Considerable differences can also be observed in the perception of working conditions from sector to sector. Thus in service industries in which unskilled white-collar workers have to cope with extremely unfavourable working conditions (in the hotel and catering industry, for example), it is all occupational categories that are affected, which further blurs the boundaries between skilled and unskilled workers.

• The results of this same survey also show that certain occupations, such as domiciliary care, report less burdensome working conditions than those for workers in retailing or in the hotel and catering industry, as if, in the case of home helps, the "constraint" seemed less oppressive. The hypothesis we formulate is that, for unskilled white-collar workers in retailing and hotels and catering, there are processes of objectification at work that increase their awareness of the harshness of their working conditions. In the case of domiciliary care, other "naturalizing" processes are at work in minimizing the recognition of both competences and working conditions (Gollac and Volkoff, 2000).[5]

Thus the transition from an industrial to a service economy and the consequent erosion and destabilization of the working class has not eliminated bad working conditions. However, the nature of those bad conditions has changed. Unskilled blue-collar workers are more likely than their white-collar counterparts to emphasize the work environment and work intensity as the main causes of the arduous nature of their work. Nevertheless, the interviews we conducted with unskilled white-collar workers show that they are not entirely spared such arduousness. In retailing, these bad working conditions are sometimes used by employers to justify the use of part-time staff. Not only shop-floor workers but check-out staff as well mention the difficulties they experience in handling goods, some of which are heavy. Furthermore, the quantitative results for this sector clearly show that work intensity and the work environment are as unfavourable as those of unskilled blue-collar workers. This can partly be explained by systems of work organization that have their roots in or seek to replicate those found in manufacturing industry with, for example, a considerable increase in repetitive work.

In the hotel and catering sector, it is issues related to posture that tend to be highlighted more (standing position), which shows that blue-collar workers do not have a monopoly on physical hardship. In the case of functionally flexible team members in fast-food establishments, the arduousness linked to the work environment and intensity is exacerbated. Workers describe the severity of the conditions they have to endure, pointing in particular to extremes of cold (caused by the need to go outside frequently) and heat (generated by the cooking equipment), as well as the dirtiness of their work environment. The hardships linked to hygiene

---

[5] These authors explain, for example, how nurses changed their view of their work between 1984 and 1991. "In 1984, 40 per cent of nurses stated that they carried or moved heavy loads; in 1991, 70 per cent of them made such a statement. The heavy loads in question are usually patients. They are usually a fair weight, they have no handles and they cannot be placed in the most convenient position for handling purposes. However, to regard a person as a load requires nurses to discard a notion of their profession based on dedication without regard for self [Kergoat, 1992] (...) They were demanding that their dedication be accorded its true value" (Gollac and Volkoff, 2000, p. 10).

Table 10.7 Working conditions of unskilled white-collar workers in three service industries: Synthetic indicators

	Service sector as a whole	Retailing	Hotels/catering	SPD
Work environment	18	20	23	10
Workplace relations	38	29	40	34
Work intensity	24	29	30	16
Temporal availability	33	33	41	30

Note on interpreting the data: see table 10.6.
Source: Gadrey et al., 2003.

conditions[6] are as much physical as psychological in nature. Workers in the fast-food industry criticize the intensity of their work and the resultant psychological burdens, which result largely from the linkage to be made between a downgraded form of functional flexibility and autonomy of execution.

True, work intensification does not automatically cause workers to perceive deterioration in their conditions and is dependent on essentially human factors. Thus, in certain cases, employees, managers and organizations adopt self-preservation strategies, which are reflected, for example, in the development of a "good general atmosphere" or "good cooperation", which makes the arduous conditions more bearable.

This perception also depends on individuals' personal trajectories. If this intensification is combined with training strategies and integrated into career management plans, it tends to be perceived in a better light by employees, who take the view that it is helping to increase their stock of competences. This very clearly applies to trainees in the hotel industry, who often report reasonable working conditions. On the other hand, when the "discordances" between the three components of occupational grade (qualifications, occupation and pay) are at their greatest, perceived hardship is exacerbated: "the level of occupational grade and training is not generally commensurate with aspirations. Perceived hardship begins when the relationship between grade, training and aspirations can no longer evolve" (Dejours, 2000, interviews conducted for this study).

For the unskilled white-collar workers in the industries we studied, it is the requirement for temporal availability rather than any other working conditions that is the main cause of the hardships they experience at work (table 10.7). This is why we investigate this topic in greater detail in the next section.

---

[6] The problems encountered in cleaning public toilets are mentioned repeatedly by employees.

10.3 UNSKILLED WHITE-COLLAR WORKERS AND TEMPORAL AVAILABILITY

10.3.1 *The need to go beyond statistical analysis, or the importance of interviews in identifying temporal availability*

In his analysis of decent working time, Messenger stresses the need to take account of both the number of hours worked and the timing of those hours (Messenger, 2004, p. 2). After all, when it is analysed from a quality perspective, working time turns out to be multidimensional; this, in turn, raises questions about its duration, timing, variability and predictability.

Working time and the flexibility associated with it lie at the heart of human resource management strategies in many service activities. The various waves of working time regulations recently introduced in France, which were reflected before 2004 in a reduction in working time in exchange for greater flexibilization (with variations usually decided by employers), have further reinforced the already existing trend towards a fairly pronounced variability of working schedules. This in turn raises the questions of "family-friendly"' working hours and of healthy working time, both of which issues are highlighted by Messenger (2004, p. 30 ff.) and which are obviously of concern in countries other than France. We will return to these questions later.

This increased flexibilization is very evident in service activities that require contact with the public, which is the case with very many unskilled jobs in industries such as hotels and catering, retailing and personal services. Direct relations with customers or users are often analysed as service relations. From this perspective, such relations not only involve face-to-face contact but are also above all human relations, with all that this implies in terms of social and, particularly, gender relations. The question Messenger raises about the gendered inequality of working time takes on its full meaning here (Messenger, 2004, p. 33).

Thus, far from being protected in this respect by virtue of being frequently at the centre of the service relationship, unskilled white-collar workers report a considerable degree of flexibility in their work schedules. This is not unconnected with the high part-time rates that are characteristic of this category. They also point to time in all its various aspects as one of the principal causes of their difficult working conditions. In the light of our statistical analysis, this temporal availability and workplace relations are the aspects of their work that unskilled white-collar workers regard as the most unfavourable.

10.3.2   The forms of temporal availability

Unskilled white-collar workers and the rapidly increasing part-time rate

The use of part-time contracts is increasing, particularly when it comes to recruiting unskilled white-collar workers. It may seem surprising or paradoxical to include part-time work among the aspects of temporal availability because of the shorter working hours it implies compared with the working time norm. Nevertheless, our interviews show that in France it is part-time workers who suffer the greatest hardships linked to increased temporal availability – mainly because of the number of hours worked and how the timing of those hours is imposed by employers.

Part-time working has increased in all occupational categories, with the part-time rate rising from 10.2 per cent in the mid-1980s to 16.2 per cent in 2002. However, the increase has been significantly greater in the unskilled categories. Among unskilled white-collar workers, the part-time rate rose from 28 per cent in 1984 to almost 41 per cent in 2002, a level significantly higher than that for unskilled blue-collar workers (17 per cent in 2002). This statistical observation requires further examination.

Everything would seem to suggest that the unskilled white-collar category is becoming synonymous with part-time work, with employers increasingly making an equation between temporal availability and part-time work, on the one hand, and between part-time work and contact with the public, on the other (Guignon and Hamon-Cholet, 2003). Thus part-time work is becoming a prerequisite for the temporal availability that employers require.

The timing, variability and predictability of unskilled white-collar workers' schedules

Examination of the greatest differences between unskilled white-collar and blue-collar workers in matters of temporal availability shows that the main area of differentiation is so-called "unsocial working hours", with more than one-third of unskilled white-collar workers working on Sundays compared with 15 per cent of their blue-collar counterparts. Thus when asked "Are there certain days or weeks when you work longer hours than the usual schedule?", 56 per cent of unskilled white-collar workers reply in the affirmative, compared with only 52 per cent of unskilled blue-collar workers. And when asked "After the shift changeover, do you have to stay at work longer than scheduled?", almost one-third of unskilled white-collar workers reply in the affirmative compared with just 18 per cent of their blue-collar counterparts (table 10.8).

Unskilled blue-collar workers are also more likely than their white-collar counterparts to be entitled to two consecutive days off work: 40 per cent of

Table 10.8   Temporal availability in France, 1998: The variables (percentages)

	SWC	UWC	SBC	UBC	Total EAP
No choice of break times or have to ask permission	53	69	60	73	63
Must agree choice of work schedules with colleagues	24	23	14	13	22
Have to stay on after a change of shift	45	30	32	18	35
Schedules laid down by management and fixed schedules (neither *à la carte*, nor freely chosen)	76	85	89	92	67
Some Sunday work	25	32	19	15	29
No opportunity to change schedules when unexpected events occur	25	31	41	46	31
Work longer hours than usual on certain days or during certain weeks	27	29	25	23	33
Night work	15	9	22	14	15
Have to work longer hours than usual on certain days or during certain weeks	66	56	60	52	69
Do not have 48 consecutive hours off work	18	40	16	18	27
Do not know next day's work schedule	45	34	36	32	43
Do not know next month's work schedule	18	24	24	25	27
Do not know next week's work schedule	61	47	65	59	64

Source: Gadrey et al., 2003.

unskilled white-collar do not enjoy this right, compared with 18 per cent of unskilled blue-collar workers.

The most extreme form of temporal availability is probably encountered in retailing, where individuals are defined by their part-time status and, more generally, by their work schedules. Thus employees are personified by their working time. Employers refer to their employees by the length of their contractual working time, as this statement made by a human resources manager in a department store during our interviews illustrates: "We need two 20 hours and a full-time manager to operate the stand."

10.3.3   Specific forms of temporal availability

The interviews we conducted in three industries confirm this trend and add some additional dimensions to this analysis. Thus, in the case of home helps and workers in the hotel and catering industry and in retailing, our interviews show very clearly that the working conditions survey is ill suited to capturing the particular difficulties of temporal availability that are characteristic of part-time jobs (staggered hours, split shifts, unpredictable changes to timetables, etc.).

"Potential" availability

This is a form of availability often found among part-timers. Usually when first hired, more rarely on a regular basis, part-timers are required to offer a wide range of possible working hours on which the employer will draw in order to meet the demands of day-to-day business. Thus a restaurant worker explained that, when he was hired, his employer asked him for a potential weekly schedule of 60 hours from which a working week of just 20 hours was to be constructed.[7] When this form of potential availability is not simply required on recruitment, but is used as a form of daily job management, it can be regarded as a constraint, but one that employers are careful not to present as such.

Fragmented work

This affects the vast majority of home helps. Virtually all women, home helps attend each day to three or four elderly persons in their homes. The shortening of work sequences mentioned by both employees and employers in the domiciliary services sector further aggravates the constraints associated with fragmented schedules. Thus one worker explained that she works a 34-hour week. Her working week is divided into 17 work sequences and she attends to a total of 11 people. Her daily schedule comprises seven one-hour sequences, which all take place either very early in the morning or late in the evening in order that she can get dependent persons up and/or put them to bed.

Split shifts

The use of split shifts is a form of working time management that is frequently encountered in the hotel and catering industry as well as in domiciliary care services. Split shifts affect the length of time employees spend at the workplace. The intervals between the periods of duty, usually between two and four hours, are often too short to allow workers to return home.[8] Thus workers in fast-food restaurants or cafeterias feel, paradoxically, that they are devoting their whole lives to work, while actually being employed only part time.

Extreme unpredictability

The variability of their work schedules often makes employees feel as if they spend their whole lives in the workplace. Employees tell their supervisor

---

[7] Another restaurant worker said he had drawn up a potential 90-hour schedule for an actual working week of just 30 hours.

[8] Because of transport timetables as well as the time required to change, to "feel clean", etc.

when they are available and the supervisor then organizes the teams' schedules. Employees seldom have more than a week's notice of their schedules. In the restaurant trade, there is a high degree of unpredictability, with schedules sometimes being changed literally at the last minute. The practice of adding amendments to employment contracts represents the most extreme form of this temporal availability and is common among new recruits. Other retail workers[9] complain that schedules and the advance notice they receive are unpredictable, as one assistant in a hypermarket noted during our interviews:

> Getting advance notice of our schedules, that's the big problem. We should be told three weeks in advance what hours we'll be working . . . At Christmas, I was told at the last minute that I wasn't working, which was good news, but I would have had the same notice if I had been working. On the Friday before Christmas, I didn't know whether I was working the following Monday.

Unpaid work

The practice of not paying employees for all the time they spend at the workplace is widespread in the restaurant trade. Workers are often obliged to arrive before the beginning of their shift (often between 45 minutes and 1 hour in advance) in order to eat, change and possibly attend a briefing on the day's activities. This time is not paid for. Thus one worker calculated that, for a shift involving 4 hours' paid work, the actual time spent at the restaurant was about 5.5 hours.

In the case of home helps, these forms of unpaid work are a consequence of the fragmentation of their work. Between each work sequence, there is an interval of approximately 15 minutes that is unpaid except for those workers covered by the "Domiciliary service organizations" collective agreement; even for these workers, the agreement is applied restrictively, since only the intervals between two work sequences in the same half-day are remunerated, and travel costs are excluded.

Unpaid time and voluntary work

Another, more qualitative, aspect of temporal availability is specific to domiciliary care services, where the tradition of unpaid work by female carers is still an element in the provision of such services for the elderly. It involves devoting unpaid time to elderly clients as carers seek to develop the relational aspect of a home help's work. All the (female) workers we interviewed mentioned forms of unpaid work linked to their paid work, but there are

---

[9] This mainly applies to students or new recruits who combine involuntary short-hours part-time jobs with staggered hours, and have considerable uncertainty as to their future schedules. More established employees tend to have negotiated contracts offering longer working hours and more stable schedules.

considerable differences between those who attempt to control their working time and those who do not count the hours and minutes they spend with their elderly clients. The unpaid work takes different forms. Over and above their "constant concern", even outside working hours, for their elderly and dependent clients, home helps give their own telephone numbers to families so that they can be called at any time should problems arise. If necessary, they will even spend the night at a client's home.

All these aspects, which we were able to capture in the course of our in-depth field survey, are seldom regarded as constraints arising out of working conditions. Under these circumstances, can we really talk of "decent working time"?

10.3.4   The five dimensions of "decent working time"

According to Messenger (2004), five dimensions should be taken into account in evaluating the impact of working time on employees' lives.

1. Long working days and unsocial hours are damaging to workers' health and have negative effects on their families and on their social life as a whole.

2. The unpredictability of working time is incompatible with the regular activities and rhythms of domestic life, particularly for the parents of young children.

3. These first two aspects impact differently on men and women, who are not time-constrained in the same way by the demands of family life.

4. Extended working days and other factors (e.g., work schedules) can have negative effects on productivity.

5. Many employees have little control over the choice of their working hours and schedules.

Various measures are proposed in order to promote working hours conducive to good health, family life, gender equality, productivity and increased freedom of choice for employees: protection against excessively long working hours and unsocial hours; collective working time reductions; equal treatment for full-timers and part-timers; and a greater role for employees in choosing their working times and schedules.

10.3.5   Part-time work in services and "decent working time"

Let us set our findings against these five dimensions of decent working time.

Long working days and unsocial hours, unpredictable working hours and no freedom of choice with regard to schedules are the lot of many workers in the service industries in France studied in the course of the research for this chapter. Part-timers are increasingly affected by specific forms of temporal availability: work fragmentation and split shifts, unpaid work, a requirement for considerable potential availability and a failure to provide sufficient notice of schedules. These forms of temporal availability particularly affect jobs that are mostly held by women, and are one of the causes of the very high labour turnover observed in these industries, as employers who fail to secure their workers' loyalty recognize.

It can be concluded, therefore, that unskilled white-collar service workers whose work involves direct contact with customers or users seldom enjoy "decent working time". In France, part-time work and decent working time scarcely seem to go hand in hand, at least in the service industries investigated here. In order to understand this paradox, it is necessary, as Maruani and Reynaud (1993) already have, to investigate the social construction of part-time work in France, in which two fundamentally opposed principles are at work. The first, which might be described as "shorter working time", is driven by employees' desire for a reversible reorganization of their working time. The second, which might be described as "part-time employment", is driven by employers seeking to create part-time jobs. This latter process is largely irreversible, and it is taking place outside of employees' control and indeed against their wishes. The forms of temporal availability outlined above have emerged as part-time employment has taken hold.

Can the notion of decent working time be deployed in order to analyse this temporal availability in depth and put forward corrective measures for workers in the industries investigated? By breaking down the notion into five constituent dimensions, it certainly provides some interesting starting points. Nevertheless, further work needs to be done in order to link the various dimensions. Messenger (2004) suggests part-time work as one potentially valuable way of reconciling paid work and family responsibilities (dimension 2 of "decent working time"). However, what kind of part-time work does he have in mind? Is equality of treatment for full-timers and part-timers sufficient to ensure real equality of treatment for men and women (dimension 3)?

The regulation of excessively long working hours and unsocial hours (dimension 1) is presented as a measure likely to lead to improved productivity (dimension 4). However, this does not seem to be a view shared by employers in the service industries we have investigated in France. This analysis is indeed pertinent, but it takes insufficient account of the question of power relations within firms.

The question of employee choice and influence over working time and work schedules (dimension 5) is a fundamental one. Unskilled part-time white-collar workers in some service industries in France often have no control at all over their work schedules. The issue cannot be reduced to the right to request changes to working time. It is the whole notion of flexibility as an organizational principle, orchestrated by firms and, in these industries, inextricably linked with the use of part-time jobs that is called into question here.

Thus, in the light of the study of temporal availability as it affects unskilled white-collar workers presented in this chapter, it seems essential to extend the decent working time approach by linking its various dimensions.

10.4   CONCLUSION

Our analysis of unskilled work in today's service societies has enabled us to develop a broader framework for interpreting the working conditions of white-collar employees. Our focus on unskilled white-collar workers, who have replaced manual workers as an archetypal figure in advanced economies, has led us to examine the close links between employment conditions and working conditions.

Although the notions of job quality and "decent work" include the time dimension to some extent, studies based on these notions are not always able to capture unskilled white-collar work in all its complexity. By placing unskilled white-collar workers at the heart of our analysis, new questions are raised about the quality and decency of working time as reflected in the part-time jobs or "half-jobs" that are being created in massive numbers in these industries. The proliferation of such jobs is being driven by a new productive and organizational logic.

Against this background, the temporal availability demanded of workers seems increasingly to be becoming a real criterion for recruitment. As they go about their work, employees experience the fragmented work and the split shifts that are part of the process of rationalizing working time. The standardization of time to which white-collar workers are subjected has its roots in industrialist logic, but frequently comes up against the particularities of certain situations or clienteles. Under these circumstances, other forms of temporal availability, such as unpaid work or voluntary work, develop in order to meet customers' demands. In these forms, temporal availability seems very closely linked to competences, particularly relational competences, but this is not recognized in terms of remuneration.

References

Amossé, T. 2001. "L'espace des métiers, de 1990 à 1999", in *Insee Premières*, No. 790, July.

Bisault, L.; Destical, V.; Goux, D. 1994. "Emploi et chômage des non qualifiés en France", in *Économie et Statistique*, No. 273, INSEE.

Blank, R.; Card, D. (eds.). 2000. *Finding jobs: Work and welfare reform* (New York, Russell Sage Foundation).

Burnod, G.; Chenu, A. 2001. "Employés qualifiés et non qualifiés, une proposition d'aménagement de la nomenclature des catégories socioprofessionnelles", in *Travail et Emploi*, No. 86, DARES, Apr. 2001.

Chardon, O. 2002. "La qualification des employés", in INSEE, *Série des Documents de Travail*, No. F 0202, Mar.

Cottrell, M.; Letreny, P.; Macaire, S.; Meilland, C.; Michon, F. 2002. "Le temps de travail des formes particulières d'emploi", in *Économie et Statistique*, Nos. 352–53, pp. 169–89.

Dejours, C. 2000. *Travail, usure mentale* (Paris, Bayard).

Devetter, F.-X. 2004. "Disponibilité temporelle: Quelles différences entre hommes et femmes?", International Symposium on Working Time, Paris, 26–28 February.

European Commission, DG Employment and Social Affairs. 2001. *Employment in Europe* (Brussels, European Commission).

—. 2004. *Employment in Europe* (Brussels, European Commission).

European Foundation for the Improvement of Living and Working Conditions. 2001. *Third European Survey on Working Conditions, 2000* (Luxembourg, Office for Official Publications of European Communities).

Gadrey, N.; Jany-Catrice, F.; Pernod-Lemattre, M. 2003. "Les enjeux de la qualification des employés. Conditions de travail et compétences des non qualifies", Rapport pour le Ministère de l'emploi et de la solidarité – DARES, June.

Guignon, N.; Hamon-Cholet, S. 2003, "Au contact avec le public, des conditions de travail particulières", *Premières Informations et Premières Synthèses*, No. 09.3, DARES, February.

Gollac, M.; Volkoff, S. (eds.) 2000. *Les conditions de travail*. Coll. Repères (Paris, La Découverte).

—; —. 2001. "Intensité et fragilité", in G. Jeannot and P. Veltz (eds.): *Le travail entre l'entreprise et la cité* (Paris, Editions de l'Aube).

ILO. 2001. *Reducing decent work deficit, A global challenge*, International Labour Conference, 89th session, Geneva.

INSEE. 2002. *Enquête Emploi* (Paris, INSEE).

Macaire, S.; Michon, F. 2002. *Le travail intérimaire: Rapport national France* (Dublin, European Foundation for the Improvement of Living and Working Conditions).

Maruani, M. 1996. "L'emploi féminin à l'ombre du chômage", in *Actes de la recherche en sciences sociales*, December, No. 115, pp. 48–57.

—. 2000. *Travail et emploi des femmes*. Coll. Repères, No. 287 (Paris, La Découverte).

—; Nicole, C. 1989. *La flexibilité à temps partiel, conditions d'emploi dans le commerce* (Paris, La Documentation Française).

—; Reynaud, E. 1993. *Sociologie de l'emploi* (Paris, La Découverte).

Méda, D.; Vennat, F. (eds.). 2004. *Le travail non qualifié, permanences et defies*. Coll. Recherche (Paris, La Découverte).

Messenger, J. 2004. "Finding the balance, working time and workers' needs and preferences in industrialized countries", paper presented at the 9th International Symposium on Working Time, Paris, 26–28 February.

Mishel, L.; Bernstein, J.; Schmitt, J. 1999. *The state of working America* (Ithaca, NY, Cornell University Press).

OECD. 1996. *Employment outlook* (Paris, OECD).

—. 2001. *Employment outlook* (Paris, OECD).

MANAGERS AND WORKING TIME IN FINLAND

11

Jouko Nätti, *Timo Anttila** and Mia Väisänen****

11.1   INTRODUCTION

11.1.1   *The changing working time regime and decent working time*

The relations of work to time, place and household are central questions of social research in general and working life research in particular (Adam, 1995; Kalleberg and Epstein, 2001). In the industrial working time regime, paid work is connected with (normal) working time in contrast to free time (or "produced time", Adam, 1995), and leisure outside paid work. Correspondingly, paid work is connected with the workplace (factory, office) in contrast to free time and unpaid housework in the household. The core features of the industrial working time regime are crystallized in the concept of normal working time, which has been designed to be an approximately 8-hour working day with daytime work and free weekends (Boulin, 1998). Normal working time and temporal institutions that guarantee time off work (free evenings, weekends, annual holidays and retirement) have established the grounds for shared time rhythms in society (Garhammer, 1999). However, during the last two decades of the twentieth century the core elements of normal working time have been eroding, and a new post-industrial working time regime has been emerging.

There is much international discussion on the new trends of working time from diverse perspectives, such as working time research (Boulin, 1998;

* Academy Research Fellow in the Department of Social Sciences and Philosophy at the University of Jyväskylä, Finland.
** Senior researcher in the Department of Social Sciences and Philosophy at the University of Jyväskylä, Finland.
*** Researcher in the Department of Social Sciences and Philosophy at the University of Jyväskylä, Finland.

Roberts, 1998), information society, networking theories (Castells, 1996, 1997; Sennett, 1998), and studies on work culture in expert occupations (Casey, 1995; Hochschild, 1997). Instead of diverse starting points, the characterization of the new working time trend is similar. The new working time regime is characterized by deregulation of collective norms, diversification of the length and pattern of working time, blurring of the limits of working time, and an erosion of normal biographies. Especially those in dynamic sectors and a good labour market position – managers and others with a great deal of autonomy, a good salary, high productivity and career prospects – tend to work long hours. Demanding knowledge and managerial work seems to require a marginalization of private life and a concentration on paid work (Casey, 1995; Hochschild, 1997).

Compared to the industrial working time discipline, the post-industrial regime creates both new opportunities and risks. At its best, the emerging working time mosaic (Sennet, 1998) provides an opportunity for individuals to choose the length and rhythm of their working time. On the other hand, there are new risks concerning the relationship between work and private life, the time and energy available for family and social life, alertness and performance (Härmä, 1998; Kalimo, 1999). Furthermore, working time trends have even deeper effects; they restructure the nature of our culture and community (Castells, 1997; Garhammer, 1999). The erosion of old, shared time rhythms (e.g. Sundays) disintegrates society.

The opportunities and risks associated with the evolving post-industrial working time regime are analogous with the core dimensions of decent working time: healthy working time, family-friendly working time, gender equality through working time, productive working time, and choice and influence regarding working time (Messenger, 2004). Decent working time signifies an appropriate match between individual needs, preferences, hours of work and working time arrangements; the lack of decent working time constitutes a gap between the hours of work that individuals need or would prefer and the ones that they are required to work (Messenger, 2004)

11.1.2   Working hours in Finland

The statutory regular working time in Finland is 8 hours per day at most, or 40 hours per week. In most branches the agreed working time per week in collective agreements is shorter, usually 37.5 hours per week, which is near the EU-15 average (38 hours; EIRO 4/2004). The estimated annual hours in Finland are 1,673 hours while the EU-15 average is 1,697 hours. In Finland, overtime work is restricted and an increased salary must be paid for overtime working. In general, no more than 250 hours of overtime per year is allowed. In practice, however, unpaid overtime is common. In the study by Lehto and Sutela (2004), 31 per cent of Finnish employees reported that they do unpaid overtime work.

In the mid-1990s, regular working hours were quite uniform in Finland, concentrating around the collectively agreed working hours (37 to 39 hours per week); the gender differences were also minor. On the other hand, shift, evening and Sunday work were more common in Finland when compared to the EU average (Julkunen and Nätti, 1999). Although there was no dramatic change in working times in Finland during the 1990s, by the end of the decade the portrait of working time had diversified slightly (Julkunen and Nätti, 2002). Still, as Antila and Ylöstalo (1999) conclude, the old working time paradigm yields only gradually; old and new paradigms now live side by side.

According to the Third European Working Conditions Survey (2000), usual weekly working hours in Finland (39 hours) were the third longest among the EU-15 countries (Paoli and Merllié, 2001), while the EU average working time among employees stood at 37 hours per week (Boisard et al., 2002). The longer working hours in Finland were mainly the result of the low proportion of part-time work in Finland (9 per cent of workers work 1 to 29 hours per week) compared to the EU average (17 per cent). On the other hand, the proportion of employees working 45 or more hours in Finland (15 per cent) was near the EU average (14 per cent) (Boisard et al., 2002). Furthermore, it is characteristic of the Finnish labour market that the working hours of men and women are similar; in 2000 the difference was 3 hours per week, which is the smallest in the EU.

In a wider international context, long working hours seem to be more common in the United States, Australia and Japan, where 25 to 35 per cent of men and 10 to 15 per cent of women work more than 48 hours a week. However, comparing evidence from different surveys is not unproblematic, since there are often significant differences among them in how working hours are defined (i.e., actual or usual hours, annual or weekly hours, for a main job or total hours, and whether commuting time is included), and how this information is collected (Kodz et al., 2003).

11.1.3   Managerial work and working time

> By working faithfully eight hours a day, you may
> eventually get to be boss and work twelve hours a day.
> *Robert Frost* (cited in White et al., 2003)

Managerial work has been defined as "a stream of disjointed, fragmented activities occurring at an unrelenting pace" (Tétard, 2000); consequently managers' jobs are ambiguous and undefined (Konrad et al., 2001). Time pressure (such as having constant interruptions, unscheduled meetings, and dealing with many issues in a short period of time) has been found to be a feature of managerial work (e.g. Konrad et al., 2001), yet at the same time, it is the feature of the work least preferred by managers in a five-country comparative study (Konrad et al., 2001). Another temporal aspect of managerial work is the fragmentation of time, which according to Tétard (2000) – drawing on Mintzberg's (1973, 1991) characterization of managerial work – has always existed and remains an element of the work. Interestingly, the fragmentation of time is increasingly also often a feature in non-managerial work (Tétard, 2000).

The contractual boundaries of time and wage (see Fagan, 2001) may also affect how working hours are defined and perceived. For some occupational groups, such as blue-collar workers, the amount of time exchanged for wages can be explicitly defined, whereas for others, e.g. those in professional or managerial positions, the time–money exchange is often hidden and time boundaries are more ambiguous (Kalleberg and Epstein, 2001). Consequently, among manual occupations overtime is usually paid, whereas among managerial and professional occupations overtime is usually unpaid (Kodz et al., 2003).

Working hours vary according to professional status and, as the poet Frost observed at the beginning of the last century, it is especially true that people in managerial positions work long hours. According to the Third European Working Conditions Survey, managers often worked very long working weeks: 39 per cent of managers worked 45 hours or more, in comparison with 5 per cent of office workers and 17 per cent of industrial workers (Boisard et al., 2002). According to the same study, when including only those working full-time, managers worked an average of 45 hours per week, which is 5 hours more compared to all full-time employees. Among managers, as in general among employees, there is a slight gender difference in working time; male managers worked an average of 46 hours per week and women managers an average of 42 hours per week (Boisard et al., 2002). According to the Finnish Labour Force Survey, in 2002 the average working time among managers was 42 hours per week, which was the longest in comparison with other occupational groups. During the 1990s the length of working time of managers increased by approximately 2.5 hours per week (Hulkko and Luomala, 2003).

11.1.4 Knowledge workers as forerunners of the changing working time regime: Threat or opportunity for decent working time?

Managerial work has traditionally been differentiated from the standard working time practice and lacked the protection of legislation on working time (e.g. Messenger, 2004). A more recent development is the increase of knowledge workers, which has implications for the relations of work to time and place, and shares some similarities with managerial work. Therefore, we examine managers and working time in the context of knowledge work.

Although it is commonly agreed that the share of knowledge work is increasing, the concept of knowledge work is far from unambiguous (Cortada, 1999; Julkunen et al., 2004). In simple terms, knowledge work includes two dimensions, which are in principle independent of each other; namely a high level of education and the use of information technology at work (Blom et al. 2001). Autonomy of work can also be added as a third criterion in defining knowledge work. Knowledge workers can be defined as those who regularly use information technology at work, and whose work requires planning and who have an upper secondary or higher level of education. Thus knowledge workers are similar to the concept of the "symbolic analyst" used by Reich (1991). In this chapter, too, the criteria for knowledge work are a high level of education, knowledge of work content, and the use of information technology at work.

Knowledge workers are assumed to be especially affected by the new working time regime as a consequence of the nature of the work. Knowledge work can be captivating and interesting in itself; besides economic success, it can also offer other rewards. Similar to managerial work, it is typically personal and endless; you can always do it better, and then work more and longer hours. In addition, demanding knowledge work or symbolic–analytical work is, in principle, detachable from a certain time and place (e.g. Bentley and Yoong, 2000). Consequently, it is usually assumed that knowledge work cannot be controlled by counting working hours, and work does not remain in the workplace; on the contrary, it spills over into the private sphere and can be carried out at home or during travel. One possible cost of more autonomous forms of work is a reduction in the right to separate working time from non-working time, coupled with pressures towards increased work intensity (Rubery and Grimshaw, 2001; Van den Berg and Schlak, 1997), thus creating a possible threat to "decent working time".

Essentially, knowledge and managerial work capture an interesting interplay of the core dimensions of "decent working time" (Messenger, 2004). On the one hand, managers and knowledge workers enjoy high working time autonomy and control over timing of work, enabling a better match between individual needs and organizational demands. On the other hand, they are affected by the lengthening of working time, and the blurring of the boundaries between work and non-work – which may have negative outcomes – for example, increasing adverse health and productivity outcomes and worsening the work–family balance (Kodz et al., 2003).

A recent Finnish study on IT professionals (Kivistö and Kalimo, 2002) found that IT professionals have long working hours (the average working week was 43 hours), and over 80 per cent of them worked weekly overtime (an average of 10 hours). Furthermore, their work was mentally exhausting, time pressure was hard, and health problems were common, even among the younger age groups. On the other hand, IT professionals had good possibilities to influence their own work.

11.1.5 Factors behind long working hours

There seems to be a consensus that a long working week "comes with the job" in managerial work. For example, Moen and Sweet (2003, p. 27) state that "some jobs simply have (or employers expect) high demands and long hours" (see also Tengblad, 2001). Factors behind stretching working hours among managers can be divided between individual and job-level characteristics, organizational culture-level aspects and economic factors.

The individual-level factors include demographic, personality and family status factors. Accordingly, managers who are more likely to work long hours are usually male, single, carrying the role of the family breadwinner, have a higher level conscientiousness and achievement motivation, and a low investment in hobbies and leisure (Feldman, 2002). Similarly, Kodz et al. (2003) report that respondents working long hours are highly committed to their work and by working long hours they secure good career prospects. People wish to devote more time to what they are most valued for, e.g. a high-status job (Hochschild, 1997). However, there are also gender differences. Men working long hours are likely to be married and with children, while women working long hours are likely to be single and without children (Kodz et al., 2003).

The job-level factors of the lengthening of working hours include, on the one hand, a high visibility of work, less specific appraisal criteria and procedures, a high amount of job challenge and good working conditions (Feldman, 2002). On the other hand, Kodz et al. (2003) suggest that on the basis of reviewing research literature, a major reason for long working hours, particularly when they are unpaid, is the volume of work. Factors increasing the volume of work relate to new organizational initiatives, including a flattening of organizational structures due to delayering; increases in project-based work; a greater emphasis on customer focus; a meetings culture; staff shortages; information technology and email overload; and an increasing need for some employees to travel for their work.

The organizational culture, with its informal rules and norms, has an impact on workplace behaviour, including leadership, selection and the socialization process in the organization. As a result, managers' long hours can be produced by a narrow range of employees acting as managers (sharing similar values, attitudes and beliefs), and an institutionalized socialization process within the organization (Feldman, 2002). Also, according to Kodz et al. (2003), the attitudes and expectations of managers and co-workers can be critical in engendering a long-hours culture in which "being present" is valued as a sign of commitment to work. The availability of time for work is often regarded as evidence of high performance and motivation for advancement (Perlow, 1998; Florida, 2002). Rutherford (2001) claims that a long-hours culture may also act as a mechanism reinforcing patriarchal structures: where the ability to work long hours has become one of the most desired management attributes, women are less likely to have equal opportunity to advance towards managerial positions because of the gendered division of domestic labour. Working time is also affected by economic factors facing the organization as a whole. The threat of declining profitability, layoffs and job insecurity can increase the number of hours worked (Feldman, 2002; Kodz et al., 2003).

All in all, earlier research findings show that many employees working long hours do so for a combination of reasons. Furthermore, the reasons given for working long hours depend, to a certain extent, on who is asked and how the questions are asked (Kodz et al., 2003).

11.1.6 Preferred hours

In the framework of decent working time, a crucial dimension is to what extent preferred and actual working hours match each other. In economic literature, it is often assumed that employees' preferred working hours correspond to their actual working hours (Lee and McCann, Chapter 3 in this volume; Messenger, 2004; Stewart and Swaffield, 1997). However, in empirical studies there is often a discrepancy between preferred and actual hours (although it is clear that preferences should be interpreted very carefully), partly because it depends on the wording of the preference questions. In addition, preferences are dependent on the situational context within a specific economic and social framework – as is the development of working time itself (see Bielenski et al., 2002; Väisänen and Nätti, 2002). Furthermore, Lee and McCann (Chapter 3 in this volume) stress the role of social and institutional conversion factors (e.g., available working time options and workplace culture) affecting employees' ability to realize these preferences.

Bielenski et al. (2002) have hypothesized six factors influencing working time preferences across countries, including the employment situation; regulation of labour markets; work organization; individual and household characteristics; and household economic situation. Although covering extensively the main macro- and micro-level components, their study does not recognize gender-specific working time culture, which is influenced by norms and role expectations and, in turn, influences both behaviour and preferences (e.g. Pfau-Effinger, 1999; Väisänen and Nätti, 2002; Stier and Lewin-Epstein, 2003).

According to the Employment Options for the Future study, conducted in 1998 and covering 15 EU Member States and Norway, about half of employees want to reduce their working time; only 12 per cent prefer longer hours. On average, employed men preferred a 37-hour week and employed women a 30-hour week, which means an average reduction of 6 hours per week for men and 3.5 hours for women (Fagan, 2002). In Finland, the preferred working week was 36 hours for men and 33 hours for women, and the average preferred reduction was 5 hours for men and 4 hours for women (Bielenski et al., 2002).

Working time preferences are influenced to a considerable extent by actual working times. On the one hand, the longer actual working time is, the longer preferred working time tends to be. On the other hand, more employees with long working hours would like to reduce their working time than those with short working hours. Furthermore, working time preferences are more homogeneous than actual working times, converging towards working times of between 30 and 40 hours per week. Men's preferred hours are influenced primarily by their actual working hours, while for women household-related factors also play a role; e.g., when there are children in the household, then women would prefer reduced working hours. In addition, age increased willingness to reduce working hours (Bielenski et al., 2002).

Fagan (2002) has reported similar results when specifically examining full-time employees' likelihood of wanting a substantial reduction (5 hours or more) in their working hours. Full-time employees preferred reduced hours if they were working long hours and had a managerial position; were older (men); had young children and a spouse; and worked in large private sector companies (men). In addition, living in certain countries (especially in France, Sweden and the United Kingdom) increased the likelihood to prefer reduced hours.

A comparative analysis of 22 countries based on the 1997 International Social Survey Program (ISSP) data (Stier and Lewin-Epstein, 2003) found that working time preferences were affected by both individual- and country-level characteristics. At the individual level, those whose standard of living is better secured (higher education, high household income and older age) would prefer to reduce their working hours, while the opposite is true for less educated workers with low incomes. At the country level, the greatest dissatisfaction with the number of hours worked is found in countries that experience economic hardship (low rates of economic growth, high rates of inequality and low levels of social welfare).

11.1.7 Aims and study approach

In the empirical analysis we investigate three questions that address dimensions of "decent working time" and the process of creating "decent working time" among knowledge workers. First, we examine how unambiguous working times are. In the literature there is an assumption that the limits of working time are blurring and employees have difficulties drawing a line between what is work and what is not work (although this has not often been investigated in surveys). On the basis of the literature, we assume that managers, in particular, have difficulties in defining their working hours.

Second, we analyse the extent and antecedents of long working hours. In the literature it is often assumed that knowledge workers, especially those in dynamic sectors (as in information and communication technology, ICT) and who have good labour market positions (e.g., managers and professionals), tend to work long hours.

Third, we study the extent and antecedents of stretching working hours: how employees see factors contributing to stretching hours. On the basis of the literature, we assume that factors stretching working hours may be linked to both the attractions and rewards of the work; to one's position in the organization (i.e., managerial position); and to tight schedules or other problems in work organization.

Fourth, we examine preferred working hours and their relation to actual hours. In particular, we examine the extent and antecedents of those employees who prefer a substantial reduction (5 hours or more) in their working hours. On the basis of the literature, we assume that work-related factors promote, and family-related factors inhibit, working long hours.

In studying these three research aims, which demonstrate aspects of the changing working time regime, we are especially interested in the gender differences. Are there differences between women and men concerning the extent and antecedents of the three phenomena? The predictors of ambiguous, long and preferred working hours include both individual (e.g., age, family situation, work commitment), and job-related (e.g., occupational status, time pressure, time autonomy) factors, as well as the organizational culture.

11.2 METHODS

11.2.1 Participants and procedure

Our empirical analyses are based on a representative survey among highly educated Finns, conducted by Statistics Finland in the spring of 2001. The random sample consisted of 3,000 people between 25 and 64 years of age, who had finished tertiary education (ISCED level 5A and 6). The postal questionnaire was answered by 1,839 people (63 per cent). In the present study, data analysis was restricted to those who were employed (1,643 people).

Of the employed respondents, 49 per cent were women and 51 per cent were men, and a majority of them were between 35 and 54 years of age (63 per cent). The mean age was 42 years (men 43, women 41 years). Three out of four were living with a partner, men more often compared to women. Four out of five partners were also employed; more often among women (88 per cent) compared to men (77 per cent). About half of the subjects had children, most commonly one or two.

Between the genders, the most obvious differences concerned occupational status and the industrial sector. Despite the similar educational background, men (34 per cent) were more often managers compared to women (14 per cent). The largest occupational group consisted of (university-level-educated) professionals (73 per cent of women, 56 per cent of men). The rest of the respondents were employed either as technicians and associate professionals, or clerks and other types of professionals. Another clear gender difference concerned industrial division, reflecting the strong horizontal gender segregation of the Finnish labour markets. Men were concentrated in manufacturing, and women were concentrated in health and social services and in the educational sector.

Knowledge work is defined in this chapter on the basis of a high level of education and the use of information technology at work. Almost all survey participants had finished tertiary education (96 per cent), and almost all (98 per cent) used information technology (e.g., a personal computer at work). Therefore, in practice all participants can be defined as knowledge workers. Sample attrition analysis, measures, methods and statistical analyses are described in Appendix 11.1.

11.3   RESULTS

11.3.1   Blurring working hours

On the basis of the literature and public debate, we can assume that the concept of working time is no longer unambiguous. For a growing number of employed people, describing how much they usually work is ambiguous and inexact. The borders of working days are obscure. Many people do part of their work at home, at meetings, in training, or by travelling.

The first aim of the empirical analysis was to examine to what extent working hours are unambiguous. Participants were asked if they could express their total working hours without ambiguity. Overall, about half of the respondents (55 per cent of women and 47 per cent of men) said that for the most part, they could express their working hours without ambiguity. Correspondingly, half of the respondents had problems to some degree. About one-third of respondents (31 per cent of women and 36 per cent of men) stated that expressing the average total working hours was somewhat problematic. Furthermore, 14 per cent of women and 18 per cent of men said that it was rather difficult to draw a line between what is work and what is not work. Thus men often felt more difficulty in defining their working hours compared to women ($p = 0.002$).

We continued our analysis by examining the antecedents of problems in defining working hours among women and men, and investigated if knowledge worker managers in particular have problems in defining their working hours by using a logistic regression analysis (table 11.1). The dependent variable was having problems and difficulties in defining working hours (1 = yes, 0 = no). Based on the hypothesized factors, the analysis included three groups (individual, work and organizational culture) of explanatory variables. A positive value (Exp (B)) indicates an increase in the likelihood that the phenomenon will occur.

The most important factor in predicting problems and difficulties in defining working hours was occupational status. Among women, managers were 5.0 and professionals 4.4 times more likely to have problems in defining working hours when compared to technicians. The corresponding figure among male managers was 2.3. Besides occupation, industry also mattered. Among women, working in education (6.4) and "other industries" (2.5) increased the odds when compared to those working in public administration. The corresponding figures among men were 3.5 and 2.4, respectively. On the other hand, and contrary to our assumptions, working in the ICT sector was not linked to problems in defining working hours.

In addition, problems in defining working hours were linked to working time culture, time autonomy and time pressure. A workplace culture favouring long working hours increased the likelihood of having problems in defining working times (2.4 times among women and 1.7 times among men) when compared to a workplace culture favouring normal working hours. Working time autonomy increased the likelihood of having problems in defining working time (1.6 times among women and 2.4 times among men). Similarly, high levels of time pressure increased problems in defining working time by 1.9 times among women – but not among men – compared with low levels of time pressure. Age, family situation, children or work commitment were not linked to difficulties in defining working hours.

Table 11.1 Factors affecting having problems and difficulties in defining working hours, by gender, logistic regression

	Women Exp(B) (sig.)	Men Exp(B) (sig.)
Age (ref. 55–64)		
25–34	0.914	1.077
35–44	0.67	1.415
45–54	0.891	1.653
Living with a partner (ref. No)	1.077	1.029
Children (ref. No children)		
Child 0–7 years	1.059	0.909
Child 8+ years	1.048	1.133
Work commitment (ref. Low)	1.088***	1.329**
Occupation (ref. Technicians and associate professionals and clerks)		
Manager	4.989***	2.311**
Professional	4.363***	1.337***
Industry (ref. Public administration)		
Manufacture	1.491	0.668
ICT	1.091	0.78
Finance	0.994	1.119
Education	6.396***	3.486***
Health, social services	0.862	1.07
Other industries	2.475*	1.875*
High time pressure (ref. Low)	1.897***	1.19
Working time autonomy (ref. No)	1.580*	2.425***
Long working hours are desirable (ref. Normal working hours are desirable at the workplace)	2.410***	1.665***
Constant	0.044***	0.175***
Chi Square	215.090***	118.123***
–2LL	825.896	967.762
N	761	785

Note: Sig.: <0.05*, <0.01**, <0.000***. Dependent variable: having problems or difficulties in defining working hours (1 = yes, 0 = no).

11.3.2   Long working hours

The second aim was to investigate the extent and antecedents of long working hours. Participants were asked how many hours per week they normally put into their main occupation, including job-related work performed at home and overtime work. Actual working hours varied from 1 to 84 hours, the average being 41.6 hours per week (43 hours for men and 40 hours for women). Only a small proportion of employees (11 per cent of women and 7 per cent of men) worked on a part-time basis (1 to 34 hours per week). Half of all women (52 per cent) and 40 per cent of men had normal working hours (35 to 40 hours). One-third of women (37 per cent) and half of men (53 per cent) worked more than 40 hours per week. Thus men worked longer hours compared to women (p = 0.000).

Besides gender, working hours also varied by occupational status. The mean hours among managers stood at 46 hours among men and 44 among women, while the corresponding figures were 43 among all men and 40 among all women. The proportion of managers who work excessive hours, at least 48 hours a week using the threshold found to be particularly harmful for workers' health (Messenger, 2004), stood at 35 per cent among men and 27 per cent among women, which is significantly higher compared to all knowledge workers (18 per cent).

In table 11.2 we continue the analysis by examining the antecedents of a long working week among women and men using a logistic regression analysis. The dependent variable is a long working week (41-plus hours per week; 1 = yes, 0 = no). The most important factors in predicting long working hours were occupational status, high time pressure, and the working time culture. Among women, managers were 3.3 times, and professionals 2.0 times more likely to work long hours when compared to technicians and other occupations. The corresponding figure among male managers was 2.2. High time pressure increased the likelihood of working long hours by 3.3 times among women, and 1.9 times among men, compared to low time pressure. A workplace culture favouring long working hours increased the likelihood of having long working hours by 2.5 times among women, and 2.6 times among men, when compared to a workplace culture favouring normal working hours.

In addition, working time autonomy and high work commitment increased the likelihood of working long hours by 1.5 and 1.9 times among women, respectively. Among men the corresponding figures were 2.2 and 2.2 times, respectively. Among women, industry also mattered. Working in education (2.2 times) increased the odds when compared to those working in public administration. Furthermore, among women, having children at home

Table 11.2   Factors affecting long working week (41+ hours per week), by gender, logistic regression

	Women Exp(B) (sig.)	Men Exp(B) (sig.)
Age (ref. 55–64)	*	
25–34	0.899	1.184
35–44	0.539	1.117
45–54	1.202	1.075
Living with a partner (ref. No)	1.256	1.012
Children (ref. No children)	**	
Child 0–7 years	0.503**	0.636
Child 8+ years	0.547**	0.856
Work commitment (ref. Low)	1.900***	2.164***
Occupation (ref. Technicians and associate professionals and clerks)	**	***
Manager	3.312***	2.220**
Professional	2.021*	0.863
Industry (ref. Public administration)		
Manufacture	2.098	1.088
ICT	1.546	0.73
Finance	1.802	1.081
Education	2.150*	0.631
Health, social services	1.282	1.25
Other industries	1.554	1.255
High time pressure (ref. Low)	3.283***	1.936***
Working time autonomy (ref. No)	1.534*	2.201***
Long working hours are desirable (ref. Normal working hours are desirable at the workplace)	2.510***	2.567***
Constant	0.059***	0.243**
Chi Square	176.200***	180.008***
–2LL	804.789	894.978
N	746	777

Note: Sig.: <0.05*, <0.01**, <0.000***. Dependent variable: long working hours (1 = 41+ hours per week, 0 =1-40 hours per week).

reduced the likelihood of working long hours compared to those without children at home. On the contrary, age and family situation were not linked to difficulties in defining working hours.

11.3.3   Reasons for stretching working hours

The third aim was to investigate the extent and antecedents of stretching working hours. Having a long working week partly indicates the stretching of working hours. In addition, participants were asked directly if their work hours (including overtime) stretched beyond the agreed or ordinary (about 37 to 40 hours per week) working hours. According to the results, 28 per cent of women and 41 per cent of men reported that their working hours regularly stretched beyond the ordinary working hours. Furthermore, 42 per cent of women and 35 per cent of men reported that sometimes the work piled up. The rest of the respondents (30 per cent of women and 24 per cent of men) said that this was seldom the case. Thus men more often reported stretching working hours compared to women (p = 0.000). Predictors of stretching working hours were similar to those in the case of long working hours. Therefore we were more interested in the reasons for stretching reported by the respondents.

Reasons for the stretching of working hours were obtained by presenting 14 factors and asking how important each of them was. The items were rated on a 3-point scale (1 = no impact, 2 = some impact, 3 = major impact) (table 11.3). The most important factors included nature, challenge and "infinitude" of the work (89 per cent of the respondents put major or some impact on it); one's own enthusiasm and commitment (88 per cent); a position with responsibility (75 per cent); and scarcity of personnel (70 per cent). The least important factor was willingness to work overtime (17 per cent). Overall, men saw most factors as more important compared to women.

To examine the factors behind stretching working time, three sum variables were constructed by using factor and reliability analysis. The first sum variable indicates the nature of work, including four items: (i) the nature, level of challenge, infinitude of the work; (j) one's own enthusiasm and commitment; (g) having a responsible position; and (l) work as a lifestyle (Cronbach alpha = 0.71). The second sum variable indicates career orientation including two items: (k) desire to succeed and acquire wealth, and (n) aspirations to advance one's career (alpha = 0.73). The third sum variable indicates problems with work organization including five items: (a) the company has too few employees in proportion to the amount of work to be done; (b) poor management of duties, poor planning and delegation; (c) the project's scheduling is too stringent; (d) the schedules demanded by the customers; and (e) co-workers who don't fulfil their own duties (alpha = 0.62).

Table 11.3   Reasons for stretching working hours by gender (major or some impact) (percentages)

	Women	Men	Total (Sig.)
The nature, level of challenge, infinitude of the work (i)	87	90	89
One's own enthusiasm and commitment (j)	88	88	88
A position with responsibility (g)	69	80	75***
The company has too few employees in proportion to the amount of work to be done (a)	71	69	70
Schedules demanded by the customers (d)	57	68	63***
The projects scheduling is too stringent (c)	56	64	60***
Poor management of duties, poor planning and delegation (b)	57	57	57
Desire to succeed and acquire wealth (k)	47	60	54***
Work is my lifestyle (l)	42	45	43
Aspirations to advance one's career (n)	41	45	43
Pressure from the work community (h)	35	31	33
Social interaction is integrated with work (m)	30	34	32
Co-workers who don't do their own duties (e)	28	30	29
Willingness to work overtime or secondary job, for pay (f)	16	17	17

Note: Sig.: <0.05*, <0.01**, <0.000*** (chi-square test).

The means of the sum variables indicated that both women and men ranked the nature of work as the most important (women 2.08 and men 2.12), followed by problems in work organization (women 1.74 and men 1.78), and career orientation (women 1.54 and men 1.64). Overall, men stressed the importance of the three sum variables more compared to women.

In table 11.4, we continue our analysis by examining factors affecting the importance of different sum variables (nature of work, career orientation and work organization) behind the stretching of working hours among women and men by using a logistic regression analysis. For the analysis the dependent variables (nature of work, career orientation, work organization) were dichotomized (values 2.00–3.00 = 1 indicating major or some impact; values 1.00–1.99 = 0 indicating no impact).

In the first analysis we concentrated on the importance of the nature of work as a factor stretching working hours. In the final model the most important factor was again occupation. Among women, managers were 5.3 and professionals 2.3 times more likely to stress the importance the nature of the work when compared with technicians and those in other occupations. The corresponding figures among male managers were 4.0 and 1.4, respectively. In addition, the

Table 11.4 Factors affecting the importance of different sum variables (nature of work, career orientation, work organization) behind the stretching of working hours, by gender, logistic regression

	The nature of work		Career orientation		Problems in work organization	
	Women	Men	Women	Men	Women	Men
	Exp(B)(sig.)	Exp(B)(sig.)	Exp(B)(sig.)	Exp(B)(sig.)	Exp(B)(sig.)	Exp(B)(sig.)
Age (ref. 55–64)			***	***		
25–34	0.628	1.019	6.190***	7.890***	0.86	1.264
35–44	0.591	1.439	3.050**	4.833***	0.994	1.625
45–54	0.995	1.017	2.401*	3.054***	0.962	1.131
Living with a partner (ref. No)	1.023	1.201	0.688	1.11	0.988	1.254
Children (ref. No children)						
Child 0–7 years	0.96	1.113	0.911	0.949	0.728	0.659
Child 8+ years	0.929	2.180***	0.99	1.271	0.744	1.017
Work commitment (ref. Low)	3.117***	2.898***	3.073***	3.021***	1.228	1.039
Occupation (ref. Technicians and associate professionals and clerks)	***	***	*	***		
Manager	5.305***	3.952***	2.297*	2.458**	0.85	1.096
Professional	2.338**	1.349	1.778*	1.248	0.778	1.439
Industry (ref. Public administration)	**		**	**		**
Manufacture	0.737	0.701	0.781	1.132	1.11	1.411
ICT	1.055	1.11	0.731	2.230*	0.682	1.342
Finance	1.168	1.234	0.954	1.886	0.961	1.16
Education	2.304*	1.161	0.602	0.686	0.557	0.417**
Health, social services	1.107	0.899	0.300***	0.724	0.991	0.73
Other industries	0.995	1.556	0.516	0.841	0.845	1.031
High time pressure (ref. Low)	2.004***	1.865***	1.31	1.262	3.309***	4.187***
Working time autonomy (ref. No)	1.498*	1.704**	1.585*	1.881***	1.346	0.962
Long working hours are desirable (ref. Normal working hours are desirable at the workplace)	1.722**	2.274***	1.577*	1.361	2.110***	1.588**
Constant	0.255**	0.185***	0.089***	0.034***	0.324**	0.155***
Chi Square	151.114***	172.614***	135.470***	183.357***	111.824***	138.237***
–2LL	877.58	854.853	833.766	877.194	866.801	919.992
N	761	785	761	785	761	785

Note: Sig.: <0.05*, <0.01**, <0.000***. Dependent variables: The nature of work (1 = yes, 0 = no); Career orientation (1 = yes, 0 = no); Problems in work organization (1 = yes, 0 = no).

nature of work was linked to work commitment, time pressure, working time autonomy and working time culture. High work commitment increased the likelihood of stressing the importance of the nature of work by 3.1 times among women and 2.9 times among men. The high odds result from the fact that both variables indicate (partly) the same phenomenon ($r = 0.21$). High time pressure increased the odds by 2.0 times among women and 1.9 times among men, compared to low time pressure. Similarly, working time autonomy increased the odds 1.5 times among women and 1.7 times among men. A workplace culture favouring long working hours increased the likelihood of stressing the importance of the nature of work by 1.7 times among women and 2.3 times among men. Furthermore, among women, working in education (2.3 times) increased the odds, when compared to those working in public administration.

In the second analysis, we examined the importance of having a career orientation as a factor in stretching working hours. In the final model the most important factor was age. Younger age increased the odds when compared to older (55 to 64 years old) employees. Besides age, occupational status mattered as well. Among women, managers were 2.3, and professionals 1.8 times more likely to stress the importance of career orientation when compared to technicians and those in other occupations. The corresponding figures among male managers were 2.5 and 1.2 times, respectively. Working in the industrial sector was also linked to the importance of career orientation. Among women, working in health and social services (0.3 times) reduced the odds when compared to those working in public administration. Among men, working in the ICT sector (2.2 times) increased the odds. In addition, working time autonomy increased the odds by 1.6 times among women and 1.9 times among men. Furthermore, among women, a workplace culture favouring long working hours increased the odds by 1.6 times, when compared with a workplace culture favouring normal working hours.

In the third analysis we looked at the importance of work organization problems as a factor in stretching working hours. In the final model the most important factor was high time pressure, which increased by 3.3 times among women, and 4.2 times among men, compared with low time pressure. Again the high odds result from the fact that both variables indicate (in part) the same phenomenon. In addition, a workplace culture favouring long working hours increased the odds of work organization problems by 2.1 times among women and 1.6 times among men. Furthermore, among men, working in education (0.4 times) reduced the odds when compared to those working in public administration.

11.3.4 Preferred working hours

The fourth aim of the study was to investigate preferred working hours. Participants were asked the ideal number of working hours per week at their

Table 11.5   Actual and preferred working week by occupational group and gender (hours)

Occupational status	Preferred hours			Actual hours			Difference (preferred – actual hours)		
	Women	Men	Total	Women	Men	Total	Women	Men	Total
Manager	34	38	37	44	46	45	–9	–8	–8
Professional	32	35	33	40	41	41	–8	–7	–8
Technicians and others	32	37	34	37	43	40	–5	–6	–5
Total	32	36	34	40	43	42	–8	–7	–8

present stage of life. Based on this question, the preferred working hours reported varied from 0 to 80 hours; the average was 34 hours per week (36 hours for men and 32 hours for women). Half of women (49 per cent) and more than one-quarter of men (27 per cent) preferred part-time work (1 to 34 hours per week). Normal working hours (35 to 40 hours per week) were preferred by half of women (48 per cent) and 62 per cent of men. Only a small proportion of women (3 per cent) and men (11 per cent) preferred more than 40 hours per week.

Compared to their actual working week, employees prefer a reduction of 7 hours on average (men 7 hours and women 8 hours) (table 11.5). Thus women prefer just a slightly larger reduction in working time compared to men. Besides gender, the preferred reduction of the working week is larger among managers and professionals compared with technicians and others.

In table 11.6, we complete our analysis by examining the antecedents of a substantial reduction (5 or more hours) in the working week among women and men by using a logistic regression analysis. The dependent variable is a preferred substantial reduction of the working week (1 = yes, 0 = no). Based on the hypothesized factors, the analysis included three groups of explanatory variables (individual, work, and organizational culture). Furthermore, we also added into the model actual long working week (0 = 1–40 hours, 1 = 41 hours or more); problems in defining working hours (1 = yes, 0 = no); stretching working hours (1 = yes, 0 = no); and the three reasons for stretching working hours – the nature of work (1 = yes, 0 = no), career orientation (1 = yes, 0 = no), and problems in work organization (1 = yes, 0 = no), in order to examine their role in preferred working time reductions. A positive value (Exp B) indicates an increase in the likelihood of the phenomenon to occur.

Overall, 63 per cent of employees preferred a substantial reduction of weekly working hours. In the final model, the most important factor was

Table 11.6   Factors affecting preference for substantial reduction of working week (5 hours per week or more), by gender, logistic regression

	Women Exp(B) (sig.)	Men Exp(B) (sig.)
Age (ref. 55–64)		
25–34	0.343**	0.966
35–44	0.67	1.311
45–54	0.627	1.117
Living with a partner (ref. No)	1.144	1.225
Children (ref. No children)	***	
Child 0–7 years	2.647***	0.902
Child 8+ years	0.992	0.731
Work commitment (ref. Low)	0.975	0.811
Occupation (ref. Technicians and associate professionals and clerks)	*	
Manager	2.680**	1.538
Professional	2.101**	1.156**
Industry (ref. Public administration)		
Manufacture	0.478	0.669
ICT	0.846	0.872
Finance	1.04	0.567
Education	0.909	1.898
Health, social services	0.684	1.981
Other industries	0.656	1.285
High time pressure (ref. Low)	1.151	1.246
Working time autonomy (ref. No)	0.716	1.072
Long working hours are desirable (ref. Normal working hours are desirable at the workplace)	1.345	1.1
Long working week (41+ hours) (ref. 1–40 hours)	6.019***	8.265***
Problems in defining working time (ref. No problems)	1.245	1.301
Reasons for stretching working hours		
The nature of work (ref. No)	0.912	0.704
Career orientation (ref. No)	1.151	0.941
Problems in work organization (ref. No)	1.348	1.795**
Constant	0.782	0.358*
Chi Square	165.859***	203.522***
–2LL	789.714	817.81
N	746	777

Note: Sig.: <.05*, <.01**, <.000***. Dependent variable: preferred substantial reduction of working week (5+ hours per week) (1=yes, 0=no.).

current working time. Among women, those working a long working week (41 hours or more) were 6.0 times more likely to prefer a substantial reduction of weekly hours, when compared to those working 1 to 40 hours per week. The corresponding figure among males was even higher (8.3).

Among women, occupational status, children and age also mattered. Female managers were 2.7 and professionals 2.1 times more likely to prefer a substantial reduction of weekly hours when compared to technicians and others. Among women, having young children (0 to 7 years old) accounted for their willingness to reduce the working time, increasing the odds 2.6 times when compared to respondents with no children (under the age of 18) at home. In addition, among women, young age (25 to 34 years old) compared to the oldest age group (55 to 64 years old), reduced willingness to cut working hours. Furthermore, problems in work organization as a reason for stretching working hours accounted for the willingness to reduce working time, increasing the odds by 1.8 times among men, when compared to respondents with no problems in work organization.

11.4 DISCUSSION

The aim of the chapter was to discuss, in the context of knowledge workers and especially managers, four interrelated aspects of working time: the extent and antecedents of ambiguous, stretching and preferred working hours, and to examine if there are significant gender differences.

Ambiguity of working time is a reality for many knowledge workers in Finland: half of them had difficulties in defining their total working hours, men more often compared to women. As expected, knowledge workers seem to be more affected by the ambiguity of working time, at least compared to the findings from the United States (Appelbaum and Golden, 2003), where the proportion of wage and salary workers who cannot specify the typical ending time of the workdays stood at 14 per cent in 2001. In the United States the proportion of workers working an "open-ended workday" has increased markedly in just a few years; in 1997 it stood at only around 9 per cent.

Occupational status was the best predictor of ambiguity of working hours; in particular managers and professionals had a much higher probability of having problems in defining working hours compared to technicians and others. In addition, those in teaching or research had more problems in defining work-hours compared to those working in public administration. Furthermore, in a long working hours culture, working time autonomy and high time pressure increased problems in defining working hours. Thus blurring of working hours was produced by work-related factors (such as content of work and time pressure) and organizational culture, but not individual-level factors, such as age or family situation. There was a slight gender difference; women had slightly fewer problems than men in defining their hours worked in paid employment.

The ambiguity of working time is produced, to a great extent, by the nature of the work (such as the independence of work tasks from the place of work). Working at home might be interrupted by household or other private tasks, which adds to the ambiguity of working time. Also, work tasks can penetrate into non-work time; although no intention is made to work, a teacher might come up with an idea for tomorrow's class, and a manager solve a work-related problem. By its very nature, knowledge work is often personal and endless.

Another feature of the post-industrial working time regime is the erosion of collectively agreed upon weekly (or annual) working time, as well as stretching working hours. While around half of the knowledge workers reported working between 35 and 40 hours per week – the normal working time – many did not. One out of three women and half of all men worked more than 40 hours per week.

Among knowledge workers, managers in particular work a long working week, which is a threat to decent working time. Occupational status predicted long working hours: female managers were 3 times and male managers 2 times more likely to work long hours compared to technicians. In addition, high time pressure, a long working hours culture, working time autonomy and high work commitment increased the likelihood of working long hours. On the other hand, among women, having young children (0 to 7 years old) reduced the likelihood of working long hours compared to those without children at home. Therefore, long working hours are connected with both the work and non-work situation. It can be assumed that the work-related factors promote, and family-related factors inhibit, working long hours (see also Feldman, 2002). The Third European Survey on Working Conditions (2000) also showed that working times vary considerably according to professional category; managers' work was characterized by both long working hours and very intensive work (Boisard et al., 2002).

Overall, long hours seem to "come with the job" for managers, who therefore are in danger of suffering from a decent working time deficit, namely that their working hours do not meet their needs and preferences. Additionally, it holds an implicit gender equality issue; the more that managers are forced to work long hours which do not meet their needs and preferences, the more likely women – who often carry the main care responsibility in the family – are to be excluded from managerial positions, reinforcing hierarchical gender inequality (Rutherford, 2001).

Besides structural factors behind long working hours, we were interested in how employees themselves see the reasons for stretching working hours.

The most common reason reported for stretching working hours was the nature of the work (following problems in work organization and career orientation). All these reasons were stressed slightly more often by men compared to women. The nature of the work was best predicted by managerial position; career orientation by young age; and problems in work organization by high time pressure. In addition, a long working hours culture predicted all of these three reasons for stretching working hours. Thus the reasons for stretching working hours were predicted by both work- and individual-level factors and organizational culture.

In the framework of decent working time, a crucial dimension is to what extent preferred and actual working hours match each other. Therefore we examined preferred working hours and their relation to actual hours. In particular, we examined the extent and antecedents of those employees who preferred a substantial reduction (5 hours or more) in their working hours. Overall, 63 per cent of employees preferred a substantial reduction of weekly working hours. As in the earlier studies, the most important factor was current working time (e.g., Bielenski et al., 2002). Those employees working a long week (41 hours or more) were 6 to 8 times more likely to prefer a substantial reduction of weekly hours when compared to those working 1 to 40 hours per week. Among women, occupational status, children and age also mattered, but not among men (see also Bielenski et al., 2002). In particular, women with managerial positions, young children and older age prefer a substantial reduction in working hours.

An interesting finding was also that the preference to reduce working hours was linked to a specific reason for stretching working time. Those reporting problems in work organization as a reason for stretching working hours were more likely to want to reduce their working time, compared to respondents with no problems in work organization. On the other hand, other reasons for stretching working hours, indicating more individual-based willingness to work long hours – such as the nature of work and/or career orientation – were not linked to a willingness to reduce working hours.

The gender differences in the extent and antecedents of preferred hours were mainly similar to earlier studies (Bielenski et al., 2002; Fagan, 2002). Women preferred shorter hours and even a larger reduction in working hours compared to men. In addition, among women the willingness to reduce their hours was linked to both work-related (long working hours, managerial position) and individual-level (age, children) factors, but among men it was only work-related factors (long working hours).

The results of this study are based on representative data among highly educated Finns. However, there are some limitations. First, the data are concentrated on highly educated knowledge workers, and therefore it is not possible to compare knowledge workers with other employees. In addition, on the basis of cross-sectional data it is not possible to examine changes over time or causal relationships. Furthermore, it is outside the scope of this study to investigate in more detail the central question regarding the relation of work and working time to place(s) of work and to the household. The expansion of information and communications technology, and the nature of knowledge work have not only changed working time issues, but changed the dependence on the place of work as well. Working time issues are also affected by non-work factors. Individuals do not live in isolation from their surrounding community and institutions. One of the most important and closest communities is the household (family). The composition and situation of the household have a role to play in the individual's social and economic behaviour, placing restrictions, making demands, and providing different possibilities and benefits.

All in all, the majority of knowledge workers and managers in Finland report the realization of the new working time regime in their everyday life; they often have problems in defining their total working hours; they often work long hours; and their working time regularly stretches beyond the "ordinary" (normative or collectively agreed) hours. The managerial position was the most important predictor for reporting ambiguity of working time and long working hours. Managerial work fuses positive and negative aspects related to various dimensions of "decent working time", enjoying in principle high autonomy, but suffering from the possible adverse effects on health and family created by long hours and stretching working time. A particular problem for policy is that many managers, who work the longest hours and have a strong preference for a reduction in their hours, often fall beyond the "safety net" of working time regulations. Therefore special measures may be needed for employees in managerial positions (see, e.g., Fagan, 2002).

APPENDIX 11.1 SAMPLE ATTRITION ANALYSIS

For the sample attrition analysis characteristics of the participants were compared to results from the 2001 annual labour force survey, collected by Statistics Finland. A similar sample (n = 2651) was selected from the LFS survey data with same criteria (age 25 to 64 years, finished tertiary education ISCED level 5A and 6). The sample attrition analysis showed that in respect of gender, age, family situation, children and occupational status our sample represented well the LFS results. In our sample 49 per cent were women, in the LFS sample 51 per cent. The largest age groups were 35 to 54 (63 per cent in our sample, 59 per cent in the LFS sample). The mean age was 42 years both in our sample and in the LFS sample. Both in our sample (82 per cent) and in the LFS sample (80 per cent) most were living with a partner. Half of respondents had children, both in our sample (49 per cent) and in the LFS sample (47 per cent). Regarding occupation, the study participants represented quite well the LFS sample. In our sample 18 per cent of the participants were managers and 68 per cent were professionals compared to 20 per cent and 68 per cent in the LFS sample, respectively. The comparison regarding industrial classification was not possible because of the different classification in our questionnaire compared to LFS questionnaire.

All in all, we may conclude that even though the response rate was not very high (63 per cent), our sample was quite representative – at least in relation to the background data we had available (i.e., gender, age, family situation, children, and occupational status).

Measures and methods

Ambiguity of working hours. To examine to what extent working hours are unambiguous, participants were asked if they could express their total working hours without ambiguity. The questionnaire is published in Finnish on the internet (http://www.jyu.fi/yhtfil/tietotyo3.htm). (See Appendix 1 of the questionnaire for detailed description of the measures and methods.)

Duration of working hours. The number of weekly working hours was asked as follows: "How many hours per week do you normally put in to your main occupation, including the job-related work you do at home and overtime work?"

Stretching working hours. The extent of stretching working hours was asked as follows: "Do your work hours (including overtime) stretch beyond the agreed or ordinary working hours?" Reasons for the stretching of working hours were surveyed by presenting 14 factors and asking how important they were.

Preferred working hours. The number of preferred weekly working hours was asked as follows: "At this stage of your life, what would be the ideal number of working hours per week?"

Statistical analyses

In the empirical analysis we use – besides cross-tabulation and factor and reliability analysis – logistic regression analysis separately for women and men. *Independent variables* included individual- and job-level factors.

Individual-level factors included age, family situation, children, and work commitment. A sum variable (values 1 to 5) was formed to indicate commitment to work, which was dichotomized for logistic regression analysis.

Job-level factors included occupational status, industry, time pressure, working time autonomy and working time culture. On the basis of occupational title the respondents were classified in three occupational groups: managers, professionals, and technicians and associate professionals. Industry was based on respondents' own classification. Working time autonomy was measured based on influence over starting and finishing times of the workday; men (60 per cent) more often than women (35 per cent) enjoyed working time autonomy. Time pressure at work was investigated through four questions, which were evaluated on a 5-point scale. A sum variable indicating time pressure at work was formed, and further dichotomized for the logistic analysis; 45 per cent of respondents reported severe time pressure.

Working time culture was measured by asking what was the most prevalent working hour norm in the workplace. Half of the respondents (56 per cent) said that normal working hours were desirable, 24 per cent reported no reaction to longer working hours, and 21 per cent said that longer working hours were desirable. The variable was dichotomized for the logistic analysis; the latter two response alternatives indicate a long working time culture in contrast to workplace culture favouring normal working hours. A long working hours culture was more common among men (48 per cent) compared to women (41 per cent).

References

Adam, B. 1995. *Timewatch: The social analysis of time* (Oxford, Polity Press).

Antila, J.; Ylöstalo, P. 1999. "Enterprises as employers in Finland", Flexible enterprise project. Työpoliittisia tutkimuksia 205 (Helsinki, Työministeriö).

Appelbaum, E.; Golden, L. 2003. "The failure to reform the workday", in *Challenge*, Vol. 46, No. 1, pp. 79–92.

Bentley, K.; Yoong, P. 2000. "Knowledge work and telework: An exploratory study", in *Internet Research*, Vol. 10, No. 4, 346–56.

Bielenski, H.; Bosch, G.; Wagner, A. 2002. *Employment options for the future: Actual and preferred working hours. A comparison of 16 European countries* (Dublin, European Foundation for Improvement of Living and Working Conditions).

Blom, R.; Melin, H.; Pyöriä, P. 2001. *Tietotyö ja työelämän muutos. Palkkatyön arki tietoyhteiskunnassa* (Vastapaino, Tampere University Press).

Boisard, P.; Cartron, D.; Gollac, M.; Valeyre, A. 2002. *Time and work: Duration of work* (Dublin, European Foundation for the Improvement of Living and Working Conditions).

Boulin, J.-Y. 1998. "Social and societal issues of working time policies in Europe", in *Vritijd Studies*, Vol. 16, No. 1, pp. 57–67.

Casey, C. 1995. *Work, self and society after industrialism* (London and New York, Routledge).

Castells, M. 1996. *The rise of the network society: The information age, economy, society and culture*, Vol. I (Oxford, Blackwell).

—. 1997. *The power of identity: The information age, economy, society and culture*, Vol. II (Oxford, Blackwell).

Cortada, J. 1999. *Rise of the knowledge worker* (Boston, Butterworth–Heinemann).

EIRO. 2004. Working time developments, European Industrial Relations Observatory, pp. 2–3 (Dublin, European Foundation for the Improvement of Living and Working Conditions).

Fagan, C. 2001. "The temporal reorganisation of employment and the household rhythm of work schedules", in *American Behavioral Scientist*, Vol. 44. No. 7, pp. 1199–212.

—. 2002. "How many hours? Work-time regimes and preferences in European countries", in Graham Crow and Sue Heath (eds.): *Social conceptions of time: Structure and process in everyday life*, pp. 67–87 (Basingstoke, Palgrave).

Feldman, D. 2002. "Managers' propensity to work longer hours: A multilevel analysis", in *Human Resource Management Review*, Vol. 12, No. 3, pp. 339–57.

Florida, R. 2002. *The rise of the creative class: And how it's transforming work, leisure, community and everyday life* (New York, Basic Books).

Garhammer, M. 1999. "De-institutionalisation of work time and its consequences in everyday life and in the life course", paper presented in the 4th ESA Conference: Will Europe Work?, Amsterdam, 18–21 August.

Härmä, M. 1998. "New work times are here – are we ready?", in *Scandinavian Journal of Work, Environment and Health*, Vol. 24, suppl. 3, pp. 3–6.

Hochschild, A. 1997. *The time bind: When work becomes home and home becomes work* (New York, Metropolitan Books).

Hulkko, L.; Luomala, H. 2003. "Työaika 1990-luvulla", in L. Hulkko (ed.): *Työajan muutokset.* Statistics Finland, pp. 8, 9–26.

Julkunen, R.; Nätti, J. 1999. *The modernisation of working times* (Jyväskylä, SoPhi).

—; —. 2002. "Reforming working times: Institutions and behaviour in Finland during the 1990s", in P. Koistinen and W. Sengenberger, Werner (eds.): *Labour flexibility – a factor of economic and social performance of Finland in the 1990s* (Vastapaino, Tampere University Press).

—; —; Anttila, T. 2004. *Aikanyrjähdys: Keskiluokka tietotyön puristuksessa* (Vastapaino, Tampere University Press).

Kalimo, R. 1999. "Knowledge jobs - how to manage without burnout?", in *Scandinavian Journal of Work, Environment & Health*, Vol. 25, No. 6, pp. 605–09.

Kalleberg, A.; Epstein, C.F. 2001. "Temporal dimensions of employment relations", in *American Behavioral Scientist*, Vol. 44, No. 7, pp. 1064–75.

Kivistö, M.; Kalimo, R. 2002. "Tietotekniikan ammattilaisen työ, voimavarat ja hyvinvointi", in M. Härmä and T. Nupponen (eds.): *Työn muutos ja hyvinvointi tietoyhteiskunnassa.* Sitran raportteja, Vol. 22, pp. 91–107 (Helsinki, Sitra).

Kodz, J. et al. 2003. "Working long hours: A review of the evidence", in Department of Trade and Industry, *Main Report*, Employment Relations Research Series, Vol. 1, No. 16.

Konrad, A.; Kashlak, R.; Yoshioka, I.; Waryszak, R.; Toren, N. 2001. "What do managers like to do? A five-country study", in *Group & Organization Management*, Vol. 26, p. 4.

Lehto, A.N.; Sutela, H. 2004. *Uhkia ja mahdollisuuksia. Työolotutkimusten tuloksia 1977–2003* (Helsinki, Tilastokeskus).

Messenger, J. 2004. "Finding the balance: Working time and workers' needs and preferences in industrialized countries. A summary of the report and its implications for working time policies", paper presented at the Ninth Conference of the International Symposium on Working Time, Paris, 26–28 February.

Mintzberg, H. 1973. *The nature of managerial work* (New York, Harper and Row).

—. 1991. "Managerial work: Forty years later", in S. Carlson (ed.): *Executive behaviour* (Stockholm, Uppsalaiensis Academiae).

Moen, P.; Sweet, S. 2003. "Time clocks: Work-hour strategies", in P. Moen (ed.): *It's about time: Couples and careers* (Ithaca, NY, Cornell University Press).

Paoli, P.; Merllié, D. 2001. *Third European survey on working conditions 2000* (Dublin, European Foundation for Improvement of Living and Working Conditions).

Perlow, L. 1998. "Boundary control: The social ordering of work and family time in a high-tech corporation", in *Administrative Science Quarterly*, Vol. 14, No. 2, pp. 328–57.

Pfau-Effinger B. 1999. "Welfare regimes and the gender division of labour", in J. Christiansen, P. Koistinen and A. Kovalainen (eds.): *Working Europe* (Aldershot, Ashgate).

Reich, R. 1991. *The work of nations* (London, Simon & Schuster).

Roberts, K. 1998. "Work and leisure: The recent history of a changing relationship and the related research issues", in *Vrijetid studies*, Vol. 16, pp. 1, 57–67.

Rubery, J.; Grimshaw, D. 2001. "ICTs and employment: The problem of job quality", in *International Labour Review*, Vol. 140, No. 2, pp. 165–193.

Rutherford, S. 2001. "Are you going home already? The long hours culture, women managers and patriarchal closure", in *Time & Society*, Vol. 10, Nos. 2–3, pp. 259–76.

Sennett, R. 1998. *The corrosion of character: The personal consequences of work in the new capitalism* (New York and London, W.W. Norton & Company).

Stewart, M.; Swaffield, J. 1997. "Constraints on the desired hours of work of British men". *Economic Journal*, Vol. 107 (Mar.), pp. 520–35.

Stier, H.; Lewin-Esptein, N. 2003. "Time to work: A comparative analysis of preferences for working hours", in *Work and Occupations*, Vol. 30, No. 3, pp. 302–26.

Tengblad, S. 2001. "Examining the stability of managerial behaviour: A replication of Henry Mintzberg's classic study 30 years later", Gothenburg Research Institute, GRI report 2001, at: http://www.handels.gu.se/gri.

Tétard, F. 2000. "Fragmentation of working time and smarter IS-solutions", in *Proceedings of the 33rd Hawaii International Conference on Systems Sciences*.

Väisänen, M.; Nätti, J. 2002. "Working time preferences in dual-earning households", in *European Societies*, Vol. 4, No. 3, pp. 307–29.

Van den Berg, P.; Schlak, R. 1997. "Type A behavior, well-being, work overload, and role-related stress in information work", in *Journal of Social Behaviour & Personality*, Vol. 12, No. 1, pp. 175–87.

White, M.; Hill, S.; McGovern P.; Mills C.; Smeaton, D. 2003. "High-performance management practices, working hours and work-life balance", in *British Journal of Industrial Relations*, Vol. 41, No. 2, pp. 175–95.

CAN NORMS SURVIVE MARKET PRESSURES? THE PRACTICAL EFFECTIVENESS OF NEW FORMS OF WORKING TIME REGULATION IN A CHANGING GERMAN ECONOMY

12

*Thomas Haipeter**

12.1 INTRODUCTION: FLEXIBILIZATION AND EROSION

For some years now, efforts have been under way to redraw the map of working time regulation in Germany. New regulatory models are emerging everywhere, and they have little in common with the principles that governed the previous, long-established system. Flexibilization and decentralization are the new watchwords encapsulating the principles driving the current changes. Working times are becoming more flexible and individual establishments and companies are becoming increasingly important as the locus of working time regulation, at the expense of industry-level collective agreements (Schmidt and Trinczek, 1999). In German literature, this process has been denoted by the term "*Verbetrieblichung*", which might best be rendered as "decentralization" or "devolvement to establishment level". The starting point for these changes was the introduction of derogation clauses into industry-level collective agreements specifying the periods of time within which variations in the distribution and scheduling of working time had to be balanced out. These derogation clauses created the conditions for decentralized negotiations on new forms of working time regulation between works councils and company or establishment management.

Increasing attention is now being paid to the risk that the delegation of negotiating competences to parties at company or establishment level may lead to an uncontrollable erosion of the collective bargaining system (König et al., 1998). It is feared that the foundations of Germany's dual system of industrial

* Institut Arbeit und Technik, Munscheidstraße, 1445886, Gelsenkirchen, Germany. Email: haipeter@iatge.de.

relations, with its delicate balance between actors at central and local levels, trade unions and employers' associations, on the one hand, and works councils and companies on the other, could be completely destabilized (Hassel, 1999; Bispinck and Schulten, 1998). The decentralization of regulation is seen as the main driving force behind the process of erosion, because it is suspected that regulations based on industry-level collective agreements are losing their power to influence behaviour at the local level. From this point of view, the shift in the levels of regulation has led to a continuous decline in the capacity of collectively agreed upon norms to shape regulatory practices at the company or establishment level.

I would like to contribute to this debate using three approaches. The first is that of a detailed empirical analysis. The fact is that little is known about how new forms of working time regulation are actually operating at the company or establishment level. However clearly the trend towards flexibilization has been identified in empirical terms (Herrmann et al., 1999; Promberger et al., 2002), we still have very little information on how new forms of working time regulation are manifesting themselves in the practical organization of individual working time. It is by no means clear, therefore, whether, and under what conditions, flexibilization and decentralization inevitably lead to the erosion of regulation through collective agreements by weakening the normative binding power of such arrangements.

The second approach is that of collective learning. The term "erosion" denotes an unidirectional process that can hardly be said to be opening up new prospects for the future structuring of working time regulation through collective agreements. If this erosion becomes firmly established on a broad front, there will be little left of the German system of industrial relations and its collective forms of regulation. However, crises can also be the starting point for new developments. From this perspective, new approaches to regulation through collective agreement can also be seen as new attempts to get the industrial relations system moving again. From this point of view, the key issue for industrial relations is the direction in which these attempts are going. Are they pointing the way towards erosion or opening up new prospects for working time regulation?

The third approach is individual participation in the negotiation of "decent working time". The new forms of working time regulation harbour within themselves the seeds of a third level of industrial relations, in addition to collective agreements and co-determination through works councils. This level is individual employee participation, the formal foundations for which are contained in the new working time regulations in the form of legitimate claims. Consequently, the new collectively agreed upon working time regulations are always associated with the promise of a "decent working time" arrangement that will enable employees to assert their own individual working time interests and requirements. Thus the extent to which this promise can be realized, and whether it will give rise to new interactions between the various levels of the system, will be a decisive factor in maintaining the normative binding power of working time regulation, and for the future of the German industrial relations system as a whole.

In examining these three approaches, I draw on the results of a research project funded by the Hans Böckler Foundation. In the course of this project, Steffen Lehndorff and I examined the practical effectiveness of new working time regulations in firms and establishments. I carried out a total of five intensive case studies in various companies in a number of different industries. In each case, 15 to 33 interviews were conducted with experts and employees.

12.2 WORKING TIME REGULATION AND CHANGES IN PRODUCTION SYSTEMS

The regulation of working time by collective agreement does not take place in a vacuum. On the one hand, it is embedded in the institutional characteristics of the industrial relations system. It is the collective actors in this system, that is, the bodies representing the interests of employees and employers (or individual employers), who negotiate the agreements that govern working time. In doing so, they are bound by the institutional framework of the respective systems. On the other hand, however, working time regulation is also directly linked to production systems in the workplace, because working time is an important variable in the organization of production.

In this section, therefore, we outline the general trends and inter-connections between working time regulation, industrial relations and production systems in Germany. This general context is crucial to any assessment of the "knock-on" effects of the new forms of regulation. It will become clear that the normative binding power of the new working time regulations will stand or fall by their ability to make working time an independent variable in the production system (and the collective actors' power to enforce the new rules), and at the same time to offer employees new scope for individual planning and participation in the process of establishing a "decent working time".

The regulation of working time in Germany has traditionally been shaped by the hierarchical interaction of two regulatory levels: industry-level collective agreements, on the one hand, and workplace co-determination, on the other (table 12.1). The outline of collective agreements on working time laid down clear standards governing the duration, scheduling, and distribution of working time that severely limited the scope of arrangements agreed at firm or

Table 12.1   The dual structure of the German industrial relations system

Regulatory level	Legal basis	Actors	Agreements	Objects of agreement
Free collective bargaining	Collective Agreements Act: primacy of collective agreement over other arrangements	Associations: trade unions and employers' associations	Industry-level collective agreements	Wages and salaries Working time Wage systems and principles of remuneration
Works constitution/ workplace labour relations	Works Constitution Act: rights of co-determination for works councils	Parties in the workplace: works councils and management	Company agreements	Implementation of industry-level collective agreements and of employment and performance conditions in the workplace

Source: Author.

establishment level. These standards were the 5-day work-week and 8-hour day, creating a total weekly working time of 40 hours (later reduced in the metal and engineering industry to 35 hours). Thus the only standards negotiated at the local level concerned specific working time systems, such as shift systems for production departments, but not separate regulatory systems governing the scheduling, distribution or duration of working times.

Conversely, this meant that all deviations from the largely definitive norms laid down in the outline agreements had formal status as exceptions. These exceptions were also governed by collective agreements and associated with additional costs in the form of premium payments. Thus there was a differentiated system of premium payments for overtime, night work, and Saturday and Sunday working. At the same time, in accordance with the provisions of the Works Constitution Act (BetrVG, 1952), these exceptions were subject to the approval of works councils. Thus flexibility in the form of deviations from the normative standards was perfectly possible in practice, but it was associated with additional costs and could also be forbidden by the works councils.

Although they were the product of sometimes bitter political disputes, these old forms of working time regulation fit so well with the functional principles of the Fordist production system and its standardized products, that a high degree of functional compatibility – in the sense of *ex-post* functionality – can be said to have existed between them (Lipietz, 1985). Thus the strong working time norms constituted an important precondition for the de-coupling of production from market fluctuations and uncertainties – which for its part was an essential condition for the exploitation of economies of scale by means of standardized products and processes. The standardization of working time meant that it was no longer a factor in competition, and at the same time created incentives for productivity gains, which were achieved through intensive use of Taylorist rationalization strategies, standardization, and by the reduction of the standard times allowed for each operation.

So it was no accident that the collapse of the Fordist production system (cf. Boyer and Durant, 1997) gave rise to a crisis in the old system of working time regulation. The old system was simply no longer compatible with the new production systems that have been emerging since the 1990s, and whose fundamental characteristic is that they bring organizations into more direct contact with the market. Nor is it any coincidence that the subsequent period has seen the enforced flexibilization of working time (Hermann et al., 1999). Firms have been striving to bring the production of goods and services as close as possible to the market. Perhaps the most incisive description of this development is found in VolksWagen manager Peter Hartz's metaphor of the factory that "breathes" with the market (Hartz, 1996), an image that is now firmly lodged in the cognitive processes of many German managers.

Thus the emergence of new forms of working time regulation can be understood only against the background of the change in production systems. In the German debate, this change has been denoted by terms such as "marketization" (Moldaschl and Sauer, 2000), or the introduction of "market-driven management systems" (Dörre, 2002). In my view, the second term is the more accurate one, since the organizational change that has taken place is characterized both by the harnessing of the market as a new instrument for coordinating internal processes, and by an attempt to manage these processes centrally.

Market-driven management systems operate on two levels, that of strategic management (which is corporate governance), and that of the operational management of decentralized units (Haipeter, 2003). At the level of corporate governance, the new element in market-driven management systems is that strategic decision-making competences are invested to a greater extent than previously in company management. As a consequence, greater emphasis is placed on strategies geared towards the interests of the capital markets that seek to maximize returns and increase the value of companies' quoted shares (Streeck and Höppner, 2003). This reference to capital markets helps corporate management to justify internally the demands for increased returns that individual operational units have to meet. This "financialization" of corporate decision-making is probably widespread (Dore, 2000; Kädtler and Sperling, 2001; Kädtler, 2003).

The "financialization" of strategic decision-making at the central level has its counterpart in the decentralization of operational decision-making competences. Strategies formulated at the central level define the general conditions in which operational units have to accommodate themselves as they exercise the responsibilities devolved to them, whether for costs or profits. In firms that have implemented operational decentralization (Faust et al., 1994), it is left up to the decentralized units to decide how to manage with the budget allocated to them or how to meet the financial targets laid down by central management. As far as the evolution of work organization is concerned, the most significant consequence of market-driven management is that employees themselves are directly confronted by the demands of the market as an objective exigency. They have to make their own individual contribution to the fulfilment of market-driven objectives in order to ensure their unit's survival, or to protect their jobs. This confrontation between employees and the market is also denoted by the term "indirect management" (Glißmann and Peters, 2001).

It is the processing of market demands associated with indirect management that gives such great impetus to demands for working time flexibilization. It is only on this basis that there can be any spontaneous response to demands emanating from the market and from customers, and only on the basis that "breathing" processes are organizationally conceivable. However, since they have to be adapted to the actual needs of companies or individual establishments – or even individual groups of employees – flexible regulations are decentralized regulations that operate at the company or establishment level. That is why companies exerting pressure for working time flexibilization in response to changes in the production system are always associated with pressure for the decentralization of working time regulations through collective agreements.

In a market-oriented production system, however, it is individual employees who are most knowledgeable about market requirements. This is why working time flexibilization is closely associated not only with the decentralization of collective working time regulations, but also with the individualization of working time organization. This individualization, in turn, can give rise to a certain degree of legitimate employee participation. The more working time regulations are intended to give employees increased room for manoeuvre in organizing their own work, the more they necessarily contain participatory elements. In this sense, flexibility regulated through collective agreements becomes an instrument for increasing employee autonomy in matters of working time organization. At the same time, however, it can also be associated with shifts in influence or importance between the various levels of the industrial relations system. In particular, it may be the starting point for

Table 12.2   Flexible working time regulation and industrial relations

Regulatory level	Legal basis	Actors	Agreements	Objects of agreement
Free collective bargaining	Collective Agreements Act	Associations	Collective agreements on working time	Framework regulations on the duration, scheduling and distribution of working time
Works councils' rights of co-determination	Works Constitution Act	Parties in the workplace	Company agreements on working time	Flexible regulations
Employee participation	Company agreements/ collective agreements on working time	Employee and supervisor	Consultations on working time organization	Resolution of individual problems with working time organization

Source: Author.

the emergence of a new regulatory level – one that is the locus for individual participation (table 12.2).

However, problems are likely to arise at the interface between self-organization and market-driven management, problems that could fundamentally call into question the binding power of collective working time regulations. Thus it is entirely conceivable, first, that their direct exposure to the requirements of the market will make employees realize that in fact all forms of collective working time regulation can be obstacles to fulfilment of their own individual work goals. Working time would become a dependent variable for employees as they seek to cope with their workloads. In this situation, the collective norm would lose its binding power because it no longer met the interests of the individual employees as they tried to organize their own work.

This applies all the more since, second, the new pressure to increase profits and reduce costs, which is linked to the "financialization" of strategic decision-making, leads to a reduction in the resources available to the operational units. The result is a personnel policy in the operational units driven by the "bottom line", the main effect of which is to reduce staffing levels to a minimum. The more restrictively this policy is pursued, the more increases in actual working times will be used as a means of dealing with temporary increases in workloads. Thus, if indirect management creates incentives for increasing working times, these incentives become inherent necessities when combined with a personnel policy which, in the wake of "financialization", is driven solely by the "bottom line".

12.3 THE CHARACTERISTICS OF NEW FORMS OF WORKING TIME REGULATION – THE CASE STUDIES

Against this background, the key question is whether, in market-driven management systems, collective regulations can still exert any normative influence at all on the organization of working time at the local level. Thus it seems reasonable to suppose that the main problem with the erosion of regulation through collective agreement lies not so much in the shift of regulatory levels itself, but rather in the fact that the shift is taking place *within a market-driven* system. This is precisely the question I will be addressing in what follows.

The most important instrument used in German companies that have introduced flexible working time systems is the working time account. Such accounts are technical tools for managing working times that deviate from agreed-upon average working times – whether enshrined in individual or collective agreements (Seifert, 2001). According to the latest surveys, it is reasonable to assume that between 30 and 40 per cent of employees in Germany now have working time accounts (Bauer et al., 2002; Seifert, 2001). However, it should be noted, in assessing these figures, that working time accounts can take very different forms, ranging from simple flexi-time systems to those whose equalization periods are much more long-term or even encompass the entire working life. The longer the equalization period within which fluctuations in working times have to be balanced out, and the higher the upper limit on the number of hours worked that can be accumulated on an account, the greater the potential for flexibility that an account provides.

In the case studies, the results of which are presented in what follows, we investigated systems of working time regulations that are part of the "avant-garde" within the new forms of regulation in Germany.[1] They belong to the avant-garde because they are designed to replace traditional regulatory systems, and to open up room for manoeuvre and hence produce particularly far-reaching forms of working time flexibility. They can be identified by three general characteristics that they all share, and that distinguish them from the typical working time account systems:

---

[1] "Components", "Supplier", "Software", "IT Services", and "Communicator" are all pseudonyms for the firms studied and are used for purposes of protecting their confidentiality.

- the particularly widespread conversion of paid overtime into normal working time: flexibility is no longer achieved through the use of overtime, which is expensive and requires the approval of the works council, but by varying normal working time. In this way, flexibility is reinterpreted, becoming a formal rule rather than a formal exception;

- the use of different account systems: the new forms of regulation combine certain types of accounts. These are generally flexi-time accounts, on the one hand, and new long-term accounts, on the other. Long-term accounts are those that allow for long equalization periods and permit employees to take their time off in extended blocks (also known as sabbaticals);

- new procedural rules: first, opportunities are provided for employees to take part in the negotiations with their supervisors and managers. The regulations provide "handholds" or points of intervention (Lehndorff, 2003) for employees by giving them certain rights to which they can have recourse should problems arise and establishing certain procedural norms for decentralized negotiations between employees and managers. In this way, the foundations have been laid for a new "arena" for decentralized bargaining (Müller-Jentsch 1986). Second, points of intervention for co-determination are stipulated. These "codetermination thresholds" (Haipeter and Lehndorff, 2002; Lehndorff, 2003) bring works councils' rights of co-determination into play when problems arise in the decentralized negotiations between employees and supervisors.

It is particularly interesting to investigate these pioneering cases because they indicate where innovations are taking place in working place regulation, and the directions new developments are going in. They are particularly suited to detailed empirical analyses. At the same time, they are likely to give some clues as to possible new means of regulation that might offer starting points for exemplary learning. Table 12.3 presents details of the various regulatory systems studied.

All the regulatory systems combine various types of accounts – such as flexi-time and long-term accounts – and thereby provide management with new and extended instruments for converting paid overtime into a more flexible form of normal working time. The flexi-time accounts either have short equalization periods or strictly defined and tightly drawn upper limits. In most cases, the long-term accounts have no equalization periods or upper limits, which is why they can also be described as lifelong working time accounts. Employees can use these lifelong accounts in two ways. The accumulated hours can either be withdrawn as an extended block of time off

Table 12.3   Summary of working time account systems

	Account types	Equalization periods	Upper limits	Compensation options/ requirements
Components	Working time account	WTA: none	WTA: +105/−35 hours	WTA: credits withdrawn in whole days or blocks of days
	Long-term account	LTA: none	LTA: +300 hours as an average of all employees	LTA: longer blocks of time, early retirement
Supplier	Flexi-time account	FTA: 1 month	FTA: +20 hours	FTA: in hours or days
	Long-term account	LTA: none	LTA: none	LTA: mandatory entitlement for further/ advanced training; transition to retirement; minimum withdrawal 3 months
Software	Flexi-time account	FTA: none	FTA: +/−60 hours	FTA: in hours or days
	Long-term account	LTA: none	LTA: up to age 45: 1,800 hours, then unlimited	LTA: block of free time; part time on full pay, early retirement
IT Services	Flexi-time account	FTA: 1 month	FTA: +/−50 hours	FTA: in hours and days
	Medium-term account	MTA: 5 years	MTA: 550 hours; 135 hours worth of accruals each year	MTA: mandatory entitlement for training; blocks of time off (fixed entitlement to 6 weeks in 5 years); working time reduction through working time budgets
	Long-term account	LTA: none	LTA: none	LTA: early retirement; lump sum payment for care services from age 45
Communicator	Flexi-time account	FTA: 1 month	FTA: +/−40 hours	FTA: in hours and days
	Long-term account	LTA: none	LTA: none	LTA: in days

Source: Own survey.

(i.e., a sabbatical) or they can be used to bring forward retirement or the transition to part-time working for older employees – in other words, to reduce working time over the course of the lifetime. In this latter option, long-term accounts function as retirement savings accounts (Haipeter and Lehndorff, 2002).

The points at which new procedural norms and co-determination come into play, and when employees themselves can begin to intervene, differ from system to system. True, all of the agreements give employees rights of participation, but in all cases employees are given the responsibility for organizing their own working time within the limits laid down for the various accounts. However, there are differences with regard to procedural norms. In this area, it is only the agreement at Communicator that has weak regulatory content. It stipulates no normative requirements at all for negotiations between employees and management. The only normative element is that management has the final decision regarding disputes. Otherwise, if the limits laid down for the flexi-time account are exceeded, then the account in question is simply capped, therefore, any excess working time, or rather any entitlement to time off in lieu, is forfeited.

In contrast, the other regulatory systems we investigated lay down strong procedural norms. At Components, for example, so-called "trigger limits" have been set, which, once reached, set in motion negotiations between the workforce and management. At Software and IT Services, working time budgets have been introduced as a replacement for, or supplement to, paid overtime. Such budgets have to be agreed upon as a matter of urgency between the workforce and management when required, that is, when flexi-time accounts are likely to be overloaded for a long period. The transfers of worked hours to the long-term accounts must also be agreed upon at a decentralized level. The same applies to the use of long-term accounts at Supplier. In addition, at Software, employees are free to choose whether or not they should join the working time account system at all. They have two options: they may either withdraw altogether from the system and switch to a "fiduciary" working time system (i.e., one which is based on trust, with working time not being recorded at all); alternatively they may remain formally within the account system, but be exempted from the obligation to negotiate (in this case, they are assigned to a no-preference list).

The variable degrees of regulatory power are also reflected in the works councils' rights to co-determination. Thus at Communicator, the requirement that the final decision should rest with management rules out co-determination. In essence, the works council has no real opportunity for intervention unless it opts to go down the formal legal route. The situation is quite different in the other four cases. At Components, the works council can be called in not only when disputes arise, but also when trigger limits are set and decisions are taken on transfers to long-term accounts. At Software, the works council also enjoys a right of co-determination in disputes. Moreover, it has veto power with regard to the approval of working time budgets, and operates as an equal partner on a working time committee that monitors the functioning of the working time regulatory system. The regulatory system at IT Services also calls on the works council when disputes arise and accords it full codetermination rights, with regard to both the establishment of working time budgets and the withdrawal of time credits.

12.4   THE PRACTICAL EFFECTIVENESS OF WORKING TIME REGULATORY SYSTEMS

How effective are the working time regulatory systems in establishing norms? Do they influence employees' everyday behaviour in respect to working time? And do they act as a counterbalance to the effects of the market-driven forms of management outlined above? In the course of our investigation, I identified a total of six problem areas that could adversely affect the practical effectiveness of working time regulations, which play a decisive role in determining their binding power.

12.4.1   The change in the function of flexi-time

It is flexi-time arrangements that constitute the actual success story of the new working time regulatory systems. It is the very flexibility of these arrangements that employees are primarily exploiting in their day-to-day behaviour. It should be remembered that today's flexi-time systems bear little resemblance to those of the 1980s. At that time, flexi-time was still used as a measure designed to improve corporate culture; today, in the companies used in the case study, it is regarded as a privileged instrument for dealing with the operational demands of day-to-day business. The room for manoeuvre in the organization of flexi-time is no longer determined solely by individual working time interests, but rather by a balance between those interests and operational requirements. This change has also been fully internalized by employees. This is not seen as generating potential conflict. Indeed, to the contrary, flexi-time is appreciated for two reasons: because it makes it possible, first, to adjust working time to business or operational requirements and, second, to satisfy individual demands for flexibility.

And yet, under the cover of the high regard for flexi-time and its practical effectiveness, a second shift in the function of flexi-time systems is currently taking place as a consequence of market-driven forms of management. Indirect management has affected work organization, and customer demands and general market pressures are giving rise to greater fluctuations in working time. Furthermore, indirect forms of management have led employees to internalize the concerns of their employers and customers, thereby making the company's economic problems, on the one hand, and its customers' requirements, on the other, their own problems. This forces them to adopt a completely new approach to working time. Adhering to agreed-upon working times becomes a secondary issue compared with the need to resolve the problems of both the company and its customers. It is no coincidence that in all of our case studies we found employees prepared to deliver a high degree of flexibility – sometimes even beyond the limits of the working time arrangement.

Yet indirect management is only one side of the coin. At the same time, organizations are being systematically starved of the human resources they need. The reason for this is the increased pressure to boost profits and cut costs to which operational units are now subject as a result of the "financialization" of corporate strategy. The result is a personnel policy driven by the bottom line, with the main objectives being to operate with the lowest possible staffing levels, and to deal with temporary increases in workloads by extending working times. This makes it increasingly difficult for employees to make use of their time credits. The extension of actual working times is becoming an inherent necessity that individual employees find it virtually impossible to avoid. For this reason, structural overtime is the "hidden agenda" of indirect management (Lehndorf, 2003).

12.4.2 The dominance of paid overtime

The route that most of the companies in our samples have taken in seeking to manage structural overtime is the traditional one of paid overtime. At IT Services, for example, this is the approach that is preferred in the working time arrangement. For employees, an application for paid overtime is a self-evident and perfectly valid alternative to the agreement of working time budgets. It is even more than that, since the procedure for agreeing on a working time budget is, in comparison, laborious and uncertain. To date, in any event, on average only one in twenty employees has actually agreed a working time budget. All the others applied for paid overtime. The volume of such additional hours worked is up to 60 or 70 per month. The reason for this, however, lies not only in the incentives contained in the working time arrangement, but also in the working time policy adopted by the works council. First, the works council has not exactly been keen to promote the new system of working time regulation. Indeed, many of the employees we interviewed were unaware that working time budgets existed. Second, through its practice of approving overtime more or less without reservation, the works council has played a major role in maintaining the dominance of paid overtime.

Thus the question of paid overtime, or time off in lieu, is decided essentially by the working time policy of the various interested parties, and principally that of the works council. This can be demonstrated by taking the example of Supplier. Here, the working time regulations stipulate that half of any increase in contractual working time is credited automatically to the long-term account, which is then recompensed in the form of time off. This is a policy decision in favour of compensatory time off that is enshrined in the regulations. Moreover, the working time practices of the various parties are consistent with the nature of the regulations. Management and the works council have agreed to be more restrictive in the use of paid overtime. Consequently, it is no longer available for use on the same scale. At the same time, actual working times are becoming shorter because a part of the increased contractual working time is recompensed with time off in lieu. One important consequence of this policy is that in many areas of the organization there is a concentration on what is absolutely essential. The demand for efficiency and effectiveness is greater than ever.

However, all this takes place in the context of a personnel policy driven by the bottom line. What will happen at Supplier if the volume of work begins to increase more rapidly again is unclear. Will the pendulum swing back towards increased use of overtime? Or will the restrictive overtime policy be maintained? And will this then put pressure on staff recruitment? In this situation, the consequences of market governance become a political problem, with which those responsible for working time regulation will have to grapple sooner or later.

12.4.3 The forfeiture of working time

Compared with the third problem area, the forfeiture of working time, paid overtime seems to be a trivial problem. With paid overtime the works council still has rights of co-determination (in theory at least), and retains an overview of the volume of hours worked. This is no longer the case when the forfeiture of working time becomes part of daily practice. In our sample, this is the case only at Communicator, but it is clear from the literature that the phenomenon is more widespread (Ahlers and Trautwein-Kalms, 2002; Glißmann and Peters, 2001; Moldaschl and Voß, 2002).

At Communicator, it is a common practice for working time to be neither recorded nor paid. Employees do not record the hours they work, or do not do so truthfully. The reason for this is that, for most employees, working time has become a parameter of only secondary importance. What is really important for individual employees is to meet customer demands and to manage their own workloads. Working time is a lesser concern. In indirect management, it is a dependent variable. Working time does not become really important until the company regulations or working time legislation are infringed. Individuals seeking to cope with the demands of their workloads regard these norms as barriers. They try to surmount these barriers while at the same time avoiding sanctions. It is for this reason that they do not accurately record the hours they work.

This practice is not only knowingly tolerated by management and supervisors but also actively supported. True, most supervisors indicate that they will not sign any time sheets that reveal infringements of the working time norms. At the same time, however, they do accept time sheets from which it is evident that the employees' output could not have been produced within the times recorded. In formal terms, all the proper procedures are followed, but in reality the collective regulation of working time no longer has any structuring effect on employees' working time practices. Rather, those practices are determined by the demands of a system of indirect management implemented against the background of a restrictive personnel policy.

There are two reasons why, at Communicator and certainly elsewhere as well, the forfeiture of working time is encouraged as a "solution" to the problem of structural overtime. The first one lies in the working time arrangement itself, which relies on automatic mechanisms without providing any opportunities for employees or the works council to intervene. One of these automatic mechanisms is the capping rule that applies to excess flexi-time credits. Any such credits exceeding the limits stipulated for flexi-time accounts are simply forfeited without compensation. What is more, there is no mechanism for triggering negotiations. Neither the forfeiture of flexi-time credits nor applications for overtime can be the object of dialogue or negotiation, because the regulations do not provide for any procedures. Nor is there any provision for the works council to intervene.

This weakness in the regulations points to the second problem, namely the weakness of the works council, which is reflected in its working time policy. The works council is caught in a predicament which might be described as a dilemma of representation. The fact is that the works council is currently the only actor that still has any interest in the practical effectiveness of collective regulation. The company and its managers and supervisors are relying on the development of indirect management, while for employees working time regulation has become a disruptive factor. When the works council intervenes to uphold working time regulations, it is pursuing a collective interest that no longer seems to coincide with the interests of individual employees. This creates a crisis of legitimacy for the works council, further weakening its already precarious position in the workplace.

The consequence of this dilemma is not only that working times lack transparency and are unpaid, but also that they are extremely long. In the interviews we conducted, employees frequently mentioned the health problems caused by such long hours. Yet these problems are not seen as an occasion to reconsider the practice. Rather, employees tend to take the view that there is no alternative. The reason for this is that anxiety over job security has been fuelled by the considerable number of jobs that have been cut in recent years. Pressure emanating from the labour market has become a significant driving force in the system of indirect management.

However, this practice of forfeiting working time threatens to become a serious problem not only for individual employees but also for the development of the organization as a whole. It is true that increasing working time at no additional cost reduces wage costs in the short term; but in the longer term it undermines the organization's learning capacities. When working time becomes a free resource, there is no longer any reason to use it economically. Nor is there any incentive to conduct a debate on questions of efficiency or effectiveness. Individual abilities are not systematically transformed into generalized and explicit knowledge (Brödner, 1997). Improvements in productivity remain individualized and compartmentalized, thereby preventing organizational learning processes from becoming firmly established.

12.4.4   The withdrawal of time credits from long-term accounts

Long-term accounts have not to date shown themselves to have any practical effectiveness. The main cause of this is the withdrawal of time credits, which is the so-called "Achilles heel" of such accounts. At the same time, this brings us back to the problem of structural overtime as a product of market-driven management systems.

The main criticism voiced by employees was that, in their view, the withdrawal of time credits, at least in the form of sabbaticals, was simply unfeasible. The reason cited was their experiences with a personnel policy driven by the bottom line. The constraining environment in which they operate means that the possibility of ever being able to make a withdrawal from an account is little more than a remote prospect, likely to remain forever out of reach. It is no accident that in none of the case study companies was a successful attempt to withdraw time credits from a long-term account for the purpose of a sabbatical reported to us. Such withdrawals simply do not happen. As a result, there are no positive examples around of narratives developing within organizations about the opportunities that do exist and which might serve to shape employees' perceptions. Thus long-term accounts have not yet been through their "baptism of fire", leaving employees' expectations to become sceptical.

To date, therefore, the only realistic option for using long-term accounts is their capacity as retirement savings accounts, enabling older workers to either take early retirement or go part time. Both of these uses of long-term accounts are very much appreciated by employees, and the opportunities are viewed much more positively. Nevertheless, these uses are obviously not sufficient to make long-term accounts more widely attractive.

12.4.5   Individualized bargaining

A key element in the new forms of working time regulation is the creation of an arena for decentralized bargaining on working time. Working time issues are no longer treated as problems for the actors at the central level, for works councils and for management at the establishment or company level. Rather, they are decided on in negotiations between employees and their managers at the local level. However, the problem here is that virtually no such decentralized negotiations have hitherto taken place.

Our case studies reveal two main reasons for the practical ineffectiveness of decentralized bargaining. The first is the persistence of old organizational forms. The disruptive factor here is hierarchy, which results in working time practices being shaped by management instructions rather than negotiations. It is true that, in our sample, this problem situation predominated only at the Components production plant. However, in light of the recent debate on the "re-standardization of labour policy" (Schumann, 1998) or the "back-swing of the labour policy pendulum" (Dörre, 2002), it may well be absolutely typical of many plants in the manufacturing sector.

The second reason is the successful introduction of market-driven forms of management. Prime examples in our sample are Components and IT Services, where market-driven management is the dominant organizational element. It is clear from these examples that market-driven management is not dependent on the existence of participatory instruments and processes in order to function. On the contrary, the most favourable conditions for rigorous implementation of market-led management, with its combination of indirect control and a personnel policy driven by the bottom line, seem to exist precisely where its effect is not compromised by rights of participation and their corresponding processes. Conversely, the use of conciliation as a coordinating mechanism may well restrict the effects of market-led management. At the same time it may create decisive advantages for the long-term development of an organization.

Both can be illustrated by taking the example of Software. Here, discussions on working time budgets and those on target setting are predominantly conciliatory in nature. They involve genuine negotiation, not just top-down target setting. Employees are able to insert their concerns about working time and job content into the decision-making process. As a consequence, working time remains an independent parameter in the participants' decision-making calculus. It is not reduced to a mere dependent variable. Working time remains a scarce commodity. Moreover, and precisely for this reason, working time and target-setting discussions increasingly function as a locus for organizational learning. The very scarcity of working time gives rise to questions about the efficiency and effectiveness of activities; as a result, individual productivity improvements can also be stored in the organization's collective "memory".

12.4.6   The anchor role of co-determination

However, decentralized bargaining cannot become established unless it is strongly supported by a works council exercising its rights of co-determination. Working time regulation needs advocates at the company or establishment level; these are primarily the works councils which, unlike employees, can draw on the Works Constitution Act, and have experience in disputes and professionalized structures to rely on in their negotiations with management.

Software provides an impressive illustration of the interaction between co-determination and decentralized bargaining, an interaction that has a decisive influence on the practical effectiveness of working time regulation and at the same time strengthens the works council's position. The works council's principal arena in the sphere of working time policy is the joint working time committee. This committee functions as a monitoring and controlling body. It compiles data on time account balances, instances of capping, working time budgets, and employees who have voluntarily withdrawn from the working time account system. At the same time, the committee intervenes as arbitrator in individualized negotiations when requested to do so by employees. However, the committee also acts proactively to monitor compliance with working time regulations. Thus employees and managers are approached when flexi-time accounts are about to be capped and encouraged to consider countermeasures. The committee also exercises its veto power when working time budgets accumulate in certain areas or among certain members of the workforce.

However, the real driving force on the committee is the works council. It is the works council which, through its representatives on the committee, constantly seeks to remind individual actors of the importance of working time and working time regulation. It is also the works council that exercises its veto power in problem situations. In this way, the works council has made the practical effectiveness of working time regulation an issue within its own policy. In doing so, however, it has clearly parted company with traditional forms of representing interests. Works council members treat employees as mature and responsible citizens of the company. Another factor is the libertarian nature of the working time system. Employees are free to choose whether or not they wish to take part in the working time account system. This gives them the impression that it is not they who are being monitored by the working time committee, but that they are simply complying with a regulatory system that they are adhering to voluntarily, with the works council helping employees to help themselves.

The veto power on working time budgets is an important instrument, by means of which working time can be used to make the effects of market-driven management on the organization a political issue. Such a veto inevitably raises the question of how, and by whom, the volume of work is to be managed. Simply posing this question is problematic for a personnel policy driven by the bottom line. By making the practical effectiveness of working time regulation a problem for its own policy, the works council has at the same time committed itself to politicizing market-driven management and keeping it in check.

12.5   CONCLUSION

One unambiguous conclusion can be drawn from this analysis of the six problem areas in working time regulation: such regulation cannot acquire normative power unless the effects of market-driven governance are kept in check. Only if this condition is met can working time regulation become effective in practice, since it is only then that working time retains – or acquires – the status of a dependent variable in the day-to-day operations of a company or establishment. Indeed, one of the most significant consequences of market-driven forms of management, with their combination of indirect control and restrictive personnel policies, is that working time can be reduced to a dependent variable in the decision-making calculus of the actors at the local level. However, when working time is subordinated to other variables in the decision-making process, working time regulations are unable to exert any significant influence over workplace behaviour.

Against this background, strong regulatory norms are a necessary condition for a system of working time regulation that is effective in practice. This is shown by the example of Communicator. If both the works council's rights of co-determination and employees' rights of participation are weak, working time norms, and with them the opportunities for works councils and employees to exert any shaping influence, are a lost cause. Working time regulation cannot function without strong procedural norms. However, even a regulatory system with strong norms does not by itself keep the effects of market-led governance in check. Without vigorous advocacy in the workplace, working time regulations exist only on paper and can have no practical application.

However, the most important advocates of decentralized working time regulations are the works councils. Only they can make working time regulations effective in practice. Two crucial preconditions have to be met if they are to succeed in this task. The first is that the works council should function as a stable countervailing power within the firm or establishment. The case of Communicator shows what happens when this condition is not met. There can be no agreement on the incorporation into the working time regulations of points of intervention for individual employees or the works council, nor is the works council capable of implementing any working time policy at all. The second precondition is that the works council should also pursue an active working time policy. It must make the practical effectiveness of working time policy a problem for its own policy-making and keep working time issues alive as policy issues within the organization.

However, such a policy depends crucially on a third precondition: the interaction between co-determination and decentralized bargaining. However hard the works council strives, working time regulation will not function properly if it seeks to regulate everything from the top down. It must not only tolerate the room for manoeuvre accorded employees in individualized bargaining, but also, when necessary, defend them against management. Employees must come onto the scene as new actors in industrial relations and the works councils must accept this fact for what it is, and understand how to make use of it. As the case of Software shows, if these conditions are met, individualized bargaining can help to strengthen the works council's position, even though such bargaining is actually based on the delegation of the rights of co-determination that it previously enjoyed. The collective representation of interests can derive fresh strength from employee participation and autonomy, provided that the relevant bodies try to make themselves the defenders of individual employees' rights in this area. There are opportunities here for the development of a form of positive feedback based on the prospect of "decent working time". The demand for "decent working time" geared to the interests and needs of individual employees can strengthen the ability of interest representation bodies in the workplace and, hence, increase the normative binding power of collectively agreed regulations that contain formal starting points for a "decent working time".

If these conditions are met, working time accounts can become not only an instrument for implementing important aspects of "decent working time", but also, through the creation of a third bargaining level to supplement the established levels of free collective bargaining and works councils' rights of co-determination, a new pillar of the industrial relations system as a whole. However, this positive scenario should not deceive us into thinking that it is a panacea for all problems. The new approaches to industrial relations have many conditions attached to them. The most important one is probably the strength of the works councils in the workplace bargaining system. In theory, keeping market-led forms of management in check is an open political process; in reality, however, this is only the case if the works council can act as a countervailing power. A weak works council can achieve little.

Trade unions also have a role to play here, both as parties to collective bargaining and organizations that have interests in common with works councils. Collective agreements are perhaps the most important instruments for strengthening the representation of interests in the workplace. Thus trade unions can, for example, deploy their negotiating power in local-level collective bargaining in order to improve works councils' bargaining position. In this sense, collective agreements can act as "guide rails" (Lehndorff, 2003) in the local organization of working time, providing crucial support for weak works councils in particular.

In addition to their guiding role in the collective bargaining process, however, trade unions must also become more active in the representation of interests in the workplace. This applies in particular to their frequently invoked function as advisers and service providers to works councils. Works councils must become acquainted with the new responsibilities that the new working time regulations place on them. In order to do this, they need trade union expertise and assistance. However, if trade unions are to be able to provide this, they need independent and consistent models of working time organization at the local level. In particular, these models should be based on two main principles: employee autonomy, and the independent role of working time as a starting point for the "politicization" of market-led management.

References

Ahlers, E.; Trautwein-Kalms, G. 2002. *Entwicklung von Arbeit und Leistung in IT-Unternehmen: Betriebsratsinformationen aus erster Hand* (Düsseldorf, Edition der Hans-Böckler-Stiftung).

Bauer, F.; Groß, H.; Munz, E.; Sayin, S. 2002. "Arbeits- und Betriebszeiten 2001. Neue Formen des betrieblichen Arbeits- und Betriebszeitenmanagements", in *Ergebnisse einer repräsentativen Beschäftigtenbefragung* (Köln).

Bispinck, R., Schulten, T. 1998. "Globalisierung und das deutsche Tarifvertragssystem", in *WSI-Mitteilungen*, Vol. 4, pp. 241–48.

Boyer, R.; Durant, J.P. 1997. *After Fordism* (Basingstoke, Macmillan).

Brödner, P. 1997. *Der überlistete Odysseus: Über das zerrüttete Verhältnis von Menschen und Maschinen* (Berlin, Edition Sigma).

Dore, R. 2000. *Stock market capitalism: Welfare capitalism. Japan and Germany versus the Anglo-Saxons* (Oxford, Oxford University Press).

Dörre, K. 2002. *Kampf um Beteiligung: Arbeit, Partizipation und industrielle Beziehungen im flexiblen Kapitalismus* (Wiesbaden, Westdeutscher Verlag).

Faust, M.; Jauch, P.; Brünnecke, K.; Deutschmann, C. 1994. *Dezentralisierung von Unternehmen. Bürokratie- und Hierarchieabbau und die Rolle betrieblicher Arbeitspolitik* (München, Mering, Hampp Verlag).

Glißmann, W.; Peters, K. 2001. *Mehr Druck durch mehr Freiheit: Die neue Autonomie in der Arbeit und ihre paradoxen Folgen* (Hamburg, VSA).

Haipeter, T. 2003. "Erosion der Arbeitsregulierung? Neue Steuerungsformen der Produktion und ihre Auswirkungen auf Arbeitszeit und Leistung", in *Kölner Zeitschrift für Soziologie*, Vol. 55, No. 3, pp. 521–42.

—; Lehndorff, S. 2002. "Regulierte Flexibilität? Arbeitszeitregulierung in der deutschen Automobilindustrie", in *WSI-Mitteilungen*, Vol. 5, pp. 649–55.

Hartz, P. 1996. *Das atmende Unternehmen. Jeder Arbeitsplatz hat einen Kunden* (Frankfurt and New York, Campus).

Hassel, A. 1999. "The erosion of the German system of industrial relations", in *British Journal of Industrial Relations*, Vol. 3, pp. 483–05.

Herrmann, C.; Promberger, M.; Singer, S.; Trinczek, R. 1999. *Forcierte Arbeitszeit-flexibilisierung: Die 35-Stunden-Woche in der betrieblichen und gewerkschaftlichen Praxis* (Berlin, Edition Sigma).

Kädtler, J. 2003. "Globalisierung und Finanzialisierung: Zur Entstehung eines neuen Begründungskontextes für ökonomisches Handeln", in K. Dörre and B. Röttger (eds.): *Das neue Marktregime: Konturen eines nachfordistischen Produktionsmodells* (Hamburg, VSA), pp. 227–49.

—; Sperling, H.J. 2001. "Worauf beruht und wie wirkt die Herrschaft der Finanzmärkte auf der Ebene von Unternehmen?", in *SOFI-Mitteilungen* Vol. 29, pp. 23–43.

König, O.; Stamm S.; Wendl, M. (eds.). 1998. *Erosion oder Erneuerung? Krise und Reform des Flächentarifvertrages* (Hamburg, VSA).

Lehndorff, S. 2003. "The long good-bye? Tarifvertragliche Arbeitszeitregulierung und gesellschaftlicher Arbeitszeitstandard", in *Industrielle Beziehungen*, Vol. 2, pp. 527.

Lipietz, A. 1985. "Akkumulation, Krisen und Auswege aus der Krise: Einige methodische Überlegungen zum Begriff der Regulation Prokla", Vol. 58, pp. 109–37.

Moldaschl, M.; Sauer, D. 2000. "Internalisierung des Marktes – Zur neue Dialektik von Kooperation und Herrschaft", in H. Minssen (ed.): *Begrenzte Entgrenzungen: Wandlungen von Organisation und Arbeit* (Berlin, Edition Sigma), pp. 205–24.

—; Voß, G.G. (eds.). 2002. *Subjektivierung von Arbeit* (München, Mering, Hampp Verlag).

Müller-Jentsch, W. 1986. *Soziologie der industriellen Beziehungen: Eine Einführung* (Frankfurt and New York, Campus).

Promberger, M.; Böhm, S.; Heyder, T.; Pamer, S.; Strauß, K. 2002. *Hochflexible Arbeitszeiten in der Produktion: Chancen, Risiken und Grenzen für die Beschäftigten* (Berlin, Edition Sigma).

Schmidt, R.; Trinczek, R. 1999. "Der Betriebsrat als Akteur der industriellen Beziehungen", in W. Müller-Jentsch (ed.): *Konfliktpartnerschaft: Akteure und Institutionen der industriellen Beziehungen* (München, Mering, Hampp Verlag), pp. 103–28.

Schumann, M. 1998. "Frißt die Shareholder-Value-Ökonomie die Modernisierung der Arbeit?", in H. Hirsch-Kreinsen and H. Wolf (eds.): *Arbeit, Gesellschaft, Kritik: Orientierungen wider den Zeitgeist* (Berlin, Edition Sigma), pp. 19–30.

Seifert, H. 2001. "Zeitkonten: Von der Normalarbeitszeit zu kontrollierter Flexibilität", in *WSI-Mitteilungen*, Vol. 2, pp. 84–90.

Streeck, W.; Höppner, M. (eds.). 2003. *Alle macht dem Markt? Fallstudien zur Abwicklung der Deutschland AG* (Frankfurt and New York, Campus).

PART IV

QUALITY, EFFICIENCY AND INEQUALITIES

TIME MANAGEMENT IN A SERVICE ECONOMY: THE CASE OF JAPAN 13

*Thierry Ribault**

13.1   INTRODUCTION

The hypothesis that seems crucial to improving our understanding of the social construction of employment in Japan runs as follows: there are in Japan three levels of convention – defined here as "a form of agreement between individuals"[1] – the common denominator of which is the "social management of age", a notion we have borrowed from Nohara (1999). These three levels are: pay conventions, family conventions and the convention on temporal availability. These different levels do not operate independently of each other and may in fact reflect a three-level analysis of the production and reproduction system (Ribault, 2002). Our objective here is to examine what this hypothesis could contribute to an analysis of the impact of the tertiarization of the Japanese economy on time management. In other words, our main empirical question is the following: is the increasing dominance of the service sector leading to radical changes in the conventions on temporal availability that currently prevail in Japanese society? What are the changes that might be observed in the future in the way individuals manage their time in light of new constraints – or indeed opportunities – that the service society brings with it? More specifically, we will examine two areas of temporal availability:

---

* Chargé de recherche au Centre National de la Recherche (CNRS).

[1] The following definition drawn up by Gadrey (2003, p. 105) could be adopted: "widely shared cognitive frameworks, often implicit, that generally have a long history. They are values, concepts of what is good and fair. They can hardly be identified directly except in texts and speeches. However, they can be identified indirectly on the basis of some of their outcomes (and the lack of controversy surrounding those outcomes) in the countries in question over long periods of time."

- Working time: is the tertiarization of economic activity and jobs leading to a destructuring of working time? Who (employment status/gender) is bearing the consequences of this destructuring?

- Domestic time: is women's employment, of which the expansion of the service sector is assumed to be largely a corollary, leading to the increased externalization of tasks that used to be carried out within the family? The care of children and the elderly are particularly interesting cases in this regard.

Empirical observation of the changes taking place has to be combined with an interpretation that seeks to assess the extent and scope of these changes. As we shall see, the hypothesis that age plays a key role in the definition of the societal conventions will provide us with a fairly pertinent interpretative framework.

We will begin, therefore, by outlining this hypothesis. We will then proceed to an empirically based presentation of the significant changes taking place in temporal availability. Finally, we will attempt to interpret these developments in light of our initial hypothesis.

13.2 AGE AS A KEY FACTOR IN SOCIETAL CONVENTIONS ON PAY, THE FAMILY AND TEMPORAL AVAILABILITY

As Nohara (1999, p. 43) has shown, the Japanese wage convention "reinforces the homogeneity of the male wage-earning class by reducing the pay differentials attributable to the diversity of occupational situations", while at the same time "considerably exacerbating pay discrimination against women". The "social management of age", which lies at the heart of this wage convention, operates through two mechanisms. The first is the construction of skills through apprenticeship – any return on investment in qualifications or skill is, *a priori*, seldom realized in the short term. The second is the lifetime wage, which covers all basic consumption needs, including the reproduction costs that often fall on individuals in a context in which the state makes little provision in this regard.

Second, "the family convention in Japan is characterized by the relative autonomy of the family space as a locus of reproduction and hence as a producer of domestic services. This characteristic reinforces the gender division of labour within the family, which is regarded as a private space" (Nohara, 1999, p. 44). The state reinforces the autonomy of the family through its non-interventionism (such as no or low levels of child benefit allowances or student grants), and a tax system in which the household is the basic unit. Thus the principle of the social management of age reinforces the gender division of status that is a fundamental element of the male bread-winner model. We fully concur with this analysis, although we would wish to extend it.

Let us take the case of the impact – often assumed to be negative – of increasing educational levels among young women on their marriage and fertility rates. Shirahase (2000) shows that this idea cannot be verified in the case of Japan. True, women are delaying the age at which they marry as they remain in education longer. On the one hand, however, the period between completion of education and marriage is in reality shorter than for women who have not attended a university; on the other hand, the probability of a female university graduate marrying is twice as high as that for a woman with a lower level of education. In other words, while the age of marriage certainly rises as the length of time spent in education increases, this delay does not signify an upheaval in the timetable of marriage and of the other family events that proceed from it. These findings support our hypothesis that family events in Japan are closely synchronized with age – particularly for women. This is less true in France, where the state influences family strategies, or in the United States, where occupation and educational levels seem to exert a strong influence on the timing of these events (Brinton, 1988). Since the timetable of family events in Japan is fairly compressed, the role that age plays in that country is all the more important. Thus the existence of a strict timetable based on age, and structured in a systematic and hierarchical way, reduces the influence of socio-economic factors, such as the level of education, occupation or social origin, and on whether or not to marry, continue working, or to have children. It is thus this timetable's relative rigidity, which is a product of the high degree of synchronization between family events and age, which makes women's choices, and indeed those of young people in general, conflicted.

Finally, the third level of convention, that of temporal availability, is seldom mentioned since it is regarded as dependent on the other two and, as it were, implicit. Nevertheless, it seems to us that it plays an equally fundamental role as the other two and, therefore, deserves to be made more explicit. It is at this level that the linkage between working time and non-working time is made. In Japan, it reflects the existence of a "time regime"[2] whose geometry varies with age in particular. Whereas some authors

---

[2] For Devetter (2001, p. 23), "working time regimes are stable and relatively durable states of equilibrium between contradictory aspirations (of employers and employees) expressed under pressure from various natural, technical, economic and social rules. They implicitly determine the type of work schedules and degree of availability that are inherent in a job. Thus these states of equilibrium, which have developed in accordance with the behaviour of actors on the demand and supply sides of the labour market, in turn influence behaviour and determine which of the various rules are selected."

(Devetter, 2001) have attempted to uncover the traces of the transition from a Fordist to a post-Fordist working time regime in Europe, the working time regime that has emerged in Japan since the 1980s is becoming highly diversified and increasingly complex. It is diversified because it no longer privileges (did it ever?) a single norm governing a worker's temporal availability. There are in fact a plurality of norms that apply at different stages in individuals' life cycles depending on their gender and age: young women or men, graduates or otherwise, middle-aged women, middle-aged men, elderly women and elderly men. Rather than the disintegration of the previous time norm, what we are witnessing is in fact a segmentation of that norm (Gadrey et al., 1999). This regime is complex, since it links a multitude of micro-regimes, the actors of which do not necessarily share the same objectives – not even with regard to time. What is striking is that, as with the wage and family conventions, it is age that lies at the heart of this third level of convention. Here too, there is a rigid timetable that governs temporal availability in accordance with age. This does not mean that gender does not itself also play a decisive role in the conventions on pay, the family, and temporal availability, but we hypothesize here that gender conventions are themselves the result of the aforementioned three levels of conventions in Japan.

Therefore, the social construction of employment (that of working and non-working time and the linkage between them) takes place in Japan at the intersection of societal conventions on pay, the family and temporal availability – with age as the factor bringing these three levels of conventions into synchronicity with each other.

Synchronization with age does not mean that the conventions are set in stone. There are certain indications that some degree of desynchronization is taking place, which is worthy of examination, as is the way in which these phenomena are reshaping the existing conventions. They include the growing dissatisfaction among young part-timers with the mismatch between their work schedules and their private lives (as well as the increase in mid-career recruitment), which leads to a growing concern among young part-timers, particularly women, to acquire "regular" employee status. However, if we wish to analyse these social changes in a way that misrepresents them as little as possible, then they must be assessed in light of the developments affecting the extent to which the various phases of individuals' wage trajectories, family events and periods of availability for work are synchronized with age.

The wage and family conventions were the subject of a previous paper, in which we analysed the duality of the Japanese wage-labour nexus (Ribault, 2000). Let us confine ourselves here, therefore, to an empirical investigation of changes in temporal availability, before suggesting how these changes might be interpreted.

13.3 SOME EMPIRICAL DATA ON TEMPORAL AVAILABILITY IN JAPAN AND ITS EVOLUTION[3]

We will focus on changes relating to time in the work and domestic spheres.

13.3.1 Working time

Is working time being destructured as service activities and jobs come to dominate the Japanese economy? If so, who is bearing the main brunt of this destructuring? What is their employment status and gender?

Work schedules

The following analysis of labour mobilization is based on data covering all economic activities. Our field surveys showed that in catering, for example, rates of labour mobilization on atypical schedules were much greater than in the economy as a whole. And in retailing, according to the Labour Inspectorate in Saitama (an outer suburb of Tokyo), almost 40 per cent of supermarkets schedule their employees to work very late into the night, whereas only 70 per cent of stores had offered them the health checks required by law.[4] Nevertheless, the advent of the 24-hours-a-day, 7-day-a-week service society is far from becoming a reality, and a large majority of the workforce continue to work relatively "normal" schedules.[5] *Nevertheless, could developments specifically affecting certain populations be detected at the end of the 1990s? And what is the link between these developments and economic tertiarization?*

First, for the labour force as a whole, rates of deployment during normal working hours were lower in 2001 than in 1996.[6] Normal working hours are defined as beginning around 8:00 to 12:00 and ending around 13:00 to 17:00. This can certainly be explained in part by the trend towards shorter working times. On the other hand, rates of deployment during the late time slots between 18:00 and 23:00 were slightly higher, as they were for the night time slots from midnight to 6:00. This trend is even more pronounced on Sundays.

Differentiation by gender shows that both men and women are affected by this trend. This parallel evolution of male and female deployment rates can certainly be linked to the tertiarization of economic activity, which requires

---

[3] The analysis developed here is based on data from the Surveys on Time Use and Leisure Activities by the Ministry of Public Management, Home Affairs, Posts and Telecommunications (2001).

[4] *The Japan Labor Flash*, No. 12, Email journal, 1 April 2004 (http://www.jil.go.jp/foreign/emm/bi/12.htm).

[5] This finding is in line with the results obtained by Devetter (2001) for France.

[6] The data used here relate to those individuals who state they are actually in work, rather than the whole of the population irrespective of employment status. They also relate to an "average day", that is the average of the deployment rates for normal workdays (excl. weekends), Saturdays and Sundays.

working hours to be staggered in order to match staffing levels more closely to the extended opening hours that are characteristic of the service sector, and to reduce wage costs – particularly against a background of recession.

Who is involved in the increasing mobilization of the workforce during atypical time slots? Full-timers (regular employees or *"seishain"*) are playing an important role in this mobilization, particularly in the evenings. As far as part-timers are concerned (the mainly female *"pâto"*[7]), they are being deployed less frequently in the standard time slots; on the other hand, however, they are not being deployed more in atypical slots. Their employment status is associated with conventions on temporal availability that remain fairly stable over time, with a particularly focused view on making paid work compatible with domestic activities. In fact, it is the *"arubaito"*[8] who are the main protagonists in this increase in atypical schedules. Not only are they deployed in large numbers during the evening time slots (18:00 to midnight) but also, unlike regular employees, during the night time slots as well (1:00 to 6:00). Thus there are two groups of employees, with very different employment statuses, who are absorbing the cyclical and structural shocks: regular employees and the *arubaito*.

Once again, can differentiation by gender help to refine the analysis? In fact, it is female *arubaito* who are most heavily involved in the increased allocation of this employment category to atypical time slots. This change can be explained by the relaxation of the legislation regarding women's work, by an increasing desire among young women to become independent of their parents and, above all, by the increasing pressure of unemployment on this population – particularly the 15–24-year-old age group (Ribault, 2002).

We turn now to workforce mobilization at weekends.

Weekend work

There has certainly been a trend over the last 15 years towards a decline in rates of working on Saturday and Sunday, which reflects the widespread acceptance of the principle of two days off per week. Nevertheless, the various age groups, occupations and employment statuses are not all affected in the same way by weekend working.

---

[7] This term is used to denote female part-timers in Japanese companies. This employment status, which also implies a social status (frequently that of a "housewife who works"), may involve a "long-hours" part-time job.

[8] In 2002, there were 4.2 million *arubaito* in Japan, 1.1 million of whom were in education. *Arubaito* are often young people employed on "short-hours" contracts and limited schedules. This type of job is not strictly equivalent to the American student job, since for many workers it is a job that forms part of the queue for better, more highly paid jobs. The average age of *arubaito* is also illuminating: it is 18 for those still in education and 34 for those who are not (source: Employment status survey 2002). The hourly wage rate for *arubaito* is low, at between 800 and 1000 yen, about one-third of the average hourly rate for "regular" employees irrespective of age. *Arubaito* receive virtually no bonus payments and have virtually no entitlement to social protection.

Thus, between 1996 and 2001, there were considerable disparities in the evolution of deployment rates by day of the week. It is true that all age groups (and both the men and the women in them) saw their deployment rates fall during the "normal" working week (excluding weekends), but it was the age groups at either end of the spectrum that were most affected: 15–24-year-olds, on the one hand, and those over 80 years old, on the other (although this latter group can be regarded as marginal!). There was also a fall in rates of Saturday working in all age groups, most markedly among 15–19-year-olds. On the other hand, the decline in rates of Sunday working among the 30 and over age groups contrasts sharply with the increase in Sunday working among the 30 and under group, and more particularly among those 24 and under. Rates of Sunday working among the 15–19-year-old age group rose by 5 and 4 percentage points respectively for males and females; the corresponding figures for the 20–24-year-old age group were 9 and 6 percentage points respectively.[9] These increases are very significant, since over the 5-year period in question they represented a rise of between 10 and 30 per cent in Sunday working in these age groups.

An analysis of labour mobilization by occupation provides some interesting additional information. On average, over the week as a whole, rates of deployment differ little with occupation. Nevertheless, when a distinction is made between the standard working week and Saturdays and Sundays, we find with no surprise that such atypical work schedules are common in agriculture and service occupations. Among the professional and technical categories, the education professions have high rates of mobilization on Saturdays (70 per cent) and Sundays (33 per cent). Similarly, weekend working is very frequent in sales occupations, with 64 per cent working on Saturdays and 44 per cent on Sundays. In the "other service occupations" category, deployment rates on Saturdays are almost as high as those for the other days of the week, while the share of those working Sundays, at 60 per cent, is the highest of any occupational category. It is true, of course, that this category includes catering workers and those employed in the leisure and entertainment industries.

Are there any differences in weekend working by gender and employment status? It should be pointed out immediately that many Japanese workers are scheduled to work at weekends, even though rates of deployment are on the decline, as we have already seen. In 2001, more than half of regular employees, part-time employees and *arubaito* worked on Saturdays, while more than a quarter of regular employees, one-third of part-timers and almost half of *arubaito*, worked on Sundays. In what ways can this simple observation be qualified?

---

[9] The rise in Sunday working applies solely to young people who have left education.

First, it should be noted that, irrespective of employment status, men are more likely than women to work on Saturdays and Sundays. Second, both male and female part-timers and *arubaito* are more likely to work on Saturdays than regular employees when weekly working time exceeds 35 hours. On the other hand, when weekly working time is less than 35 hours, fewer male and female part-timers work on Saturdays; this reflects the need of women at least, to make work and domestic schedules compatible. The gap between the scheduling of regular and atypical employees is even greater on Sundays, particularly in the case of male *arubaito*. It should also be noted that this time, it is the *arubaito* with shorter weekly working hours who are more likely to work on Sundays than the others. This may reflect the fact that the jobs in question are held by students whose temporal availability is constrained by their school or college timetables, or it may be that these jobs are held by workers waiting in the queue for higher-status jobs who do not really have any choice when it comes to work schedules.

13.3.2 Domestic time

Is there a tendency for domestic functions to be outsourced to professional providers? It is undeniable that, on average, economically inactive married women devote more time to domestic tasks, that is, housework, childcare and elder care, and shopping, than those who are in paid employment. In 2001, the inactive married women spent about 7 hours per day on such tasks, compared with the 4 hours devoted to them by economically active married women. However, this gap has existed at least since the 1970s.

Since the end of the 1980s, women have reduced the time they devote on average to domestic tasks. However, the reduction is only slight: in 1986, they spent 4 hours a day on average on such tasks, compared with 3 hours and 45 minutes in 2001, a reduction of just 15 minutes in 15 years. In relative terms, the change seems even more minimal: on average, domestic tasks took up 16 per cent of women's time budgets in 2001, compared with 17 per cent 15 years previously. Similarly, the gap between men and women in this regard is narrowing but still remains very wide. In 2001, the average time men spent on domestic tasks was just one-seventh of that spent by women (33 minutes per day); in 1986, men devoted 19 minutes per day to such tasks, 13 times less than women. Thus women's labour force participation has not significantly changed either the distribution of domestic tasks between men and women or the ways in which these tasks are performed. It might reasonably have been expected, after all, that an increasing proportion of these tasks would have been entrusted to organizations outside the household. It is true that the meagre level of service provision in the Japanese welfare state scarcely increased at all during this period.

In order to more thoroughly test the hypothesis that domestic tasks are being outsourced, we will focus on elder care, which is one of the major domestic activities likely to be outsourced to commercial or non-commercial providers outside the household.

A complex relationship between work and care

Over the 10-year period for which we have comparable data (1991 to 2001), women's labour force participation rate has stabilized at around 50 per cent (which in fact constitutes a slight decline), while at the same time there has been a reduction in the share of the total time (men and women together) given over to care activities (from 78 per cent to 73 per cent). This finding is not indicative of a strong trend towards the substitution of paid work for domestic activity, which in turn is supposed to be generating a significant market for services provided outside the household. The alternative calculation we have carried out, based on the share of care tasks in women's daily schedules, produces the same results. The evolution of women's involvement in elder care (which rose from 2.6 to 3.3 per cent) seems to be more consistent with a stagnating rate of labour force participation among women.

An analysis by age group sheds light on this surprising and complex relationship between work and care over the period 1991 to 2001. *The first finding is that women in the 15–19 and 20–24-year-old age groups have reduced their labour force participation rates, while at the same time considerably reducing the share of their time devoted to care activities.* On the one hand, this phenomenon can certainly be explained in part by the increased length of time spent in education, and, on the other hand, by the increasing delay in leaving the parental home, the postponement of marriage, and the increase in healthy life expectancy, which means that older family members do not need care until later in their lives. Nevertheless, an increasing proportion of women in this age group are involved in the care of elderly family members, even though that involvement is on average less intensive. *The second finding is that, at the other end of the life cycle, the 60–64 and over-65-year-old age groups are going through changes similar to those experienced by young women, although with some differences and, obviously, for different reasons.* Labour force participation rates among women between the ages of 60 and 64 are declining slightly, as is the proportion of their time spent on care tasks. At the same time, as is the case for young women, increasing numbers of older women are involved in such tasks. The major difference between these older women and those in the younger age groups is that, for women between the ages of 60 and 64, the time spent on care tasks fell only very slightly over the decade in question here (from 2 hours and 9 minutes per day in 1991 to 2 hours and 2 minutes in 2001). Women in this older age group remain among the most generous providers of care. We also notice that labour force participation rates among women aged 65 and over have also declined as has the share of their time spent on care tasks.

The third significant development is that labour force participation rates for women in the 25–29 and 30–39-year-old age groups are rising, while at the same time women in these age groups are devoting an increasing share of their time to care tasks. Increasing numbers of women in these age groups are involved in providing care with the average length of time they spend each day on such work increasing. Between 1991 and 2001, it rose from 1 hour 15 minutes to 1 hour 49 minutes for the 25–29-year-old age group, and from 1 hour 56 minutes to 2 hours 7 minutes among 30–39-year-olds. These are the age groups most affected by the "double schedule", whereby women are engaged simultaneously, and in increasingly large numbers, in production, social and reproduction activities. *The fourth significant development concerns women in the 40–49 and 50–59-year-old age groups.* For these women, the substitution of paid work for care tasks follows a more or less "normal" pattern, with labour force participation rates rising and the share of their time devoted to caring for others declining. Like women in the 20–24-year-old age group, increasing numbers of them are involved in care activities but the average time they spend on such tasks has declined considerably. For women between the ages of 40 and 49, it has declined from 2 hours 28 minutes in 1991 to 1 hour 34 minutes, and for those between the ages of 50 and 59, it has declined from 2 hours 40 minutes to 2 hours 22 minutes. This period in women's working lives seems to be the one in which their children between the ages of 20 and 24 are most actively engaged in care activities (see above), while at the same time experiencing increased financial needs linked to their education. Furthermore, in part as a result of the longer time spent in education, women in the 25–29-year-old age group tended to increase significantly the share of their time given over to care tasks throughout the decade. At the same time, such an increasing number of them became involved in care activities that the average time thus spent increased considerably. This suggests that the age at which the younger members of a household take over responsibility for older family members is changing. What we are observing here is undoubtedly a strengthening of the intergenerational exchange between, on the one hand, women with children who are devoting most of their time to paid work in order to earn the second income required to fund their children's expensive education, and, on the other hand, their children who, in exchange for these financial resources and the material protection afforded by the family, undertake to commit themselves to a greater extent than usual to domestic activities such as the care of elderly family members. In some cases, this responsibility may become a reality at a somewhat later age than previously.

Contrasting patterns of development in the time allocated to care

Between 1991 and 2001, the total amount of time women spent on care activities increased slightly by (5 per cent), while that spent by men increased substantially by 53 per cent. The amount of time spent on paid work increased by a meagre 1 per cent for women and 2 per cent for men. However, women still accounted for 79 per cent of the total time spent on care tasks in 2001, compared with 84 per cent 10 years earlier; and for 36 per cent of the total time spent on paid work, which is the same as in 1991.

The average time women spend looking after elderly members of their households has declined in each age group, whereas men in the over-50 age groups have seen rapid increases in the time spent on such activities. For women, detailed examination of the populations concerned shows that when the family member in need of care is under 65 years old, the average time devoted to his or her care rises slightly over the period (particularly when the person is cared for in the household, as opposed to an institution outside the home), despite an overall trend towards a reduction in the average time given over to care tasks. The same phenomenon can be observed among men. It is true that the number of people involved in care activities is rising sharply in the case of people aged 65 years and over, and declining steeply in the case of those under 65.

The question of paid work

There was no significant change between 1991 and 2001 in the distribution of female carers between those in paid work and those who are economically inactive. Nevertheless, in the case of women looking after people under 65 years old, 58 per cent were economically active in 1991 – compared with 52 per cent in 2001. This would seem to suggest that, when they are in paid work, women tend to reduce their involvement in the care of elderly household members under 65 years of age, and to increase their contribution to the care of family members over 65. This interpretation is confirmed, incidentally, by the evolution of the total amount of time spent on care tasks by economically active women between 1991 and 2001: it increased by 64 per cent for those looking after a person over 65 years old, and fell by 50 per cent for those caring for a person under 65. The changes in the corresponding figures for economically inactive women were less dramatic but of the same order.

Care in the home and care outside the home

Care for people 65 years old and older. In 1991, 80 per cent of the time economically active women devoted to care tasks was spent looking after elderly relatives in the home (as opposed to the time spent in an institution outside the home). In 2001, on the other hand, this figure fell to 55 per cent. The figures for economically inactive women were 74 per cent and 66 per cent in 1991 and 2001, respectively. This means that in the course of the 1990s, there was a shift in the location of women's care work from the home to institutions outside the home. This shift was particularly marked in the case of women in paid work. However, does this mean that the time devoted to care tasks decreases as the location where the care is provided changes? The answer is no. Even though the increase between 1991 and 2001 in the amount of time spent on care activities in institutions was significantly greater than that in the time allocated to such tasks within the home, the growth was positive in both cases.

Care for people under 65 years old. In this category in 2001, there was a relative balance between the amount of time devoted to care in the home and the time spent on care outside the home (49 per cent and 51 per cent respectively). In 1991, the distribution was significantly less favourable to home care (41 per cent of total time spent on care activities). This trend towards a return to the home as the place where elder care is provided can be observed among both economically active and economically inactive women, as well as among both women and men.

Although some reservations have to be expressed as to the validity of the statistics used, it can be hypothesized that this transition is probably linked to the effects of public policies intended to discourage elderly people from remaining in institutions, particularly hospitals (a phenomenon known as "social hospitalization"). Thus both the number of hospital stays and the duration of those stays were reduced significantly during the decade in question here. If this is so, why is the same phenomenon not observed in the case of over-65-year-olds? One possible answer is that people in this age group are being increasingly cared for partly in short-stay institutions (day centres, respite care centres, etc.), which were being developed rapidly during the 1990s, in part through the impetus given by local authorities. These institutions enable users to remain in their own homes (which may be either shared with or close to their children), while giving them access to more professional services when they need them. What is certain is that the total time devoted to the care of older people under 65 years of age declined considerably during the 1990s – particularly in the case of care provided outside the home. Another interpretation of this development, which is not incompatible with the previous one, is that rising labour force participation rates among women (however slight the rise may be) have encouraged them to reduce their share of the time devoted to the care of family members under 65 years of age, whose health is improving in any case, in order to be able to give more time to older, more dependent family members. This would reflect a shift in the distribution of temporal availability arising out of the constraints of labour market participation, on the one hand, and changes in the rate of dependence by age, on the other.

The 2001 time budget survey sheds light on the question of whether care behaviour changes with the use of external assistance. Almost 30 per cent of men and 25 per cent of women who reported caring for a family member also called on external assistance such as home help services. However, when these caregivers call on this type of assistance to help with an elderly relative, no reduction in the average time spent on care tasks can be observed. Indeed, the opposite tends to happen: the more frequently external assistance is called on, the longer the average time devoted to care tasks becomes. This phenomenon can certainly be explained by the fact that an elderly person who needs at-home help requires all the more additional care provided by a relative. *In other words, care provided by the family and that provided by professionals are not as substitutable in practice as might be thought in theory.* All this shows, once again, how complex the relationship is between paid work and the time devoted to the care of elderly family members, and indeed, domestic time in general.

How should we interpret the scale of these developments in the wider context of social change and the forms it takes? In our attempt to find some answers to this question, we now return to the central role that, we hypothesize, age plays in the societal conventions on pay, the family and temporal availability.

13.4 THE THREE CONVENTIONS: STRUCTURAL OR MARGINAL CHANGES?

13.4.1 *Limited individualization of life histories*

Briefly, the three levels of convention we have identified reflect basic characteristics of the productive and reproductive spheres of the Japanese economy. More specifically, the pay conventions reflect the lifetime employment system and the accumulation of skills through apprenticeship; the family conventions reflect the independence of the family from national or local public bodies and the high level of interdependence between household members (i.e. forms of solidarity inside rather than outside the family); the conventions on temporal availability reflect a segmented and complex time regime that helps to ensure the coherence of the pay and family conventions. The timetables for the various phases of lifetime wage trajectories, family events, and of periods of temporal availability are synchronized with age, which means that individual life histories have only a minor influence on the chronology. Thus it is not only social temporalities (i.e., social structures of time including work, domestic life, leisure and solidarity) that are structured differently or are the object of variable levels of commitment from individuals depending on their age, but also the age structure of individual life histories: hence the timing of the various phases of lifetime wage trajectories, family events and periods of temporal availability. In other words, the individual-ization of life histories seems to be very restricted.

As a contrast, let us take the case of Sweden, whose economic and social system is very different from that of Japan. In Sweden, family events and periods of temporal availability have become decoupled from age through a mechanism that has been described as the "complete individualization of society" (Daune-Richard and Nyberg, 2003; Håkan and Bjørn, 2004). In other words, beginning studies at a university, leaving the family home, marriage, birth of the first child, graduation and obtaining a first job – all events that punctuate the life cycle – no longer take place in accordance with a strict timetable (if they ever did).[10] Incidentally, this desynchronization, which is not confined to Sweden, is a major factor in the emergence of new social risks in countries that are not prepared for it (Taylor-Gooby, 2005). In the Japanese reference system that governs social and family policy, the public authorities are involved only in a very limited way in the autonomous space in which the family produces domestic services (Nohara, 1999). Studies have shown that the ideology of a strict separation between the domestic and public spheres is particularly influential. It is men in the upper social classes who are the main supporters of this ideology; irrespective of social milieu, women tend to favour the use of professional services, whether in the provision of care for the elderly or for childcare (Yamato, 2000). There is no Japanese equivalent of the "public childcare service" that exists in Sweden (Letablier, 2003). The autonomy of the family reinforces the inequality of the gendered division of domestic labour, which already gains considerable support from the dominance of the male breadwinner model. Moreover, in the Japanese family, children are not the focus of parental concern as autonomous individuals with rights, as is the case in Sweden (although this does not prevent the ideology that a mother's care is essential for young children from being highly influential).[11] Thus a survey carried out in 2001 in the Tokyo region showed that 60 per cent of women subscribe to the "myth of the 3-year-old child", according to which a child must be looked after by his or her mother until the age of 3 (Japan Institute of Labour, 2003). Finally, the relationship between family events and individual life histories is still largely structured around a relatively rigid timetable (Brinton, 1988; Ribault, 2002). The persistence of a high degree of synchronization between family events and age certainly helps

---

[10] This does not prevent the principle of equality of rights and obligations with regard to work and family responsibilities from producing inequalities (see Estévez-Abe, 1999; Lallement, 2002; Daune-Richard and Nyberg, 2003).

[11] For example, the rates of breastfeeding are as high as in Sweden.

to minimize the emergence of new social risks such as those that can be observed in Western countries. Thus it is this synchronization of life events (whether family- or work-related) with age that is the basis for the persistence of the various forms of family solidarity that function as a safety net for family members. This is why skills, educational level, occupation and social origin have little impact on individual choices as to whether or not to marry, continue working or have children.

What are the mechanisms – particularly the economic ones – that underlie this relatively static situation, in which age continues to play a dominant role in the structuring of individual timetables, despite the changes that have been taking place at the various levels of societal conventions?

13.4.2　Conventions on availability and welfare and competency regimes

There are many studies that characterize Japan in terms of the predominant position occupied by its skill formation system and its dualist consequences. What can this perspective contribute to our exploration of the conventions on temporal availability and their modes of change?

A firm-specific competency regime

The dominant competency regime in Japan is described as one that privileges the construction and use of firm-specific competencies, as opposed to one that privileges general competencies (Aoki, 1988; Koike 1994; Estévez-Abe, 1999; Estévez-Abe et al., 2001). A guarantee of job security is necessary in order to encourage both individual employees and their employers to invest in competencies that can be exploited only by the firm in which they were acquired. In this context, job security can be guaranteed by law or collective agreements, as well as by non-legal mechanisms such as the transfer of employees to subsidiaries.

A general competency regime is generally associated with a welfare regime in which neither employment nor unemployment protection is highly developed. This gives workers a strong incentive to protect themselves against insecurity in the labour market by investing mainly in "transferable" (i.e. general) skills. In contrast to this institutional pairing, where there is a high level of protection against job insecurity and unemployment, workers may find it more attractive to invest in competencies specific to a particular firm or industry. Japan is located in an intermediate position between these two extremes. Japanese companies offer a high level of protection for a core segment of their workforces against the background of a societal system that offers little protection against unemployment. This obviously encourages employees to take advantage of the career opportunities offered to them internally by investing heavily in firm-specific competencies (Estévez-Abe et al., 2001). Since there does not seem to have been any fundamental weakening of the positive relationship between pay and age or seniority during the 1990s, it can be said that, at the beginning of the twenty-first century, there is still a high level of job protection in Japan (Sparks, 2004).

Thus the first major characteristic of the Japanese firm-specific competency regime lies in the fact that *it is based on a social protection regime in which employees enjoy the status of breadwinner, which guarantees security not so much of earnings as of employment*, depending on size of firm. In this system, employees of small and medium-sized firms are extremely vulnerable. Thus from the welfare point of view, we are dealing with a strong breadwinner regime whose fiscal and social protection arrangements alone bear witness to the obstacles it places in the way of the development of full-time work for women, and the way which it gives women's employment a particular dynamic. In fact, when structural changes occur in the productive system, workers who are made redundant have to find a job in an emerging industry as quickly as possible, since they do not have access to high levels of unemployment benefit over a long period of time. In reality, when male breadwinners see their job security threatened or their earnings cut, their wives generally seek employment in order to compensate for the loss of household income. This mobilization of female labour takes place in a context in which the costs of social protection are low because of the limited scope of public programmes in this area. As a result, employers in sectors in which a high share of the workforce has general competencies have a plentiful supply of labour from which to recruit workers on terms and conditions that can hardly be described as restrictive (Estévez-Abe et al., 1999).

A second major characteristic is that *demographic constraints weigh all the more heavily on a competency regime of this kind, since age is one of the factors that helps to synchronize the various levels of convention on pay, family and temporal availability.* As Estévez-Abe (1999, p. 36) notes: "Japan is more vulnerable in the long term to a shortage of young, male labour since it has to try to keep the age of its workforce relatively low." Incidentally, this is what explains the more intensive use of female labour during periods when there is a shortage of young workers, a general reduction in the labour supply or a mismatch between supply and demand in the labour market. During the 1960s, demographic changes and the unprecedented increase in the time spent in education resulted in a significant reduction in the supply of young male graduates. As more and more graduates enter the labour market at a relatively advanced age, so the average age of the labour force rises, which has an inflationary effect on wage costs. Since Japan maintains a restrictive immigration policy, women have seen considerable employment opportunities open up for them, including skilled jobs for those who have been able to access the necessary training. Thus in an employment system in which skill formation is stimulated and rewarded by seniority-based pay and lifetime employment, a labour shortage poses an extreme set of problems for companies. How, for example, can they keep the average age of the workforce as low as possible in order to prevent labour costs from rocketing? The entry of women into waged work during the 1980s and 1990s can also be explained in part by the rise in the cost of male labour.

A firm-specific competency regime compatible with the development of jobs requiring general competencies

In theory, the predominance of a firm-specific competency regime is an obstacle to the development of jobs requiring more general competencies, and in particular, therefore, to the development of a certain number of service jobs. In reality, however, it is clear that what has characterized the evolution of employment since the late 1970s in Japan is precisely the development of services requiring general competencies.[12] True, a number of field studies and broader statistical surveys have shown that some service jobs in Japan, including part-time jobs, fall more within the scope of a "quasi-internal market" than a real general competency regime. There is plenty of evidence of particularly high levels of seniority among this category of female workers. Nevertheless, in the absence of any guarantee of pay levels sufficiently high to meet a family's needs – in other words, in light of the supplementary nature of the financial resources generated by this type of job – they cannot really be regarded as part of a firm-specific competency regime. Thus, as recent studies have confirmed, once the variables such as seniority and educational level are controlled for, most of the gender pay gap is due to the unequal value attached to age in determining pay levels; this applies, incidentally, to both full-time and part-time jobs (Iwata, 2004). Furthermore, it is well known that the opportunities – when they exist – for career development in this type of service job cannot be compared with those on offer to male *seishain*. This confronts us with a first paradox: *the dominant competency regime in Japan, which is based on firm-specific competencies, does not seem to be an obstacle to the development of jobs requiring general competencies such as those found in service industries.*

It is true that the Japanese welfare regime, which is characterized by a relatively low level of unemployment protection and a relatively high level of job protection (particularly for full-time male employees), encourages the

---

[12] The vast majority of the jobs that fall within the scope of the "Daieist" wage–labour nexus (so called after one of the large Japanese retail chains) require general competencies (Ribault, 2000).

development of jobs requiring general competencies in two ways. First, in the strong male breadwinner model, as already mentioned above, any challenge to the family wage constitutes a threat, which means that in a crisis (and any resulting downward pressure on pay levels) women are drawn into the labour market, taking jobs requiring general competencies in order to compensate for any possible losses of income. Second, labour shortages or other tensions in the labour market (whether quantitative or qualitative – the Japanese employment system is particularly vulnerable to age factors) encourage women to seek jobs requiring general competencies.

It is interesting to note – and this is the second paradox – that *this mobilization of female labour has been accompanied by the development of public (or under public licence) childcare facilities. This is paradoxical, since the "standard" theories of the welfare state suggest that a strong male breadwinner model like that in Japan does not favour the development of an infrastructure for the care of young children.* However, Japan has been putting in place just such facilities, most of them public or partly funded by the public authorities and in no way inferior in either quantity or quality to those in European countries (even though the Scandinavian countries are outstanding in this regard) or, even more so, in North America.[13] What may seem surprising is that a shortage of labour with firm-specific competencies can encourage the introduction of social policy measures that "normally" reflect a "women-friendly" approach. It is true that the entry of large numbers of women into the labour market all at once made it essential to put in place facilities for the care of young children; first so that those women not yet working could contemplate entering the labour market, and second, so that those already in work could be trained and maintain continuity of employment after the birth of their child(ren).

Societal conventions and their stability

The expansion of jobs requiring general competencies, which tends to encourage women to enter the labour market, should have a negative impact on the system for protecting male workers with firm-specific competencies. In fact, the cost associated with providing such protection increases as the employment system moves from a regime in which firm-specific competencies predominate, towards one in which general competencies prevail. In other words, an increase in the transferability of the principal competencies deployed and most highly rewarded brings increasingly burdensome economic

---

[13] This does not of course mean that all problems with these facilities have been eliminated (opening hours, waiting lists, etc.). Nevertheless, the problems that persist are a result of the fact that the childcare facilities are not really suited to the purpose of establishing real gender equality in the workplace.

constraints to bear on the initial model and begins to call in question the breadwinner status of specialized workers (which in turn stimulates women's employment). It is then up to political leaders and policy-makers to decide whether or not to attempt to modify such economic developments by putting in place protective measures such as those introduced in the social democracies of Northern Europe. In these societies, the welfare state itself has become the employer of a relatively unskilled labour force (also offering qualified jobs at the same time), and has taken it upon itself to put in place social protection measures designed, on the one hand, to maintain the economic and social stratum of workers with firm-specific competencies and, on the other, to promote gender equality in a way that is compatible with the maintenance of that stratum. What is the situation in Japan?

Although the specific characteristics of the Japanese competency and welfare regimes, taken together, tend to favour the development of jobs for women with general competencies, particularly in personal and business services, these types of jobs are not institutionally dominant, despite the fact that they predominate numerically. Our hypothesis – which does not exclude the influence of political factors further upstream – is that one of the explanations for this lies in the persistence of age as an important factor in the societal conventions on pay, the family and temporal availability.

In a system in which the timing of the various phases in individual wage trajectories, family events and periods of availability is governed principally by age, the most appropriate mode of skill formation and accumulation is one that privileges firm-specific competencies, since it is this mode that offers the most efficient and effective means of establishing a balance (in both quantitative and qualitative terms) between the supply of and demand for labour (depending on the temporal availability offered and required). Thus the gradual transition from a firm-specific to a general competency regime can lead to significant changes in the evolution of societal conventions, particularly those on temporal availability (see Gadrey et al., Chapter 10 in this volume).

As far as the family conventions are concerned, these changes give rise to doubts about the durability of the strong breadwinner model. After all, any challenge to the dominance of the firm-specific competency regime is not unconnected with the entry of women in large numbers into waged work (particularly on a part-time basis), and hence with the transition from a strong to a weak breadwinner model (one full-time and one part-time wage earner), along the lines of the model that became established in the Netherlands during the 1980s.

As far as the conventions on temporal availability are concerned, significant changes may occur when age is no longer the main vector structuring the timing of availability. On the one hand, atypical work schedules are no longer preserved for male workers or for certain age groups. On the other hand, the distribution of domestic tasks is likely to become more equal, since individuals' availability for domestic tasks will depend less on gender than on the residual availability that paid work brings with it. Now if women work more and their schedules are less standardized, it is very likely that they will rethink their commitment to domestic tasks. Finally, some of these tasks, particularly the care of children and of the elderly, could well be increasingly outsourced. In none of the following areas have we observed any significant change in Japan:

*   atypical work schedules are increasing among young workers (*arubaito*, particularly women) and among "regular" male workers; however, *pâto* jobs remain the preserve of middle-aged women seeking to work hours that are compatible with their responsibility for domestic tasks;

*   the distribution of domestic tasks by gender has not changed significantly over time;

*   the stability of the shares of their total time budget that both men (a quarter of their available time) and women (about 10 per cent) spend on paid work is evidence of the limited nature of the changes taking place;

*   households are being slow to externalize certain domestic tasks, despite the mechanisms put in place by government; furthermore, we have already seen, in the case of elder care, that the externalization of tasks can be accompanied by a simultaneous increase in the overall amount of time devoted to the care of elder members of the household.

This forces us to conclude that the transition to a general competency regime has not yet occurred and that the absence of any fundamental challenge to the central role that age plays within the currently prevailing firm-specific competency regime bears eloquent testimony to this fact.

13.5   CONCLUSION

The conventions on temporal availability provide the linkage between those on pay and the family, which is why they are worth investigating, since they are the means of adjustment between two spheres: production and reproduction. By placing age at the heart of its societal conventions on pay, the family and temporal availability, the Japanese economic and social system puts a curb on the marketization of the productive and reproductive spheres, while at the same perpetuating a certain number of inequalities (particularly those relating to gender). To adopt the terminology of specialists in the welfare state, this arrangement guarantees a high level of "decommodification". This decommodification reflects the extent to which the power of market forces over individuals' lives is reduced by the welfare state (Esping-Andersen, 1990). It is generally measured by the earnings replacement rate of welfare benefits. In Japan, however, it is rather job security (the effect of which might be measured by seniority, for example) that is the most reliable yardstick. The weakness of the transfer effects of domestic time to the market sphere, as observed in the case of elder care, for example, shows how firmly rooted this decommodification is.

If a society that places age at the heart of its conventions on wages, the family and time may suffer from the major disadvantage of subjecting the socio-economic system to the uncertainties of demographic change (see, for example, the effect of an ageing population on inflationary wage costs), it also has the advantage – age, unlike gender, being a transitional state – of being able to adapt itself to changes in that variable without making structural changes to the system as a whole. As far as wages are concerned, the ages at which *seishain* join a company, retire or reach the end of their careers with that company can be postponed or brought forward, and employers can make up (certainly within limits) for the costs of such changes by demanding greater flexibility from part of their workforce. As far as the family is concerned, the average age of leaving the parental home, of first marriage, and of having the first child, can also be postponed without fundamentally altering the sequencing of the various phases of the life course. Finally, as far as the temporal dimension is concerned, the combination of rapid demographic change and rising female labour market participation rates should, logically, lead to a widespread increase in atypical schedules and periods of work, including the increasing externalization of some of the work of caring for children and elderly family members, as well as a redistribution of domestic tasks and time between the sexes. To date, however, such phenomena remain very limited. Work schedules are becoming more flexible, but this requirement for increased flexibility still mainly concerns workers at an age that is compatible with the temporal availability expected of them in the reproduction sphere. On the domestic side, not only is the division of labour still very unequal by gender and age, but as the example of elder care shows, the entry of women into the labour market, far from fostering the emergence of market services, has merely delayed the age at which such care begins to be provided, with caregivers and the cared-for ageing together.

In theory, the dual protection afforded to male employees as the holders of firm-specific competencies and as breadwinners could be under threat from a dual shift, first, towards a more individualistic and less family-based welfare state, and second, towards a more general, less specific competency regime.

Will tertiarization, through the economic specificities it brings to bear depending on the economic and social systems in which it unfolds, unleash an irreversible wave of job creation in which the competencies in greatest demand will be largely general in nature?

However, let us return to our initial question, which is whether the tertiarization of the Japanese economy is leading to a radical desynchronization between the societal conventions on wages, the family and temporal availability, on the one hand, and age, on the other. In theory, this should be the case, since tertiarization is associated, as we have seen, with an increase in jobs requiring general competencies – particularly in a context in which state support for new social services is strictly limited. As Estévez-Abe (1999) mentions, there is usually a higher level of gender equality in a general competency regime, or at least this type of regime is more neutral with regard to gender than a specific competency regime; furthermore, the family model associated with such a regime is often of the weak breadwinner type (one full-time and one part-time provider) rather than the strong breadwinner type (one full-time provider). In principle, therefore, the transition from a regime dominated by firm-specific competencies to one dominated by general competencies constitutes a shock to the productive system that requires a structural adjustment in the reproductive sphere. From the point of view of wage conventions, careers and pay are no longer evolving mainly in line with age; as far as the family conventions are concerned, the timing of family events may be disrupted, with births occurring before marriages, and women gaining greater financial autonomy as a result of growing recognition of their competencies and qualifications. Finally, as far as the conventions on temporal availability are concerned, a new distribution of domestic tasks is leading to structural changes in women's availability for work and making it possible to reshape the wage convention, with age no longer being the driving force of individual wage trajectories. Availability for work and non-work activities is less rigid and less predetermined by age.

For all that, the conventions on family and temporal availability in Japan do not seem to be undergoing any spectacular changes. The time that women have "freed up" is being channelled towards jobs in market personal services that are both poorly paid and offer little in the way of social protection. These jobs are in part a response to a labour supply that is constrained by the still considerable burden of domestic tasks for which women are responsible and are also part of the dominant family structure, that of the male breadwinner. Social protection is provided by family solidarity, by the main breadwinner's employer and, to a very limited extent, by the state. If changes to these conventions can take place without challenging the synchronization with age that lies at its heart, such changes can be regarded as marginal.

We can also conclude from these results that the most significant dimensions of "decent working time", namely, "working time arrangements should be healthy, family-friendly, promote gender equality and facilitate workers' choice and influence over their hours of work",[14] are not particularly advanced in contemporary Japan.

References

Aoki, M. 1988. *Information, incentives and bargaining in the Japanese economy* (Cambridge, Cambridge University Press).

Brinton, M. C. 1988. "The social-institutional bases of gender stratification: Japan as an illustrative case", in *American Journal of Sociology*, No. 94, Sept., pp. 300–34.

Daune-Richard, A.M.; Nyberg, A. 2003. "Entre travail et famille: À propos de l'évolution du modèle suédois", in L'État providence nordique, *Revue française des affaires sociales*, No. 4, Oct.–Dec.

Devetter, F.X. 2001. *L'économie de la disponibilité temporelle au travail : La convention fordiste et ses remises en cause*, Thèse de sciences économiques à l'Université de Lille–1, Dec.

Esping-Andersen, G. 1990. *Three worlds of welfare capitalism* (Cambridge, Polity Press).

Estévez-Abe, M. 1999. *Multiple logics of the welfare state : Skills, protection, and female labour in Japan and selected OECD countries*, USJP Occasional Paper 99-02, (Harvard University).

—; Iversen, T.; Soskice, D. 2001. "Social protection and the formation of skills: A reinterpretation of the welfare state", in P. Hall and D. Soskice (eds): *Varieties of capitalism – The institutional foundations of comparative advantages* (Oxford, Oxford University Press).

Gadrey, J.; Jany-Catrice, F.; Ribault, T. 1999. *France, Japon, États-Unis: L'emploi en détail – Essai de socio-économie comparative* (Paris, Presses Universitaires de France).

—. 2003. *Socio-économie des services* (Paris, La Découverte).

Håkan, J.; Bjørn, H. 2004. *New welfare states – new forms of citizenship? On the implications for social protection systems of the turn to active citizenship*, paper presented at the COST A 15 Conference "Reforming Social Protection Systems in Europe: Co-ordination and Diversity", Nantes, France, 22–24 May.

Iwata, K. 2004. "Diverse working situation among non-standard employees", in *Japan Labor Review* (Japan Institute for Labor Policy and Training), Vol.1, No.1.

Japan Institute of Labour. 2003. *Research report on the child-care leave system: Findings of a study of women's work and family life*, Research Report No. 157, July.

---

[14] See Messenger (2004).

Koike, K. 1994. "Learning and incentive system in Japanese industry", in M. Aoki and R. Dore (eds.): *The Japanese firm* (Oxford, Clarendon Press), pp. 41–65.

Lallement, M. 2002. "Régulation des temps sociaux en France et en Suède", in *Économies et Sociétés*, No. 22, pp. 1349–67.

Letablier, M.-T. 2003. "Les politiques familiales des pays nordiques et leurs ajustements aux changements socio-économiques des années quatre-vingt-dix", in L'État providence nordique, *Revue française des affaires sociales*, No. 4, Oct.–Dec.

Messenger, J.C. 2004. "Finding the balance: Working time and workers' needs and preferences in industrialized countries", paper presented at the Ninth International Symposium on Working Time, Paris, 26–28 February.

Nohara, H. 1999. "L'analyse sociétale des rapports entre activités féminine et masculine - Comparaison France-Japon", in *Revue française de sociologie*, July–Sept., No. 3, pp. 531–58.

Ribault, T. 1999. *Care services for the Japanese elderly: Between family arrangements and market mechanisms*, Discussion Paper No. 116, Economic Research Center, School of Economics, University of Nagoya.

—. 2000. "Toyotisme et Daiéisme: Deux pôles complémentaires du rapport salarial au Japon", in *Economies et Sociétés*, No. 11, pp. 71–100.

—. 2002. "La construction sociale de l'emploi des jeunes au Japon: Au carrefour des conventions salariale, familiale et de disponibilité temporelle", *Revue Française de Sociologie*, Vol. 43, No. 3, pp. 485–519. Translated as "The social construction of youth employment in Japan: At the intersection of societal conventions on pay, the family and temporal availability", in *Revue Française de Sociologie*, No. 45, Supplement, 2004, pp. 63–95.

Shirahase, S. 2000. "Women's increased higher education and the declining fertility rate in Japan", in *Review of Population and Social Policy* (Tokyo, National Institute of Population and Social Security Research), No. 9, pp. 47–63.

Sparks, C. 2004. *Changes in Japanese wage structure and the effect on wage growth since 1990*, Preliminary draft report, July, Japan Institute of Labour, Tokyo.

Taylor-Gooby, P. (ed.). 2005. *New risks, new welfare: The transformation of the European welfare state* (Oxford, Oxford University Press).

Yamato, R. 2000. "Preferences for personal care in Japan: The influence of gender and socioeconomic status", in *The International Scope Review*, Vol. 2, No. 4 (Winter), pp. 1–12.

TWO OCCUPATIONAL GROUPS FACING THE CHALLENGE OF TEMPORAL AVAILABILITY: HOSPITAL NURSES AND BANK MANAGERIAL STAFF IN FRANCE, BELGIUM AND SPAIN

14

Paul Bouffartigue* and Jacques Bouteiller**

14.1   INTRODUCTION

Many studies dealing with working time have demonstrated both the convergence of trends within the EU and the continuity of specific national features (Anxo et al., 1998; Daune-Richard, 1996; Freyssinet, 1999; Lallement, 2000). The conclusions reached, however, depend on the level of the comparison. On the one hand, drawing on statistical indicators or transformations of institutional regulation accentuates the convergences, while on the other hand, privileging comprehensive qualitative investigations emphasizes the singular aspects of the national contexts. Only multi-level, comparative approaches – which are still rare – offer the possibility of going beyond such a dichotomy (Michon, 2003).[1] This is the paradigm adopted here to study relationships between the *formalized*, *represented* and *experienced* dimensions of working time with regard to two occupational groups – female hospital nurses and bank managerial staff – in the countries of Belgium, France and Spain.[2]

After defining the sociological perspective and methodological approaches of this study (section 14.2), we provide certain background information about the three national contexts with regard to labour market participation, employment, unemployment, and working time by gender and

---

* Sociologist, Research Director, National Centre for Scientific Research, LEST (Institute of Labour Economics and Industrial Sociology), Aix-en-Provence, France.

** Socio-economist, Associate Researcher, National Centre for Scientific Research, LEST (Institute of Labour Economics and Industrial Sociology), Aix-en-Provence, France.

[1] Among the exceptions, see Baret (2002).

[2] This research, coordinated by P. Bouffartigue (LEST), involved: P. Bouteiller (LEST, France); E. Martinez and M. De Troyer (Belgium); and C. Prieto, R. Ramos-Torre, P. Messeger, J. Lago, J. Callejo and R. Moron-Prieto (Spain).

age group; and (section 14.3) the formalized regulation of working time. We then present the main findings concerning the three levels of working time in the three countries; first for nurses (section 14.4) and then for bank managerial staff (section 14.5). The conclusion emphasizes the distance separating the two groups in all three cases, and suggests how the approach can shed light on trade unions' difficulties in keeping in check the growing power of neo-liberalism's policies of flexibilization, fragmentation and the imposed individualization of temporal availability.

14.2   A MULTI-LEVEL APPROACH

Our approach is distinguished by the importance given to the level of *"experienced time"*, in its relationships to *"formalized time"* and *"represented time"* (box 14.1); by a conception of work times which encompasses both the *time on the job* and the *time in the working life*; by the attention paid to *differentiations among wage earners*, notably with regard to *gender*; and by the examination of *societal diversity*.

The notion of *experienced time*, according to Grossin (1996), is taken here to mean *qualitative time*, that of each person's overall *temporal experience*, within which working time – even in the narrow sense of the *time of the provision of labour* – constitutes a pivotal component among employed persons, but one which is always part of the larger complexity of mixed social times. Work times are not limited to the time of labour provision: they involve the *time of the job* (the time stipulated in the work contract) and the *time of working life*. A comprehensive approach to reviewing the dynamics of working time standards in France has convinced us that, with the decline of the Fordist norm, we are dealing not with one single standard of flexibility on the rise, but two. The first, *"heteronomous"*, is not controlled by wage earners, is not well recognized in terms of wages and status, and has little relevance for researchers. Most notably, it is found in the world of unskilled service employees.[3] The second, *"autonomous"*, is the exact opposite of the first; that is, it is exemplified by certain managerial posts and intellectual or artistic professions (Bouffartigue and Bouteiller, 2003a). In principle, female hospital nurses occupy a middle position between these two patterns as they are subject to time constraints linked to the continuity of treatment, but enjoy a protective wage status relative to women without qualifications; the bank managers are closer to the autonomous pattern.

This temporal experience emerges from a series of social contexts, where *formalized working time* (regulated by explicit rules) is one of the essential

---

[3] Cf. the contribution by Gadrey et al., Chapter 10 in this volume.

Box 14.1   Methodology

Each of the three levels of temporal representation was subject to specific forms of investigation.

Formalized time, or the *formal standard* of the regulation of working time, was studied on the basis of an analytical grid distinguishing four levels of regulation (national law; national agreements; sector-based collective agreements; and company, plant, and hospital agreements and rules), three dimensions of time worked (provision of labour, work contract and working life) and three registers within the provision of labour (duration, distribution and predictability).

The *time represented* by collective bargaining participants was investigated on the basis of documentary sources (leaflets and lists of demands) and interviews carried out at the national level of the sectors or companies studied, as well as at the local level of the establishments and departments. Sources used in this study were kept confidential to protect the anonymity of the participating firms and employees; therefore, pseudonyms are used in lieu of the names of participating institutions. The nurses worked at the following institutions: in France, Vital, a public hospital in the provinces (2,000 employees); in Belgium, Erasme, a university hospital (3,000 employees); and in Spain, Clinico, also a university hospital (5,600 employees). The managerial staff of the commercial banks worked at the following: in France, the CGP was chosen (40,000 employees, 35 per cent managerial); in Belgium, Fortis (25,000 employees, 50 per cent managers); and in Spain, Banco (32,000 employees, 70 per cent in the "technician" category).

The study on *experienced time* was conducted through biographical interviews carried out on the basis of a common grid. In France, these were conducted with about 15 employees from each occupational group (female nurses from two medical units, cardiology and diabetology–nephrology; bank managers from a group of CGP branches with 500 employees, 30 per cent of them being managers mainly devoted to sales and marketing). In Belgium, nine female nurses working in medicine (endocrinology–diabetology and neurological rehabilitation) and ten managers from Fortis (half back office, half front office) were interviewed. In Spain, six interviews were carried out with female nurses from the cardiology unit. The *experienced time* of the bank managers was analysed on the basis of materials produced by two discussion groups (one male, the other female) and four interviews with "technicians" from Banco (three front office, one back office).

components. The configuration of relations between the levels and actors of this regulation varies from one country to another, with the actors conveying *representations of time*, notably in collective bargaining, which itself functions largely on the basis of *formalized working time* (Thoemmes and de Terssac, 1997).

Differentiations among wage earners are clearly increasing. The central role of gender justifies the comparison of the two groups, which are at once sharply gender based. "Femininity" is at the foundation of the socio-historical construction of the nursing profession, while "masculinity" is at the origin of the managerial category (subsequently, this gender identification is being modified). The forms of temporal availability are also highly differentiated. The growing domination of productive and market times over "human times" is imposing itself on a body of wage earners who are unequally equipped to resist it or organize it positively. Here, women are in a relatively unfavourable position. The necessity for continuous medical treatment confronts largely female nurses with socially abnormal schedules imposed as an occupational norm, while bank managers, largely male, have only recently been subject to the pressure for results (which has now become a career criterion along with temporal availability). In each of these cases we ask to what extent, and in what ways, is temporal availability socially recognized, controlled, and legitimized by those concerned?

Comparing the ways in which work times are constructed in specific national contexts implies articulating them with other social times within *societal constructions*. Therefore, here we must take into account the respective roles of the family, women, and the state, in the sphere of reproduction. The "national forms of employment" (Groupe emploi exclusion, 1998; Barbier and Lindley, 2002) are themselves embedded in wage–society and welfare state models (Esping-Andersen, 1999), which determine "gender conventions" (Letablier and Lurol, 2000). Such an approach thus runs into the methodological problem of "comparing the incomparable" (Maurice, 1989).

14.3 THREE NATIONAL CONTEXTS

14.3.1 *Statistical overview*

The difference in labour market participation rates by gender is greatest in Spain (27.8 per cent), lowest in France (12.8 per cent), and more pronounced among women between the ages of 55 and 64, two-thirds of whom are economically inactive in Spain and Belgium. Older men are also unlikely to have paid employment in Belgium. In France, nearly half the women in this age group are economically active. In Spain, the absence of paid employment among women from 25 to 54 years old is still much more common (one-third, compared to one-quarter in France and Belgium).

The activity rate by age and gender also shows the degree to which, in France, and even more so in Belgium, labour market participation is concentrated among prime-age individuals. Nearly half the male members of the labour force over 54 years old are no longer actively working in Belgium. Unemployment rates are at similar levels. The Spanish rate comes closer to the other two but is higher, as is the percentage of precarious jobs, which affect nearly one-third of the active population, with men affected almost as often as women. This configuration is reversed for the rate of part-time employment. Part-time status is still rare in Spain for the population as a whole (8 per cent), although it is starting to affect women significantly (18 per cent), but it exceeds the European average for Belgian women (37.7 per cent, compared to 33.5 per cent). In France, the part-time rate remains slightly under the European average (29.7 per cent).

Taken as a whole, these figures lead to the classic hypothesis of a certain substitutability between the two forms of employment, which serves as a tool of flexibility and a means of sharing available work.

The weekly work-hours ("customary" and "actual") of people working full time differ less from one country to another. Spain is the only country where the "customary" full-time work-week exceeds 40 hours. The number of part-time hours is highest in France, where it exceeds the European average, and is lowest in Spain. The situation in France suggests the generalized influence of a French-style employment standard, that is, an unlimited-term and full-time contract throughout the entire labour force, including those groups most recently employed (women in part-time employment). When we combine the frequency and length of part-time work, the cases vary from country to country. In Spain, we find part-time work which is still infrequent and with a limited number of weekly hours; in France, rather frequent part-time work with a long work-week; and in Belgium, part-time work that is even more frequent and lasting, indeed, almost as long as in France. The use of this atypical form of employment in Europe follows distinct models, which reveal "differentiated societal logics" (Lallement, 2000).

The data on schedules show that habitual night work remains marginal in all three countries. Belgium stands out for the frequency of shift work (in alternating teams), and Spain for weekend work in which one-third of the labour force works on Saturday and 15 per cent on Sunday.

From this initial overview, we may note that France and Belgium are similar in terms of most of the indicators, while Spain is set apart by the low rate of female labour market participation (outside of the young age groups, which indicates a recent upsurge in the entry of women into the world of wage earners) and the frequency of weekend work.

14.3.2 Formalized regulation of working time

The changes in industrial relations that have taken place in the three countries over the past 20 years are similar, but they exist within different structures (box 14.2). In France, the state plays a central role in the regulation of labour and employment, even if the industrial sectors have played an important role at certain critical historical moments (Fidenson and Reynaud, 2004). Once again, it was through legislation (the so-called "Aubry" laws) that the legal working week was reduced to 35 hours for companies with more than 20 employees and the civil service. But we may speak of "negotiated law" to the extent that it stimulated a renewal of collective bargaining around working time at sector and company levels. The rate of unionization is also low in France, especially in the private sector, and the numerous trade unions are divided, notably with regard to the issue of working time. In Belgium and Spain, the state and the rule of law have less weight and sectoral collective agreements play a more active role, along with the infra-national levels, including the Flanders–Wallonia division in Belgium, and the role of the provinces and autonomous communities in Spain. The trade unions are much less fragmented and divided in these two countries, each of which has two main federations: in Belgium, the "Fédération Générale du Travail de la Belgique" (FGTB), "Confédération des Syndicats Chrétiens" (CSC), and the smaller "Centrale Générale des Syndicats Libéraux de Belgique" (CGSLB); in Spain, the "Confederacion Sindicál de Comisiones Obreras" (CC.OO) and the "Unión general de Trabajadores" (UGT), along with a few nationalist unions. The rate of unionization is higher than in France (50 per cent in Belgium, 15–20 per cent in Spain). But it is at the company and establishment levels that collective bargaining and unilateral employer-driven regulation is on the rise. Common to all three countries is the same trend of "reversing the working-time *problematique* of the past 25 years" (Freyssinet, 1999).

14.4   FEMALE HOSPITAL NURSES

In all three countries, the nursing occupation is distinguished by the frequency of irregular hours, and more broadly, difficult working conditions. In a context where the continuous increase in healthcare needs comes up against the limitation of public health expenditures, treatments are more technical and more often subject to protocols, and the lengths of hospital stays are shorter with patients hospitalized more often suffering from multiple pathologies. Despite the profession remaining highly feminized, it has nonetheless departed from the stereotype of the nurse as a young single woman. Most

Box 14.2   Formalized regulation of working time: Main provisions

In France, education is compulsory until the age of 16, but in practice schooling continues much longer. While the legal retirement age of 60 years (with the exception of specific occupations) was not lowered by recent pension system reforms, the length of the required contribution period (37.5 years until 1996) was extended (42 years in 2010), first in the private sector and then in the public sector. Alongside the unlimited-term work contract, "atypical forms of employment" (notably the fixed-term contract (FTC), "temping", part-time work, and subsidized jobs) have been on the rise for the past 20 years. The category that has received the most encouragement is female part-time employment, in one of two contrasting forms: one involving a protected job (in which part-time is usually chosen and often associated with parental leave), and the other a non-protected job (in which part-time is more often imposed). The rationale underlying working time was "reversed" in the 1980s, thanks to a number of factors including an element of redistribution of the fruits of growth, and the collective reduction of working time (RWT), which became one of the possible components of a labour–management trade-off involving greater flexibility of times worked and sharing of available work. Depending on the period, emphasis has been placed on one term of this trade-off or the other. The determined intervention of public authorities in recent years enforcing the Aubry laws in organizations, and the reduction of working time (known in France as the ARTT – *aménagement et reduction du temps de travail* – or simply the "35 hours"), should not mask the broader margins of freedom given to negotiators, or the extended possibilities of flexible organization of work hours (annualization, wage adjustment, and wage packages for managers based on days worked). As a result, the differences in the situations among different sectors, companies and categories of employees have become even more pronounced.

In Belgium, education is compulsory until the age of 18, with the possibility of part-time schooling from age 16 on. The legal retirement age is 65 years for men (full career of 45 contribution years), and 63 for women (who will be aligned with men by 2009). The system of "pre-pensions" (early retirement with unemployment benefits) at age 58, and even as early as age 53, remains in force. As in France, FTCs, "temping", and subsidized jobs constitute the main precarious forms of employment and come under comparable legislation. Possibilities for parental leave are slightly greater in Belgium (full or part-time leave until the child is 4 years old), as are the possibilities for full or part-time career breaks for personal reasons ("time credits"). Notwithstanding resistance at the branch level of regulation, public authorities have closely supervised wage negotiations and directly encouraged policies regarding working time. They have done this following two main rationales: the sharing of available work (through

/cont'd

Box 14.2   (/cont'd)

the massive use, until recently, of "pre-pensions" and the encouragement of part-time work) and negotiated flexibility. Even if unions were unable to obtain the 35-hour week, certain sectors and companies have come closer to it, generally at the price of concessions in the area of flexibility in the arrangement of working hours (with the spread of the reference period to an annual scale). This is the case for the banking sector, where the average yearly working week is fixed at 35 hours, and also in the healthcare sector for wage-earners over 45 years old (with a sliding scale of 36 hours at age 45; 34 hours at age 50; 32 hours after age 55).

In Spain, compulsory school attendance ends at age 16. The legal retirement age is 65 years for men and women alike, with just 35 contribution years necessary for a full pension. But pre-retirement and early retirement plans have led to a drop in the real retirement age. The rate of labour market participation among men between 60 and 64 years old went from 67 per cent in 1980 to 43 per cent in 2000. As elsewhere, measures have been taken to encourage the labour market activity of older workers. Fixed-term contracts (FTCs) have been easy to use, and have been used frequently since the 1980s, with the result that they now represent nearly one-third of total employment. This situation has, in turn, led to a high level of labour turnover and a large proportion of unemployed workers receiving little or no compensation. Despite recent measures to encourage it, part-time employment has shown little increase in Spain. Since 1999, Spanish legislation, like that in other countries, has followed European directives on the "reconciliation of work and family life" by introducing rights to leave for the care of children or other family members.[1] A series of legislative modifications over the past 20 years has tended to weaken the normative framework of the law in favour of collective bargaining at the sectoral and company levels, which has also allowed for greater flexibility. If the "workers' statute" of 1980 included initial provisions promoting flexibility, it still maintained strict controls and subordinated those provisions to the existence of collective agreements. This limited the number of working hours per day (9) and per week (43), and also limited overtime by imposing an extremely high premium (more than 75 per cent above the normal wage). But the 1994 reform of this statute was designed to disrupt the institutional framework by raising the ceiling on the number of daily and weekly hours. This was done in the spirit of the annualization of working time, and also by modifying the hierarchy of norms so as to accord considerably more latitude to collective bargaining at the sectoral and company levels. As in Belgium, trade union activity in Spain in favour of the 35-hour week has had effects on the contractual and actual duration of working time; but these are uneven and often associated with trade-offs in the area of greater flexibility.

Note: [1]European integration has helped to harmonize these forms of time regulation.

Table 14.1   Percentage of women, age of female nurses in France and
             Spain, age of nurses (male and female) in two French and two
             Belgian hospitals

	Female nurses		Nursing staff (including nurses' aides)	
	France	Spain	Vital Hospital (Fr.)	Erasme Hospital (Belg.)
Age 25 and under	3.0	4.4	4.0	7.2
Ages 25–34	25.4	23.5	30.0	27.3
Ages 35–44	29.9	39.3	33.0	45.1
Ages 45–54	29.1	27.1	28.3	18.0
Age 54 and over	12.5	5.9	4.6	2.4
Women as percentage of total	87.0	86.0	88.0	87.0

Sources: Female nurses – France: DREES, 2003. Spain: EFT, 2001. Nursing staff include both males and females: Administrations of hospitals studied. While the four columns are not strictly comparable, since nearly 90 per cent of nursing staff are female, some very rough comparisons are possible.

female nurses live with a partner and continue working within their profession despite old and new occupational hardships.[4]

The ageing of female nurses seems more pronounced in France (table 14.1), but the phenomenon does not have a simple explanation. It may reflect different rhythms of increasing the number of nurses and thus of recruitments (in Spain, the development of the public health system is more recent), or inequalities in the number of departures before the legal retirement age (in Belgium, these are encouraged thanks to recent agreements). In all three countries, single women have become a small minority of all nurses.[5] Part-time status has spread, especially in France (where it concerns one-third of the profession), and in Belgium. And in all three cases, we can observe a diminution of irregular schedules over the course of the career.

Certain specific country features in the regulation of the occupation are likely to have an effect on employment and working conditions. Belgium has two certification levels, "certified" (*baccalauréat* level) and "graduates" (*baccalauréat* + 3 years of study). The latter, who are more numerous and better paid, nonetheless provide the same patient care, from the most technical procedures to "nursing" per se.[6] The public authorities' discourse on the nursing "shortage" is more pervasive than in France. As for female

---

[4] For the French case, cf. Le Lan and Baubeau (2004): the constraints of pace and deadlines showed significant aggravation between 1998 and 2003.

[5] In France and Spain alike, only one female nurse out of five in the 35 to 44 age group lives alone.

[6] This distinction does not coincide with the French distinction between nurses' aides and nurses: Belgium has a separate category of "nursing auxiliaries" or "health auxiliaries", but they are few in number and hold no specific diploma.

nurses in Spain, training flows are less strictly controlled by the public authorities, which may explain why they face greater unemployment.[7]

14.4.1   France

Formalized time comes under the L'Aménagement et la Réduction du Temps de Travail (ARTT) agreement concluded at the end of 2001 between the Ministry of Health and certain unions, in the context of the new Aubry laws. This type of working time introduced a double wage scale (annual and weekly), a definition of "actual working time" and rules for maximum hours worked and rest periods. The "35 hours" (due to become 32 hours for night work) are conceived as a yearly average with variable modalities depending on the specific rules. This agreement does not eliminate pre-existing differences between hospitals and personnel categories.[8] At Vital Hospital, it has led to longer hours for the night shift, which in turn benefits from a greater number of reduction of working time (RWT) days than the day shifts. The dominant feeling among the nurses is that working conditions have declined and that the RWT is more limited than was previously hoped. In case of absences in the care units (since there is practically no recourse to temping and the supply posts have few staff members), the main form of regulation consists of calling nurses to work on their days off.

The *represented time* of the social partners reflects sharp divergences. The Nursing Care Department at Vital Hospital calls for greater flexibility in the management of working time, and sees the notions of "chosen time" and "part time" as closely related. The unions are divided over this notion. The main union among those signing the agreement, the Confédération Française Démocratique du Travail (CFDT), which is not represented locally, approves the national agreement, but at the same time disapproves of the minimal role left for local bargaining. Meanwhile, the unions which did not sign, Confédération Générale de Travail (CGT) and Force Ouvrière (FO), represented at the local level, stress the limited effectiveness of the reduction of working time given the insufficient number of jobs created, as well as the dangers of greater flexibility of working time.[9]

The investigation of *experienced time* confirms the critical role of time issues in the nurses' lives. Their competence as "jugglers" – a term used by several of them – is a central aspect of their professional abilities. Nurses nonetheless work minor miracles every day in order to withstand their

---

[7] In 1997, 16 per cent of Spanish nurses (male and female) underwent at least one period of unemployment, including 4 per cent who were unemployed during the entire year.

[8] These disparities were revealed in 1999 by the Roche mission preceding the ARTT in the civil service.

[9] Since the new personnel supposed to compensate for the RWT were insufficient, the public health sector was the first to "relax" the 35 hours, in early 2003, with a special exemption from the maximum limit on overtime hours.

accumulated time constraints, both at work and outside of it (especially in the coordination of the two space-times). These daily acrobatic feats, which relate to the majority of interviewees (that is, those with children), become extremely dangerous when they are prolonged or when the partner also works atypical or irregular hours, and/or when there is no extended family to help with the care of young children.

In fact, these temporal competencies are largely invisible, with little or no statutory recognition. They are constructed socially, on three temporal levels:

- *The process of socialization and work socialization*, in which the attitude towards the profession is most often positive and often already explicitly anchored in the maternal model, that is, in the sense of a plan for self-fulfilment through an activity in the service of children and/or others. Here, the preservation of a strong interest in the work nourishes and sustains time-management abilities, especially since atypical hours, although considered "socially abnormal", are at the same time seen by these nurses as "professionally normal".

- *The modalities of personal appropriation of the hours proposed*, which is, in particular, the possibilities for mutual aid and arrangements through scheduling within the care units between colleagues or with the head nurse, as well as the possibilities for switching to part-time status once they have children.

- *The hopes for better schedules in the course of working life*, that is, hopes which are made credible by career possibilities.

The nurses are critical with regard to the way the reduction of working time is applied.[10] Being badly represented by the trade unions is less on the scale of major demands. The fact that female experience of time is badly reflected in the dominant union approach probably also plays a role, as certain women leaders in the CFDT and CGT health-workers' federations recognize. The nurses still have the feeling, moreover, of not really being "represented as female nurses", which reflects the objective distance between the socio-occupational and gender composition of the union teams, and female nurses as a group. But it also reflects the distance between certain of their aspirations concerning time and the traditional union viewpoint. This gap is expressed in two ways: first, there is the nurses' attachment to time arrangements on the fringes or outside of regulations. These arrangements are based on a social exchange in which longer and/or more intensive daily schedules (10 or even 12 hours comprising the "swing" shift from

---

[10] An extensive survey carried out at the same period (2002, i.e. at the beginning of the application of the ARTT in the hospitals) arrives at a similar conclusion (Tonneau, 2003).

the "night" team to the "morning" team, with a rest period under the legal minimum) are accepted and sometimes even requested in order to benefit from longer days off or vacations. Second, there is the shift to part-time status. While this is an extremely important issue in the experience of these female nurses, it was practically absent from public debate at the hospital when the RWH (reduced working hours) was introduced.

14.4.2 Belgium

Formalized working time, as demonstrated by a recent agreement covering the health-care sector, attempts to compensate for the insufficient attractiveness of nursing jobs. Provisions have thus been introduced for the gradual reduction of work hours from the age of 45 on. Other measures are aimed at harmonizing and upgrading remunerations, stabilizing personnel, increasing training flows, developing bridges between the two certification levels, establishing a better definition of tasks, and improving work schedules. Nurses benefit from "pregnancy leave" which is remunerated from the beginning of their pregnancy at 80 per cent of their wages. In the hospital studied, the regulations seem to be better respected than elsewhere. It has become common practice to have every other weekend or public holiday off, and to have three weeks of paid vacation during July and August rather than two for family reasons. Nearly two-thirds of the nurses over 45 have chosen to adopt the voluntary RWT, while the remaining third have opted for maintaining the length of their working time. Among the tools that permit administrators of the care units to deal with workload fluctuations and absences is recourse to temping, which plays a key role (there are some 100 temporary nurses working at Erasme Hospital). These may be beginners who are learning about the different situations involved in the practice of their profession, or experienced nurses who have deliberately chosen this form of employment. Their favourable situation in the labour market – as attested by the fact that they are remunerated for their seniority – leaves them a certain degree of choice among institutions, units and schedules. They are seen as having a more detached relationship to their work than the "permanent" nurses. Part-time status also plays a large role (half of the nurses at this hospital are part time) in so far as part-timers can be asked to increase their working time as the need arises without exceeding the limits on work hours.

With regard to *represented time*, employers in the sector would like to see greater flexibility in working time, such as extending the daily hourly limit from 11 to 12 hours, the replacement of the quarterly reference period by the annual system, greater possibilities for converting overtime into compensatory days off, and easier utilization of fragmented work periods.

Conversely, the unions would like to see more control of exemptions and better compensation, in time and wages, for exceeding the limit on work hours. At Erasme Hospital, where the rate of union membership is 35–40 per cent, the unions are vigilant about the application of rules on working time, including a 50-hour maximum allowed per week, breaks at a minimum of every 11 hours, and recognition of the (frequent) extra hours in the late evening as "night work". The nurses sometimes criticize this attitude because it can reduce possibilities for their own work arrangements within the units. As a result, the unions adopt a more pragmatic attitude in practice. But at the same time, they criticize the excessive use of temping and the inadequate number of personnel. The question of working hours in the nurses' real career paths – the switch to part-time status and/or regular daytime schedules – does not seem to be a subject of discussion or action, any more than in the French case.

On the level of *experienced time*, work rhythms, and the way the nurses adjust to them, resemble the situations observed in the French hospital, but with a few slight differences. The morning shift begins working later at Erasme (7 a.m. rather than 6 a.m.), but the large size of the metropolitan area means a longer commuting time and having to get up almost as early. The night shift works one hour more. The advantage of having every other weekend off was introduced earlier. The changing of the shifts lasts slightly longer. And the hours of nurses on fixed shifts vary less because of a more sophisticated system for mobilizing replacements.[11] Otherwise, the rotation between morning and evening hours for the day shift, like that of the night shift, is quite similar, as is day-to-day work organization. The nurses show the same abilities for coordinating and planning personal and family time and, within the units, the same kinds of time arrangements. On the other hand, the hospital administration seems more willing to take into account differences in temporal availability in relation to family situations. In spite of the great number of arrangements, however, tensions associated with the double availability required – for an ever more demanding job and for the family – also remain quite sharp.

14.4.3 Spain

The *formalized regulation* of the health-care occupations is undergoing profound changes in the wake of the decentralization of authority over health-care management from the state to the autonomous communities, which got under way in 2001. The ongoing collective bargaining deals with training, professionalization, and working conditions and hours. As elsewhere, the general context is one of pressure on health-care expenditures, the search for shorter

---

[11] Such differences might also be found in France, however, from one hospital to another.

waiting periods before hospitalization, more flexibility in the conditions of recourse to outside personnel, and greater managerial autonomy for the individual institutions, including the management of work hours. In practice, the regulation of working time already seems to take place largely at that level.

Formalized working time comes under the general civil service rules, that is, overtime is not remunerated but compensated with days off. The average annual work week is 37.5 hours, and in addition to 22 vacation days, agents are entitled to 6 personal days each year. The draft law on the status of health-care personnel provides for a maximum work-week of 48 hours on a 6-month basis; the definition of night work as that carried out between 11 p.m. and 6 a.m.; and a minimum break of 12 hours between two periods of service. A specific agreement covers the health-care personnel of the autonomous regional communities, which allows for a notable exemption for health reasons from stand-by duty and rotations for personnel over 55 years old. At Clinico Hospital, the argument of the "unit's needs" is increasingly used to call upon replacements because the possibility of recourse to a back-up team has been eliminated and personnel resources must now be found within the care units themselves. In the cardiology unit studied, there was also an increase in "internal" management of scheduling through sporadic arrangements between the head nurse and the other nurses.

At the level of *represented time*, the profession has a high degree of collective organization, mainly on the occupational model. Thirty-seven per cent of the female nurses, for example, belong to trade unions and only 8 per cent to the CC.OO and UGT unions. Beyond the objective of the 35-hour week, union action is focused on closer control of work hours and better monetary compensation for "abnormal" hours (Sundays, nights, etc.), in the face of a decrease in the additional remuneration specific to night work.

In Spain, nurses typically have a "double career" determined by professional and family considerations. The beginner's alternating daytime schedule gives way to night work with the birth of children. Since this schedule is better paid, it also helps in the purchase of a home. As the children grow up, the nurses seek a fixed daytime schedule, with work in a community clinic, which is often seen as the ideal position at the end of their careers. Comments made in a nurses' discussion group (similarly as in one-to-one interviews) show that the possibilities for individual scheduling arrangements in line with their family situations are important; indeed, this is what determines most of their informal exchanges of hours. As in the other two countries, nurses in Spain suffer above all from the lack of weekend availability for family life and the unforeseeable nature of their working time. This lack of availability itself is perceived as more severe than the quantitative shortage. In addition, these nurses feel (as is common in the other two countries as well) that their workload is increasing. They also expressed the opinion that their position in the labour market is declining because of the surplus of nurses relative to the number of jobs available, and that as a result, they face reduced margins for negotiating where and under what conditions, notably temporal, they will work within their profession.

14.4.4 Comparative remarks

It is at once necessary and difficult to take into account all the facets of the working situation of such an occupation in order to grasp the potential national features of its *experienced times*. Certain aspects of the Belgian nurses' *formalized time* appear less favourable than in France (such as a lower training level for some of them or longer normal and maximum weekly hours), but others are more favourable, including the reduction of working hours for those approaching retirement and "pregnancy leave". By contrast, the conditions of Spanish nurses appear less favourable. In both cases, however, the position of the occupational group in the labour market seems to play an important role. In Belgium, it is the scarcity of nurses that has forced employers to modify end-of-career working time. And this situation is even more the case where *practised, experienced times* are concerned. The way, for example, that female nurses in France, and even more so in Belgium, have massively seized upon part-time status to regain a certain control of their time has to do with the "scarcity" of labour (Baret, 2002). And in all three countries, phenomena of individual organization of schedules (whether sporadically or throughout the life cycle) may be largely invisible in labour–management agreements, but have a customary existence nonetheless with regard to extremely localized power relations within establishments, care units and territories.

14.5 BANK MANAGERS

The banking sector in all three countries shows convergent economic and social dynamics, with deregulation and disintermediation (i.e., reduction in the use of intermediaries between producers and consumers) going along with the entry of the major banks into a more competitive world. In certain cases, as in France, this development has been associated with a privatization process. The sector's shift from administered to market regulation has resulted in radical changes, which are more or less pronounced from one country or company to another. Everywhere, however, feminization, higher training levels and an increase in managerial staff – as well as ageing tied to the decline in overall numbers – characterize banking personnel. France shows the greatest degree of feminization and the clearest ageing of the labour force, while these two

Table 14.2   Percentage of women and managers, age of bank managers

	France (AFB, 2002)	Spain (AEB, 1997)	Belgium (ABB, 1997)
% women/total personnel	55.0	27.0	47.0
% managers/total personnel	30.0	60.0 ("technicians")	40.0
Age 30 and under	16.2	16.4	19.5
Ages 30–39	20.8	29.3	26.4
Ages 40–49	30.5	36.8	29.5
Ages 49 and over	32.0	17.6	24.6

trends are the least marked in Spain, and Belgium occupies a middle position (table 14.2). The proportion of "managerial staff", however, must be considered with a great deal of caution, given the specific sense of this notion in each case.[12] This "category" has little institutional and symbolic coherence in Belgium (De Troyer and Martinez, 2002), and even less in Spain, where (and this is the case with banking) it often becomes dispersed within a larger group of "technicians" (Prieto, 2002).

14.5.1   France

Formalized time is determined through ARTT negotiations, which are themselves embedded in larger issues (bringing the sectoral collective agreement back into play). All the unions ultimately signed the latter, notwithstanding the conflicts involved in the course of negotiations. The negotiation of the "35 hours" at the sectoral level was marked by even greater conflict, with sharper inter-union divisions over this issue than over the collective agreement as a whole (Dressen, 2003). At the bank selected for this study (the "CGP"), the CFDT is the most influential union at sectoral and company level, while this union has more moderate positions than its federation. Indeed, the CGP is one of the rare major banks where the union signed the agreement. The climate of that negotiation and the subsequent application of the "35 hours" suffered less than elsewhere.

In terms of *represented times*, however, we find the classic divergences between unions and management. The latter seeks to limit job creation, make working time more flexible and moderate wage increases, while the former seek to increase hiring, obtain the maximum number of RWT days chosen by the

---

[12] Cf. Bouffartigue (2002) on the specifically French notion of *cadre*, a term which encompasses "professionals" or "experts" as well as "managers". In English, it is often translated as "professional and managerial staff".

employees, and protect wages. At CGP, the question of the measurement and the reduction of managers' working time in "wage packages based on days worked" (*forfaits en jours*) seems to have been the subject of specific compromises and controversies which concerned, on the one hand, the possibility offered to some of the managers to opt voluntarily for this modality and, on the other, an amendment to the agreement extending the list of managerial posts involved, against the CFDT's position. But for the SNB (CFE–CGC), the main trade union organization among managers (which signed this amendment), CGP management's determination to offer managers a form of RWT clearly differentiated them from non-managers, and met the desires of a significant part of the managers constituting the union's electorate.

To understand the *experienced time* of the managers in the CGP sales and marketing network studied requires taking into account two contrasting social profiles. The older managers, nearly all of who were men, were recruited with low diploma levels and came from modest social backgrounds and local geographical origins. They started out in support posts, became managers in the course of their careers, and remained close to the union movements. The young managers, half of whom were women, all had higher-education diplomas and came from diverse social and geographical backgrounds. Since they had begun their careers as managers, they were removed from union culture. Although we cannot really speak of a "generation gap", certain tensions existed between the two categories. In both groups, time constraints were much less severe than among the nurses, and the distance between their experienced time and the time represented by the unions seems smaller. The "35 hours" were better accepted than at the hospital. The slight difference between the managers' actual experience and the union's benchmarks had to do with the breakdown, and thus the reduction, of working time. Certain recent graduates even found the formula of a wage package in days more flexible (because it does not imply the "constraint" of taking an RWT day off each month), and more adapted to the organization of their work and lives.

Nonetheless, the reasons behind the low level of time constraints are considerably different for the two generations. Among the older, male managers, career stakes were a thing of the past, and their domestic situations made them more disposed towards a professional investment which was ultimately rather limited (with relatively regular, predictable work schedules), and combined with personal activities. Among the young generation, career stakes were crucial. Optimistic about their career prospects, they were concerned with investing themselves in their work and proving themselves, especially since they were conscious of the heightened competition resulting from greater pressure over profits. Would they have to accept a geographic change in order to pursue their individual careers, or would they opt for maintaining a certain quality of family life, in which the career of their partner often counted as much as their own? Ultimately, the evolution of work pressures and the way tensions between strategies of professional fulfilment and the division of domestic tasks are handled within the "two-career" couples of this new generation will determine the extent of the emerging changes in CGP managers' experienced time.

14.5.2 Belgium

Banking is one of the sectors in which a significant proportion of managers are distinguished between their functions and those of other employees in the job classifications. They are thus placed between "managerial/trustworthy staff" (*personnel de direction/de confiance*), who are 4 per cent of total banking personnel and not covered by regulations on working time, and support staff. The definition of this "managerial/trustworthy staff" constitutes a major issue in union–management conflicts. Branch managers are generally placed in this category.

The *formalized time* of the collective agreement notes the union demand for a 35-hour week without trade-offs in terms of flexibility (the annual guideline of 1,621 hours goes along with weekly and monthly limits which are still quite strict) and wages. It is true that the decrease in working hours has not led to the creation of jobs; that a number of banks were already close to the new guidelines; and that its effectiveness is not guaranteed for managers and "managerial /trustworthy staff". The most contested points, such as the definition of "trustworthy staff" and the increased numbers of branches open on Saturdays, have been consigned to moratoria or work groups. The possibilities for pre-pensions at age 58 have been maintained. For the rest, the company remains a major locus for collective bargaining. At Fortis Bank, the work-week is 36 hours long but employees benefit from 12.5 "extra-legal" holidays and managers from 15.5. Apart from the tiny fraction of "managerial/ trustworthy staff", managers are in principle subject to the same working time regime as other employees, with a combination of daily and monthly scales. Only "managerial/trustworthy staff" have their remuneration indexed to earnings in any significant way, which reflects the trade union's vigilance and influence. This factor is essential for understanding the different attitudes of bank managers with regard to working time in the three countries. These compromises over working time are very recent and could prove unstable, especially since the company itself is the result of a recent merger, whereby the system of time regulation carried over was the one most favourable to the personnel.

The *represented time* of human resources development (HRD) has three objectives: broadening the notion of "trustworthy staff" who are not covered by working time regulations; increasing real work-hours; and revoking compromises deemed too "generous" in the areas of variable hours and extra-legal holidays. The FGTB and CSC unions present a united front at the bargaining table but exhibit differences in the area of working time. The FGTB believes that applying the system of time accounting and recovery of extra hours to all managers will encourage a time-clock mentality. The CSC, meanwhile, is distrustful of an overly rigid approach, has reservations about the demand for extending badges to branch personnel, and feels that the increase of recovery days disorganizes work. The union presence is much stronger in the "back office" than in the sales and marketing network, where the personnel are more dispersed and subject to greater mobility as well as greater pressure over earnings coming from the branch managers.

"The advantage of the bank is that you can pursue your career and still have a family life." This statement from a young female manager working in the Fortis sales and marketing network shows that such a representation of social mobility remains possible among the new generation of bank managers and that *experienced time* is inseparable from career issues. It also indicates, as in the French case, the distance separating these managers from female nurses in terms of time constraints. Compared with available data on managers' real work hours, it shows that position in the chain of command and gender are the determining variables in the relationship to working time. For example, the practices of middle managers are closer to those of office employees than those of top managers, and women, regardless of their category, are more likely to measure their presence at work, as well as to have less daily overtime and to work part time. Overall, expecting to advance in the company ranks, or in the internal labour market more generally, means not counting the number of hours worked. The application of the rules comes up against the weight of tacit agreements on what a manager is, and on the form of commitment to the work and company that are associated with the job. As in France, above all it is the feminization of the managerial staff that is calling into question a model presented as universal when it is in fact gendered in the masculine. Unlike female nurses, whose domestic constraints are legitimated and integrated into the management of their working time, the managers' temporal availability eclipses their domestic situation.

14.5.3 Spain

Formalized time depends mainly on the private bank's national collective agreement. This agreement makes it easier to stop working before the legal retirement age and indeed, among the three countries studied, Spain is the one with the lowest percentage of wage earners over 50 years of age. The provisions concerning work hours also represent an advance over the legislation in force, but their effectiveness is uncertain given the low number of collective agreements at company and establishment levels. Working days are traditionally continuous in the sales and marketing network (8 a.m.–3 p.m.) and discontinuous in the back office (i.e., administrative functions). Saturday work in the bank branches is either excluded or limited during the period from October to May.

The *time represented* by the two main unions, CC.OO and UGT (which have 60 per cent of the representatives' mandates), is aimed at reducing the length of the work-week and work-year, eliminating Saturday work, lengthening holidays, and broadening rights to leaves for family or personal reasons. Union representatives denounce the considerable distance between the formal and actual norms of working time, whereby contractual work-hours are frequently exceeded under the impact of a model of temporal availability in one of two forms. In the back office, the workload is increasing in the context of organizational changes and greater competition over promotions. In the branch, there is also pressure over sales figures through the indexing of remunerations to earnings. The excessive lengthening of the work-day has become a major issue of contention, along with the denunciation of its negative effects on employment and free time. In Spain, the category of bank employees which comes closest to French and Belgian notions of managerial staff is that of "technicians", although this term is broader.[13] Union representatives divide them into three groups: recent graduates recruited on precarious terms waiting for a stable position and thus subject to a high level of professional demands; those over 45, who have no prospects for promotion and are waiting to stop working; and those in the 30–45 age group, who have to deal with the tension between the risk of an early levelling off of their careers and the demand for intense involvement in their work and the company. These same representatives indicate that they are taking into account changes arising from the rapid feminization of the personnel. This has led them to develop a critique aimed at both the formal homogeneity of collective agreement provisions and their ineffectiveness because of the individualized nature of managers' practices in the area of working time. Between the extremes of excessive rigidity and total deregulation, they proposed a schedule which would vary according to the personal needs of the wage earners, but which would come under specific rules. This representation of time, as expressed by union activists, seems much closer to *experienced time* than what the official demands suggest.

---

[13] A distinction is made between "fully dedicated managers", who are younger and have more diplomas, and others who have the manager title but neither the responsibilities nor the wage level of the first group.

Experienced time as it emerges from two discussion groups of mid-career bank managers (men and women, ages 30–45) reflects several divisions depending on the work situation (in the sales and marketing network or the central departments), gender and life-cycle stage. The branch managers denounce the "tyranny of the ratio", where daily extra hours are tied above all to pressure over objectives in a context of limited personnel. In the back office, what counts most is the importance of temporal availability as a promotion criterion. In both cases, the criteria for determining objectives and promotion are opaque and outside the control of the unions, despite their repeated demands. But gender constitutes the main division. Female managers, regardless of their family situation, are quite exacting in their double roles as professionals and women, with the latter always linked to motherhood. Since their own mothers generally remained outside the labour force, they have inherited a conception of motherhood entailing a great amount of availability for the children. The "reconciliation" of these two activities thus seems impossible for them. But far from resigning themselves to this situation, resorting to simple personal arrangements or counting on their partners to take over domestic tasks, they expect the company to create more room for family life, through shorter work-hours, part- or full-time parental leaves and so on. As for the men, while the chauvinist model still dominates, some accept a far more measured relationship to their work and considerable involvement in family life.

But this trade-off between mid-career bank managers and their employers, that is, greater temporal availability at the price of a status-enhancing career, is starting to be perturbed by a series of factors, including the improvement of their position in the labour market and a feeling of imbalance between their contributions and their compensation. The result, in a number of cases, is the decision to resign. The "exit" wins out over the "voice" (Hirschman, 1995). As for the *experienced time* of this group of managers, who are objectively and subjectively at the end of their careers from about 45 years on, there is nothing in common with the preceding groups, a distinctive feature which is not the case with *represented* and *formalized time* alike.

14.5.4   Comparative remarks

The situation of middle-aged managers in the Spanish bank, and especially that of the women, shows the same trends found in the other two countries. Here, the employer's adoption of management methods privileging profit-sharing appears to meet with less collective and/or union resistance than in Belgium and even in France. This phenomenon assumes even more specific features because the entry of Spanish women into the labour market is still quite recent;

seemingly "prisoners" of a very strict vision of their role as mothers, they are faced with a choice which is more radical than elsewhere: extensive professional availability based on the male model or withdrawal into the family sphere.

14.6   CONCLUSION

For each of the two groups studied, the prevailing trend would seem to be the converging dynamics of work time in all three countries. The social logics that construct these occupations and distinguish them from each other (notably the logic of gender) seem to be stronger than the social logics rooted in societal differences and similarities.

But the latter exist nonetheless, which means that the outlines of the two occupational groups cannot be compared with any degree of precision in isolation from an entire group of intertwined social relations. A Belgian nurse is not a French or Spanish nurse. Her certification levels are different, as is her place in the division of labour within the hospital. She does more nursing *per se* because she cannot rely on the same number of auxiliary nurses. Similarly, Belgian bank managers are not French bank managers. Their status is more recent and more fragile in institutional terms, while their social identity is less clear. And what can we say about the vast group of "technicians" in the Spanish bank? The limited amount of part-time employment in Spain is reflected among female nurses, whereas in France and even more so in Belgium, part-time work is a key element in their mode of regulating the responsibilities they "juggle". Bank managers in Spain face considerably more pressure over temporal availability, with the realities of their experienced time far removed from formalized work time. In addition, pressure over sales figures is now combined with a recent surge in female activity, leading these two trends to come up against the symbolic resistance of the traditional housewife model.[14] If female managers emancipate themselves from such a model, it appears likely to occur at the price of extremely high existential tensions.

Our investigation nonetheless confirms the general trend towards a decrease in the average length of working time, associated with an increase in its intensity, flexibility and diversity, phenomena which are themselves rooted in the spread of company regulations and the decline of legal safeguards. In all three countries, neo-liberal policies have now gained the upper hand over union-initiated advances in the area of the collective reduction of working time, advances which have most often been emptied of their meaning in a context of unequal social dialogue.

---

[14] For Schmidt et al. (2000), the resistance of the traditional family model in Spain would explain why working women avoid recourse to part-time activity, seen as synonymous with the danger of a pure and simple return to the home.

Even if the two groups share a strong subjective involvement in their work, the distance separating the nurses from the bank managers is reflected by very different forms of temporal availability, as well as the concomitant blurring of boundaries between work and life outside of work. The availability of the first group is at once less controlled by its members and less well recognized in statutory terms. This distance stems above all from the gender-based identity of both groups, with female roles underlying the first and male roles the second. It is also related to differences in the forms of subordination to their respective economic and social temporalities: that is, the imperative of continuous treatment imposes schedules outside of social norms on nurses, who are also faced with the unpredictability of their schedules, which is not the case for bank managers. To some extent, the nurses sometimes succeed in drawing on the legitimacy of their domestic responsibilities to limit their temporal availability at work, notably through informal arrangements within the care units. This is not (or not yet) the case for female bank managers. But the fact remains that the role of gender in the constitution of these occupations and in their situation of time management issues is not eternal. If the masculinization of nursing is still very limited, the feminization of bank managers is occurring rapidly. And it is potentially the main resource for questioning the model of extensive temporal (and geographic) availability in this occupational group for all three countries.

Beyond differences in the strength of the trade unions, *experienced time* in these two groups, and the unions' *represented time* converge with slight differences.[15] This *represented time* goes back to complex processes of the collective representation of time, including the unions' representations of workers' temporal problems and expectations. But our investigation does not provide sufficiently precise data on this issue. If we limit ourselves to the explicit formulation of union demands related to working time, this seems much more dependent on the state of *formalized time*, which it seeks to influence in relation to a realistic evaluation of the balance of power with employers. In all three cases, union representatives may find themselves in an awkward position relative to nurses' or bank managers' expectations if they opt for a strict application of regulations or propose new rules too directly inspired by the "Taylorist" vision of the evaluation and control of time. In all three countries, men are over-represented in the union leadership of hospital workers, and the same is true for older men with few diplomas among the leadership of the banking unions. This disproportional representation may explain part of the distance in question.

---

[15] The French case shows that the membership rate is not automatically a factor. While the distance seems greater for the female nurses than in the two other countries, this is not the case for bank managers, as demonstrated by the common approval of the majority unions and at least part of the managers themselves for the fixed annual wage package in days. For lack of such a formula in Belgium, and especially in Spain, the gap between the rule and actual practice is considerable.

In the French case, a complementary interpretation has also been advanced regarding the difficulty of maintaining the prospect of "collective guarantees of a possibility of individual choice" (Leuthold and Lichtenberger, 1981), notably in the area of work times. This is true especially when action in favour of collective and/or union control of objectives and workload is both crucial and difficult everywhere. On the first issue, certain rights already exist and are largely used by female nurses; moreover, this is the case with the right to part-time status or the possibility of opting for RWT after age 45 in Belgium. But these rights remain limited and are not without disadvantages in the context of limited personnel: imposed multiskilling, less scheduling of hours, and the reduction of pensions. Other personal arrangements of work-hours during the course of a career are practised in all three countries, such as fewer alternating shifts and more fixed daytime hours. Personnel management in the hospitals takes temporal aspirations into account to a certain extent. But this does not involve universal, collective rights. Would such practices seem to point the way towards union action more in tune with *experienced times*?

It is important to stress the fruitfulness of linking the various temporal levels on which the social experiences of professional times are based. "Job time" sheds light on "working time". This occurs, for example, when temporary Belgian nurses (who occupy a strong position in this segment of the labour market) manage to choose their working hours – unlike some of those who have stable jobs, or when young Spanish bank managers starting out with fixed-term contracts are immediately subject to heavy demands for temporal availability. "Professional lifetime" also sheds light on "working time". In both groups, activity is particularly coming to an end before the legal retirement age, which reflects the issues of workload and work intensity (professional or, for women, professional and domestic) throughout working life. How will the patterns of mobilization for work evolve if professional life comes to last considerably longer? Or how can the possibility of workers' individual choice and collective control over working time – that fifth dimension of "decent working time" – be expanded without spacing these possibilities over the whole of working life?[16] This is just one illustration of the fact that all the dimensions of "decent working time" are at once interdependent and inseparable from work that is "sustainable" in terms of its responsibilities and remuneration level alike.

---

[16] On "decent working time", see Chapter 16 (Conclusion) by J. Messenger in this volume.

References

Anxo, D.; Boulin, J.-Y.; Lallement, M.; Silvera, R.; Lefèvre, G. 1998. "Recomposition du temps de travail, rythmes sociaux et modes de vie: Une comparaison France Suède", in *Travail et emploi*, No. 74, pp. 5–20.

Barbier, J.C.; Lindley, R. 2002. "La précarité de l'emploi en Europe", *Quatre pages*, No. 53, Centre d'Etudes de l'Emploi.

Baret, C. 2002. "Le temps de travail sous tension: Une comparaison Belgique, Italie, France, Grande-Bretagne, Pays Bas et Suède", in *Sciences sociales et santé*, No. 3, pp. 75–105.

Bouffartigue, P. (ed.). 2002. *Cadres et comparaisons internationales: Les "cadres" dans les pays d'Europe occidentale*, Les cahiers du GDR Cadres, No. 2.

—; Bouteiller, J., 2003a. "A propos des normes du temps de travail", in *La revue de l'IRES*, No. 2, pp. 137–60.

—; —. 2003b. *Temps professionnels institués, représentés, vécus: Une recherche européenne coordonnée sur les infirmières hospitalières et les cadres de la banque. Résumé de la monographie française et synthèse comparative* (Aix-en-Provence, LEST).

Brun-Hurtado, E. 2003. "Les classifications d'emploi à l'épreuve des transformations organisationnelles du travail dans la banque", Communication aux 9èmes journées de sociologie du travail, Paris, 27–28 November.

Daune-Richard, A.M. 1996. "How does the 'societal effect' shape the use of part time work in France, the UK and Sweden?", in J. O'Reilly and C. Fagan (eds.): *Part-time paradoxes* (London, Routledge).

De Troyer, M.; Martinez, E. 2002. "Les cadres en Belgique", in P. Bouffartigue (ed.), 2002.

Dressen, M. 2003. "Nouvelle articulation entre la négociation de branche et d'entreprise dans les banques en France (1997–2001)", in *La revue de l'IRES*, No. 2, pp. 47–48.

Esping-Andersen, G. 1999. *Les trois mondes de l'Etat-providence: Essai sur le capitalisme moderne* (Paris, Presses Universitaires de France).

Fridenson, P.; Reynaud, E. (eds.). 2004. *La France et le temps de travail* (1814–2004) (Paris, Odile Jacob).

Freyssinet, J. 1999. "Réduction et reorganisation des temps de travail dans les pays de l'union européenne", in *Chronique internationale de l'IRES*, No. 61, pp. 43–48.

Grossin, W. 1996. *Pour une science des temps: Introduction à l'écologie temporelle* (Toulouse, Octares).

Groupe emploi exclusion. 1998. "Rapports entre formes d'emploi et temps de travail. Une comparaison européenne", in *Sociologia del lavoro*, No.74–75, pp. 124–132.

Hirschman, A.O. 1995. *Défection et prise de parole: Théorie et applications* (Paris, Fayard).

Lallement, M. 2000. "Les comparaisons internationales des temps de travail: Apports, portées, limites", in G. Groux (ed.): *L'action publique négociée: Approches à partir des 35 heures* (Paris, L'Harmattan).

Le Lan, R.; Baubeau, D. 2004. "Les conditions de travail perçues par les professionnels des établissements de santé", in *Études et résultats*, No. 335, DREES.

Letablier, M.T.; Lurol, M. 2000. "Les femmes entre travail et famille dans les pays de l'Union européenne", in *La lettre*, Centre d'Études de l'emploi, No. 63.

Leuthold, P.; Lichtenberger, Y. 1981. "Enjeu collectif ou débrouille individuelle", in *CFDT Aujourd'hui*, Vol. 19, No. 48, pp. 55–64.

Maurice, M. 1989. "Méthode comparative et analyse sociétale", in *Sociologie du travail*, No. 2, pp. 175–91.

Michon, F. 2003. "Sur les difficultés méthodologiques de la comparaison internationale des temps de travail", in M. Lallement and J. Spurk (eds.): *Stratégies de la comparaison internationale* (Paris, Editions du CNRS).

Prieto, C. 2002. "Techniciens, professionnels et cadres: Les cadres en Espagne", in P. Bouffartigue (ed.), 2002, pp. 81–91.

Schmidt, M.; Cebrian, I.; Davia, M.-A.; Hernanz, V.; Malo, M.-A. 2000. "Transitions through part time work in Spain and the United Kingdom: A route into secure employment?", in J. O'Reilly, I. Cebrian and M. Lallement (eds.): *Working time changes: Social integration through working time transition* (Cheltenham, Edward Elgar).

Thoemmes, J.; de Terssac, G. 1977. "La négociation du temps de travail et les composantes du référentiel temporel", in *Loisirs et Société*, Vol. 20, No. 1, pp. 51–72.

Tonneau, D. 2003. "La réduction du temps de travail dans les hôpitaux publics: Des difficultés liées à l'organisation", Document de travail No. 35, DREES.

WHO IS WORKING AT WEEKENDS? DETERMINANTS OF REGULAR WEEKEND WORK IN CANADA[1]

15

Isik U. Zeytinoglu* and Gordon B. Cooke**

15.1   INTRODUCTION

In the last few decades, part-time work, temporary jobs and work schedules have expanded throughout most industrialized countries (Boisard et al., 2003, p. 1; Presser, 2003, p. 2; Zeytinoglu, 1999, p. ix). The majority of new jobs created since the 1980s in Canada are part-time and temporary employment contracts (Tabi and Langlois, 2003, p. 13; Vosko et al., 2003, p. 20; Zeytinoglu, 2002, p. 15). This trend is evident in all sectors of the economy, including the public sector (Ilcan et al., 2003, p. 636). With the political, economic and technical changes of the last few decades, as well as the socio-cultural changes in work, personal and family lives, there is a move toward a 24-hour, 7-day work society in Canada. The traditional 5-day schedule of 7–8 hours of work per day starting somewhere between 6 a.m. and 9 a.m. and ending between 3 p.m. and 6 p.m. is no longer applicable to many workers. Working time is encroaching on social and personal time for many workers, and it is now not unusual to be regularly employed at weekends.

The ILO report, *Working time and workers' needs and preferences in industrialized countries: Finding the balance* (see also Messenger, Conclusion in this volume) shows that Canada's experience with working time issues is

---

* Professor of Management & Industrial Relations, DeGroote School of Business, McMaster University.

** Assistant Professor of Industrial Relations, Faculty of Business Administration, Memorial University of Newfoundland.

[1] This is the revised version of our paper presented at the International Symposium on Working Time, Ninth Meeting, Paris, 26–28 February 2004. This study is supported by a grant from the Social Sciences and Humanities Research Council of Canada. Data used in this chapter were accessed through Statistics Canada McMaster Research Data Centre. The chapter represents the views of the authors and does not reflect the opinions of Statistics Canada. For correspondence contact either zeytino@mcmaster.ca or cookegb@mcmaster.ca.

similar to that of other industrialized countries. Of the five dimensions of decent working time discussed by Messenger, we will focus here on the healthy working time dimension (though the gender equality through working time and family-friendly working time dimensions are also closely related). The healthy working time dimension focuses on enhancing workers' well-being by addressing the health and safety implications of working excessively long hours, night work, and various types of shift work schedules (Messenger, this volume). We will then extend this focus to weekend work in Canada. Weekend work is an unsocial schedule that can be disruptive to personal life as it affects leisure time, such as pursuing personal interests, spending time with family, and socializing with friends, neighbours and the local community.

The underlying theme of this chapter is that healthy working time is an important component of workers' health. As a starting point, we will use the World Health Organization's definition of health as "a state of complete physical, mental and social well-being and not merely the absence of disease or infirmity" (Zeytinoglu et al., 1999, p. 23). Meaningful employment, economic stability, and healthy and supportive work and social environments are all recognized as being of central importance to the health of individuals (Hamilton and Bhatti, 1996, p. 3). Social life is also an important component of an individual's health and well-being (Zeytinoglu et al., 1999, p. 23).

This chapter focuses on workers whose regular work-week includes Saturdays, Sundays and sometimes both days (hereafter referred to as workers regularly employed at weekends). The purpose of this chapter is to examine the determinants of regular weekend work in Canada. We use Statistics Canada's 1999 Workplace and Employee Survey (WES). The WES data are collected from employers and their employees, and contain a large number of identifying variables for weekend work and its determinants not usually available in other data sets in Canada. Using these data will also allow us to generalize about the general population of Canada.

The topic of regular weekend work can be examined from employers', consumers' and workers' perspectives, since each category is a key player in the weekend work issue. In this chapter, however, the analysis will be from the individual workers' perspective, since we believe that it is the workers who are most disadvantaged by the weekend work issue. In weekend work, employers and consumers are the main beneficiaries. Employers keep their businesses open at weekends earning profits and/or using their capital more efficiently by not keeping it idle, while consumers get extended hours of service. The workers, therefore, are the main source of labour who provide the services and produce the goods in order to supply the demands of employers and consumers at the weekend. Weekend workers are employed at a time when most other people, including their family and friends, are resting or socializing.

Moreover, they often lose out on socializing within their communities, as many community activities take place during this customarily restful time. We point out, too, that workers are also consumers, and although they might not want to work at weekends, many do demand service at this time.

15.2 THE CONTEXT, THEORETICAL BACKGROUND AND FACTORS ASSOCIATED WITH WEEKEND WORK

Starting with the Industrial Revolution, and later in the 1930s, a certain life-style was created for workers in Canada, thanks to strong unionization in mass-production manufacturing and related industries. Workers had two days per week as a rest period, and most wives did not work outside the home since a single-earner income in the family was sufficient in providing a middle-class lifestyle (Forrest, 1996, n.p.; 1998, p. 83). In the last three decades global restructuring of economies, major innovations in the information technology sector, increased growth of the service sector, and changes in social values and family structures (including many women entering the labour force and remaining there) have led to substantial changes in the hours worked and demanded in Canada (Zeytinoglu and Muteshi, 2000, p. 108). For example, in 1991, 11 per cent of the workforce worked regularly on Saturdays or Sundays (Winters, 1994, p. 45). This percentage increased to 18.5 per cent in 1999 (see table 15.3). Studies from the European Union (Boisard et al., 2003, p. 24) and the United States (Presser, 2003, p. 8) show similar trends.

In terms of the theoretical background, weekend work can be explained by both the dual labour market theory (Doeringer and Piore, 1971, p. 2) and core–periphery conceptualization (Atkinson, 1987, p. 93; Osterman, 1992, p. 280). The literature suggests that people who work during the traditional work-week are full-time "core" workers in jobs with primary labour market characteristics. These are the workers in good quality jobs with good pay and benefits, as well as access to training, promotion possibilities within the company and relative job security. These core jobs are surrounded by a variety of peripheral work arrangements (Zeytinoglu, 1999, p. 52; 2002, p. 18.). Of those peripheral work arrangements, we will focus only on part-time work, temporary work and seasonal work.

In this chapter, we argue that these peripheral work arrangements are one of the important factors contributing to the increase in weekend work. It is the availability of labour in a variety of work arrangements that allows employers to create weekend jobs. There seems to be an abundance of individuals working, voluntarily or involuntarily, in a variety of non-standard jobs and work schedules, including regular weekend work.

Part-time and temporary jobs are particularly conducive to weekend work. Recent figures show that 62 per cent of Canadian workers are employed on a full-time basis, 9 per cent in both regular part-time and temporary full-time employment respectively, 6 per cent in temporary part-time employment, with the other 14 per cent being self-employed (Kapsalis and Tourigny, 2004, p. 6). Focusing on hours worked, a Statistics Canada study (Kapsalis and Tourigny, 2004, p. 7) showed that temporary full-time workers worked fewer hours than temporary part-time workers, and both groups worked fewer hours than regular full-time workers. In particular, temporary employment accounts for almost one-fifth of overall growth in paid employment between 1997 and 2003 (Galarneau, 2005, p. 6).

The idea of core–periphery conceptualization, usually relegated solely to the periphery of part-time and temporary workers who work in unsocial work schedules of evenings and split shifts, should, as this chapter argues, include weekends as well. Part-time and temporary workers employed in the "periphery" of their organizations work in secondary labour market conditions (Beechy and Perkins, 1987, p. 142; Zeytinoglu, 1999, p. 49; Zeytinoglu and Cooke, 2004, p. 20). Thus we expect to find those in part-time and/or temporary jobs to be more likely to be regular weekend workers.

Seasonal workers in the secondary labour market, therefore, are accordingly placed in the periphery of their workplaces. These workers are hired for only a fixed period of time, such as only in summers or during holiday seasons. Seasonal workers often work extended hours or consecutive days (Osberg et al., 1995, p. 3) during less desirable working hours. We expect to find in our study that there are significant numbers of seasonal workers employed regularly at weekends.

It is well known that unionization tends to protect workers from undesirable working conditions (Akyeampong, 2002, p. 5; Marshall, 2003, p. 12). There is also ample research showing the benefits of unionization for workers (Fang and Verma, 2002, p. 18). Unions were at the forefront of the legislated two-day-per-week rest period. Though many non-standard workers are not covered by collective agreements (Gunderson and Hyatt, 2001, p. 103), and even if covered, endure inferior conditions to regular full-time workers (Zeytinoglu, 1991, p. 408), we presume that in unionized environments there will be protection against weekend work. Perhaps those working at weekends will be non-union workers, who are often part-time, temporary or seasonal workers. Thus we expect to find that unionized workers will be less likely regularly to work at weekends.

Non-standard work is typically found in the service sector, while the manufacturing sector generally uses full-time workers on an overtime or shift basis, or contracts out the work (Zeytinoglu and Muteshi, 2000, p. 100). It is mostly the workers in retail trade who tend to work at weekends

(WES Compendium, 2001, p. 33; Zeytinoglu et al., 2003, p. 32). We expect to find in our study that workers in the service sector will be more likely regularly to work at weekends.

Well-educated, white-collar professionals generally have "standard" work hours during the usual Monday through Friday work-week, though they might work longer hours during the workday. They may also choose to work at weekends, due to the occupational culture of long hours, corporate culture and management strategies (Romaine and Zeytinoglu, 1999, p. 264). Nonetheless, they tend to consider themselves as sometimes, but not regularly, weekend workers. They are generally employed in good-quality jobs with core labour market characteristics. Thus we expect to find that these white-collar managerial and professional workers will not be working regularly at weekends. That is, we expect that workers in low-level white-collar jobs or blue-collar jobs will be more likely to work regularly at weekends.

There is mounting empirical evidence demonstrating that non-standard work has come to represent a particularly female option where work is being contracted in a gender-differentiated way (Zeytinoglu and Muteshi, 2000, p. 102). The literature suggests that many of the workers employed at weekends are disadvantaged populations of the society, including women, parents with dependent children (Cranford et al., 2003, p. 459), and ethnic minorities who are, in Canada, mostly recent immigrants (Chard et al., 2000, p. 191; Zeytinoglu and Muteshi, 2000, p. 110). It is likely that workers in weekend jobs will be drawn from these populations in the labour force. Thus we expect to find that women, recent immigrants, many of whom are ethnic minorities, and parents with dependent children are more likely regularly to work at weekends.

To better demonstrate this hypothesis, the following model represents our analysis and the factors associated with weekend work. The model shows the relationships between possible different factors involving weekend work such as the workplace, industry, and a number of individual characteristics that are associated with it. These relationships are presented in figure 15.1.

15.3   METHODOLOGY

Data from the Workplace and Employee Survey (WES), which is a new data set of Statistics Canada, is based on a survey of employers (workplaces) and workers employed by those workplaces. The analysis presented here is based on the responses provided by workers, which are then merged with some of the workplace characteristics obtained from the workplace data. Details of the data are provided in box 15.1.

In this chapter, we focus on whether the worker's regular work-week includes Saturdays and/or Sundays. This is the dependent variable in our

Figure 15.1   Job, workplace and individual factors that affect regular
weekend work

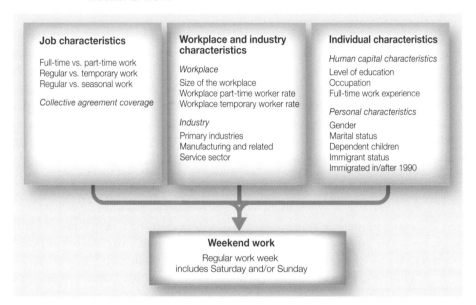

Job characteristics	Workplace and industry characteristics	Individual characteristics
		Human capital characteristics
Full-time vs. part-time work	*Workplace*	Level of education
Regular vs. temporary work	Size of the workplace	Occupation
Regular vs. seasonal work	Workplace part-time worker rate	Full-time work experience
	Workplace temporary worker rate	
Collective agreement coverage		*Personal characteristics*
	Industry	Gender
	Primary industries	Marital status
	Manufacturing and related	Dependent children
	Service sector	Immigrant status
		Immigrated in/after 1990

Weekend work
Regular work week
includes Saturday and/or Sunday

multivariate analysis. Variables that can affect regular weekend work are
grouped into four categories: job characteristics, workplace characteristics,
industry sector and individual (i.e. human capital and personal) characteristics.
While most variables come from the employee data, the size of the workplace,
workplace part-time and temporary worker rate, and industry variables are
from the merged employer data set. These variables and how they are coded
are explained in table 15.1.

In analysing the data we begin with the frequency distributions and
descriptive statistics. Following that, we will proceed to a multivariate analysis
in order to isolate the relationships between weekend work and several potential
factors associated with it. The following analysis uses weighted microdata
accessed at the McMaster Research Data Centre.

Although we are interested in a range of variables that may be associated
with regular weekend work, we are particularly interested in assessing the
relationships between part-time, temporary and seasonal work status, and
regular weekend work. We examine the associations between the dependent
variable of regular weekend work and the key variables of whether a worker is
in a part-time, temporary or seasonal job, and whether the worker is covered
by a collective agreement. In addition, the interaction variables of the
following associations are used in the analysis: part-time and temporary work,
part-time work and work covered by a collective agreement; and temporary

Box 15.1   Data source and explanations

Data

Statistics Canada's Workplace and Employee Survey (WES) 1999 employee microdata linked to workplace (i.e. employer) microdata are used. WES surveys firms in all industries, with the exception of agriculture, fishing, fur trapping and public administration. WES covers all firms regardless of size, and examines a range of workplace issues. The 1999 WES has data on 24,597 employees from 6,351 workplaces, with a response rate of 83 per cent and 94 per cent respectively. Data were collected first from the employers, followed by surveying selected employees from each workplace. For larger workplaces, up to 12 employees were randomly chosen. For very small organizations – with four or fewer employees – all employees were selected. (For more on sampling and sample design, see WES Compendium, 2001.)

Limitations of the data

The WES data probably under-represent individuals with part-time and/or temporary employment contracts because only employees of the workplaces are eligible for sampling under the WES methodology. Thus, for example, workers employed by the temporary help services (agency workers) can be included only if that agency is captured as a separate workplace. If, however, these workers are on temporary assignment in another workplace, they are not surveyed since they are not employees of that employer.

work and work covered by a collective agreement are included as part of the key set of variables. We also include a number of other variables to control for their effects on the regular weekend work variable. Thus other workplace, industry and individual characteristics variables are included. For each analysis, we record the odds ratio, coefficient and significance level of each variable as well as the overall (pseudo) R^2 (i.e. how much of the variance is explained).

It should be noted that Statistics Canada strongly recommends the use of bootstrapping[2] in statistical analysis using the WES data set due to its complex survey design. All presented significance levels are bootstrapped results, using Statistics Canada's recommended set of 100 bootstrapped weights for this data set via the Stata function developed and discussed by Pierard et al. (2004, p. 20). One effect of using such a large data set and a bootstrapping procedure is that results may indicate strong statistical significance even when substantive significance is unclear. Therefore we will discuss particular variable results only when statistical significance is found and the magnitude of the

---

[2]"Bootstrapping" is generally used as a method of testing the reliability of a data set.

Table 15.1   Description of variables

Variable name	Question/explanation, coding
Dependent variable	
Regular weekend work	Does your usual workweek include Saturdays and/or Sundays? 1 = Yes, 0 = No
Key variables of interest	
Job characteristics	
Part-time work	Not counting overtime, how many paid hours on average [usually] do you work per week at this job? 1 = Part-time, working 29.9 hours or less per week 0 = Full-time, working 30 hours or more
Temporary work	Which of the following describes your terms of employment in this job? 1 = Temporary work, i.e. casual or on-call work where hours of work vary substantially from one week to next, called in whenever work is needed, or term employment ending at a specified date 0 = Regular work arrangement with no contractual or anticipated termination date
Seasonal work	Which of the following describes your terms of employment in this job? 1 = Seasonal work, 0 = Not seasonal
Covered by a collective agreement	In current job, are you a member of a union or covered by a collective bargaining agreement? 1 = Yes, 0 = No
Interaction variables	
Part-time and temporary work	Work part-time and temporary? 1 = Yes, 0 = No
Part-time and covered by a collective agreement	Part-time worker covered by a collective agreement? 1 = Yes, 0 = No
Temporary and covered by a collective agreement	Temporary worker covered by a collective agreement? 1 = Yes, 0 = No
Other associated variables	
Workplace characteristics	
Workplace size	Total employment at [the workplace] in the last pay period of March 1999, number of workers
Log of workplace size	Transformation to reduce skewness in the data
Workplace part-time worker rate	Total number of part-time employees in the workplace in the last pay period divided by total employment at the workplace in the last pay period of March 1999 (% part-time)

Variable name	Question/explanation, coding
Workplace temporary worker rate	Total number of temporary (i.e. non-permanent) employees receiving a T4 slip at the workplace in the last pay period divided by total employment at the workplace in the last pay period of March 1999 (% temporary)
Industry characteristics	
Primary industries	1 = Yes, 0 = Otherwise
Manufacturing and related	1 = Yes, 0 = Otherwise (reference group)
Service sector	1 = Yes, 0 = Otherwise
Individual characteristics	
Human capital characteristics	
Highest education attained:	
Less than high school	1 = Yes, 0 = Otherwise
Completed high school	1 = Yes, 0 = Otherwise
Some post-secondary (including degree/certificate diploma but excluding university degree)	1 = Yes, 0 = Otherwise
University degree or higher	1 = Yes, 0 = Otherwise (reference group)
Occupation:	
Manager	1 = Yes, 0 = Otherwise
Professional	1 = Yes, 0 = Otherwise
Lower white-collar	1 = Yes, 0 = Otherwise
Blue-collar	1 = Yes, 0 = Otherwise (reference group)
Full-time work experience	Number of years
Full-time work experience squared	Number of years squared
Personal characteristics	
Gender	1 = Female, 0 = Male
Marital status:	
Married/common law partner	1 = Yes, 0 = Otherwise (reference group)
Other marital status (single, separated, divorced, widowed)	1 = Yes, 0 = Otherwise
Dependent children	1 = Yes, 0 = No
Immigrant status:	
Immigrant	1 = Yes (not Canadian-born), 0 = No (Canadian-born)
Recent immigrant	1 = Yes (immigrated in/after 1990), 0 = No

significance is sufficient to suggest noteworthy associations. We will do this by looking at the odds ratio, which, if below 0.9 or above 1.1, will give us a crude indication of substantive significance.

15.4   CHARACTERISTICS OF THE WORKERS

Our study indicates that about 19 per cent of workers in Canada regularly work at weekends. As presented in table 15.2, roughly 15 per cent of our sample is involved in part-time work arrangements, while the shares of those in temporary or seasonal jobs are 5 per cent and 2 per cent respectively. Among a weighted sample of 10.8 million, those in part-time, temporary and seasonal arrangements represented 1.6 million, 0.5 million and 0.3 million workers, respectively.

About 28 per cent of the workers in this survey were either unionized or covered by a collective agreement, but only a small percentage of part-time and temporary workers were covered by a collective agreement. The average worker was in a workplace of over 400 employees, while the percentages of part-time and temporary employees per workplace were 28 per cent and 12 per cent, respectively. Almost two-thirds of surveyed workers were in the service sector, with one-third in manufacturing and related industries, leaving only a very small proportion in primary industries. Of the total workers in this survey, over 70 per cent had some post-secondary education, college degree, diploma or university degree. Close to two-thirds were in blue-collar occupations and about one-fifth were in lower-level white-collar occupations, with the remainder being managers and professionals. The average full-time work experience was 16 years. Slightly more than half the respondents in the survey were female, more than two-thirds were married or in common-law relationships, and slightly less than half had dependent children. Most respondents were Canadian-born, while 18 per cent were immigrants, of whom only about 3.5 per cent had immigrated during or after 1990.

15.5   PERCENTAGE OF WORKERS IN REGULAR WEEKEND WORK

As a starting point, descriptive statistics were reviewed to discover which worker sub-groups were more likely to be employed at weekends. Among all surveyed workers, 18.5 per cent regularly work at weekends. On a weighted basis, that equates to just under 2 million among the sample of 10.8 million workers. In comparison to the earlier cited estimate of 11 per cent in 1991, this study confirmed that weekend work in Canada was not confined to an unlucky few. Moreover, as the following statistics show, all segments of the labour force were affected.

Table 15.2   Characteristics of workers

Variable label	Mean	Standard deviation	Percentages
Regular weekend work (% workers)			18.5
Part-time work			15.2
Temporary work			4.8
Seasonal work			2.4
Covered by a collective agreement			27.9
Part-time and temporary work			2.5
Part-time and covered by a collective agreement			4.4
Temporary and covered by a collective agreement			2.1
Workplace size	412.16	1 144.49	
Workplace size – logarithmic form	1.79	0.86	
Workplace part-time worker rate	0.28	0.29	
Workplace temporary worker rate	0.12	0.22	
Industry:			
Primary sector			1.7
Manufacturing and related sector			33.6
Service sector			64.7
Highest education attained:			
Less than high school			10.7
Completed high school			17.5
Some post-secondary			52.4
University degree or higher			19.5
Occupation:			
Manager			15.1
Professional			16.2
Lower white-collar			22.4
Blue-collar			46.4
Full-time work experience	16.17	10.71	
Full-time work experience squared	376.14	421.58	
Gender (percentage female)			52.1
Marital status:			
Married/common-law			69.1
Other marital status			30.9
Has dependent children			47.2
Immigrant status:			
Immigrant			17.5
Recent immigrant			3.5

Figure 15.2 Part-time, temporary and seasonal workers regularly working at weekends (percentages)

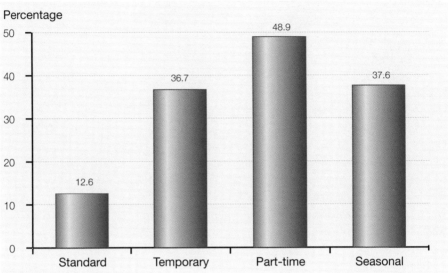

As shown in figures 15.2 and 15.3, the differences among job status categories were dramatic: 49 per cent of part-time workers and 37 per cent of temporary workers regularly work at weekends. That compares to only 13 per cent of standard (i.e. neither temporary nor part-time) workers who regularly work at weekends. Since part-time and temporary workers may have lower tenure inside organizations and therefore may be assigned to less desirable (leftover) work schedules, we looked at only those with less than 30 months of tenure with their current employer. Surprisingly, among this group of recently hired employees, only 25 per cent worked at weekends (versus 16 per cent among those with higher organizational tenure). While the percentage working weekends among those recently hired was higher than the average for all workers, it was much lower than the percentages for the part-time and temporary groups. (Since this effect size is smaller than expected, we instead included the role of full-time work experience in our multivariate analysis.) Seasonal workers frequently exhibited a similar work characteristic, with 38 per cent regularly working weekends.

Interestingly, there is little difference between those covered by a collective agreement and those who are not, with the proportions of workers regularly working weekends among these categories being 20 per cent and 18 per cent, respectively. On the other hand, there were major differences between occupational groups, with 26 per cent of lower-level white-collar employees working at weekends, versus about 17 per cent among blue-collar

Figure 15.3   Recently hired workers regularly working at weekends (percentages)

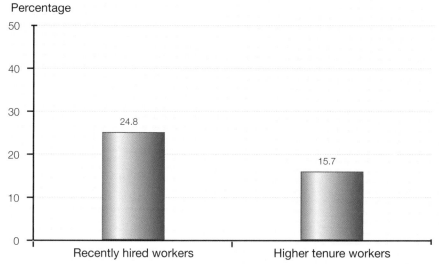

Figure 15.4   Women and men regularly working at weekends (percentages)

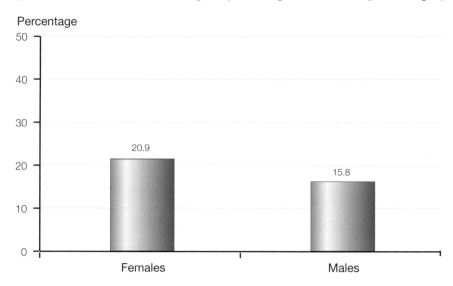

workers, and only about 14 per cent among workers in managerial jobs. Similarly, there were meaningful differences between the genders, with 16 per cent of males regularly working weekends versus 21 per cent among females, as shown in figure 15.4.

These distributions show that those who regularly worked weekend unsocial hours were likely to be employed in part-time, temporary, seasonal jobs and/or possibly covered by collective agreements. Moreover, they were also more likely to be female and/or in lower-level white-collar jobs.

15.6 MULTIVARIATE ANALYSIS RESULTS

Now, we turn to the multivariate results shown in table 15.3. As expected, workers in part-time and/or seasonal jobs were significantly more likely to work at weekends. On the other hand, workers in temporary jobs were only somewhat more likely to work weekends when controlling for the effect of other factors. Unexpectedly, workers covered by a collective agreement were more likely to work at weekends. Since we were controlling for the impact of industry, occupation, gender and other factors, these were not related factors for workers covered by collective agreements to work regularly at weekends. The interaction of part-time status with other variables yields unusual results as well. Workers in part-time employment covered by collective agreements were much more likely to work at weekends, but those who were part-time and temporary were much less likely to do so (when controlling for those two pairs of categories separately).

Our research of the past two decades on part-time and temporary employment suggests some explanations for these findings (see, e.g., Zeytinoglu, 1999, p. xix; 2002, p. 16). Since the early 1980s there has been a steady change in unionized workplaces. First part-time work increased in unionized workplaces, then casual work also began to increase. Unions were initially reluctant to represent these workers, but as time passed and their numbers continued to increase in the workplaces they represented, unions began negotiating for these workers. They principally negotiated for full-time and part-time workers who were in more or less regular and continuous employment. Unions also negotiated for temporary workers, although these negotiated wages, benefits and employment conditions were generally lower than those that full-time and part-time workers received. For example, unions were able to provide more predictable schedules for their members by negotiating with the employer to post schedules a few days before the assigned shift, enabling workers to plan ahead better for events in their own lives. Before such collective agreements the employer would have simply called the worker the day before the workday, necessitating unplanned availability on the part of the worker. If the worker refused the unplanned work schedule a few times, the employer would simply no longer call, which would lead to the worker losing their job.

In another example, in some collective agreements unions were able to negotiate longer shifts (that were at least 5 hours long) for part-time workers

Table 15.3   Determinants of regular weekend work in Canada (logistic regressions)

	Odds ratio	Regression coefficient	Standard error	Significance
Key variables of interest				
Part-time work	2.721	0.998	0.179	***
Temporary work	2.024	0.705	0.361	*
Seasonal work	1.898	0.641	0.257	**
Covered by a collective agreement	1.299	0.262	0.132	**
Part-time and temporary work	0.491	−0.712	0.420	*
Part-time and covered by a collective agreement	1.774	0.573	0.263	**
Temporary and covered by a collective agreement	1.020	0.019	0.311	
Other associated variables				
Workplace size (log form)	0.861	−0.149	0.053	***
Workplace part-time worker rate	5.244	1.657	0.180	***
Workplace temporary worker rate	0.620	−0.479	0.214	**
Industry: Primary sector	1.638	0.493	0.264	*
Industry: Manufacturing and related (ref.)				
Industry: Service sector	2.514	0.922	0.106	***
Education: less than high school	1.810	0.593	0.253	**
Education: completed high school	1.886	0.634	0.213	***
Education: some post-secondary	1.636	0.492	0.202	**
Education: university degree or higher (ref.)				
Occupation: manager	0.843	−0.171	0.206	
Occupation: professional	0.498	−0.697	0.161	***
Occupation: lower white-collar	0.962	−0.039	0.107	
Occupation: blue-collar (ref.)				
Full-time work experience	0.952	−0.050	0.013	***
Full-time work experience squared	1.001	0.001	0.000	*
Gender (1 = female)	0.656	−0.422	0.098	***
Marital status: married/common-law (ref.)				
Marital status: single/divorced/widowed	1.392	0.331	0.117	***
(Has) dependent child(ren)	0.930	−0.073	0.123	
Immigrant	1.157	0.146	0.162	
Recent immigrant	0.840	−0.174	0.240	
Constant		−2.469	0.300	***
Number of observations prior to weighting	23,209			
Wald chi-square	717.160			
Probability > chi-square	0.000			
Pseudo R-square	0.193			
Log pseudo-likelihood	(9,001)			

Note: Significance levels: *** $p < 0.01$, ** $p < 0.05$, * $p < 0.10$.

by stipulating that these shifts be at the weekends or in the evenings. Before these negotiated longer shifts, employers assigned workers 2- or 3-hour shifts during times when there was greater demand for their services. These workers would end up spending so much time commuting to and from work that they would have spent an hour's earnings on travel. Under these conditions, part-time and temporary workers covered by collective agreements agreed to work at weekends or evening shifts, but it was stipulated that they must be allowed to work a minimum 5-hour shift. Although some workers were not always satisfied with the time or day of the designated shifts, at least it was worth the time and effort to get to work. In fact, our recent research shows that many of these workers are showing symptoms of stress and reduced job satisfaction due to the unfavourable working conditions in part-time and/or temporary jobs (Zeytinoglu et al., 2003, p. 29).

Concluding this issue, it is important to note that part-time and temporary workers are less likely to work in weekend jobs, precisely because employers are able to fill those weekend shifts with part-time workers regularly scheduled for weekends (of the unionized type that was discussed previously). Temporary workers are offered employment at weekends only if these regular workers do not show up for work.

Continuing with our presentation of the multivariate analysis results (in table 15.3), employees in larger workplaces (determined by the number of workers) or with a higher proportion of temporary employees are less likely to work at weekends. However, those workplaces with higher proportions of part-time employees are more likely to have weekend work accomplished than others. In fact, the results suggest that part-time job status and the workplace part-time worker rate are among the most indicative signals of regular weekend work.

In terms of the industry relative to manufacturing workers, those in the primary and especially service sectors are also more likely to work regularly at weekends. Therefore, as expected, and similar to the European Union experience (Boisard et al., 2003, p. 29) and the United States experience (Presser, 2003, p. 8), regular weekend work seems to be more common in the service sector than elsewhere.

Human capital characteristics are also important. Higher levels of education, which indicated a greater investment in human capital, help workers to avoid regular weekend work. In comparison, workers without university degrees are more likely than workers with higher levels of education to work regularly at weekends. The level of education is also closely related to the level of occupational group a worker belongs to. Our results show that, except for professionals, there are no substantive differences in the level of regular weekend work between occupational groups when controlling for other factors. To be more precise, professionals are significantly less likely to regularly work weekends, but managers and lower-level white-collar and blue-collar workers all have essentially the same likelihood of regular weekend work. The fact that managers are regularly working at weekends is an unexpected result of the study, although blue-collar and lower white-collar workers working at the weekend are in the expected parameters of the study. Managers who regularly work at weekends are increasing in Canada. If workplaces are open at weekends, there will often be managers in them. Some of those managers may even be hired regularly to work at weekends. For the time being, professionals appear to be immune to regular weekend work. It is possible that they may be working at some weekends at home on work-related business, such as preparing reports or reading work-related publications, but they are not regularly assigned to do this work at weekends. The study also illuminated the fact that full-time work experience has essentially no effect on the likelihood of working weekends regularly.

In terms of personal characteristics, after controlling for other factors, being male is associated with a higher likelihood of regular weekend work than being female, which is unexpected based on the earlier descriptive statistics. Consequently, the reason why more females (than males) work weekends is due in large part to being overrepresented in jobs, occupations, or other industries in which regular weekend work is prevalent, rather than due to gender *per se*. In other words, in terms of overall numbers, more female workers regularly work at weekends than male workers because more females work in part-time jobs; in lower-level white-collar clerical, sales and personal services occupations; and in the service sector. Women's customary weekend employment does not occur because employers create these regular weekend jobs specifically for women. In other words, these are not what some people call the "mom's shift part-time work" that exists in the United Kingdom or in Germany (the former West Germany). The jobs were not created with women in mind, to accommodate women's hours of work with children's schooling hours, for instance, but because there is consumer demand for services at weekends and employers want to keep their workplaces open and working for reasons of competitiveness.

The fact that more women than men are regularly working at weekends suggests that there is discrimination against females due to the patriarchal societal system that operates in Canada and most other countries. As the theory of patriarchy discusses (Walby, 1990, p. 19), society separates women and men according to their gender, giving specific roles to each and expecting different work roles and caregiving responsibilities from each based on their gender. In households, it is usually the women who perform the domestic work, including caring for children and working adults. In addition, women

411

want to, and need to work in paid jobs. Since men are generally employed full time, and women take care of the household chores and caregiving responsibilities in the home, they end up working at times of the week that are left over after family responsibilities have been performed. Since weekend or evening hours are the times that employers seek to fill, times that also correspond with the male partner in the family being home to oversee any household or caregiving activities, women end up applying for and working during those weekend hours. We should, however, keep in mind that these are not the work-hours and schedules that women voluntarily choose, but are the hours and schedules that the patriarchal society, family unit, and social system dictate are suitable for women; thus these hours are involuntarily chosen hours for women workers. As Messenger (in this volume) discusses, these are tightly constrained choices for women, particularly where childcare services are limited or impractical.

In terms of marital status, our results show that in comparison to married workers, those who are single are more likely to be engaged in regular weekend work. Those who have fewer family commitments and, possibly, students who are in school during the weekdays are regularly working at weekends.

Finally, contrary to our expectations, there are no significant differences between Canadian-born workers and immigrants in terms of weekend work. In addition, there are no differences between Canadian-born, pre-1990 immigrants, and recent immigrants in terms of weekend work. All are equally likely regularly to work at weekends. Other research shows that recent immigrants in Canada are largely in overall poor-quality jobs. Being a recent immigrant is a significant factor in earning lower wages (Thompson, 2002, p. 21) and benefits (Zeytinoglu and Cooke, 2005, p. 54) than the Canadian-born and immigrants who came to Canada before 1999. Overall, this suggests that although recent immigrants work in jobs with lower pay and fewer benefits, when it comes to regular weekend work there are no differences, suggesting that new immigrants are not discriminated against in the weekend work aspect of their jobs.

15.7 SUMMARY AND CONCLUSION

In the last few decades there have been major changes in working time in Canada. Canadians are experiencing an extension of working hours to evenings and weekends, as well as moving towards a 24-hour, 7-day work society. As our study indicated, since 1991, the last time a study of weekend work was conducted in Canada using Statistics Canada data, there has been an increase in the percentage of workers regularly working at weekends from 11 per cent to 18.5 per cent. The object of this study was to examine the determinants of weekend work in Canada.

There is strong evidence in our data that workers in part-time, temporary and/or seasonal jobs are more likely to work regularly at weekends. Workers covered by collective agreements, particularly those in part-time jobs covered by such agreements, are more likely, on average, to work regularly at weekends. Workers in workplaces with a high percentage of part-time workers and those employed in the service sector are also more likely regularly to work at weekends. An overall analysis of these findings suggests a certain scenario for regular weekend workers. Many of them work in part-time and seasonal jobs, with some others in temporary jobs. These workers are employed in workplaces where the employer relies largely on part-time workers, and they are predominantly in the service sector. Our accumulated research on this topic suggests that part-time workers are predominantly covered by collective agreements. To a lesser degree, temporary and seasonal workers are working at weekends in return for some security in the number of hours the employer assigns them, including some continuity and regularity in work schedules, which includes longer shifts (of 5 hours or more), making it financially feasible for them to commute to work. We argue that these are the underlying reasons for part-time, temporary and seasonal workers, particularly the part-time workers covered by collective agreements regularly to work at weekends.

We also found that those with higher education, including professionals, are less likely regularly to work weekends, which shows the value of investment in education and the importance of the professional occupation from a worker perspective.

On the other hand, although a higher percentage of females than males regularly work at weekends, that difference changes course when controlling for workplace, industry, and individual worker characteristics. The difference between the descriptive statistics and multivariate results allows us to infer that female workers are more likely regularly to work at weekends due to other factors, such as being overrepresented in part-time, temporary and seasonal jobs, rather than due to gender or occupation *per se*. In other words, employers are creating regular weekend jobs that are part-time, temporary, and seasonal, and filling them with available workers. Employers are creating these regular weekend jobs because there is consumer demand for services at weekends, and because they want to keep their workplaces open and operational for competitiveness reasons. More women than men regularly working at weekends suggests that this is discrimination against females due to the patriarchal societal system. In our society, femininity and masculinity are constructed differently, placing women and men at different jobs in workplaces and in different roles in society. As a result of this, women spend more hours performing household tasks and caregiving work, and fewer hours in paid work (at times when their spouse can assume the responsibility for these housekeeping tasks). Since men

413

tend to work in full-time jobs in a standard schedule of weekdays, women opt – for lack of other options – regularly to work at weekends.

Interestingly, we also found less variation regarding the level of weekend work between Canadian-born workers and immigrant workers, and pre-1990 immigrants and recent immigrants. This suggests that regular weekend work has penetrated into the working life of all workers. It is not only new immigrants, or immigrants in general, who are undertaking these undesirable hours of work. Canadian-born workers are enduring a similarly unsocial schedule.

Regular weekend work is an unsocial schedule that can be disruptive to personal life, affecting leisure time activities such as pursuing personal interests, being with the family, and socializing with friends, neighbours and the local community. Weekend work can also be unhealthy, as we showed in another study – a detrimental factor contributing to increased stress, with the resultant physical and mental health problems for workers and consequently their workplaces (Zeytinoglu et al., 2003, p. 49, Messenger in this volume). Similar concerns are being raised for working time schedules and their correlations with workers' health in Europe (Boisard et al., 2003, p. 44). It was noted that meaningful employment, economic stability, healthy work environments, and supportive social environments are important, but also that an active social life outside the workplace is a vital component of an individual's health and well-being (Zeytinoglu et al., 1999, p. 23). Overall, the increasing percentage of regular weekend workers in Canada, and factors associated with this trend, reveal unhealthy working time schedules for workers, suggesting that many workers may have challenges in balancing regular weekend work with social and personal time.

References

Akyeampong, E.B. 2002. "Fact-sheet on unionization", in *Perspectives on Labour and Income*, Vol. 13, No. 3, pp. 47–54.

Atkinson, J. 1987. "Flexibility or fragmentation? The United Kingdom labour market in the eighties", in *Labour and Society*, Vol. 12, No. 1, pp. 87–105.

Beechy, V.; Perkins, T. 1987. *A matter of hours: Women, part-time work and the labour market* (Minneapolis, University of Minnesota Press).

Boisard, P.; Cartron, D.; Gollac, M.; Valeyre, A. 2003. *Time and work: Durations of work* (Dublin, European Foundation for the Improvement of Living and Working Conditions).

Chard, J.; Badets, J.; Howatson-Leo, L. 2000. "Immigrant women", in *Women in Canada 2000: A gender-based statistical report* (Ottawa, Statistics Canada), pp. 189–207.

Cranford, C.J.; Vosko, L.H.; Zukewich, N. 2003. "The gender of precarious employment in Canada", in *Relations Industrielles/Industrial Relations*, Vol. 58, No. 3, pp. 454–82.

Doeringer, P.B.; Piore, M. 1971. *Internal labor markets and manpower analysis* (Armonk, New York, M.E. Sharpe).

Fang, T.; Verma, A. 2002. "Union wage premium", *Perspectives on Labour and Income*, Vol. 3, No. 9, pp. 13–19.

Forrest, A. 1996. "Heterosexuality as a workplace norm: Implications for women", paper presented at the annual conference of the Canadian Industrial Relations Association (June).

—. 1998. "Unpaid work: Invisible and undervalued in industrial relations theory", in P.-A. Lapointe, A. Smith and D. Veilleux (eds.): *The changing nature of work, employment and workplace relations: Selected papers from the XXXIVth annual CIRA conference* (Quebec, OC, ACRI/CIRA), pp. 81–90.

Galarneau, D. 2005. "Earnings of temporary versus permanent employees", in *Perspectives on Labour and Income*, Vol. 6, No. 1, pp. 5–18.

Gunderson, M.; Hyatt, D. 2001. "Contingent work: The role of the market, collective bargaining, and legislation", in *Proceedings of the 53rd Annual Meeting, Industrial Relations Research Association* (Urbana-Champaign, Illinois, IRRA), pp. 99–107.

Hamilton, N.; Bhatti, T. 1996. *Population health promotion: An integrated model of population health and health promotion* (Ottawa: Health Promotion Development Division, Health Canada). Mimeo.

Ilcan, S.M.; O'Connor, D.M.; Oliver, M.L. 2003. "Contract governance and the Canadian public sector", in *Relations industrielles/Industrial Relations*, Vol. 58, No. 4, pp. 620–43.

Kapsalis, C.; Tourigny, P. 2004. "Duration of non-standard employment", in *Perspectives on Labour and Income*, Vol. 5, No. 12, pp. 5–13.

Marshall, K. 2003. "Benefits of the job", in *Perspectives on Labour and Income*, Vol. 4, No. 5, pp. 5–12.

Osberg, L; Wien, F; Grude, J. 1995. *Vanishing jobs: Canada's changing workplaces* (Toronto, James Lorimer & Co.).

Osterman, P. 1992. "Internal labor markets in a changing environment: Models and evidence", in D. Lewin, O. Mitchell and P. Sherer (eds.): *Research frontiers in industrial relations and human resources* (Madison, Wisconsin, IRRA Series), pp. 273–308).

Pierard, E.; Buckley, N.; Chowhan, J. 2004. "Bootstrapping made easy: A Stata ADO file", *Statistics Canada Research Data Centres Information and Technical Bulletin*, Vol. 1, No. 1, pp. 20–36.

Presser, H.B. 2003. *Working in a 24/7 economy: Challenges for American families* (Thousand Oaks, California, Russell Sage Publications).

Romaine, J.; Zeytinoglu, I.U. 1999. "Work related health issues for managerial women and men: The case of chartered accountants", in M. Denton, M. Hajdukowski-Ahmed, M. O'Connor and I.U. Zeytinoglu (eds.): *Women's voices in health promotion* (Toronto, Canadian Scholars' Press), pp. 254–66.

Tabi, M.; Langlois, S. 2003. "Quality of jobs added in 2002", in *Perspectives on Labour and Income*, Vol. 4, No. 2, pp. 12–16.

Thompson, E. 2002. "The 1990s have been difficult for recent immigrants in the Canadian labour market", in *Quarterly Labour Market and Income Review*, Vol. 3, No. 1, pp. 21–25.

Vosko, L.F.; Zukewich, N.; Cranford, C. 2003. "Beyond non-standard work: A new typology of employment", in *Perspectives on Labour and Income*, Vol. 4, No. 10, pp. 16–24.

Walby, S. 1990. *Theorizing patriarchy* (Oxford, Blackwell).

WES Compendium. 2001. *Workplace and employee survey, 1999 data* (Ottawa, Statistics Canada).

Winters, J. 1994. "Weekend workers", in *Perspectives*, Summer, pp. 45–48.

Zeytinoglu, I.U. 1991. "A sectoral study of part-time workers covered by collective agreements: Why do employers hire them?", in *Relations industrielles/Industrial Relations*, Vol. 46, No. 2, pp. 401–19.

—. 1992. "Reasons for hiring part-time workers", in *Industrial Relations: A Journal of Economy and the Society*, Vol. 31, No. 3, pp. 489–99.

—. 1993. "Negotiation issues for part-time workers: The impact of occupation", in *Relations industrielles/Industrial Relations*, Vol. 48, No. 2, pp. 305–19.

—. 1999. *Changing work relationships in industrialized economies* (Amsterdam, John Benjamins).

—. (ed.). 2002. *Flexible work arrangements: Conceptualizations and international experiences* (The Hague, Kluwer Law International).

—. (ed.) 2005. *Flexibility in workplaces: Effects on workers, work environment and the unions* (Geneva, IIRA/ILO). (http://www.ilo.org/public/english/iira/studies/st10book/index.htm)

—; Cooke, G.B. 2004. "Differences in benefits within non-standard employment contracts", in *Statistics Canada Research Data Centres Paper Series*. (http://www.statcan.ca/english/rdc/papers.htm)

—; —. 2005. "Non-standard work and benefits: Has anything changed since the Wallace Report?", in *Relations industrielles/Industrial Relations*, Vol. 60, No. 1, pp. 29–62.

—; Muteshi, J. 2000. "A critical review of flexible labour: Gender, race and class dimensions of economic restructuring", in *Resources for Feminist Research*, Vol. 27, Nos. 3–4, pp. 97–120.

—; Denton, M.; Hajdukowski-Ahmed, M.; O'Connors, M.; Chambers, L. 1999. "Women's work, women's voices: From invisibility to visibility", in M. Denton, M. Hajdukowski-Ahmed, M. O'Connor, and I.U. Zeytinoglu (eds.): *Women's voices in health promotion* (Toronto, Canadian Scholars' Press), pp. 21–29.

—; Moruz, J.; Seaton, B.; Lillevik, W. 2003. *Occupational health of women in non-standard employment* (Ottawa, Status of Women Canada, Research Directorate).

—; Lillevik, W.; Seaton, B.; Moruz, J. 2004. "Part-time and casual work in retail trade: Stress and other factors affecting the workplace", in *Relations industrielles/Industrial Relations*, Vol. 59, No. 3, pp. 516–44.

PART V

CONCLUSION

TOWARDS DECENT WORKING TIME 16

Jon C. Messenger

This concluding chapter aims to synthesize some of the most important findings from the selected papers from the Ninth International Symposium on Working Time that are included in this volume and, in particular, to apply these findings to the task of further developing and refining the five dimensions of the proposed policy framework for moving towards "decent working time".

16.1 BACKGROUND

As mentioned at the beginning of this book, a recent ILO publication[1] has analysed the gaps between the working hours that individuals need or would prefer and the actual hours that they are required to work (Messenger (ed.), 2004). This report found that there are several different types of "gaps" between workers' actual and preferred hours of work that are particularly common. These include the following situations: those workers who are working "excessively" long hours and would prefer to work substantially fewer hours; those workers who are working part-time – and especially those in "marginal" part-time jobs of less than 20 hours per week – who would prefer to work more hours; and finally, those workers whose primary concern was not the number of hours they are working, but rather the *arrangement* of those hours, such as working at night, at weekends, and on irregular or rotating shift schedules.

From the perspective of decent work,[2] the "gaps" which exist between people's aspirations regarding their work and their current work situations can

---

[1] Jon C. Messenger (ed.) 2004. *Working time and workers' preferences in industrialized countries: Finding the balance* (London and New York, Routledge).

[2] A brief discussion of the ILO's concept of decent work is included in this volume. For a more in-depth treatment of the subject, see International Labour Office (ILO). 1999. *Decent work*, Report of the Director-General to the International Labour Conference, 87th Session (Geneva).

be viewed as "decent work deficits". The ILO defines a "decent work deficit" as "a gap between the world that we work in and the hopes that people have for a better life" (ILO, 2001, p. 8). Thus, the "gaps" that have been identified between workers' actual and preferred hours of work can be considered as one type of "decent work deficit". By adopting this approach, we can establish a basis from which to consider how the goal of decent work can be advanced in the arena of working time – that is, towards "decent working time".

Based upon both the existing international labour standards in the area of working time and recent research on working time trends and developments focusing on industrialized countries,[3] the ILO's Conditions of Work and Employment Programme has proposed five significant dimensions of "decent working time", as indicated in the Foreword. These five dimensions are as follows: working time arrangements should promote health and safety; be "family-friendly"; promote gender equality; advance the productivity of enterprises; and facilitate worker choice and influence over their hours of work. Advancing each of these five dimensions requires a broad range of policies, which may be articulated at the national, sectoral and/or enterprise levels. Of course, the precise mix of policies that need to be pursued will vary substantially across countries (and perhaps even across states or regions within the same country), depending upon the socio-economic realities extant in each country.

16.2 HEALTHY WORKING TIME

The first of the five dimensions of "decent working time" is healthy working time. The need for working time to be both healthy and safe is a traditional concern – one that dates back to the very first international labour standard, the Hours of Work (Industry) Convention in 1919. Long working hours and "unsocial" working hours, particularly night work, are neither preferred by workers nor healthy for them. Moreover, one must keep in mind that the effects of long hours and "unsocial" working hours (e.g., night work) are not limited to individual workers, but also affect their families and society at large (Spurgeon, 2003).

The principle that underlies this dimension of "decent working time" is that hours of work which are unhealthy should not be a means of improving firms' profitability, a principle referred to in the international standards on working time, most significantly the Hours of Work (Industry) Convention, 1919 (No. 1) and the Hours of Work (Commerce and Offices) Convention, 1930 (No. 30). This principle is also a primary objective of the European Union (EU) Directive on Working Time (93/104/EC).

---

[3] A similar research effort focusing on developing countries and countries in transition is now nearing completion, and the results of this project will be published in an ILO report on *Working time around the world* (working title) in 2007.

Nevertheless, as Golden (2004; see also Chapter 8 in this volume) points out, both employers and individual workers may not properly consider the potential negative effects on health and safety in determining working hours, which may result in the overutilization of labour or "overwork". Golden (2004, p. 6) defines overwork as the point "when the length of work hours begins to adversely affect the health and safety of individuals, families, organizations and the public, even if workers themselves voluntarily work the excess hours". He emphasizes that these negative externalities with regard to health and safety – that is, the "spillover costs of overwork", justify the need for some type of regulation to provide a "countervailing force" to restrain excessively long hours (ibid., p. 16). Golden emphasizes that the need for such regulation holds not only in those cases in which the long hours are involuntary, but even when the long hours are worked "voluntarily",[4] in order to protect the safety and health of both the workers involved and the general public. A similar justification can be applied to protective measures concerning night work and other forms of "unsocial" hours as well.

Appropriate public policies to protect workers against excessively long and "unsocial" working hours are a necessary, but not sufficient, condition for achieving the goal of healthy working time. Both Campbell (2004) and Golden (Chapter 8 in this volume) point to the relatively weak regulatory and institutional frameworks regarding working time which exist in Australia and the United States, respectively, as being important factors in the increasing incidence of long or "extended" hours in those countries (see also Lee, 2004). Noting that the move towards longer hours is the dominant trend for full-time employees in Australia, Campbell (2004) stresses the importance of unpaid overtime, particularly among managers and different categories of salaried professionals, and a lack of paid annual leave due to an increasing casualization of the Australian labour force. Clearly, these factors relate directly to the regulatory framework in Australia, which excludes most professionals and managers from overtime pay requirements that might help limit the recourse to extended hours, and excludes "casual workers"[5] from employee entitlements such as that for a minimum amount of paid annual leave. Similarly, Golden notes that the only regulatory restraints on long working hours in the

---

[4] Golden also notes that there is a tendency for workers to adjust their working time preferences in line with their current hours, so in such cases workers may actually be internalizing "preferences" for long hours based on the requirements of their jobs.

[5] The category of "casual workers" in Australia is quite broad. "There is no standard number of working hours that defines a casual worker . . . the main difference between a permanent and a casual worker is the notion that a permanent employee has an ongoing contract of employment of unspecified duration while a casual employee has not. The characteristics of casual employment that flow from this notion are:

• Limited entitlements to benefits generally associated with continuity of employment such as annual and sick leave, and

• No entitlement to prior notification of retrenchment (no security of employment) and only a limited case for compensation or reinstatement". (Kryger, 2000)

United States are the overtime premium imposed under the Fair Labor Standards Act (FLSA), as well as weekly and daily limitations on hours of work that apply only to truck drivers. However, there is no general limitation on maximum hours of work in the United States, and a broad range of managerial, professional, and technical occupations are exempt from the over-time pay requirements of the FLSA under regulations which are established by the United States Department of Labor.[6]

Nonetheless, establishing a sound national framework for regulating working time is not, in and of itself, sufficient to make healthy working time a reality. Strong economic pressures or incentives towards long or "extended" hours can reduce the effectiveness of any regulatory framework. For example, it appears that the traditional link between low pay and long hours continues to exist in many developing countries, as overtime payments provide an important source of additional income for some low-wage workers. This is particularly true for workers with low educational levels, especially in develop-ing countries such as Brazil and China (Saboia, 2002; Zeng et al., 2005). Paid overtime, while increasing the earnings of these workers, can, however, become institutionalized, often as a cost-saving strategy for firms when compared with the increased fixed costs of hiring additional workers. When this occurs, workers may gradually come to accept long hours of work – in some cases, they may even come to be "dependent" on the additional income generated by overtime working – adjusting their working hour preferences towards their current hours (as suggested by Golden in this volume) and becoming unwilling or (economically) unable to reduce their working hours. In this case, perhaps the most effective policy for encouraging reduced working hours is a minimum wage set at a level sufficient to allow workers to earn a "decent" income during the standard or "normal" work-week.

In addition, it is becoming more and more obvious that, at least in the industrialized world, those workers with the highest levels of remuneration, such as managers and professionals, exhibit the longest working hours. As Nätti et al. report in Chapter 11 of this volume, in Finland long working hours were best predicted by occupational status, with managers and professionals being substantially more likely to work long hours compared with other occupational categories. According to their study, "[a]mbiguity of working time is a reality for many knowledge workers in Finland: half of them had difficulties in defining their working hours, men more often compared to women" (p. 309). The most common reason that they found for such

---

[6] See *Defining and Delimiting the Exemptions for Executive, Administrative, Professional, Outside Sales, and Computer Personnel; Final Rule*. US Department of Labor, Employment Standards Administration, Wage and Hour Division, Federal Register 69: 22122, 23 April 2004.

"ambiguous" and "stretching" working hours among managers and professionals was the "nature of the work" (p. 311). In other cases, however, it may be that corporate culture and management strategies, as well as intense competition among colleagues, induce workers to work long hours. For example, Haipeter (Chapter 12 in this volume), working with Lehndorff on a series of case studies of German firms with innovative working time systems (see, e.g., Lehndorff, 2002), emphasizes the "'financialization' of corporate decision-making", which focuses on increasing shareholder value (and often results in cutting staff levels to an absolute minimum), combined with the use of "market-driven management systems" which require employees to achieve market-based objectives (e.g., specific performance targets) within a framework that allows individuals extensive discretion in organizing their work (pp. 323–5). This combination of high performance targets and heavy workloads, plus extensive autonomy in organizing work, including individual working time, often results in hours of work that extend "as necessary" to achieve established performance targets or business objectives. There are now, therefore, increasing concerns about the effects of excessively long hours on the health and safety of managerial and professional staff.

Combating the pressures for long and "stretching" working hours among managers and professionals is not an easy task. Despite the effects of such long hours on the health, safety and personal lives of these workers, it is often difficult to address unhealthy working time among managers and professionals, and in fact most national working hour regulations exclude many workers in these occupations from their provisions. Extending regulations on working hours, such as those for overtime pay and maximum hour limits, would be an important step towards reducing the long hours among these workers. In France, for example, the working hour laws have been extended to cover most *cadres* (a category that includes both managerial and professional staff), by limiting the total number of days that they work (via extended paid holidays) rather than limiting total hours worked as for other employees (Incomes Data Service, 2002). In some circumstances it may also be feasible to incorporate at least some of these types of workers into workplace collective agreements, but new mechanisms of regulation that centre on the amount of hours worked may also be necessary.

16.3 "FAMILY-FRIENDLY" WORKING TIME

A second important dimension of "decent working time" is providing workers with family responsibilities engaged in paid employment with the time that they need to handle those responsibilities – in line with the principle established in the ILO's Workers with Family Responsibilities Convention, 1981 (No. 156). Such responsibilities include caring for family members (children, elderly relatives, etc.) and performing other necessary household tasks (cooking, cleaning, shopping, etc.) "Family-friendly" working time allows individuals sufficient time to meet these essential domestic obligations, and therefore benefits not only workers, but also society as a whole. In particular, *"family-friendly" working time measures*[7] are designed to help meet the needs of parents – both men and women – to have sufficient time to care for their families, particularly (although certainly not exclusively) *on a daily basis*, a reality that is often forgotten in so-called "post-Fordist" working time arrangements that often function by averaging hours over a period of weeks, months, or even an entire year.

According to studies of life-cycle working time (Boulin and Hoffman, 1999; Anxo et al., Chapter 4 in this volume), working time patterns and workers' preferences regarding their hours of work are highly influenced by variations across the life cycle of individual workers – variations that have become more dramatic as individuals' biographies have become more diverse. Such studies argue that the allocation of an individual's time among paid work, domestic tasks, care, leisure and other activities is highly sensitive to household composition (e.g. the number and age of household members) and also their current phase in the life course. Indeed, in some countries, such as Japan, the entire social system is based on an individual's age – that is, their particular stage of life. In Japan, this life-cycle-based structure includes not only paid employment (which is based on seniority), but there is also "a high degree of synchronization between family events and age" (Ribault, Chapter 13, p. 347 in this volume).

Family responsibilities and the precise nature of those responsibilities – e.g. the presence of children and their age(s) – exert a strong influence on households' time allocation and gender division of labour (see e.g. Anxo, 2004). However, these impacts vary substantially across countries and societal contexts, such that the ability to combine family commitments and work exhibits a large variation among countries. For example, Ribault (Chapter 13 in this volume) points to an interesting phenomenon of "intergenerational exchange", in which Japanese women aged 50–59 substantially increase their participation in the paid labour force in order to provide extra household revenues to finance their children's (often very expensive) tertiary education; in return, their children, who are typically between 20 and 24 years old at that time, take on the primary responsibility for household tasks, such as providing elder care. While this may be an extreme example, it nonetheless provides an

---

[7] The entire range of "family-friendly" measures can include a variety of different policies and practices, including not only those relating to hours of work, but also a number of other measures such as maternity protection and affordable, accessible and high-quality childcare services.

illustration of just how complex the relationships between time use and household composition can be.

Some of these family responsibilities are already outsourced, at least in part (e.g. childcare facilities, schools and market-based services for domestic tasks). Nevertheless, not all such activities can reasonably be outsourced; thus a significant portion of these activities remains the responsibility of the family or household. Both "inflexible" working hours and limited childcare and other family-related support tend to reinforce the traditional "male breadwinner–female homemaker" division of labour within households and create difficulties in combining paid work and family duties.

However, successfully blending work with family responsibilities is also about *when* people are available, and the energy that they have available to devote to family activities (Fagan, 2004). "Non-standard" working hours in the evenings, at nights and at weekends, as well as unpredictable variations in working hours based on fluctuating market demands, tend to increase the likelihood that workers will report work–family conflicts (see Fagan, 2004; European Foundation for the Improvement of Living and Working Conditions, 2001). Of course, the inconveniences involved with working "non-standard" hours are not equally shared by all groups of workers: for example, Zeytinoglu and Cooke (Chapter 15 in this volume) demonstrate that in Canada, those workers in part-time, temporary and seasonal jobs are more likely to work at weekends than full-time, permanent employees.

The possibility of using working time arrangements to facilitate the combination of work and family commitments may be achieved by different but complementary means. These "family-friendly" working time measures include a variety of policy options, ranging from a collective reduction in full-time hours to an individual right to reduce (or adapt) working time for family reasons, such as has been recently introduced in the United Kingdom. In general, short working hours – that is, part-time work – appears to be a widely employed strategy for balancing paid employment with family responsibilities. For example, Bouffartigue and Bouteiller (Chapter 14 in this volume) find that part-time work is the "linchpin" of personal strategies for juggling paid work and family responsibilities among hospital nurses in Belgium and France.

However, there are two main problems with this reliance on part-time work as a strategy for work–family reconciliation. The first problem is that part-time jobs are, on average, of lesser quality than comparable full-time jobs. This is the case in many countries, not only in terms of hourly wages, but also with regard to non-wage benefits such as pensions (and health insurance in the United States), social insurance coverage, training opportunities and career development (see e.g., Polivka et al., 2000; Fagan and O'Reilly, 1998). In addition, "substantial" part-time hours (20–34 hours per week) are much more popular than "marginal" part-time hours of less than 20 hours per week (see, e.g., Fagan, 2004). In fact, it appears that many full-timers would prefer to switch to part-time work but for the workplace obstacles and career penalties that are currently associated with part-time work. The second problem is that part-time workers are overwhelmingly female,[8] meaning that part-time work is gender-segregated in nearly all of the countries in which it exists (see the discussion in the next section).

These findings point to the importance of improving the quality of available part-time positions as a means of achieving "family-friendly" working time. This in turn suggests the need to "normalize" part-time work vis-à-vis the full-time standard that exists in each country. As noted in the chapter by Yerkes and Visser (Chapter 9 in this volume), such a process of "normalization" has already occurred in the Netherlands and is in now in process in Germany and the United Kingdom as well. Equal treatment regulations in employment, non-wage benefits and social protection systems help to improve the conditions of part-time work, and at the same time make a substantial contribution towards promoting gender equality, a subject to which we turn in the next section (McCann, 2004).

Certain types of "flexible" working time arrangements can also contribute to work–family reconciliation, particularly those flexi-time programmes and "time-banking" schemes that permit workers to accumulate extra hours and then use them to take full or partial days of paid time off at a later date. If properly structured, such schemes can also allow workers to vary their hours of work based on their individual family situations. Finally, offering workers the possibility of "telecommuting" to their jobs by working from home can also provide them with the ability to blend work and family responsibilities on a daily basis, although care must be taken that this does not lead to excessive hours due to the inevitable blurring of the boundaries between paid work and personal life.

Maternity, paternity, parental and similar care-related leave can also advance "family-friendly" working time by providing longer-term working time adjustments for family responsibilities (and physical recovery for mothers in the case of maternity leave). For example, Sweden offers one model for using blocks of paid leave, including sabbaticals, to help individuals to better organize their working time over the life cycle. And although few countries have family leave entitlements as generous as those in Sweden, statutory entitlements to maternity, paternity and parental leave have been increased in almost all OECD countries in recent years (OECD, 2001).

---

[8] In industrialized countries, women hold nearly three-quarters of all part-time positions (OECD, 2004, p. 311), and part-time work is increasingly used in developing countries as well (e.g., Taylor, 2004).

A final point regarding work–family reconciliation measures is that take-up of working time adjustments or extended leave is often low – particularly for men – and so there is a substantial gap between policy and practice. Employees may feel that they can't afford to take advantage of such opportunities, perhaps because their line manager is unwilling to agree to these arrangements, or because they may perceive that it will jeopardize their future promotion potential and/or even their job security. In particular, take-up rates for these measures are systematically much lower for men than for women, and long weekly working hours are largely (though certainly not exclusively) a male phenomenon. All of these factors suggest that in general men have insufficient time for family life. This phenomenon and the resulting gender inequality in the sharing of family responsibilities that it spawns are addressed in the next section.

16.4 GENDER EQUALITY THROUGH WORKING TIME

The third dimension of "decent working time" involves using working time as a tool for promoting gender equality. Equality of opportunity and treatment between women and men in the world of work is a principle established in a number of international labour standards, most notably the Discrimination (Employment and Occupation) Convention, 1958 (No. 111). This ILO Convention enshrines the elimination of discrimination regarding employment and occupation as a fundamental principle – one that remains at the core of the ILO Decent Work Agenda today (ILO, 2000a). This means that the overall objective of advancing gender equality also needs to be applied in the area of working time – and integrated into the full range of working time policies – in order to ensure that policies designed to advance other "decent work" objectives do not inadvertently have a negative impact on gender equality.

An important principle in this respect is to distinguish between working time measures that are "family-friendly" *per se* and those that are both "family-friendly" *and can simultaneously promote gender equality as well*. For example, measures such as part-time work or parental leave provide parents with the opportunity to spend more time caring for their children or older relatives. However, if mothers are the only ones who make use of such leave, then, while these policies may indeed help promote work–family balance, they may simultaneously reinforce gender inequality by relegating women to marginal forms of labour market participation – rather than paving the way for a *true* equality in paid employment. To promote gender equality, working time policies must, first, enable women to be on an equal footing with men in employment (e.g., position levels, career advancement, etc.), and second, enable *"both partners* [to] combine paid work, family responsibilities, and lifelong learning . . ." (emphasis added), as suggested by Bosch in his proposed model for a new, more flexible standard employment relationship (Bosch, 2004, p. 1; Bosch, Chapter 2 in this volume). Realizing such a model will obviously require a more equal division of domestic tasks between men and women, including care responsibilities – which can be promoted via working time policies that encourage men to adjust their working hours at different stages of the life course, such as when they have young children.

From this discussion, it is clear that the gender equality dimension of the decent working time policy framework has two important implications for working time policies. First, working time policies should promote gender equality in employment through gender-neutral measures. Second, it is important to ensure that policies that advance other dimensions of decent working time do not negatively impact on gender equality.

As discussed in the ILO's recent book on working time in the industrialized countries, a coordinated combination or "portfolio" of policies is required to promote gender equality because the efficacy of one particular instrument is usually contingent upon other measures (Messenger, ed., 2004). First, policies are needed to close the "gender gap" in the number of hours of paid employment for men compared with those hours worked by women. This objective can be achieved both by limiting excessively long hours among full-time workers and encouraging longer hours for part-timers. Changing the "long-hours culture" that is often associated with the self-determined working time patterns of many managers and so-called "new economy" professionals is a particularly thorny problem, as these individuals are largely exempt from working time regulations. The long hours in such positions act as an (often invisible) barrier to the advancement of women who have family responsibilities, and hence reinforce the "glass ceiling" that already exists in these occupations.

Second, with regard to the question of part-time work, the key issues are twofold. First, it is essential that the quality of part-time work be improved if it is to be made compatible with the objective of promoting gender equality (Fagan, 2004; OECD, 2001; Fagan and O'Reilly, 1998). As mentioned earlier in this chapter, one particularly important mechanism for improving the quality of part-time work – and thus helping to promote gender equality, since (as noted above) the vast majority of part-time workers are women – is the use of equal treatment regulations in employment, non-wage benefits and social protection systems, which will help to improve the employment conditions of part-time workers. Promoting the equal treatment of part-time and full-time workers is a principle that was established in the ILO's Part-Time Work Convention, 1994 (No. 175), and has been extended to the laws of a number of countries, as well as to the European Union as a whole through the 1997 EU Part-time Work Directive (97/81/EC) (McCann, 2004). The equal treatment approach is clearly an essential step towards improving the quality of part-time work. Ultimately, this means embarking on a process whose objective is to make part-time positions equivalent to those of full-time ones in terms of their pay, benefits and career development opportunities. Such a process – sometimes referred to as the "*normalization*" of part-time work – is discussed at length in the chapter by Yerkes and Visser presented in this volume (Chapter 9).

The occupational profile of part-time positions is also important. Policies designed to promote equal treatment between part-timers and full-timers require "comparable" full-time positions with which comparisons regarding the equal treatment of part-time workers can be made. If part-time workers are concentrated in a narrow range of occupations, there may be few if any comparable positions. To address this situation, policies are needed to help "desegregate" part-time work, such as making part-time positions available in a wider range of jobs and incentivizing employers to structure part-time positions around "substantial" rather than "marginal" part-time hours (which are typically defined as less than 20 hours per week) by, for example, removing provisions in social security regulations that favour the creation of "marginal" hours jobs (McCann, 2004). With a wider range of part-time positions plus more substantial part-time hours, the underemployment (including earnings losses) associated with part-time work is reduced, as are the career advancement penalties; as a result, part-time workers become more fully integrated alongside full-timers in the workplace and the labour market as a whole (Fagan and O'Reilly, 1998). According to Yerkes and Visser (Chapter 9 in this volume), such a broad profile of part-time positions already existed in the Netherlands by the end of the 1990s.

Beyond the question of part-time work, promoting gender equality involves overcoming the "no-win" dilemma of work–family reconciliation measures: that is, policies designed to facilitate women's integration into the labour market may simultaneously reinforce gender inequality in the domestic division of labour and thus inadvertently undermine gender equity in employment (Moss and Deven, 1999). In particular, managerial resistance and the negative attitudes of colleagues can create obstacles to men's use of reconciliation measures. To help overcome such obstacles, a broad range of policies (and not just working time policies) are needed to promote the involvement of fathers in domestic tasks and care activities. One possible approach would be to provide fathers with the right to take extended leave for family reasons or reduce their working hours when they have young children – rights that are already available to mothers in many industrialized countries. In addition, enterprise-level policies designed to reduce organizational resistance to men adapting their working hours based on family needs would also have positive "knock-on" effects for female colleagues by "normalizing" a broad range of working time arrangements.

16.5 PRODUCTIVE WORKING TIME

Obviously, it makes no sense to talk about decent working time without considering its effects on the productivity of enterprises. In that sense, "decent working time" is also *productive working time*, in that more and more enterprises are recognizing that promoting a healthy "work–life balance" for their employees isn't just the "right thing" to do, but that such an approach can also serve as an effective competitiveness strategy. Enterprise policies and practices that seek to promote "decent working time" can benefit businesses in a number of different ways, as will be discussed below.

Before considering the range of positive effects that have been shown from various aspects of "decent working time" policies and practices, however, a few words of caution are in order. First, there is a fundamental normative question: whether or not economic impact is the most appropriate perspective from which to evaluate public policies, such as those embodied in international labour standards (whether on working time or other subjects), or whether one should focus primarily on their efficacy in promoting social welfare. How one answers this question will depend in large part on whether one places greater importance on economic efficiency or on social justice. Second, as emphasized by Rubery et al. (Chapter 5 in this volume), the human resource management practices associated with "post-Fordist" forms of work organization – such as the "self-regulated" working time of many managerial and professional staff and the "fragmented" time systems (e.g., very short part-time hours) often used, for example, in the retail industry – lead to flexible working hours that have the potential for a "double-edged impact"; that is, the end result can be either positive or negative depending upon how the working time arrangement is implemented. Thus, as with other employment practices, there is the potential for both a "high road" and a "low road" to achieving working time flexibility – and, as we shall see, taking the "high road" generally requires a proactive approach.

Having said that, there are nonetheless substantial business benefits that can be reaped from "decent working time" policies and practices. First, there is longstanding evidence that points to a link between reductions in working hours and increased hourly productivity, including the ILO's own research (see White, 1987 for a review of the relevant literature). Such productivity gains result not only from physiological factors such as reduced fatigue (as in the case of workers who are working long hours on a regular basis), but also from an improvement in employee attitudes and morale. The largest potential productivity gains can be expected from reductions in "excessive" hours of work – i.e., more than 48 hours per week – which also helps to advance the other dimensions of decent working time as well.[9] There is substantial empirical evidence that reductions in "excessively" long hours of work – typically linked with changes in work organization, methods of production and similar factors – have resulted in substantial productivity gains over the years (see, e.g., Bosch and Lehndorf, 2001; White, 1987).[10] Also, since long hours of work are positively related to absenteeism and staff turnover, reducing such long hours can also provide firms with benefits in terms of reduced absenteeism and lower staff turnover (see e.g., Barmby et al., 2002).

A number of enterprise studies also show the business benefits of adopting company policies that promote various aspects of decent working time, such as working time arrangements that allow workers to adjust their work schedules in response to their individual circumstances. For example, one major study in the United States found that flexi-time and tele-commuting had positive effects on productivity (Boston College Center for Work and Family, 2000). Flexible working time arrangements such as flexi-time and compressed work-weeks have also shown positive effects on employee attitudes and morale (see, e.g., Hogarth et al., 2001; Gottlieb et al., 1998). These improvements in employee attitudes and morale can, in turn, translate into a better "bottom line" – as demonstrated by a recent study that shows a statistically valid, positive relationship between employees' emotions regarding their work and firms' financial performance (Towers Perrin and Gang & Gang, 2003). A review of the literature on the effects of flexible working time arrangements (Avery and Zabel, 2001) also found benefits to firms from such arrangements due to decreased tardiness and absenteeism, as well as improved recruitment and retention of employees, particularly when labour markets are tight. Finally, some studies indicate that perhaps the most important factor is not the working time arrangement *per se*, but rather *workers' ability to choose their arrangement* – often referred to as "time sovereignty" – that shows the strongest impact on employees' job performance, and hence on firms' productivity (Gottlieb et al., 1998). Thus there appears to be substantial evidence regarding at least the potential benefits of "decent working time" arrangements for enhancing enterprise productivity.

---

[9] The ILO is in the process of developing "decent work" indicators, which include as one indicator the proportion of the workforce with "excessive hours of work", defined as having usual hours of work of over 48 hours per week in the main job. This 48-hour threshold is in line with the ILO Hours of Work (Industry) Convention, 1919 (No. 1) and the ILO Hours of Work (Commerce and Offices) Convention, 1930 (No. 30), both of which establish 48 hours as the maximum for weekly hours under normal circumstances.

[10] It should be noted that the productivity gains connected with reductions in working time tend to decrease as the length of working time decreases. More recent empirical studies of the productivity effects of reductions in working time have focused on the reduction of hours of work from a lower baseline level (i.e., 40 hours per week or less), and these studies generally show weak or no effects of working time reductions in countries in which hours of work are already relatively short (see, e.g., Anxo and Bigsten, 1989).

This is *not* to say, however, that these business benefits will *automatically* result from simply deploying working time arrangements that are consistent with "decent working time". Realizing these benefits requires firms to implement innovative arrangements that consciously seek ways of combining business efficiency with increased worker influence over their working hours. Such an approach is demonstrated in the chapter by Haipeter (Chapter 12 in this volume), in which we see a number of different German firms experimenting with innovative forms of working time arrangements, including flexi-time and various forms of "working time accounts" (i.e., "time banking" schemes that allow workers to accumulate "credits" in working hours for later use) that attempt to make just such a combination. Not surprisingly, Haipeter finds both successes and failures among his company case studies. For example, those flexi-time arrangements that actively seek to balance the interests of workers with firms' operational requirements are a particular "success story" that emerges from these case studies. On the other hand, Haipeter also finds that *long-term* working time accounts – designed to enable employees to take time off in extended blocks (i.e. "sabbaticals") – have not lived up to their promise, primarily because of practical difficulties with scheduling the withdrawal of large blocks of time credits from these accounts (in the form of sabbaticals) in an intensely competitive environment in which staffing levels are tight.

Ultimately, as Bosch (Chapter 2 in this volume) emphasizes, "Any attempt to combine business efficiency with increased time sovereignty for employees inevitably raises the question of work organization" (p. 59). Bosch goes on to cite Lehndorff's work on innovative forms of work organization (see e.g., Lehndorff, 2001), which, he says, "show[s] that such a synthesis can be made to work successfully" (p. 59). In the ILO's recent book on working time in industrialized countries, Messenger (2004), in his analysis of working time at the enterprise level, reaches a similar conclusion, but emphasizes that making such a synthesis work in practice requires firms to make a *conscious* attempt to align business objectives and strategies with workers' needs and preferences in ways that are mutually reinforcing. This point is aptly demonstrated by the experience of the lessons learned from enterprise case studies in France, in the context of the Aubry laws mandating a 35-hour average work week (Charpentier et al., Chapter 7 in this volume). Three of the four companies in this study lacked "'an associated project for change', which could have harmoniously combined the various components of decent working time . . ."; not surprisingly, therefore, all three of these companies reported negative effects from the move to the 35-hour work-week (e.g., lower productivity, increased absenteeism), while the one company (Banque) that had adopted a proactive strategy for managing this change seems to have fared much better (p. 193).

16.6 CHOICE AND INFLUENCE REGARDING WORKING TIME

Increasing demands for temporal availability at all hours of the day and during all 7 days of the week, as discussed in the chapter by Gadrey et al. (Chapter 10 in this volume), can be considered to be a type of "competence" sought by employers. These authors present evidence demonstrating that such temporal availability is particularly important when hiring employees who possess low levels of formal qualifications. According to Gadrey et al., such requirements for extensive temporal availability – at all times of the day, on all days of the week, at very short notice, for interrupted or irregular work periods, etc. – are among the most unfavourable of working conditions because of the substantial disruptions they create in individuals' lives. For example, they cite the "paradoxical" perception of part-time workers in cafeterias or fast-food restaurants, who, despite working short hours, feel that they are giving their entire lives to their work because they must be available for work at any time and on very short notice (p. 281). While these are perhaps extreme cases, they nonetheless serve to highlight the importance of workers' ability to choose, or at least influence, their working hours for achieving decent working time. This is the fifth and final dimension of "decent working time": choice and influence regarding working time.

The concept of "decent work deficits" discussed at the beginning of this chapter – with its notion of "gaps" between people's aspirations regarding their work and their current work situation – implies that increasing workers' ability to choose, or at least influence, the length of their working hours and their work schedules can help to advance "decent working time". Increasing workers' choice and influence regarding their working hours is – as discussed in the ILO's recent book on the subject – a matter of considering workers' *subjective* needs and preferences, with all of the technical difficulties that this approach entails, rather than making the assumption that actual working time arrangements reflect workers' preferences regarding their hours of work. This notion is taken one step further in the concept of "working time capability" developed by Lee and McCann in Chapter 3 of this volume. Building on the work of Sen (1999) they outline a concept of *working time capability* with a set of *real* options from which workers are able to make *genuine* choices, and then develop a model which focuses on the importance of considering the available, feasible alternatives when choices about working time are made. Expanding this kind of choice means expanding the range of opportunities for workers to structure their work and personal activities, such that their working hours can more closely approximate their individual situations.

This objective can be advanced in two related ways. First, the number of working time options available to employees can be increased, such that workers can choose from a "menu" of alternatives. Second, workers can be permitted to exercise a direct ongoing influence over the length and arrangement of their working hours. This latter approach (often referred to as an "individual influence" approach) recognizes that "decent working time" should help to promote the outcomes that individual workers prefer.

Policy measures to advance worker choice and influence regarding working time can be adopted at the national, sectoral and enterprise levels. For example, national legislation has been introduced in a number of European countries that can enhance worker influence by allowing collective agreements to implement or modify working time standards (EIRO Online, 1998). Laws have also been enacted in a few countries, such as the Netherlands, Germany and the United Kingdom, which provide individual workers with a right to request changes in their working hours. Although the specific provisions of these laws vary[11] – and both the working time regulatory frameworks and socio-economic circumstances in these three countries are quite different – such "right to request" legislation has the potential to advance workers' ability to influence their working hours, as well as to address the existing dichotomy between full-time and part-time work. In fact, this "right to request" approach favours a notion of the "*modulation*" of working hours, by promoting smoother transitions between different working time arrangements (McCann, 2004; Anxo et al., Chapter 4 in this volume).

At the enterprise level, flexi-time schemes and "time banking" accounts that allow workers to build up time "credits" for later use are tools that have the *potential* to offer workers a substantial amount of influence over their working hours. As noted above, such schemes can combine business efficiency with increased worker influence over their working hours, for example by creating working time accounts that fuse time banking with aspects of hours averaging over multi-week periods. Indeed, any firm-level practice that provides workers with a choice among alternative work schedules or facilitates worker influence over scheduling would be of some benefit to individual workers and can be encouraged through a range of government incentives.

Mechanisms such as a "right to request" changes in working hours laws and time banking accounts do not always work as intended, however. For example, Fouarge and Baaijens (Chapter 6 in this volume) investigate Dutch workers' preferences regarding their working hours in the context of the pioneering legislation in the Netherlands regarding the right to request working time changes (including changes in both the number of hours worked

---

[11] For example, the British provision, which is included in the Employment Rights Act 1996, applies only to parents with children under the age of 6 or disabled children under the age of 18.

and their scheduling). Their early findings[12] – with the Dutch "right to request" legislation in place for just two years at the time of the study – showed that, despite the law, changes in working hours are still often associated with job mobility; this finding indicates that certain "rigidities" in how enterprises structure working hours persist. Likewise, Haipeter (Chapter 12 in this volume) discusses flexi-time and other types of working time accounts, and identifies some problems with their use. In particular (as noted above), he finds problems with the withdrawal of time credits in *long-term* time accounts (e.g., for sabbaticals), often leading to the forfeiture of working time, and concludes that "(l)ong-term accounts have not shown themselves to be of any practical effectiveness. The main cause of this is the withdrawal of time credits, which is the so-called 'Achilles' heel' of such accounts" (p.334).

One must also be cautious about a tendency to assume that providing workers with greater choice and influence over their hours of work necessarily means a complete individualization of decisions regarding working hours, or that this approach can be effective entirely at the individual level. As highlighted by Lee and McCann (Chapter 3 in this volume), a strong degree of social support is essential in increasing workers' "working time capability" – that is, the range of realistic working time options from which they can choose. Such support can be provided at various levels through methods including laws that strengthen trade unions such as those on independence, recognition and the right to strike.

Finally, it is important to consider how broader social objectives can be realized in conjunction with the facilitation of individual choice. The synchronization of working hours and social times, such as those times traditionally dedicated to community and family activities, becomes increasingly difficult in a context of individualized hours. Building on the work of Supiot (2001), Rubery et al. (Chapter 5 in this volume) emphasize that certain types of "post-Fordist" human resource management practices:

> call into question collective aspects of the organization of work and life by challenging "the community time patterns that have governed life on and off the job" . . . Results-based employment relationships blur the boundaries between work and free time while fragmented time relationships often explicitly facilitate the scheduling of work in parts of the day or week that would previously have been considered "community time" (pp.126–7).

Thus working time policies also need to explicitly address these concerns wherever possible. For example, such policies need to consider the opening hours

---

[12] This study uses data from the OSA Labour Supply Panel through the year 2002, which is only two years after the Adjustment of Working Hours Act in the Netherlands came into effect (in July 2000). Therefore it was probably too early for any significant impacts of the law to have materialized.

of public and private services, including changing these hours when necessary to accommodate changing lifestyles, in order to promote an improved quality of life. The "times of the city" (*tempo della città*) initiative in Italy provides a good illustration of how this concern regarding the synchronization of working hours and social times might be addressed (see, e.g., Boulin and Mückenberger, 1999).

16.7 FUTURE DIRECTIONS

As we have seen, the five dimensions of "decent working time" provide a broad policy framework by which the goal of decent work can be advanced in the arena of working time. These five dimensions should be considered as a set of *guiding principles* that point in a direction that leads towards "decent working time" – at whatever stage a country may be in its process of development. As principles, the five dimensions of "decent working time" will of necessity vary substantially in their implementation (i.e., the specific mix of policies used to advance decent working time) from one country to another, according to variations in national, regional and perhaps even local circumstances.

It should also be emphasized that these five dimensions of "decent working time" cannot – and are not designed to – provide a comparative *analytical* framework for an empirical definition of "decent working time" on an international basis. That is not to say, however, that such a comparative analytical framework could not be developed; it is simply that this was not the original purpose of the concept of "decent working time". In fact, Boulin et al. (Chapter 1 in this volume) suggest one possible approach that might be used as a starting point for developing such an analytical framework. However, a word of caution appears to be in order here: given the well-known difficulties of making even the simplest international comparisons, developing such a framework – which would amount to an international *empirical definition* of "decent working time" – would seem to be a Herculean task.

Nonetheless, the five dimensions of "decent working time" do provide an overall structure for future research in the field of working time – in fact, each of these five dimensions constitutes an important theme for future research on working time. For example, the ILO has already published a volume (Spurgeon, 2003) focusing on the first dimension of decent working time, healthy working time, which provides a meta-analysis of the current state of knowledge regarding the effects of working time (both hours of work and working time arrangements such as shift work, night work and irregular hours) on both safety and health. Similarly, the recent work by Lee and McCann in developing the concept of "working time capability" (which is presented in Chapter 3 of this volume) helps to advance our understanding of the fifth dimension of decent working time, choice and influence regarding working time.

In its future programme of research on working time, the ILO will bring to fruition its current research project on working time in developing countries and countries in transition with the publication of a report on *Working time around the world* (working title) in 2007. The topic of working time is one that, while it has been heavily researched in industrialized countries, is unfortunately often neglected or even forgotten in many developing countries. As this report will show, it is essential to avoid making broad generalizations regarding hours of work and working time arrangements across the developing world, as even the limited evidence that is available shows that there are dramatic differences in both the regulation of working time and actual working hours and working time arrangements across different regions of the world, such as among Asia, Africa and Latin America (see, e.g., Zeng et al., 2005; Ndiaye, forthcoming; Saboia, 2002). This report will conclude with a set of policy suggestions designed to apply the "decent working time" policy framework, which was developed based on research on working time in industrialized countries, to the substantially different circumstances that exist across the developing and transition countries.

In terms of specific research topics relating to various aspects of the five dimensions of "decent working time", the following issues appear to be of particular importance. First, from the perspective of healthy working time, it remains essential to focus on the traditional question of excessive working hours – but this time in newly emerging economies such as China and India. Second, it will be crucial to further explore the obvious trade-offs between the dimensions of "family-friendly" working time and gender equality through working time, such as in the area of part-time work – seeking policies that can *simultaneously* promote work–family reconciliation and gender equality. It will also be important to expand the knowledge base regarding how various types of flexible working time arrangements, such as compressed work weeks and "time banking" accounts, can be structured to promote increased enterprise productivity (the dimension of productive working time), without detracting from workers' health and safety (the dimension of healthy working time), including flexible forms of work organization such as teleworking.[13] Finally, working time research efforts should be aimed at exploring the fifth dimension of decent working time, choice and influence regarding working time, along the lines suggested by Lee and McCann – that is, by expanding workers' "working time capability", including how this relates to the question of working time and older workers in the context of "active ageing" policies.

---

[13] While technically not a working *time* arrangement, the increasing importance of teleworking within the context of "self-managed" working time, especially among managerial and professional staff, and its profound implications – e.g., in terms of blurring the boundary between paid work and personal life and its tendency to promote "stretching working hours" (see, e.g., Nätti et al., Chapter 11 in this volume) – makes it an important topic for future research.

In addition, as discussed at the beginning of this book, the ILO has been considering the implications of the recent General Survey Report (ILO, 2005) on two of the most important international labour standards on working time, the Hours of Work (Industry) Convention, 1919 (No. 1) and the Hours of Work (Commerce and Offices) Convention, 1930 (No. 30), which concluded that the revision of these instruments is warranted.[14] A discussion of this report at the International Labour Conference in June 2005 and a subsequent discussion by the ILO Governing Body in November 2005 concluded with the suggestion to conduct a Tripartite Meeting of Experts on Working Time. In determining how to proceed, the available research on the various working time topics discussed in this volume will be crucial in informing both the decision of the ILO's Governing Body regarding the appropriate course of action to take with respect to these standards, as well as any potential future discussion of working time at a Meeting of Experts or at the International Labour Conference – the body which ultimately makes the decisions on the adoption and revision of international labour standards.

While it is hoped that all of these efforts will assist in advancing "decent working time", ultimately, however, any movement in this direction will depend on the *relative value* that both institutions and individual citizens place upon their quality of life compared with their material wealth. The economic imperatives driving societies towards the "24-7 model" of operating hours and greater diversification in working hours for individual workers appear unlikely to diminish, and may well continue to intensify. The question then becomes one of individual and societal values: what working hours do people want? And what are they willing to accept to get them, e.g., lower earnings? Even in a country such as the United States – where material incentives are strong and very long working hours are commonplace – a significant portion of workers are now saying that they would like to reduce their hours, even if that means some reduction in income (Jacobs and Gerson, 2004; Golden, Chapter 8 in this volume). Perhaps not surprisingly, in the last few years a citizen movement dedicated to fighting "time poverty" and promoting a more "balanced life" has sprung up in that country.[15] Thus, as a greater focus on quality-of-life issues emerges among individuals and in institutions across the industrialized world, we might well expect to see an increased call for policies and approaches that offer the promise of moving towards "decent working time".

---

[14] This report was prepared by the ILO's Committee of Experts on the Application of Conventions and Recommendations.

[15] Take Back Your Time is a "grass-roots" citizen movement whose stated objective is to fight "time poverty" in the United States. For more information about this organization, see www.simpleliving.net/timeday.

References

Anxo, D. 2004. "Working time in industrialized countries: A household perspective", in J. Messenger (ed.), 2004.

—; Bigsten, A. 1989. "Working hours and productivity in Swedish manufacturing", in *Scandanavian Journal of Economics*, Vol. 91, No. 3, pp. 613–19.

Avery, C.; Zabel, D. 2001. *The flexible workplace: A sourcebook of information and research* (Westport, Connecticut, Quorum Books).

Barmby, T.; Ercolani, M.; Treble, J. 2002. "Sickness absence: An international comparison", in *The Economic Journal*, June, Vol. 112, pp. F315–F331.

Bosch, G. 2004. "Working hours and the standard employment relationship", paper presented at the Ninth Conference of the International Symposium on Working Time, Paris, 26–28 February.

—; Lehndorff, S. 2001. "Working-time reduction and employment: experiences in Europe and economic policy recommendations", in *Cambridge Journal of Economics*, Vol. 25, pp. 209–43.

Boston College Center for Work and Family. 2000. *Measuring the impact of workplace flexibility: Findings from the national work/life measurement project* (Boston, Massachusetts, Boston College Center for Work and Family, Wallace E. Carroll School of Management). http://www.bc.edu/centers/cwf/research/highlights/meta-elements/pdf/flexexec-summ.pdf.

Boulin, J.-Y.; Hoffman, R. 1999. "The conceptualisation of working time over the whole life cycle", in J.-Y. Boulin and R. Hoffman (eds.): *New paths in working time policy* (Brussels, European Trade Union Institute).

—; Mückenberger, U. 1999. *Times in the city and quality of life*, BEST European Studies on Times (Luxembourg, Office for Official Publications of the European Communities).

Campbell, I. 2004. "Employer pressures and overtime: Exploring the causes of extended working hours in Australia", paper presented at the Ninth Conference of the International Symposium on Working Time, Paris, 26–28 February.

European Foundation for the Improvement of Living and Working Conditions. 2001. *European Union Survey on Working Conditions* [acceding and candidate countries] (Luxembourg, Office for Official Publications of the European Community).

European Industrial Relations Observatory (EIRO) Online. 1998. *Flexibility in working time in Europe* (Dublin, European Foundation for the Improvement of Living and Working Conditions). http://www.eiro.eurofound.ie/2001/11/study/TN0111143S.html.

Fagan, C. 2004. "Gender and working time in industrialized countries", in J.C. Messenger (ed.), 2004.

—; O'Reilly, J. (eds.) 1998. *Part-time prospects: An international comparison of part-time work in Europe, North America, and the Pacific Rim* (London and New York, Routledge).

Golden, L. 2004. "Overemployment in the US: Which workers are willing to reduce their work hours and income?", paper presented at the Ninth Conference of the International Symposium on Working Time, Paris, 26–28 February.

Gottlieb, B.; Kelloway, E.K.; Barham, E. 1998. *Flexible work arrangements: Managing the work-family boundary* (Chichester, UK, Wiley).

Hogarth, T., et al. 2001. *Work-life balance 2000: Results from the baseline study* (Norwich, United Kingdom, Department for Education and Employment).

Incomes Data Service (IDS). 2002. "France: Managers' hours and the European Social Charter", in *Employment Europe*, March, Vol. 483, p. 5.

International Labour Office (ILO). 1999. *Decent work*, Report of the Director-General to the International Labour Conference, 87th Session, Geneva.

—. 2000a. *Decent work for women: An ILO proposal to accelerate the implementation of the Beijing Platform for Action* (Geneva, ILO).

—. 2000b. *Your voice at work: Global report under the follow-up to the ILO Declaration on Fundamental Principles and Rights at Work*, International Labour Conference, 88th Session, Geneva.

—. 2001. *Reducing the decent work deficit*, Report of the Director-General to the International Labour Conference, 89th Session, Geneva.

—. 2005. *Hours of work: From fixed to flexible? General Survey of the reports concerning the Hours of Work (Industry) Convention, 1919 (No. 1) and the Hours of Work (Commerce and Offices) Convention, 1930 (No. 30)*, Report III (Part 1B), International Labour Conference, 93rd Session, Geneva.

Jacobs, J.A.; Gerson, K. 2004. *The time divide: Work, family, and gender inequality* (Cambridge, Massachusetts, Harvard University Press).

Kryger, T. (Australian Bureau of Statistics). 2000. "Casual employment: Research note 2, 1999–2000" (Canberra, Australia, Parliament of Australia, Parliamentary Library). http://www.aph.gov.au/library/pubs/rn/1999-2000/2000rn02.html.

Lee, S. 2004. "Working-hour gaps: trends and issues", in J.C. Messenger (ed.), 2004.

Lehndorff, S. 2001. *Weniger ist mehr: Arbeitszeitverkürzung als Gesellschaftpolitik* (Hamburg, VSA-Verlag).

—. 2002. "The governance of service work – changes in work organization and new challenges for service-sector trade unions", in Transfer, Vol. 8, No. 3, pp. 415–434.

McCann, D. 2004. "Regulating working time needs and preferences" in J.C. Messenger (ed.), 2004.

Messenger, J.C. (ed.) 2004. *Working time and workers' preferences in industrialized countries: Finding the balance* (London and New York, Routledge).

—. 2004. "Working time at the enterprise level. Business objectives, firms' practices, and workers' preferences", in J.C. Messenger (ed.), 2004.

Moss, P.; Deven, F. (eds.). 1999. *Parental leave: Progress or pitfalls?* (Brussels, CVBG-Centrum voor Bevolkings-en Gezinstudie).

Ndiaye, A. Forthcoming. *Étude sur le temps de travail et l'organisation du travail: Cas du Sénégal*, Conditions of Work and Employment Programme Series (Geneva, ILO).

Organisation for Economic Co-operation and Development (OECD). 2001. "Work and family life: How do they balance out?", in *OECD Employment Outlook 2001* (Paris, OECD).

—. 2004. *OECD Employment Outlook 2004* (Paris, OECD).

Polivka, A.; Cohany, S; Hipple, S. 2000. "Definition, composition, and economic consequences of the non-standard workforce", in F. Carré et al. (eds.): *Nonstandard work: The nature and challenges of changing employment arrangements* (Champaign, Illinois, Industrial Relations Research Association).

Saboia, J. 2002. "Survey report: Working week and organization of labour in Brazil", ILO Conditions of Work and Employment Programme, unpublished report.

Sen, A. 1999. *Development as freedom* (Oxford, Oxford University Press).

Spurgeon, Anne. 2003. *Working time: Its impacts on safety and health* (Seoul, ILO and Korea Occupational Safety and Health Research Institute).

Supiot, A. 2001. *Beyond employment: Changes in work and the future of labour law in Europe* (Oxford, Oxford University Press).

Taylor, O. 2004. "Working time and work organization in Jamaica", ILO Conditions of Work and Employment Programme, unpublished report.

Towers Perrin and Gang & Gang. 2003. *Working today: Exploring employees' emotional connections to their jobs* (New York, Towers Perrin).

White, M. 1987. *Working hours: Assessing the potential for reduction* (Geneva, ILO).

Zeng, X.; Liang, L.; Idris, S.U. 2005. *Working time in transition: The dual task of standardization and flexibilization in China*, Conditions of Work and Employment Programme Series No. 11 (Geneva, ILO).

INDEX